Patrizia Noel Aziz Hanna, Laura Catharine Smith (Eds.)
Linguistic Preferences

Trends in Linguistics
Studies and Monographs

Editors
Chiara Gianollo
Daniël Van Olmen

Editorial Board
Walter Bisang
Tine Breban
Volker Gast
Hans Henrich Hock
Karen Lahousse
Natalia Levshina
Caterina Mauri
Heiko Narrog
Salvador Pons
Niina Ning Zhang
Amir Zeldes

Editor responsible for this volume
Chiara Gianollo

Volume 358

Linguistic Preferences

Edited by
Patrizia Noel Aziz Hanna and Laura Catharine Smith

DE GRUYTER
MOUTON

ISBN 978-3-11-135593-1
e-ISBN (PDF) 978-3-11-072146-1
e-ISBN (EPUB) 978-3-11-072157-7

Library of Congress Control Number: 2021943955

Bibliographic information published by the Deutsche Nationalbibliothek
The Deutsche Nationalbibliothek lists this publication in the Deutsche Nationalbibliografie;
detailed bibliographic data are available on the Internet at http://dnb.dnb.de.

© 2023 Walter de Gruyter GmbH, Berlin/Boston
This volume is text- and page-identical with the hardback published in 2022.
Typesetting: Integra Software Services Pvt. Ltd.
Printing and binding: CPI books GmbH, Leck

www.degruyter.com

Essays in honour of Theo Vennemann gen. Nierfeld

Theo Vennemann gen. Nierfeld

Preface

We are very pleased to dedicate this volume to Theo Vennemann gen. Nierfeld on the occasion of his 80th birthday. *Linguistic preferences* celebrates both Theo Vennemann the scholar and his scientific oeuvre. With contributions from linguists around the globe, this volume has arisen as a result of the high regard Theo Vennemann is held in. Indeed, it reflects just a glimpse of the impact Theo Vennemann has had on the field as a researcher, colleague, teacher, and mentor.

We would like to thank all contributors and referees as well as the participants of the international colloquium "Current aspects of preference theory: A symposium on the occasion of Theo Vennemann's 80th birthday", held at the LMU Munich.

We are grateful to Birgit Sievert and Barbara Karlson from De Gruyter Mouton for their effort to make this volume possible as well as to the series editors Chiara Gianollo and Daniël Van Olmen. We would like to thank Stephen Laker (Kyushu) and Dietmar Zaefferer (Munich) for their support and those who assisted us in proofreading and formatting this volume: Eden Buchert (BYU), Christina Champenois (BYU), Carolin Cholotta (Bamberg), Jonas Inderst (Bamberg), Laura Knoll (Bamberg), Aaron Ostler (BYU), and Anna Walker (BYU).

Bamberg and Provo in February 2021
Patrizia Noel Aziz Hanna and Laura Catharine Smith

Contents

Preface — VII

Patrizia Noel Aziz Hanna und Laura Catharine Smith
Introduction: Preferences — 1

Part I: **Gradience and preference ranking**

Monica Macaulay and Joseph Salmons
Prosodic templates in Algonquian reduplication and initial change — 17

Robert Mailhammer
Amurdak intersyllabic phonotactics and morphophonemic alternations as motivated by the Contact Law — 49

Renate Raffelsiefen
Shortening as a window on phonological grammar — 71

Laura Catharine Smith
Moving from syllables to feet in the prosodic hierarchy: How foot-based templates reflect prosodic preferences — 109

Part II: **Prioritisation and the inferring of preferences from observed choices**

Hans Basbøll
Danish stød in the light of morae, the Weight Law and sonority (strength): A personal view — 143

Philip Hoole
Towards phonetic explanations for preferred sound patterns — 171

Larry M. Hyman
The first person singular subject negative portmanteau in Luganda and Lusoga — 195

Irmengard Rauch
The laryngeal preference, Saussure, and his politics — 209

Part III: **Comparative evaluation and the inherent "predictive" purpose of preferences**

Antoniy Dimitrov
Preference laws and a new interpretation of Modern Bulgarian "liquid metathesis" —— 219

Raymond Hickey
Syllable structure and sonority in Modern Irish —— 247

Donka Minkova
Preference theory and the uneven progress of degemination in Middle English —— 265

Patrizia Noel Aziz Hanna
The principle of scopal serialisation: Wackernagel position and mirrored Wackernagel position —— 293

Tabula Gratulatoria —— 319

Index —— 323

Patrizia Noel Aziz Hanna und Laura Catharine Smith
Introduction: Preferences

Preferences form a central concept of human categorisation. They contribute to decision-making, in the selection of beliefs, solutions, structures, etc. Indeed, the term "preference" comprises a wide range of meanings, such as comparative evaluation, prioritisation or favouring, and choice ranking. In linguistics, the study of preferences has been especially fruitful in the evaluation of linguistic structures and studying language change. *Linguistic Preferences* provides new insights from linguistics with both theoretical and empirical contributions to this interdisciplinary field of research with the aim of honouring the contributions made by Theo Vennemann to the field of linguistics. It offers contributions from phonology, morphology, syntax, and subsystem interactions, based on linguistic data from Algonquian languages (amongst others Menominee, Ojibwe, Cree), the Iwaidjan language family (Amurdak), Indo-European languages (Bulgarian, Danish, English, French, German, Irish, Old Saxon, Old Frisian, Slovak), and Bantu languages (Luganda, Lusoga).

1 General lines of thought

Preference theory has grown to be an interdisciplinary field of research, with substantial and sometimes conflicting contributions from disciplines such as moral philosophy, economics, psychology, evolutionary biology, artificial intelligence, and linguistics. Applied to the study of human language, preferences lead to clear-cut implications for linguistic theory. Preferences, inter alia, are related to universals in non-trivial ways, since "preference theories are meant to tell us something about preferred locations of languages in the space Q of possible languages" (Vennemann 1983: 12). Unlike descriptive theories of languages, they are characterised by rank-ordering elements along specified parameters. They imply an objective of linguistic improvement, and, at the same time, provide a benchmark for assessing collective linguistic choices in situations of language change.

Despite divergent basic assumptions (see Hansson and Grüne-Yanoff 2018 for an overview), research on preferences across the diverse disciplines reveals common lines of thought, which are pivotal to this volume:

Patrizia Noel Aziz Hanna, Department of German Linguistics, Otto-Friedrich-Universität Bamberg, Bamberg/Germany
Laura Catharine Smith, Department of German and Russian, Brigham Young University, Provo, UT/USA

1) Gradience and scales
2) Preference ranking
3) Observed choices
4) Prioritisation
5) Comparative evaluation
6) Inherent "predictive" and explanatory purpose

Preferences are represented on diverse kinds of scales and relate to relative rankings of, e.g. decisions, data, alternatives, or of preferences themselves (Herzberger 1973, Sen 1974, Bolle 1983, Liu 2011, Pigozzi, Tsouliàs, and Viappiani 2016). They are subject to rational scrutiny and employed to explain choices (Hausman 2012, Gelbukh, and Calvo 2018); choices are one major way in which preferences may be expressed (Payne, Bettman, and Johnson 1993: 258). While prioritisation may be understood as an action, comparative evaluations are often treated as mental states (Hausman 2012: 2). Furthermore, there is an inherent "predictive" and explanatory purpose in dealing with preferences (cf., e.g. Liu 2011: chap. 3, Antrup 2013).

Linguistic Preferences explores these issues from a linguistic perspective. This volume is dedicated to Theo Vennemann on the occasion of his 80th birthday.

2 Linguistic preferences from an interdisciplinary perspective

The intense study of preferences started in the 20th century. For linguistics, Theo Vennemann anchored his work on preferences in functional linguistics, more precisely in markedness theory and naturalness theory (cf. Jakobson 1941, Donegan and Stampe 1979, and Dressler 1999a for a subtheory of markedness theory as a preference theory). Theories of linguistic preferences reflect the discussion outlined above on the basis of linguistic data.

2.1 Gradience and scales: Better and worse structures

Instead of differentiating between good or bad options, preferences allow more fine-grained analyses (see Chisholm and Sosa 1966 for a discussion of the relation between "intrinsically good" and "intrinsically better"). Linguistic gradience is investigated as relative order of category members on a scale of preference relative to a specified parameter, where some linguistic structures are better or worse than others. Both better and worse linguistic structures presuppose a gradient nature of linguistic well-formedness.

The order of linguistic preferences is motivated functionally and locally. Interval scales allow meaningful comparisons of differences (e.g. onset A is better than B) but not meaningful comparisons of ratios (e.g. onset A is twice as good as onset B) (cf. Hansson and Grüne-Yanoff 2018 for references). As one prime example of an established phonological scale, relative consonantal strength (or, inversely, sonority) measures preferences on an interval scale. The relative order of the elements on this scale is subject to discussion (e.g. the relative sonority of Proto-Indo-European /m/, Cooper 2015: 317–320, Zair 2018). A second example is the scale for empirically proven preferences in evidential choices: Visual < Non-visual < Inferred (based on visual traces) < Reported < Assumed (Aikhenvald 2018: 27); the preference for visual information source matches its being less marked. A third example is the theoretical standpoint that language types are "constituted by specific constellations of choices from the various natural scales" (Dressler, Mayerthaler, Panagl, and Wurzel 1987: 11). Gradience is understood as an integral part of grammar.

2.2 Preference ranking

Another focus of research on preferences is the ranking of preferences. Either A can be preferred to B (A ≻ B), or the relation between A and B can be valued as indifferent (A~B) (Halldén 1957: 10). Major interdisciplinary topics in preference ranking focus on the notion of completeness and question whether transitivity applies.

With respect to completeness, an open question is whether complete scales of structures should be assumed or whether knowing about the most preferred structure allows neglecting worse ones. With linguistic scales such as Vennemann's (1988) consonantal strength scale, the question arises whether complete preferences have to be assumed, e.g. whether a linguistic community that abolishes the worst syllable onset is aware only that they disprefer the worst onset E to all others or whether they are aware that they disprefer E to D, D to C, C to B, and B to A. In addition to these scales, the concept of a template or templatic pattern has been introduced in linguistics as a convergence of preferences. As used in (morpho-)prosodic analyses, these templates reflect predetermined prosodic patterns, which "play a role in determining what segments or features can and will surface in the phonology and morphology of a language" (Smith and Ussishkin 2015: 264). Rather than being exceptionless absolutes, templates tend to reflect preferences for words or stems to have a particular shape.

One example of transitivity as a property of preferences is that if A is preferred to B and B is preferred to C, then A is preferred to C (see Armstrong 1948 for a discussion of the transitivity of indifference). Hansson and Grüne-Yanoff (2018) illustrate the Sorites Paradox as a counter-example to transitivity, focussing on adjacent members vs. members of a greater distance, with 1000 cups (C) of coffee, C0 containing no sugar, C1 containing one grain of sugar, C2 two grains of sugar, and so on. Since the difference between closely adjacent members is too small to tell the difference, these members might be considered equally good. This is, however, not the case for C0 and C999. The issue of indifference changing to non-indifference is a crucial factor in language change.

A variety of theoretical approaches have espoused the notion of preferences, including notably Optimality Theory (OT), in which "the way of choosing the optimal alternative naturally induces a preference ordering among the alternatives", i.e. a quasi-linear order of preferences (de Jongh and Liu 2009: 87, 91). It is worth acknowledging OT as a model partly compatible with preferences, since the ordering of constraints in linguistic output forms a central issue in OT, in which different grammars reflect different rankings of a supposed universal constraint set (Prince and Smolensky 1993). In contrast to OT constraints, the preferences of natural linguistics are not based on a generative notion of Universal Grammar (see Ritt 2001 for a comparison of the wider theoretical frameworks). Moreover, the concept of preferences within natural linguistics, in contrast to OT, has a crucial historical dimension, which allows for homogeneous definitions of well-formedness (cf. Gibbon 2001: 190–194 and for a comparison of preferences and constraints Dziubalska-Kołaczyk 2001).

Preference ranking in linguistics refers to combinations of preferences, stressing their order. This includes combinative preferences, e.g. when a given preference law has multiple scenarios, or the observation that mutally exclusive preferences like morphological and phonological naturalness can be at odds (e.g. Shannon 1991 on inflexional suffixes; cf. also Hyman and Schuh 1974: 94 on abstract phonological units vs. grammatical categories).

2.3 Observed choices

Viewing observed choices as revealed preferences is the subject of controversial interdisciplinary discussion, most notably because preferences, in contrast to choices, are understood as "subjective mental states that are not directly observable" (Grüne 2004: 382). Observed preferences, it has to be noted, are defined via choices. A major point of criticism, especially in studies within the field of economics, is that it has to be shown empirically that "the specific preference relation implied by the respective choice axiom is indeed the preference ordering on which an agent bases her deliberation" (Grüne 2004: 386).

Linguistic studies on preferences focus on preferences as observed choices. Thus, in principle, the criticism also holds for studies on linguistic principles (cf. Hill 2009 for the Neogrammarian view and Aarts 2007: chap. 2 for the scientific context of the Neogrammarian claim). The way of reasoning in linguistic preference theory, however, is not mainly inductive but abductive in the Peircean sense of creating explanatory hypotheses (Peirce 1903). It starts with an observation, such as common patterns of language change, and then seeks a hypothesis on the most simple explanation for this observation.

Collective linguistic choices are understood as evidence for preferences, since linguistic preference theory takes language change to be (local) language improvement (Vennemann 1989). Language users' choices favour preferred structures over dispreferred ones. Likewise, synchronic states of languages are considered products of optimisation, which show a reduction of markedness (e.g. Wurzel 1996). In a linguistic preference theory, these products are evaluated against historical stages of a language or against typologically unmarked structures and then interpreted as a choice for the better structure on a specified parameter.

2.4 Prioritisation

Not every preference is based on choice. It is not possible, for instance, to choose one's articulators or human processing limitations. The resulting prioritisation, which represents another focus of preference research, does not imply comparative evaluation. Some structures have worse chances than others to occur in natural languages. Answers to the nature of this kind of limitation come from interdisciplinary research. Studies from phonetics, semiotics, and evolutionary theory have offered ways of explaining why prioritisation in linguistic preferences exists (e.g. Dressler 1995, Blasi et al. 2019). Prioritisation thus provides external evidence for favoured linguistic structures from other disciplines than linguistics and thus allows for "strong" explanation in linguistics.

If we understand prioritisation as an action instead of a mental attitude (Hausman 2012) within non-linguistically determined boundaries, "strong" explanations (Vennemann 1983: 14) for linguistic structures surface; an example is the connection between the quality of a phonological structure and its phonetic complexity, since the human sound systems are shaped by human anatomy and physiology. Another example is the relation between cognition, directionality in speech planning and look-ahead (Levelt 1989). It is our hope that accessing linguistic prioritisation from an interdisciplinary perspective will give rise to a better understanding of the nature of possible human languages.

2.5 Comparative evaluation

From the perspective of preferences, options can be evaluated against one another, for instance along a scale of increasing linguistic quality or continuum for a particular feature or parameter. In order to evaluate preferences, i.e. A is better than B in some aspect, alternatives and their properties have to be identified and weighed. They are compared by (collective) agents, i.e. evaluated relative to each other. Evaluation can either be partial, i.e. a ranking for a specific aspect, or total, i.e. a ranking which takes every relevant aspect into consideration (Hausman 2012: chap. 10). Comparative evaluations of linguistic structures become discernible in variation when language users are confronted with diverse structures which stand in conflict with one another or are equally preferred yet, for instance, on different parameters. Moreover, the goals of language perception vs. language production can be at odds. The result of comparative evaluation can be synchronic variation representing structural effects of optimisation.

So then what makes some feature or preference A better than feature or preference B for a language user? Consider that linguistic preference laws are graded statements about quality in terms of linguistic markedness (Mailhammer, Restle, and Vennemann 2015: 450–451) where "less marked" can be interpreted as "more preferred". When conflicts occur between preferences, "agents strive towards maximal benefits or expected utility" (Dressler 1999b: 392; cf. Dziubalska-Kołaczyk 2001: 74). Insights into linguistic preferences are provided, for instance, by research into areal preferences; when speakers of two or more different languages are in a situation of language contact and finally "agree" on a structure for the language undergoing influence, diverse kinds of preferences surface as the result of comparative evaluation.

2.6 Inherent "predictive" and explanatory purpose

One of the aims of preference theories is to predict and explain key issues like welfare, consumption, or language change. There is, quite naturally, not one single complete, transitive, context-independent, and choice-determining ranking of factors which motivates people (e.g. Hausman 2012: 109). Preferences are either understood as choice-determining, thus allowing predictions about observable behaviour, or as later rationalisations of behaviour (cf. Hansson and Grüne-Yanoff 2018). The inherent "predictive" and explanatory purpose is the last focus of linguistic preference research addressed here.

Markedness studies partly resolve the synchronic/diachronic antinomy, because the same markedness principles are typical of language acquisition, aphasia, language change, and in synchronic states of languages (Jakobson 1941; cf. also Murray 2008: 2436). Following this line of thought, the inherent predictive and explanatory purpose of linguistic preference theory leads to an account of synchronic linguistic patterns which is not purely descriptive. Instead it serves to explain properties of individual languages, such as unidirectional serialisation (i.e. head-dependent or dependent-head). Linguistic preferences have an impact on cross-linguistic distribution; if not, they are either falsified or the decrease in statistical significance is due to naturalness conflicts (Dressler 1999a: 139–140).

Apart from the assessment of synchronic states of languages, linguistic preference theory offers a theory of change based on linguistic markedness. Research on linguistic preferences is based on the assumption that preferences result in a conscious or unconscious shift towards a more optimal state along a continuum; if language-internal change occurs, it is assumed to be towards a better instead of worse structure. This idea makes synchronic states of languages the result of optimisation with regards to a given parameter. Linguistic preferences are – unlike beliefs, values, and tastes – not subject to change. The scalar distribution of elements in a language, however, can change, for instance driven by sound laws (Vennemann 2000: 240). While predictions of single events are not possible, the set of possible changes is constrained by linguistic preferences (see Wurzel 2001: 5.3 for explanations in the arts). Linguistic preference laws serve "elucidation", i.e. knowing them, we recognize their motivation. At the same time, their external explanation accounts for their universality (Vennemann 1988: 67).

3 Theo Vennemann's linguistic preference laws

Drawing on research on linguistic preferences in general, we now turn to Theo Vennemann's own work on preference laws which has inspired the papers in this volume. Although Vennemann's preference laws built on his early work on phonology, this work almost didn't happen. As Theo Vennemann notes in an interview with fellow linguist, Haj Ross[1], he had moved on from phonology and was

---

[1] In this interview, Theo Vennemann shares his personal journey with linguistics, including how he came to re-engage with phonology and the ideas that led to the development of the preference laws. This excerpt begins at about 53:59 into the interview which can be found online

immersed in syntax research when a new student came to Munich to study phonology with him. Vennemann describes the origins of linguistic preference theory and his return to phonology from syntax as follows:

> But then unexpectedly there was a return to phonology and the way it happened was this: A student of James Foley's at Simon Fraser University in Vancouver decided he wanted to study phonology with me. He came to Munich to study here. And he was interested in phonology, because that's what he was here for and he sort of asked me to [...] teach him phonology. And so I offered courses in phonology and he took them and then something happened. He once wrote a term paper about natural generative phonology especially the work of Joan Hooper's (Bybee's) and he cited the rule that she formulated that in syllable contacts, you know at the borders, the syllable border within a word, there is sort of an ordering constraint that the more sonorous, the less consonantal sounds have to come before the less sonorous, the more consonantal, sounds. So *ar$ta* was alright but *at$ra* was not alright. And as I read it I thought, "Well that isn't correct because you have both. You have languages that have *ar$ta* and you have languages that also have *at$ra*. Of course you also have languages that have *a$tra*, but very few languages that have *a$rta*." So I said, "You can't formulate it that way. It's a graded matter, a matter of gradation." The case is this. You know *ar$ta* is a very good contact; many languages tolerate it. Hardly any languages don't tolerate it that have complex structures like that at all, you know. And *at$ra* is very bad; and it's the worst you can have as a matter of fact. And in between you have all kinds of combinations and the break off point is different from one language to the next, so you can't have a general rule. What you have is a preference for some structures and decreasing preference as you go up the scale. So I started thinking in terms of scales, you know sort of inspired by 19th century scales, also Jim Foley's scale of consonantal hierarchies, consonantal strength or sonority – the same thing, but different directions. And so I started formulating generalisations over scales. This approach was quite inspiring to a number of people, including this student from Canada, Robert Murray. He is now professor at Calgary, Alberta in Canada and he wrote a thesis on *Phonological strength and Early Germanic syllable structure*. So he was the one who sort of dragged me back into phonology. And I've been a phonologist ever since.

The theoretical insights that came from Vennemann's return to phonology in the 1980s, insights we celebrate in this volume, culminated in the view that linguistic preferences were "theorems of a general theory of the human communicative capacity" (Vennemann 1988: 4). Vennemann developed the idea of linguistic preferences as linguistic laws, thus connecting them both to Neogrammarian thought and to universals in typological research. Vennemann's early work applied these preferences to syllable structure in an attempt to provide an understanding of the factors motivating sound change. Some structures turned out to be more preferred

---

at: https://youtu.be/SshmGNs9reQ. We are grateful to Robert Murray for making us aware of the interview and to Haj Ross for making his interview available to the public.

than others, and language change was seen as a shift in concert with these preferences. This new perspective changed the theoretical landscape in two ways. First, this shift in thought helped scholars explain the motivating and at times conflicting forces behind both language change and synchronic patterns in languages, a move beyond the largely descriptive work of traditional approaches. Second, scholars began shifting their thinking from Jakobson's binary markedness system where structures were either marked or unmarked (e.g. Jakobson 1941) to a more gradient system, where structures were seen as either more or less preferred than others in relation to a given parameter. This gradience was in turn associated with the Diachronic Maxim which Vennemann (1988: 2) formulates as follows: "Linguistic change on a given parameter does not affect a language structure as long as there exist structures in the language system that are less preferred in terms of the relevant preference law". In other words, less preferred structures are the first to be targeted for language change, where changes are interpreted as language improvements relative to a given paramater. Consider an established example about the gradient nature of linguistic structures, namely word initial *k*-clusters in English and German. According to the third stipulation of the Head Law,² syllable initial clusters are more preferred "the more sharply the Consonantal Strength drops from the onset towards the Consonantal Strength of the following syllable nucleus" (Vennemann 1988: 13–14). Consequently, a *#kl* cluster at the beginning of a word is more preferred than *#kn*, while *#kn* is in turn more preferred than *#km* (Vennemann 1988). This set of preferences is attested in German and English, both of which have words in their lexicons beginning with the word-initial onset *#kl* (E *clump*, G *Klumpen*). While neither language contains the dispreferred *#km* cluster as is also assumed for Proto-Indo-European (see e.g. Zair 2018), it is the history of *#kn* that highlights 1) the effect of the Diachronic Maxim and 2) how even related languages can differ in their treatment of the same structure. Although both English and German had the initial *#kn* cluster as evidenced in the spellings in words like E *knee* and G *Knie*, English eliminated the cluster while German continues to retain it (Lutz 1991). Thus, if language change occurs at all, it will affect the worst structures first, i.e. *#km*, and then the next least preferred, i.e. *#kn* as we see in English. The most preferred structures will be the last targeted for change, if they are targeted at all.

---

2 The Head Law, which defines preferences for syllable onsets, includes three stipulations: "A syllable head is the more preferred: (a) the closer the number of speech sounds in the head is to one, (b) the greater the Consonantal Strength value of its onset, and (c) the more sharply the Consonantal Strength drops from the onset toward the Consonantal Strength of the following syllable nucleus" (Vennemann 1988: 13–14; cf. also Murray & Vennemann 1983).

Although initially and still most commonly applied to the syllable, the influence of Theo Vennemann's work on preference theory in general has had a much broader impact in linguistics beyond accounting for phonological change. Indeed, it is Vennemann's broader and more generalised notion of preferences that serves as the inspiration for this volume and ties together the wide set of perspectives on linguistic preferences found in these papers which celebrate the enduring influence of Theo Vennemann's groundbreaking work on linguistic preferences.[3]

4 This book's contributions

Linguistic Preferences reflects the general lines of thought in preference theory from a linguistic perspective. Part I deals with gradience and preference ranking, while Part II focuses on prioritisation and the inferring of preferences from observed choices. Lastly, the papers in Part III address the issues of comparative evaluation and the inherent "predictive" purpose of preferences.

Part I, "Gradience and preference ranking", focuses on the question of gradience and the order of preferences with respect to both language change as well as synchronic states of languages and language families. The articles address the question of motivations of attested patterns as well as deviations from expected choices. This entails the complementing of phonemes which hitherto were not ranked (MAILHAMMER for taps as well as intersyllabic phonotactics and morphophonemic alternations in Amurdak). In discussing the theoretical implications of gradience and preference ranking on the basis of empirical data, the chapter contributes to the ongoing discussions of the status of markedness, prosodic feet, and morphophonology. Markedness constraints and their rankings open a critical discussion in terms of linguistic input and output (RAFFELSIEFEN for a discussion of phonological preferences related to German words originating from short-

---

[3] It is important to note the contributions to other areas of linguistics and scholarship made by Theo Vennemann, including but not restricted to his bifurcation theory to explain the High German consonant shift, phonological analyses drawing on syllable cut, as well as his work on areas such as pre-historic language contacts reflected in the hydronymy and toponomy north of the Alps, in the Runic alphabet, and the Germanic lexicon and grammar. Indeed, in his interview with Haj Ross noted above, Theo Vennemann shares his scholarly and intellectual journey. His contributions have impacted a large number of fields within linguistics. This volume's focus on preferences in general serves as a common thread to connect the broad range of work of scholars studying such varied data to celebrate the various ways in which Theo Vennemann's work has inspired the work of others.

ening, including acronyms and clippings). Research on linguistic templates leads to innovative hypotheses of developmental paths (MACAULAY and SALMONS on historical prosodic templates in Algonquian reduplication and initial change) and to contrastive studies on sound change and lexical development (SMITH for an examination of the impact of foot-based templates shaping vowel loss, reduction and retention in the history of West Germanic as well as plural formation in Modern German and Dutch).

Part II, "Prioritisation and the inferring of preferences from observed choices", deals with the nature of prioritisation as well as with the question of how preferences can be inferred from observed choices. Observed choices become particularily apparent in language change and in the chronology of developments. One objective of inferring preferences from observed choices in linguistics is the precise description of particularly complex linguistic features (BASBØL on the distribution of Danish stød and word-structure non-stød, including a discussion of the relative quality of the members of the consonantal strength scale). Inferring preferences from observed choices allows for a deciphering and re-interpretation of otherwise inscrutable structures (HYMAN for portmanteau morphemes in Luganda and Lusoga). The analyses are complemented by reflections on the history of linguistics (RAUCH about de Saussure's then controversial discovery of "coefficients sonantiques" as a result of abduction from observed choices). In contrast to choices which reflect preferences stand influencing factors such as perceptual limitations and articulatory constraints, which result in prioritisations (HOOLE for electromagnetic articulography displaying gestural co-ordination which motivates (dis)preferred patterns).

Lastly, Part III addresses issues of "Comparative evaluation and the inherent predictive purpose of preferences". In sum, what motivations can be accounted for in order to evaluate one structure as better and another one a worse option on either the syntagmatic or paradigmatic axis? Part III proposes answers from different viewpoints on synchronic states of languages, i.e. from the viewpoint of linguistic concept formation, from typological data (NOEL AZIZ HANNA for the syntactic preference of scopal ordering as part of the principle of unidirectional serialisation), and from areal observations of preferred patterns (DIMITROV for the Proto-Slavic Law of rising sonority and "post-open-syllable" innovations in liquid metathesis in Bulgarian). Preferences "explain" tendencies across languages and local distributions of segments. They also lead to insights into linguistic processes (HICKEY for Modern Irish epenthesis and metathesis) Laws and principles viewed as universals lead to an interpretation of synchronic states of languages with a predictive potential in terms of phonological, morphological, and syntactic optimisation. And finally, one of the explicitly formulated aims of future linguistic research is to test theories of lexical access and diachronic stability in language (MINKOVA

for a preference-based explanation of the presence or absence of geminates in the history of English and a tentatively proposed step-wise loss of geminates). The different viewpoints from which the articles start lead to a clearer picture of an optimisation and organisation of linguistic structures in general.

References

Aarts, Bas. 2004. *Syntactic gradience: The nature of grammatical indeterminacy*. Oxford: Oxford University Press.
Aikhenvald, Alexandra. 2018. Evidentiality: The framework. In Alexandra Aikhenvald (ed.), *The Oxford handbook of evidentiality*, 1–54. Oxford: Oxford University Press.
Antrup, Andreas. 2013. Co-evolution of institutions and preferences: The case of the (human) mating market. *Journal of Theoretical Biology* 332. 9–19.
Armstrong, Wallace. 1948. Uncertainty and the utility function. *Economic Journal* 58. 1–10.
Blasi, Damian, Steven Moran, Scott Moisik, Paul Widmer, Dan Dediu & Balthasar Bickel. 2019. Human sound systems are shaped by post-Neolithic changes in bite configuration. *Science* 363(6432): eaav3218.
Bolle, Friedel. 1983. On Sen's second-order preferences, morals, and decision theory. *Erkenntnis* 20. 195–205.
Chisholm, Roderick & Ernest Sosa. 1966. On the logic of "intrinsically better". *American Philosophical Quarterly* 3. 244–249.
Cooper, Adam. 2015. *Reconciling Indo-European syllabification*. Leiden: Brill.
Donegan, Patricia & David Stampe. 1979. The study of natural phonology. In Daniel Dinnsen (ed.), *Current approaches to phonological theory*, 126–173. Bloomington: Indiana University Press.
Dressler, Wolfgang. 1995. Interactions between iconicity and other semiotic parameters in language. In Raffaele Simone (ed.), *Iconicity in language*, 22–37. Amsterdam: John Benjamins.
Dressler, Wolfgang. 1999a. What is *natural* in Natural Morphology (NM)? *Prague Linguistic Circle Papers* 3. 135–144.
Dressler, Wolfgang. 1999b. On a semiotic theory of preferences in language. In Michael Haley & Michael Shapiro (eds.), *The Peirce seminar papers: Essays in semiotic analysis. Proceedings of the International Colloquium on Language and Peircean Sign Theory, 1997*, Vol. 4, 389–415. New York: Berghahn Books.
Dressler, Wolfgang, Willi Mayerthaler, Oswald Panagl & Wolfgang Wurzel. 1987. Introduction. In Wolfgang Dressler, Willi Mayerthaler, Oswald Panagl & Wolfgang Wurzel (eds.), *Leitmotifs in Natural Morphology*, 1–22. Amsterdam: John Benjamins.
Dziubalska-Kołaczyk, Katarzyna. 2001. Phonotactic constraints are preferences. In Katarzyna Dziubalska-Kołaczyk (ed.), *Constraints and preferences*, 69–100. Berlin: de Gruyter.
Gelbukh, Alexander & Hiram Calvo. 2018. *Automatic syntactic analysis based on selectional preferences*. Cham: Springer.
Gibbon, Dafydd. 2001. Preferences as defaults in computational phonology. In Katarzyna Dziubalska-Kołaczyk (ed.), *Constraints and preferences*, 143–199. Berlin: de Gruyter.

Grüne, Till. 2004. The problems of testing preference axioms with revealed preference theory. *Analyse & Kritik* 26. 382–397.
Halldén, Sören. 1957. *On the logic of 'better'*. Lund: Library of Theoria.
Hansson, Sven Ove & Grüne-Yanoff, Till. 2018. Preferences. In Edward Zalta (ed.), *The Stanford Encyclopedia of Philosophy*. <https://plato.stanford.edu/archives/sum2018/ entries/ preferences/>. (25.11.19)
Hausman, Daniel. 2012. *Preference, value, choice, and welfare*. Cambridge: Cambridge University Press.
Herzberger, Hans. 1973. Ordinal preference and rational choice. *Econometrica* 41. 187–237.
Hill, Eugen. 2009. Die Präferenztheorie in der historischen Phonologie aus junggrammatischer Perspektive. *Zeitschrift für Sprachwissenschaft* 28. 231–263.
Hyman, Larry & Russell Schuh. 1974. Universals of tone rules: Evidence from West Africa. *Linguistic Inquiry* 5. 81–115.
Jakobson, Roman. 1941. *Kindersprache, Aphasie und allgemeine Lautgesetze*. Uppsala: Almqvist & Wiksell.
de Jongh, Dick & Fenrong Liu. 2009. Preference, priorities and belief. In Till Grüne-Yanoff & Sven Ole Hansson (eds.), *Preference change: Approaches from philosophy, economics and psychology*, 85–107. Dordrecht: Springer.
Levelt, Willem. 1989. *Speaking: From intention to articulation*. Cambridge, MA: MIT Press.
Liu, Fenrong. 2011. *Reasoning about preference*. Dordrecht: Springer.
Lutz, Angelika. 1991. *Phonotaktisch gesteuerte Konsonantenveränderungen in der Geschichte des Englischen*. Tübingen: Niemeyer.
Mailhammer, Robert, David Restle & Theo Vennemann. 2015. Preference Laws in phonological change. In Patrick Honeybone & Joseph Salmons (eds.), *The Oxford handbook of historical phonology*, 450–466. Oxford: Oxford University Press.
Murray, Robert. 2008. The place of historical linguistics in the age of structuralism. In Sylvain Auroux, E.F.K. Koerner, Hans-Josef Niederehe & Kees Versteegh, (eds.) *History of the language sciences: An international handbook on the evolution of the study of language from the beginnings to the present*, Vol. 3, 2430–2445. Berlin: de Gruyter.
Payne, John, James Bettman & Eric Johnson. 1993. *The adaptive decision maker*. Cambridge: Cambridge University Press.
Peirce, Charles Sanders. 1903. The nature of meaning. In: *The essential Peirce: Selected philosophical writings. Volume 2 (1893–1913)*. Edited 1998 by Nathan Houser & Christian Kloesel. Bloomington, IN: Indiana University Press.
Pigozzi, Gabriella, Alexis Tsoukiàs & Paolo Viappiani. 2016. Preferences in artificial intelligence. *Annals of Mathematics and Artificial Intelligence* 77. 361–401.
Prince, Alan & Paul Smolensky. 1993. *Optimality Theory: Constraint interaction in Generative Grammar*. Technical Report, Rutgers University Center for Cognitive Science and Computer Science Department, University of Colorado at Boulder.
Ritt, Nikolaus. 2001. Are optimality theoretical "constraints" the same as natural linguistic "preferences"? In Katarzyna Dziubalska-Kołaczyk (ed.), *Constraints and preferences*, 291–310. Berlin: de Gruyter.
Sen, Amartya. 1974. Choice, orderings, and morality. In Stephan Körner (ed.), *Practical reason*, 54–67. Oxford: Blackwell.
Shannon, Tom. 1991. On the syllabic motivation of inflectional suffixes in Germanic. In Elmer Antonsen & Hans Henrich Hock (eds.), *Staefcraeft: Studies in Germanic linguistics. Selected papers from the 1st and 2nd Symposium on Germanic Linguistics, University*

of Chicago, 4 April 1985, and University of Illinois at Urbana-Champaign, 3–4 Oct. 1986, 169–183. Amsterdam: John Benjamins.

Smith, Laura Catharine & Adam Ussishkin. 2015. The role of prosodic templates in diachrony and dialects: Prosodically-driven language change. In Patrick Honeybone & Joseph Salmons (eds.), *The Oxford handbook of historical phonology*, 262–288. Oxford: Oxford University Press.

Vennemann, Theo. 1983. Causality in language change: Theories of linguistic preferences as a basis for linguistic explanations. *Folia Linguistica Historica* 6. 5–26.

Vennemann, Theo. 1988. *Preference laws for syllable structure and the explanation of sound change: With special reference to German, Germanic, Italian, and Latin*. Berlin: de Gruyter.

Vennemann, Theo. 1989. Language change as language improvement. In Vincenzo Orioles (ed.), *Modelli esplicativi della diacronica linguistica: Atti del Convegno della Società Italiana di Glottologia, Pavia, 15–17 settembre 1988*, 11–35. Pisa: Giardini. [Reprint 1993 in Charles Jones (ed.), *Historical linguistics: Problems and perspectives*, 310–344. London: Longman.]

Vennemann. 2000. Triple-cluster reduction in Germanic: Etymology without sound laws? *Historische Sprachforschung/Historical linguistics* 113. 239–258.

Wurzel, Wolfgang. 1996. Morphologischer Strukturwandel: Typologische Entwicklungen im Deutschen. In Ewald Lang & Gisela Zifonun (eds.), *Deutsch-typologisch*, 492–524. Berlin: de Gruyter.

Wurzel, Wolfgang. 2001. *Flexionsmorphologie und Natürlichkeit: Ein Beitrag zur morphologischen Theoriebildung*. Berlin: de Gruyter.

Zair, Nicolas. 2018. On the relative sonority of PIE /m/. *Indo-European Linguistics* 6. 271–303.

Part I: **Gradience and preference ranking**

Monica Macaulay and Joseph Salmons
Prosodic templates in Algonquian reduplication and initial change

Abstract: Vennemann (1988) inspired broad interest in the diachrony of prosodic templates, extending the insights of syllable preferences to larger prosodic units. We examine two widespread patterns of nonconcatenative morphology in Algonquian languages, reduplication and "initial change". Reduplication takes various forms across Algonquian, but all of the languages have at least historical prefixation of a syllable consisting of a copy of the initial consonant plus a fixed vowel /a/, long or short. Initial change, which creates participles (among other functions), encompasses a set of morphological processes: ablaut (qualitative and/or quantitative) and affixation (prefixation or infixation, usually of the form -*ay*-). Prosodic templates allow us to capture previously unrecognised synchronic connections via history and to suggest possible developmental paths of initial change.

1 Introduction

Non-affixal morphological patterns like ablaut and reduplication – nonconcatenative morphology – often connect with prosodic patterns and are sometimes claimed to produce prosodically preferred outputs. Nonconcatenative morphology has been described in many languages of the world (see Wilbur's 1973 crosslinguistic survey of reduplication or the discussion of Arabic ablaut later

---

Acknowledgements: This paper began with two presentations in 2003, one at the International Conference on Historical Linguistics (Copenhagen) and the other at the Algonquian Conference (University of Western Ontario). As we began to work on the topic again, we were fortunate to be asked to contribute to this volume honoring Theo Vennemann's work. We presented the new paper at the University of Arizona in 2019. In addition to the editors and those audiences, we thank the following for comments and feedback on the project: David Costa, Amy Dahlstrom, Hunter Lockwood, Mizuki Miyashita, Adam Ussishkin, and Andy Wedel. All the usual disclaimers apply.

Monica Macaulay, Language Sciences Program, University of Wisconsin – Madison, USA
Joseph Salmons, Language Sciences Program, University of Wisconsin – Madison, USA

in this paper). Still, the morphologically rich Algonquian languages have largely been overlooked in this regard. These patterns are typologically striking in Algonquian, since we might expect that polysynthetic languages are not compatible with a high degree of fusion between morphemes (in the sense of phonological fusion rather than semantic). As Comrie puts it (1989: 49), "in practice [...] as the index of synthesis [number of morphemes per word] gets higher, the ratio of agglutination to fusion must also increase".

Two nonconcatenative phenomena are attested in most modern Algonquian languages: reduplication and "initial change" (IC henceforth, explained below). We have four goals in this paper. We first establish the robust role of nonconcatenative morphology in Algonquian. Second, we demonstrate that reduplication and IC are instantiations of closely parallel phenomena. Third, we show how a prosodic perspective allows us to unify the remarkably diverse set of ways that IC and reduplication are marked across the family and within individual languages and to show the resultant similarities. Finally, while the existence of templates is well established, their status in the grammar remains controversial and their history ill-understood. We argue that Algonquian IC reflects the rise of a prosodic pattern formally akin to reduplication. This paper takes a first step toward integrating two important prosodic phenomena into our synchronic and diachronic understanding of Algonquian and toward clarifying the diachrony of templates.

IC – so called because it involves change to the initial syllable of the word – is exemplified for the Algonquian language Menominee in Table 1, below (with relevant segments underlined in the last column). IC encompasses a set of morphological processes, namely ablaut (qualitative and/or quantitative) and affixation (prefixation and/or infixation, usually of the form -*ay*-).[1]

Reduplication, the other prosodic phenomenon in Algonquian to be considered here, is exemplified (again for Menominee) in Table 2. These examples show fixed-vowel reduplication, with or without copying of the initial consonants.

---

[1] Menominee data are presented in the practical orthography used by the Menominee: <q> represents glottal stop, <c> represents a sound which varies between a palatal and an alveolar affricate, <ae> represents the low front vowel, and vowel length is marked with a macron. Elsewhere we use a raised dot for vowel length or follow authors' original transcriptions – raised dot, colon, or doubled vowels – to the extent practical. We generally follow Americanist usage, including <y> for the IPA glide <j>, <š> for IPA <ʃ>, and <č> for IPA <tʃ>.

Table 1: Initial Change in Menominee (Bloomfield 1962: 98, 176–185).

Unchanged		Changed		
(C₁)VC₂	*ahsāmet* 'when he feeds me'	(C₁)V·C₂	Ablaut	*a͞ehsamet* 'when he fed me'
	poqsa͞ehkah 'when he dons it'			*po͞qsaehkah* 'when he donned it'
(C₁)V·C₂	*āqtaek* 'when it is extinguished'	(C₁)ayV·C₂	Prefixation	*ayāqteken* 'whenever it is extinguished'
	pōset 'when he embarks'		Infixation	*payōset* 'when he embarked'

Table 2: Menominee reduplication (Bloomfield 1962: 427–430; second author's fieldwork).

Prefix	Plain	Reduplicated
Cā-C	*mekēw* '[The dog] barks'	*mā-mekew* 'It barks again and again'
āy-V	*apēw* 'S/he sits'	*āy-apew* 'S/he keeps sitting'
ā-yV	*yātapew* 'S/he changes his/her seat'	*ā-yātapew* 'S/he repeatedly changes his/her seat'

Although details vary across the languages, one core pattern of reduplication is attested across the family – albeit only in historical reflexes in the case of Blackfoot (Berman 2006) – and is thus uncontroversially reconstructed for Proto-Algonquian (see Section 4). As illustrated in Table 2, this is the prefixation of a syllable composed of a copy of any initial consonant plus a fixed vowel, /a·/ or /a/. Vowel-initial words generally show epenthesis of /y/ after reduplicative /a(·)/, a process which is found throughout the Algonquian languages (at least on a sporadic basis) in other contexts as well, to break up VV sequences (cf. Bloomfield 1946: 93). *y*-epenthesis is illustrated in example (1):[2]

(1) Menominee (Bloomfield 1962: 83, 105)
 a. *pīt-   -aw   -an*
   bring.it- -TH   -LOC
   'if I/you (sg.) bring it'

---

[2] Abbreviations used are: 1, 2, 3 – first, second, third person; CONJ – conjunct [order]; EPEN – epenthetic; IC – initial change; ITER – iterative; LOC – local (first or second person); PL – plural; TH – theme sign.

b. *pōse-*   *-y*   *-an*
    embark- -EPEN -LOC
    'if I/you (sg.) embark'

(1a) shows the suffix *-an* attached to a consonant-final base, while (1b) shows it attached to a vowel-final base, triggering *y*-epenthesis.

Thus, reduplication and affixal (non-ablauting) IC are formally remarkably similar. We argue that the nature of IC lies in reduplication-like prosodic morphology. Whether or not initial change has *origins* in reduplication, the two processes are parallel, and in one daughter, Shawnee, IC is now realised by reduplication, as discussed below. We suggest that IC originated in the long-vowel, apparently affixational pattern and that the ablauting forms were later developments due to contraction of vowels across the glide /y/. We use the simple building blocks of prosodic morphology and phonology to argue that prefixation/infixation can be seen as templatic mapping, with reference to the syllable, foot, and phonological edges.

We define a prosodic template, following Macken and Salmons (1997: 37), as "a conventionalized unit – a single unit – that imposes constraints on the surface form of words and, in so doing, encodes a particular relationship between words thus related". In the data at hand, we have inflectional templatic patterns, rather than generalisations over the lexicon. In the growing body of work on diachronic templates, Smith and Ussishkin (2015: 284, also Murray and Vennemann 1983, Vennemann 1988, Smith 2004 and this volume) argue that "templates provide a unified approach to divergent language patterns not only within languages but cross-linguistically". On some views, reviewed by Guekguezian (2017: 84 and elsewhere), templates require special grammatical machinery, e.g. being associated with a diacritic. He instead sees templates as purely epiphenomenal, produced by "the interaction of prosodic well-formedness and recursive prosodic word structure triggered by syntactic cyclicity" (2017: 84). Following Salmons and Zhuang (2018: 568), we understand templatic patterns as "organized around preferences for certain prosodic structures", which "all create general prosodic patterns and yield a particular word structure." That is, templates instantiate prosodic preferences.

In the next two sections, we review contemporary Algonquian IC (Section 2), describing its functions across the family, and turn to previous analyses of Proto-Algonquian IC (Section 3). Section 4 introduces Algonquian reduplication and its reconstruction. We show in Section 5 that a coherent pattern of IC can be reconstructed across different stem shapes by seeing it as a nonconcatenative morphological operation closely parallel to reduplication. We close by sketching a scenario of how reduplication and IC might have developed historically. We conclude in Section 6.

2 Functions of initial change

Initial change, exemplified for Menominee in Table 1 above, is an inflectional process which applies to a particular paradigm of the verb, known as the conjunct order. The number and types of such paradigms vary across the Algonquian languages, but common to virtually all are the independent order (used for most main clauses) and the conjunct order (used for subordinate clauses and in other contexts). These paradigms are distinguished by both prefixation and suffixation. Typically, independent order makes use of prefixes which mark one of the arguments of the verb (determined by a person hierarchy), while conjunct order does not use the prefixes. The suffixes used in each order differ as well. Consider first the examples in (2), from Nishnaabemwin (a dialect of Ojibwe):

(2) Nishnaabemwin (Ojibwe) (Valentine 2001: 232, 236)
    a. INDEPENDENT ORDER
        ni-   boodwe-   -min
        1-   make.fire- -1PL
        'We make a fire'
    b. CONJUNCT ORDER
        boodweyaang
        boodwe-   -yaang
        make.fire- -1PL
        '(that) we make a fire'

In (2a), illustrating independent order, Nishnaabemwin uses a first person prefix *n-* (underlyingly /ni-/); in (2b), the prefix is lacking in conjunct order. The two examples also illustrate how different suffixes are used in the two orders.

Initial change produces a subcategory of the conjunct order, traditionally called the "changed conjunct". Typical functions include the formation of participles and what Algonquianists call iterative forms, illustrated in (3):

(3) Nishnaabemwin (Ojibwe) (Valentine 2001: 239, 240):
    a. CHANGED CONJUNCT: PARTICIPLE
        bw<u>aa</u>dweyaang
        IC+ *boodwe-*   *-yaang*
        IC+ make.fire- -1PL
        'We who make fire'

b. CHANGED CONJUNCT: ITERATIVE
b<u>waa</u>dwewaang-in
IC+ boodwe- -waang -in
IC+ make.fire- -1PL -ITER
'Whenever we make fire'

Participles (as in 3a) are verbal forms which often translate as relative clauses.[3] Iteratives (as in 3b) are forms which are translated as 'whenever [*verb*]'. Both of these examples illustrate initial change in Nishnaabemwin, which in this case takes the form of ablaut, as is illustrated later in this paper.

Another common function of changed conjunct is to mark past tense or perfective aspect. Valentine, for example, says of this use in Nishnaabemwin that "[i]n some cases verbs show initial change to indicate a specific instance of an event in the past, as opposed to a customary, habitual, or repetitive event [...] . Clauses of this sort are usually staging for a main predication, providing a time specification for the main verb of the sentence" (2001: 771). Goddard says that in Delaware "[t]he changed conjunct generally denotes actual events" and "[t]he changed subjunctive indicates an actual past event subordinate to some succeeding past event" (1979a: 50). Similarly, Bloomfield, describing Menominee changed conjunct, says, "[W]here it contrasts with other tenses, it denotes an actual prior event" (1962: 486). His example is given in (4), where the verb which describes the act of entering, which precedes the act of sitting down, is in changed conjunct form:

(4) Menominee changed conjunct (Bloomfield 1962: 486; our glosses)
payīhtiket, pes-onāpew
IC+ *pīhtike-* -t pes- onape- -w
IC+ enter- -3.CONJ come- sit.down- -3
'After he had entered, he came and sat down'

Having provided this brief survey of the functions of initial change in the modern languages, we now turn to previous historical treatments of the form of initial change.

---

3 Valentine (2001: 510) notes that in Nishnaabemwin participles may also have some nominal inflection, and this is true in some other Algonquian languages as well.

3 Historical perspectives on initial change

In the first part of this section we review the most important earlier reconstructions of initial change. While rigorous in their application of the comparative method and well-developed as segmental accounts, these works do not treat prosodic aspects of IC.[4] In Section 3.2, we turn to one previous hypothesis about the origins of IC.

Earlier researchers have reconstructed the segmental changes associated with IC for Proto-Algonquian and Pre-Proto-Algonquian. Table 3 illustrates five of these proposals. Note that Bloomfield, Goddard, Pentland, and Hockett reconstruct Proto-Algonquian, while Costa's reconstruction is of Pre-Proto-Algonquian.

Table 3: Reconstructions of Initial Change in (Pre-)Proto-Algonquian.

Unchanged	Changed				
	Proto-Algonquian				Pre-Proto-Alg.
	Bloomfield (1946)	Goddard (1979a, p.c.)	Pentland (1979)	Hockett (1981)	Costa (1996)
a	e·	e·	e·	e·	e·
i	---	---	---	---	ye·
e	e·	e·	e·	e·	e·
o/we	o·/we·	we·	we·	---	we·
a·	aya·	aya·	eya·	aya·	aya·
i·	ayi·	a·	(y)a·	a·	a·
e·	aye·	aye·	eye·	aye·	aye·
o·	ayo·	wa·	wa·	wa·	ayo·

As Oxford argues (2015: 320, following Goddard), the status of the *we/*o contrast is unclear but *we became *o either in Proto-Algonquian or "in all daughters except Proto-Eastern-Algonquian". While this is an important [to avoid repeating consequences] historical question, it has no consequences for our analysis. Likewise, the absence in (most of) Table 3 of a changed version of short *i reflects a gap in the Proto-Algonquian vowel system under some reconstructions, not in the paradigm of initial change, and it is, again, not important here. See Goddard (1979b: 75–76, 81–84) for details.

---

4 Blain (1992: 33) suggests that her floating feature account of vowel quality in Ojibwe reduplication could be extended to initial change, but she does not pursue the idea further.

Like his reconstructions of Proto-Algonquian in general, Bloomfield's (1946) reconstruction of IC is primarily based on Fox (now known as Meskwaki), Cree, Menominee, and Ojibwe, which Bloomfield viewed as exemplars of the Central Algonquian group. He reconstructs long vowel IC as having a prefixed *ay-* in all cases. Goddard (1979a: 196–197, n. 3) observes that Bloomfield's reconstruction is essentially just the Menominee pattern, and he goes on to suggest that Proto-Algonquian *i· changed to *a· and *o· changed to *wa· instead.[5]

Pentland (1979) reconstructs initial change based on data from Menominee, Ojibwe, and eastern dialects of Cree. As Table 3 shows, Pentland reconstructs the same changes for *a and *e as Bloomfield does but differs significantly from Bloomfield in his reconstruction of the changes for *o (which he actually treats as *we) and the long vowels.[6]

Hockett (1981) provides a detailed overview of the phonological changes undergone by Menominee as it evolved out of Proto-Algonquian, drawing on Bloomfield (1946) and Goddard (1979b). The reconstruction shown in Table 3 is given as part of his discussion of the Menominee forms.

Finally, Costa (1996) considers a thorough sample of the Algonquian languages to arrive at a reconstruction of IC. Because the patterns are obscure even in Proto-Algonquian, Costa reconstructs IC at the level of Pre-Proto-Algonquian, hence the additional column in Table 3. His reconstruction of IC is by far the most comprehensive, the culmination of a long tradition of historical work on Algonquian IC.

We do not suggest revisions to Costa's reconstruction. We do seek to unify the very heterogeneous set of morphological operations all serving a single function: quantitative ablaut (*e ~ *e·), qualitative ablaut (*i· ~ *a·), qualitative and quantitative ablaut together (*a ~ *e·), infixation, and prefixation. Furthermore, ablaut (of any type) is otherwise rarely if ever used for morphological purposes across the family, and prefixation is likewise relatively rare (mostly limited to person-marking and reduplication, though Blackfoot has more, see Berman 2006). A prosodic approach forms the core of our discussion in Section 5, but first we turn to the almost unstudied question of the origins of initial change.

---

[5] Ives Goddard (p.c.) has come to think that an earlier reconstruction by Bloomfield (1925) was probably correct, in which Proto-Algonquian had (unchanged) *o in all positions (rather than initial *we), with IC to *we·.

[6] Going beyond Algonquian proper to Algic (or Macro-Algonquian), Pentland further proposes that the Yurok infix *-eg-* corresponds to Proto-Algonquian *-ey-, his reconstruction of the IC affix associated with long vowels. Costa (1996: 63–64) shows that these are highly unlikely to be comparable reconstructions for reasons we will not review here. Our prosodic approach makes such a connection even less likely. Berman (2003) revisits the issue of initial change in Yurok with a different proposal, but this lies beyond the scope of this paper.

We have just seen that several scholars have proposed reconstructions of IC. Much less has been said about its actual origins. Pearson (1985) suggests that IC originated in a prefix *ye- which metathesised with initial consonants. He posits this for Pre-Proto-Algonquian and argues that after the prefix underwent metathesis with initial consonants, it "immediately coalesced with the following vowel to produce the effect now known as initial change" (1985: 532). That is, all IC originated in prefixation. That prefix, where there was a stem-initial consonant, became infixed by what he apparently conceives of as a completely regular process of metathesis. Later segmental changes then transformed some of those infixed forms into ablaut-like morphological patterns. In this way, Pearson unifies the three distinct operations attested as part of contemporary and readily-reconstructed IC.

Pearson thus addresses essentially the same questions that we ask in this paper about the ultimate source of IC. However, the heart of Pearson's proposal is an implausible *double* metathesis, both instances of which would have to be regular processes: one metathesis of an entire syllable around a single consonant, presumably followed by an additional metathesis of the glide and vowel. That is, in order to produce the well-attested CayV- pattern of IC, Pearson's proposal would entail metathesis of *ye-CV- to *CyeV-, and then a second metathesis to *CeyV- (with a lowering of *e to *a at some point in the chronology).[7] We are not aware of any parallel in the languages of the world, and it would be unusual on several counts. Mielke and Hume (2001) show that metathesis tends to occur at right edges of words, not left edges. Also, as Yu (2007: 141–148) lays out, cases of metathesis leading to infixation seem to be perceptually motivated, where the moved segment has features that can extend phonetically over a longer stretch, such as pharyngealisation or laryngealisation. That provides no motivation for Pearson's scenario, though the change would improve syllable structure in the Vennemannian sense.

A regular process of this type would be extremely unusual, either as sound change or as a morphological operation, and it seems unlikely for reasons just given. Even assuming the changes proposed, the first step, prefixation, still looks odd within Algonquian, a family richer than most in suffixation, but poorer than many in prefixation.[8] Furthermore, the proposed infixation and metathesis would have few clear parallels or models across the family. While our proposal parallels Pearson's in some ways, difficulties like two intertwined regular metatheses suggest a need for a simpler and more directly motivated account.

---

7 However, see Pentland's proposal of *-ey- as the reconstructed infix.
8 As Adam Ussishkin (p.c.) points out, Turkish is typologically similar, showing extensive suffixing but one pattern of emphatic reduplication at the left edge of some adjectives.

We turn now to a consideration of the second nonconcatenative process in Algonquian languages, reduplication, which will set the stage for our analysis of initial change in Section 5.

4 Reduplication in Algonquian

Goddard (1979b: 92–93) notes that "The comparative study of the complex patterns of reduplication exhibited by many [Algonquian] languages is hampered by the dearth of descriptive materials." This remains largely true 40 years later. We review some available descriptions, and discuss recent hypotheses on the reconstruction of reduplication in Proto-Algonquian and its broader affiliation, Proto-Algic. Leaving aside patterns like triplication (e.g. Drapeau 2014: 476–477 on Innu), three primary patterns can be observed: (a) (C)a(·)-, (b) heavy reduplication of the form (C)a·h-, and (c) disyllabic reduplication. We discuss these in turn.

Common to all descriptions of Algonquian reduplication is prefixation of a syllable consisting of a copy of the initial consonant plus a fixed vowel /a/, either long or short. If there is no initial consonant, the vowel is prefixed and /y/ is inserted to break up the ensuing vowel cluster. This pattern – with long /a·/ – has already been illustrated for Menominee in Table 2, above (see also Macaulay 2018). An example of a language which shows the same pattern, but with short /a/, is East Cree (Junker and Blacksmith 1994), as exemplified in Table 4:[9]

Table 4: Reduplication in East Cree (Junker and Blacksmith 1994).

Prefix	Plain	Reduplicated
Ca-C	*pakaasimuu* 'S/he swims'	*pa-pakaasimuu* 'S/he swims over & over/always'
	niimuu 'S/he dances'	*na-niimuu* 'S/he dances all the time'
ay-V	*asameu* 'S/he feeds her/him'	*ay-asameu* 'S/he feeds her/him over & over'

A second pattern is what Ahenakew and Wolfart (1983) call 'heavy reduplication', prefixation of *(C)a·h-*.[10] This is distinguished in Plains Cree from light reduplication, prefixation of *(C)a-* (the pattern just discussed). Table 5 illustrates:

---

[9] Junker and Blacksmith describe a few other sporadic patterns in East Cree as well, but what is shown in Table 4 seems to be the productive form.
[10] The coda [h] of heavy reduplication is described by Ahenakew and Wolfart as devoicing: "the *h*-like sound of this devoicing is strongest before a stop [...], less clear-cut before a nasal [...]

Table 5: Reduplication in Plains Cree (Ahenakew and Wolfart 1983).

Type	Prefix	Reduplicated
light	Ca-C	pa-pimohtēw 'he was walking along'
	ay-V	ay-ācimowak 'they are telling stories right now'
heavy	Cāh-C	māh-mātow 'he cries off and on'
	āh-V	āh-ācimowak 'they tell one story after another'
both	Ca-Cāh-C	ni-pa-pāh-pimohtān 'I keep walking (all year round)'
	ay-āh-V	ay-āh-ācimowak 'they kept telling stories'

The two patterns in Plains Cree are distinguished semantically: light reduplication generally signals an ongoing action, state, or progressive aspect. Heavy reduplication signals a discontinuous or intermittent action or state; or repetitive, intensive, or distributive aspect. The two can co-occur, as the final pair of examples in the table indicate.

The third pattern found is disyllabic reduplication, which copies the first two syllables of the base with no fixed elements. This is found in Meskwaki, and it too contrasts with the familiar monosyllabic reduplication, in this case *(C)a·-* (although the vowel is /e·/ when the vowel of the base is /e/) (Dahlstrom 1997). Table 6 summarises both monosyllabic and disyllabic reduplication as well as their combined occurrence:

Table 6: Reduplication in Meskwaki (Dahlstrom 1997).

Type	Prefix	Reduplicated
monosyllabic	Ce·-Ce(·)	ke·-keteminaw-e-wa 'He blesses him'
		me·-me·menat-amwa 'He vomits'
	Ca·-CV	na·-nowi·-wa 'He goes out'
		wa·-wi·tamaw-e·wa 'He is telling him'
	a·-y-a/a·/e	a·-y-ahkwi 'so far' (preverb)
		a·-y-ešawi-wa 'He does thus'
	wa·-w-o (< #o)	wa·-w-otami [< otami] 'waste time' (preverb)
disyllabic	CV(·)CV-CVCV(·C)	mena-menah-e·wa 'He makes him drink'
	V(·)CV-h-VCV	ata-h-atame·-wa 'He smokes'
both	CV·CV-Ca·-CV	wa·wi·wa·-wi·tamaw-e·wa 'He keeps telling him over and over'

---

or before /w/, and not audible at all before /s/" (1983: 370–371). This may reflect partial vowel devoicing, but they note that the phonological status of [h] is unclear.

Again, the two types of reduplication in Meskwaki are semantically distinct: monosyllabic reduplication marks continuative or habitual aspect, and disyllabic reduplication marks iterative aspect (repeated or distributed action). As shown in the table, as in Plains Cree the two types can co-occur.[11]

Although of course there is variation in the details, these three examples typify the patterns of reduplication described in the literature on Algonquian languages.[12] Some of the deviations from these patterns include the following:

(5) a. Long vowel in consonant-initial forms but short vowel in vowel-initial forms
 – Atikamekw (a dialect of Cree) *ma·-ma·konam* 'He takes it continually by hand'; *ay-a·cciw* 'He moves continually' (Beland 1978)
 b. Fixed vowel /e(·)/ (long or short) before base with /e(·)/
 – Meskwaki; see first two rows of Table 6, above
 – Ojibwe *tepwettam* 'he believes'; *te-tepwettam* 'he believes from time to time' (Nichols 1980)
 – Potawatomi *nU-wepUna*; *n-we-wepna* 'I leave him repeatedly' (Hockett 1948)[13]
 – Menominee *mē-mesāhkonam* 'he shapes it by hand into a solid mass' (Bloomfield 1962)
 – Miami-Illinois *nee-neehseeci* 'he breathes repeatedly, he pants' (David Costa, p.c.)
 c. Length of vowel in prefix depends on underlying length of vowel of base
 – Nishnaabemwin (Ojibwe) unreduplicated stem /dakamibatoo/, reduplicated *d-daakmibtoo* 'keep running across' [short *a* in initial syllable deleted by regular rules, vowel lengthened in second syllable also by regular rules]; unreduplicated stem /boontese/, reduplicated *baa-boontese* 'keep stopping' (Valentine 2001)

---

11 The historical record for Miami-Illinois also shows disyllabic reduplication, at least sporadically (David Costa, p.c.): *eenkihaata* 'he kills him (changed conjunct)'; *eenki-eenkihiwia* 'habitual killer'. In this language, it appears to have marked habitual action, unlike the pattern in Meskwaki.
12 Goddard (2010: 157) says that "Delaware has more functionally distinct types [of reduplication] than any other Algonquian language." He exemplifies five reduplicative patterns: they are all of the light variety (C plus a vowel) or the heavy variety (CVh). The differences are found in the vowel which appears, in terms of its quality and quantity.
13 Hockett uses the symbol <U> to indicate a vowel which is susceptible to syncope. The reduplicated form given, *n-we-wepna*, shows this syncope of <U>.

- Ojibwe unreduplicated *waniššin* 'he is lost'; reduplicated <u>wa</u>-*wanissin* 'he gets lost here and there'; unreduplicated *ko:ki:* 'he dives', reduplicated <u>ka:</u>-*ko:ki:* 'he dives here and there' (data from Nichols 1980; reported in Blain 1992)
    d. Sporadic *CVC*- reduplication
    - Menominee <u>kēs</u>-*kēskaham* 'he repeatedly chops it through' (Bloomfield 1946)
    - Meskwaki <u>ki·š</u>-*ki·škatahw-e·wa* 'he whips him' (Dahlstrom 1997)
    e. Sporadic *CVʔ*- or *CVh*- reduplication
    - Menominee <u>cēq</u>-*cepāēkaw* 'he repeatedly jerks'; <u>kāh</u>-*kāskaham* 'he scrapes it by tool' (Bloomfield 1962) (recall the use of <q> for glottal stop)
    - Meskwaki <u>či·h</u>-*či·pi·kwe·-wa* 'he winks' (Dahlstrom 1997)
    - Miami-Illinois <u>kiih</u>-*kiilohkimilaani* 'I doubt you, disagree with you' (David Costa, p.c.)
    - Severn Ojibwa <u>šīh</u>-*šiki* 'he urinates'; <u>tēh</u>-*tēhsipīhsē-* 'skip over water' (Todd 1970)
    f. Regular reduplicative prefixation but a change in the vowel of the base
    - Plains Cree *nitawāpamēw* 'he goes to see him'; <u>na</u>-*nātawāpamēw* 'he looks out for him' (Wolfart 1969: 200)
    - Menominee *kenuahkose-* 'be a tall tree'; <u>ka</u>-*kānuahkosewak* 'they are tall trees' (Bloomfield 1946)

This material should give readers an idea of the similarities and differences in reduplicative patterns across the Algonquian languages. Hypotheses about the reconstruction of reduplication in Proto-Algonquian have until relatively recently been limited: Bloomfield (1946: 122), for example, says that the "regular type of reduplication" is *Cā*- and lists "various irregular types." Hockett (1981: 68) agrees, pointing out that Algonquian reduplication has presumably always been heterogeneous: "There is no evidence that Algonquian has ever had a single completely dominant pattern of reduplication. Instead, there is evidence for several, one more productive in a particular period (or language), another at some other time or place." Still, he continues, "[t]he commonest pattern, undoubtedly of P[roto-]A[lgonquian] age, is [...] for *Cā*- to be prefixed to the stem, where *C* is the initial nonsyllabic of the stem; if the stem begins with a vowel then *C* is zero, but /y/ is inserted after the /ā/."

Moving beyond Algonquian to Algic, which includes Yurok and Wiyot (Haas 1958, Berman 1982), Garrett (2001) has proposed that Yurok shows reflexes of what he sees as Algic patterns of monosyllabic and disyllabic reduplication. Garrett argues that Yurok "repetitive" reduplication reflects Algic disyllabic reduplication (thus related to modern-day Meskwaki disyllabic reduplication and possibly Plains Cree heavy reduplication), while the intensive infix *-eg-* "arose from the reinterpretation of a monosyllabic (*Ce-*) reduplicative formation" (2001: 309). Conathan and Wood (2003), however, suggest that the semantics of disyllabic reduplication in Yurok and Meskwaki are too divergent for it to have a plausible common origin. The Yurok case shows clear parallels to the geographically close but unrelated language Karuk, and they conclude that a contact-based explanation is more likely. As noted above, the only case that has been described in print of an Algonquian language with both monosyllabic and disyllabic reduplication is Meskwaki (Dahlstrom 1997).[14] Dahlstrom (p.c.) considers the disyllabic reduplication pattern of Meskwaki to be of more recent origin than the monosyllabic pattern; the disyllabic pattern is phonologically regular, productive, and has predictable semantic effects, while the monosyllabic type displays a number of irregularities, is less productive, and may have idiosyncratic semantics. In addition, if both reduplication patterns apply to a single token, the disyllabic reduplicant is on the periphery (cf. Table 6). In the absence of significantly broader and more powerful comparative evidence, disyllabic reduplication in Yurok (on the one hand) and one or more Algonquian languages (on the other) appears, then, to be an innovation rather than a retention.

Reconstructions of Proto-Algonquian reduplication agree that Proto-Algonquian had *Ca·-*. There may have been additional reduplicative patterns, possibly with coda consonants (whether epenthetic or copied), which account for the now-sporadic exceptional forms of reduplication found across the family.

It is plausible that the robust types of reduplication attested across Algonquian all developed from full-copy reduplicative patterns which evolved into fixed-vowel patterns. Niepokuj (1997) proposed just such an evolutionary trajectory for reduplication crosslinguistically. There are other attempts at reconstructing full-copy reduplication in Algonquian, such as Hockett (1981: 68–69), or Cowan (1972) and Siebert (1967) on reduplication in some bird names, but such detours lie too far off the road to our goals in this paper to be considered further.

---

14 In addition to Miami-Illinois, Marguerite MacKenzie (p.c.) tells us that Innu of Sheshatshiu (Cree) also has disyllabic reduplication. Another disyllabic pattern is reported for Western Naskapi (Cree) by Julie Brittain (p.c.), who suggests that the pattern might be better understood as *CVC-* reduplication, with an epenthetic vowel after the second consonant. There may be additional examples of disyllabic reduplication in the Algonquian languages.

5 Analysis

With this empirical groundwork laid, we now turn to a new analysis of initial change in the broader context of Algonquian verbal morphology. Costa claims that "at the Proto-Algonquian level initial change was a fully developed morphophonemic process, and [...] even at that stage, the alternations inherent in initial change had no clear phonological motivation" (1996: 64). As we have seen, he goes on to reconstruct considerably clearer patterns for Pre-Proto-Algonquian, but even there a fully-developed *segmental* account cannot completely elucidate the structure and motivations of IC, nor can it unify the set of different morphological operations involved. Pearson (1985) overcomes the last problem, but his proposal is not without serious complications, as described above. In this section we show how a prosodic approach can yield better results, directly situating IC in the grammar of early Algonquian more comfortably, while capturing its profound parallels with reduplication.

A preliminary version of our hypothesis is given in (6), where we schematise the relationship between the unchanged and the changed forms. As explained below, we treat the modern long-vowel pattern (that is, the one in which -*ay*- is added) as the more basic.

(6) Reconstructed pattern of IC: first formulation
Unchanged   **Changed**
$(C_1)V(\cdot)C_2$ ~ $(C_1)ayV(\cdot)C_2$

We exemplify this proposal in Table 7. For convenience, we draw on Hewson's (1993, now https://protoalgonquian.atlas-ling.ca) reconstructions of Proto-Algonquian verb stems, but nothing in our argument hinges on the details of the particular forms; a similar exercise could be undertaken with Aubin (1975) or other sources.

Table 7: Reconstructed IC in Proto-Algonquian (verb stems from Hewson 1993).

Initial Syllable	Meaning	Unchanged Stem	Changed Stem
CV·	'whittle'	*mo·hkwetam-	*mayo·hkwetam-
	'see'	*ne·we·-	*naye·we·-
CV	'shut'	*kepwiken-	*kayepwiken-
	'drown'	*tahpene·-	*tayahpene·-
V(·)	'paddle'	*ešičime·-	*ayešičime·-
	'tell'	*a·totam-	*aya·totam-

Compare (6) with (7), which schematises reduplication in a parallel fashion:

(7) Reconstructed pattern of reduplication
Base **Reduplicated**
$C_1V(\cdot)C_2$- ~ $C_1a\cdot\cdot C_1V(\cdot)C_2$-
$V(\cdot)C_2$- ~ $a\cdot y\cdot V(\cdot)C_2$-

Table 8 exemplifies:

Table 8: Reconstructed reduplication in Proto-Algonquian (verb stems from Hewson 1993).

Initial Syllable	Meaning	Unreduplicated Stem	Reduplicated Stem
CV·	'whittle'	*mo·hkwetam-	*ma·mo·hkwetam-
	'see'	*ne·we··	*na·ne·we··
CV	'shut'	*kepwiken-	*ka·kepwiken-
	'drown'	*tahpene··	*ta·tahpene··
V(·)	'paddle'	*ešičime··	*a·yešičime··
	'tell'	*a·totam-	*a·ya·totam-

Stated this way, reduplication and IC constitute closely related prosodic patterns, where IC combines elements of consonant- and vowel-initial reduplication: The major difference is that IC moves rather than copies C_1, but like reduplication, it involves the fixed vowel /a/. The other surface difference falls out automatically from this view: in IC, moving an onset and inserting /a/ creates a V-V sequence and thus triggers intervocalic /y/ insertion, on which see below.

A traditional approach might formulate this view of IC in terms of infixation of -*ay*- after the initial consonant, or as a process of prefixation followed by metathesis, which Yu (2007: 176–177, elsewhere) shows to be a common source of infixes. Both approaches, however, make IC seem anomalous in the morphological context of Algonquian, since productive infixation appears otherwise unknown in the family. That a pattern of infixation is employed to break up consonant glide onset clusters (see Section 5.3) seems even more un-Algonquian. Prosodic morphology, however, allows us to understand seemingly disparate processes as instantiations of parallel phenomena, including in this case.

Comparing IC to reduplication, an autosegmental version of IC might treat it as the result of "movement" of C_1 to a new initial position before a prefixed *a*-. This is shown in (8), where the top tier shows the CV slots and the bottom tier the IC form:

(8) Autosegmental representation of C movement (metathesis) hypothesis for IC, parallel to reduplication

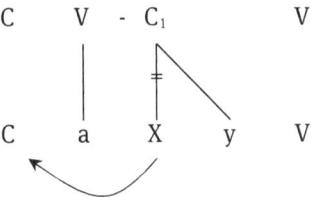

While this gives us a graphic representation of the similarity between the two operations, and the notion of moving the consonant may have some (pre-theoretical) intuitive appeal, a more expressly templatic account can bring IC yet closer to its prosodic sister, reduplication. We propose treating IC as a templatic mapping process, whereby material is inserted after an initial consonant, as illustrated in provisional fashion in (9), again using classic autosegmental formalism simply for convenience:[15]

(9) Traditional (autosegmental) representation of mapping of IC

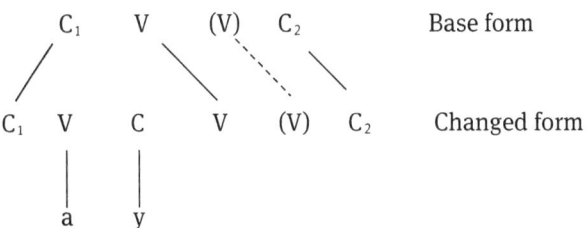

Such a view finds remarkable parallels in Heath's (1987) analysis of Moroccan Colloquial Arabic (see also Gafos 2002). There, similar morphological processes insert material into the interior of familiar Semitic word templates. Heath (1987: 11–12) treats Arabic patterns of the type described above as 'periphery-in' mapping, "whereby the leftmost and rightmost input segments are located in the corresponding peripheral output positions. After this is done, remaining medial positions in the output are filled [by a set of other processes]" (1987: 48–49), including the use of 'filler' consonants, or 'nonlexical segments' inserted into

---

15 Mizuki Miyashita notes (p.c.) that mapping also helps motivate the movement.

the templates, to occupy unfilled C slots (also called 'edge-in' mapping). These, as it happens, are the glides *y* and *w*. For example, /mik-a/ 'plastic' can form a professional noun, *mwayk-i*; that is, a noun meaning a person whose job is associated with the activity of the root. Professional nouns have the template /CCaCC-i/, where the first and last consonants are those of the corresponding root – thus, /mCaCk-i/ in our example. Filler semi-vowels then take up the remaining slots, yielding the surface form *mwayk-i*.[16] This is illustrated graphically in (10), below.

(10) Heath's 'periphery-in' mapping (Moroccan Colloquial Arabic)

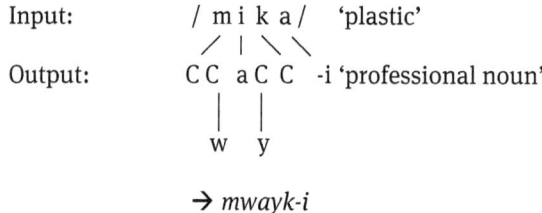

→ *mwayk-i*

Others have made similar proposals and have argued persuasively that edges of phonological domains can be the beginning point of association – e.g. Yip 1988, who argues that association might be best understood as edge-oriented.

Of course Algonquian languages – unlike Semitic languages – are not typically nonconcatenative in their morphology, and templates have not, to our knowledge, been invoked in the Algonquian tradition.[17] One might wonder what templates are at play and just what slots given segments are being mapped to. This brings us back to the relationship of IC to reduplication. Consider the revised comparison of these processes in Table 9, separating here C-initial from V-initial reduplication and representing empty consonant slots with 'C_0':[18]

---

[16] Like Algonquian initial change, Moroccan Arabic phonology and morphology involve complex patterns of ablaut, and these are, moreover, connected to reduplication.

[17] That is, aside from the relatively mundane use of templates for foot and metrical structures, as in Hayes (1995: 211–222) and elsewhere – although see Milligan (2005). Goddard (2010: 135) describes reduplicative patterns in Munsee as "templates", although he does not make theoretical use of the notion.

[18] Others have noted such parallels (e.g. Blain 1992), but to our knowledge no previous analysis connects reduplication and initial change directly.

Table 9: Templatic comparison of IC and reduplication.

		Base	Template
C-initial	IC	$C_1V(\cdot)C_2$	$C_1aC_0V(\cdot)C_2$
	Reduplication	$C_1V(\cdot)C_2$	$C_1a\cdot C_1V(\cdot)C_2$
V-initial	IC	$V(\cdot)C_1$	$aC_0V(\cdot)C_1$
	Reduplication	$V(\cdot)C_1$	$a\cdot C_0V(\cdot)C_1$

The prosodic templates involved are now virtually identical, save for the fact that the underlying stem-initial consonant of IC has been treated like the 'periphery-in' edge consonants in Heath's analysis, leaving an empty C-slot in the template stripped of its pre-specified content (represented by C_0).[19] The result is insertion of /y/, a 'filler' consonant used in Algonquian to avoid hiatus and also used in vowel-initial reduplication. (11a-c) provide examples first of IC and second of reduplication, for comparison (again using Hewson's forms):

(11) a. Periphery-in mapping of IC

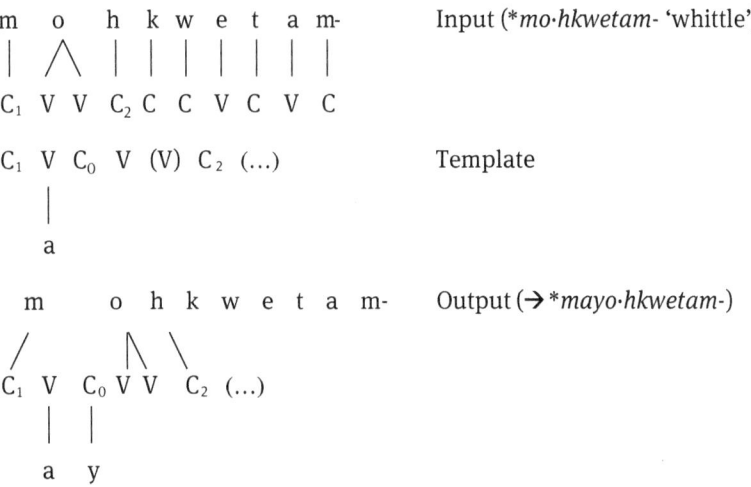

---

19 A further difference arises if the language uses a long /a·/ in reduplication, as in Menominee.

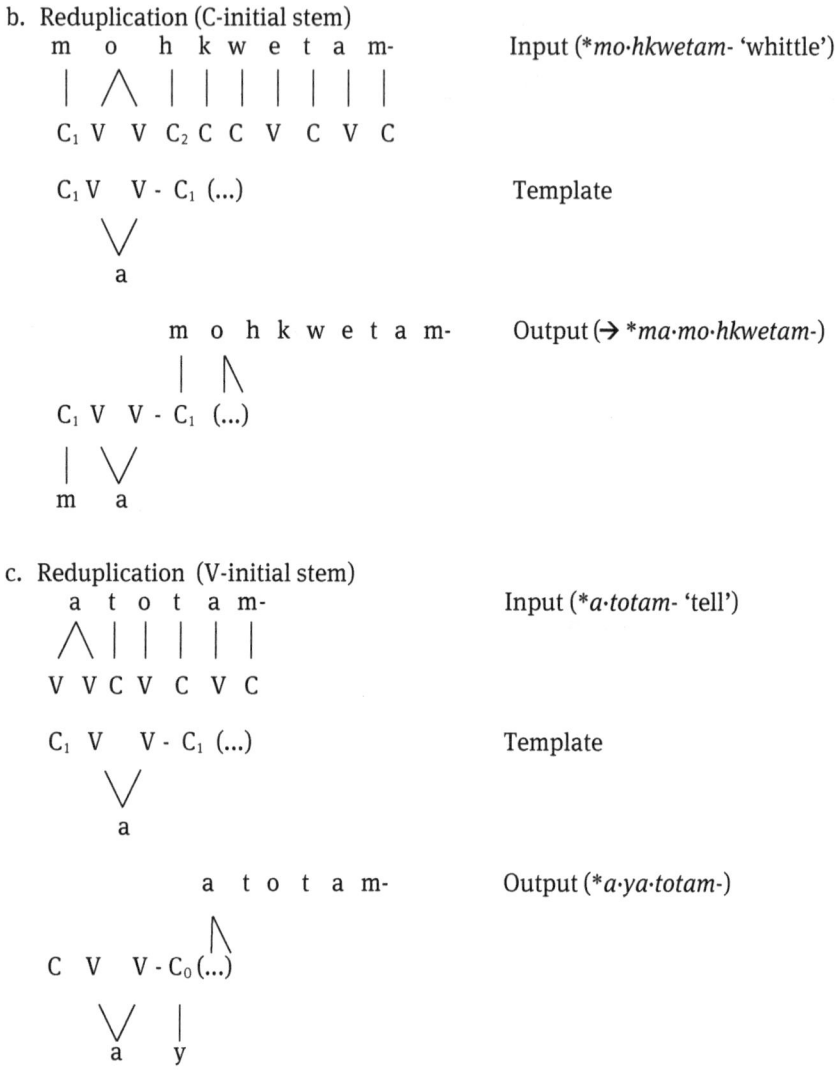

(11a) provides the input, template, and output for periphery-in mapping in the changed form *mayo·hkwetam- (from stem *mo·hkwetam- 'whittle'). (11b) shows the application of the reduplicative template, in which the initial consonant is copied, yielding *ma·mo·hkwetam-. A vowel-initial stem is shown in (11c); here, there is no initial consonant and so epenthetic [y] is inserted to break up the sequence of vowels, yielding *a·ya·totam- (from *a·totam- 'tell').

So far, our prosodic approach appeals primarily to the notion of phonological edges, specifically to the well-established principle of edge-in or periphery-in mapping. As the salient characteristic of IC – that is, movement rather than copying of an initial consonant – can be captured as edge-in mapping rather than the copying of reduplication, it is central, but we briefly note at this point two other prosodic aspects of IC not discussed in earlier work, syllable structure and foot structure. First, IC preserves word-initial consonantal onsets intact. While we certainly would not say that it came into existence for this purpose, the structure of IC does yield a universally preferred syllable structure (i.e., consonant-initial) in the important word-initial position – encoded in Vennemann's "Head Law" (1988: 13–21). Like other aspects of IC, this too can be thought of in familiar prosodic terms, well known across the world's languages, namely the strong tendency to move or preserve material not only in syllable onsets, but especially in prosodically prominent positions – in particular the edges of phonological domains. These patterns are also consistent with work like Wedel, Ussishkin, and King (2019), showing that left edges are prone to retain contrasts and right edges more likely to neutralise.

Second, IC obviously alters foot structure (consider the proto-forms posited in Table 8). Biedny et al. (2019) argue that Proto-Algonquian was iambic and, as discussed below, reduplication and IC produce iambic forms in numerous cases. For instance, Valentine (2001: 429) points out that reduplication creates iambic feet; when the vowel of the base is short, reduplication creates a light-heavy (LH) foot by prefixing a short syllable and lengthening that vowel.

If Proto-Algonquian was iambic, long-vowel IC (whether consonant- or vowel-initial) would improve metrical structure, creating a LH foot in place of a monosyllabic H foot, a form that Hayes (1995: 82) argues to be the maximal and canonical iamb. Thus, the hypothetical changed forms of our *mo·hkwetam- 'whittle' and *a·totam- 'tell' begin with LH: *mayo·hkwetam- and *aya·totam-. If we assume that consonants count for weight,[20] then closed initial syllables would also fit in this category: unchanged *kepwiken- 'shut' ~ changed *kayepwiken-, and *tahpene·- 'drown' ~ *tayahpene·-. This would leave a modest residue of words where an unchanged initial short syllable yields LL, such as *ešičime·- 'paddle' ~ *ayešičime·-. In fact Hayes argues that iambic feet of the shape H or LL should be rare and exist only because of the "need to parse most or all of the syllables in the string" (1995: 82). Guekguezian understands templatic morphology as the emergence of "optimal prosodic structure" (2017: 82) and an iambic Proto-Algonquian prosody would have been a motivation for the rise of these kinds of forms. Still, the metrical history of the family is not yet well understood, and both H and LL feet exist and have been created in Algonquian, as discussed by Biedny et al. (2019).

---

[20] That said, we note that consonants do not count for weight in, e.g., Menominee.

A striking typological parallel comes from Montler (1989), who describes a morpheme marking "actual" aspect in Saanich (a dialect of North Straits Salish) which manifests itself, in different contexts, as infixation, reduplication, and metathesis. Montler unifies the three superficially divergent processes by showing that all three produce structures conforming to an underlying CVCC template. We argue that a number of superficially quite different processes were tightly unified at an earlier stage of Algonquian, and the Saanich processes, implicitly treated by Montler as nonconcatenative ("a system in themselves, distinct from prefixation and suffixation" 1989: 106), cover basically the same range of surface patterns as those at hand here. In Saanich, these processes represent the same morpheme, reinforcing our claim that the kinds of patterns we treat in Algonquian are plausibly related. More importantly, Montler proposes an expressly templatic analysis, formulating a rule "whose primary goal is to produce a CVCC stem", a procedure which "produces a target stem shape through mechanisms of copying or moving available material" (1989: 106).

Returning to Algonquian, with the basic prosodic foundation sketched above, we can propose an account of the full set of IC forms. As already illustrated, many languages still prefix *ay-* to stems beginning with a long vowel. This corresponds exactly to the original pattern we posit and requires no further discussion; indeed, it does not require a prosodic perspective at all. Let us turn to those environments where IC has evolved into something somewhat different and more complex.[21]

5.1 Pattern for long vowels

Under our proposal, long-vowel IC forms still evince the original pattern across much of Algonquian. That is, it seems likely to us that the earliest form of initial change must have involved a prosodic pattern that looks like infixation in consonant-initial stems, which then reduced in some cases to the present ablauting patterns. This analysis seems also to be assumed in previous work, especially Pearson (1985), and is summarised in (12):[22]

---

[21] Other possibilities exist. McCarthy and Prince (1999: 248–254) pursue an "infixing reduplication" analysis for similar phenomena in a number of languages. Scholars like Wiese (2001) broaden the definition of "reduplication" to include cases where no material is actually copied. One could treat IC as an instance of such infixing reduplication.

[22] Pentland (1979: 409) also assumes this when he says of his reconstructed IC infix *-ey- that, "[...] such a sequence would normally contract with the following vowel to yield a long vowel."

(12) Pattern of IC for long vowels:
 CV· ~ CayV·
 In some languages; in some forms:
  CayV· > CV· (with ablaut)

In other words, a plausible way for this to have arisen would have involved edge-in mapping: the addition of surface infixal material which then contracted to create qualitative ablaut. Assuming that IC was once a unified process, this is also consistent with the usual direction of change, where reduction of material is presumed, rather than later, ad hoc addition of new material. In some sense, this point is anticipated by Costa (1996: 59–60), who writes that the "prefixing of *ay- in long vowels for initial change is definitely old, since it is found throughout the Algonquian areas. The use of *ay- is the only way of changing long vowels in Menominee and Arapaho-Gros Ventre, and the most common way of changing all vowels in Blackfoot."[23]

In terms of basic reconstruction, there is one major oddity in the (Pre-)Proto-Algonquian paradigm, as noted earlier – the infix-less changed form of *i·, reconstructed by Costa (among others) as changing to *a· rather than the expected *ayi·, as reconstructed by Bloomfield. Some of the modern languages do show /ayi·/ (e.g. Menominee and some dialects of Cree, while other dialects of Cree have *iyē* or *iyī*), but both Hockett and Costa posit *i· ~ *a· as the original pattern, and Goddard (1979a: 196–197) regards this as "likely". While this seems eminently reasonable, we suggest that Bloomfield's (1946: 100–101) Menominee-like pattern reflects an earlier stage of the process, as illustrated in (13):

(13) Pattern of IC for long vowels – the case of **i:
 **i· ~ **ayi·
 In some languages:
  **ayi· > **a·

Why then do we find /i·/ ~ /a·/ in most of the modern languages? The sequence of palatal glide plus high front vowel may have been elided, in a sort of process common with adjacent, overly similar segments (cf. the Obligatory Contour Principle). David Pentland (p.c.) points out that Proto-Algonquian did allow sequences

---

23 The evidence for initial change with long vowels is absent in several languages (e.g. Meskwaki-Kickapoo, much of Eastern Algonquian) or fragmentary (e.g. Potawatomi, Miami-Illinois, Shawnee). Still, everyone reconstructs the process for Proto-Algonquian.

of *yi· after both vowels and consonants, and so this hypothesis remains speculative (also see the literature on contraction in Algonquian, e.g. Goddard 2001).

Bloomfield's proposal would then have represented the earlier pattern, while Costa's reconstruction of *i· ~ *a· would reflect a later development, quite possibly by Pre-Proto-Algonquian.

We turn now to similar patterns of reductions in short-vowel IC.

5.2 Pattern for short vowels

The securely reconstructed basic pattern for IC in short vowels – short vowels becoming long (with some qualitative ablaut) – likely reflects reduction of an original VyV sequence (note that we address the special status of *i ~ *ye· below), as in (14):

(14)   Pattern of IC for short vowels:
       CV ~ CayV > CV· (with or without ablaut)

In fact, Haas argues that Algonquian *i and *o are "reduced variants of *ye (or *ya) and *we (or *wa) [...] . This suggests that at an earlier period *i and *o were vocalic *y and *w" (1966: 488). Whether the specifics of that proposal are correct or not, there is certainly ample evidence for alternations between vowels and glide+vowel sequences in the Algonquian languages. In the phonology of the languages of the world, similar patterns abound, including Sievers' Law in Indo-European or some of its daughters, where glides and vowels vary according to phonological context. Such phenomena are often driven by metrical or prosodic considerations (as in Sievers' Law, with motivations in syllable and foot structure, e.g. Smith 2004).

Recall that Costa's reconstruction posits a changed form *ye·· for unchanged short *i, which would point toward exactly the vowel-glide alternation we have in mind. For his *a ~ *e· and *e ~ *e· changes, we assume later reductions from *aya and *aye to *e·.[24] Pearson's view – drawing on Haas – of straightforward segmental reductions in such cases may prove right, but it is impossible to know. Other

---

[24] Again, we follow Costa (1996) in positing *-ay- as the affix involved, while Pentland (1979) argues that the affix must be *-ey-, specifically referring to particular processes of contraction across *y. The resolution of these early developments does not change the core point at hand about higher level prosodic structure.

possibilities for resolving this matter include the murky prehistory of Algonquian metrics and perhaps even directly morphological developments.[25]

5.3 Pattern for CGV-

One additional environment, verb stems beginning with a consonant-glide sequence, was not sketched out above because the evidence for it is so seldom discussed in sufficient depth for either IC or reduplication.[26] In spite of the sparse evidence, though, it is significant because it shows another way in which IC and reduplication are similar in at least some of the Algonquian languages: In reduplication and in regular forms of IC, consonant-glide clusters are broken up. That is, reduplication copies only the stem-initial consonant but not the glide. In IC – at least in Menominee, the only language for which we have sufficient data – the cluster is similarly broken up by infixation. The pattern is illustrated in (15) for Menominee, where underlying initial clusters of consonant plus glide are relatively uncommon but do exist.

(15) CGV- Initial Change and reduplication in Menominee
Initial change:
Unchanged: *mw-akeht-* → *mwākeht-* → *muakehtuaq* 'when we eat them'[27]
Changed: *ma̱yuakehtuawen* 'whenever we eat them' (Bloomfield 1962: 99)
Reduplication:
kiasōhāēw 'he hides from him' (stem = /kyāsw-/)
Reduplicates with *kā-*: *kā-kiasōhāēw* 'he keeps hiding from him' (Bloomfield 1975: 96)

nianan 'five' (stem = /nyānanw/)
Reduplicates with *nā-*: *nā-nianan* 'five each, five at a time' (Bloomfield 1975: 160)

---

25 We consider analogical accounts the least likely of scenarios, but given the complex restructurings associated with similar patterns (see again Sievers' Law), they are not impossible.
26 Milligan (2000: 248) argues that these sequences are better understood as CVV in Menominee, understanding apparent GV sequences as nuclei, rather than as part of the onset plus the nucleus. It is unclear whether this analysis extends to other Algonquian languages.
27 The first vowel of the inflectional suffix *-akeht* '1pl acting on 3' undergoes an irregular lengthening process when attached to the short stem *mw-* 'eat'. /wā/ is treated as a long diphthong (Bloomfield 1962: 97) and is conventionally written <ua>.

Nichols (1980) provides similar patterns from Ojibwe, where *CwV-* is treated as in Menominee except in the case of *kwVV-*. (16) illustrates:[28]

(16) CwV- Reduplication and Initial Change in Ojibwe
  kwVV-:
    kwaapa'ike 'he dips'
    Initial change: *kw<u>a</u>yaapa'ikeet* [presumably 'the one who dips']
    Reduplicated with *kwaa-*: <u>*kwaa*</u>-*kwaapa'ike* 'he keeps dipping'

    kwaaškwani 'he jumps'
    Initial change: *kw<u>a</u>yaaškwanit* [presumably 'the one who jumps']
    Reduplicated with *kwaaš-*: <u>*kwaaš*</u>-*kwaaškwani* 'he jumps here and there'
  Other CwV(V)-
    nimpwaanawittoon 'I can't deal with them'
    Reduplicates with *paa-*: *nim<u>paa</u>-pwaanawittoon* 'I can't deal with them in different places'

    twaa'ipii 'he cuts [a] hole in ice'
    Reduplicates with *taa-*: <u>*taa*</u>-*twaa'ipii* 'he cuts holes in ice here and there'

    kwayakkwentam 'he thinks straight'
    Reduplicates with *ka-*: <u>*ka*</u>-*kwayakkwentam* 'he thinks straight now and then'

Dahlstrom (1997) also notes irregularities in the reduplication of words beginning in CGV-:[29]

(17) CGV- reduplication in Meskwaki
  kʷV·-:
    kʷa·škʷat-amwa
    Reduplicates with *kʷa·-*: <u>*kʷa·*</u>-*kʷa·škʷat-amwa* 'he drops it [food] while eating'

    kʷe·hta·nite·he·-wa
    Reduplicates with *kʷe·-*: <u>*kʷe·*</u>-*kʷe·hta·nite·he·-wa* 'he feels terrible'

---

28 Nichols does not provide parallel forms with initial change; David Pentland (p.c.) was kind enough to supply us with the ones shown in (16).
29 True CG sequences (excluding /kʷ/) are always followed by an underlyingly long vowel in Meskwaki, and since IC does not affect long vowels in Meskwaki there are no parallel IC data (Amy Dahlstrom, p.c.).

Other CGV·:
kya·t-amwa
Reduplicates with *ka·*: <u>*ka·*</u>-*kya·t-amwa* 'he keeps it for himself'
Or, reduplicates with *kya·*: <u>*kya·*</u>-*kya·t-amwa*

šwa·šika
Reduplicates with *ša·*: <u>*ša·*</u>-*šwa·šika* 'eight each'
Or, reduplicates with *šwa·*: <u>*šwa·*</u>-*šwa·šika* 'in groups of eight'

That is, in Meskwaki /k^w/ acts like a single consonant when reduplicated, but other sequences of CGV optionally act like the CGV sequences in Menominee and Ojibwe (the latter with its one exception).[30]

The currently available evidence indicates that in some of the Algonquian languages IC and reduplication treat word-initial consonant clusters in parallel fashion, namely copying/moving only the first consonant rather than full clusters. This provides another prosodic link between the processes.

If we can be allowed a moment of speculation, the arguments and evidence suggest a plausible, if unprovable, developmental path. Proto-Algonquian, like virtually all languages, had reduplication of at least one type. At some point in early prehistory, reduplication could easily have provided a model for what became IC. The key difference, in terms of phonological edges, is edge-in vs. periphery-in mapping. IC involves edge-in mapping and movement of a consonant rather than the copying of reduplication. Proto-Algonquian was probably an iambic language and if so, these processes lead to preferred prosodic structures, optimisation in the sense of Guekguezian (2017). Much of the further history of IC, its development into the complex set of ablauting and other patterns found today, revolves around the patterns of glide insertion, *y, to avoid hiatus and later patterns of glide loss. In one daughter language, Shawnee, IC has come to be marked by reduplication, which strongly suggests that speakers recognised the similarities between the formal patterns, motivating a merger. This process has only come to completion in the historical record, given that Schaefer (2019) shows ablauting IC in early 20th century writing. Whether this speculation is ultimately borne out, this specifically historical prosodic approach uncovers fundamental unity underlying disparate modern patterns. Key parts of the story find striking support from other languages of the world, including Moroccan Colloquial Arabic and Saanich.

---

30 Dahlstrom says that "the version with no glide in the reduplicative prefix is more common" (1997: 212). Note also that Dahlstrom treats /k^w/ as a single (complex) consonant, while Nichols treats /kw/ as a sequence of consonant plus glide.

6 Conclusion

This paper has synthesised what is known or claimed about both initial change and reduplication in the Algonquian languages. While these look quite different across the modern languages, from a historical perspective they reveal powerful unity. Costa's meticulous reconstruction for Pre-Proto-Algonquian posits four related but distinct processes: quantitative ablaut, qualitative ablaut, prefixation, and infixation, not to mention alternations involving both types of ablaut together. As is well recognised today, higher-level prosody molds segmental structure both synchronically (cf. Fougeron and Keating 1997, Sluijter 1995) and diachronically (cf. Page 1999). In particular, prosodic approaches to language history often uncover previously unseen patterns of regularity and motivate formerly disparate segmental changes (Murray and Vennemann 1983, Macken and Salmons 1997). This and the synchronically attested hodgepodge of segmental processes in Algonquian reduplication and IC led us to seek a more unified analysis by considering the prosodic level.

A historical prosodic analysis of IC shows that profoundly different surface realisations in the family can be captured with a single prosodic pattern closely akin to the most broadly attested and surely ancient pattern of reduplication. IC involves a type of nonconcatenative morphology employing edge-in mapping rather than copying. Our templatic analysis treats IC as close structural kin to reduplication, if not reduplication in the narrow sense, since no elements are copied. If, as some suspect, Proto-Algonquian was an iambic language, improvement in foot structure could have motivated the rise of these kinds of structures and might thus provide a link between two similar phonological manifestations of very different types of morphology. Biedny et al. (2019) begin to explore these issues.

Our proposal for IC treats it as nonconcatenative in the sense of McCarthy (1999), emphasising its status as a sister process to reduplication. Even if the origins of IC are not found in reduplication itself, the parallels have had consequences in at least one language. As noted, modern Shawnee has come to mark IC with reduplication, closing the circle in a sense.

The stark differences in function argue against a common origin for the two processes. In brief, reduplication marks aspectual notions such as iterativity, intensification, and continuity, while IC creates participles – noun-like forms which function much like relative clauses – and marks past tense or perfective aspect. Instead, IC reflects a second, nonconcatenative pattern in Algonquian. This ties reduplication to IC and the range of modern reduplicative patterns not necessarily dating back to Proto-Algonquian (light vs. heavy, mono- versus disyllabic, full copy reduplication), as well as the more difficult case of Yurok -*eg*-, all carrying various functions across the languages. In light of such widely attested but diverse patterns, nonconcatenative processes are surprisingly robust within Algonquian.

This paper provides new support for the value of historical prosodic templates in understanding synchronic prosodic patterning. Our proposal allows us to posit relatively straightforward developments into the attested modern forms of IC, although we have hardly accounted for all of the details. The major advantage of treating IC as a prosodic operation comes in showing it to be close formally to reduplication in Algonquian. If our arguments are correct, they suggest a direction for future research on the reconstruction of IC, as well as a foundation for hypotheses about the sound changes which would have had to occur to produce the synchronically occurring forms in the modern languages.

References

Ahenakew, Freda & H. C. Wolfart. 1983. Productive reduplication in Plains Cree. In William Cowan (ed.), *Papers of the 14th Algonquian Conference,* 369–377. Ottawa: Carlton University.
Aubin, George. 1975. *A Proto-Algonquian dictionary.* (Canadian Ethnology Service, Mercury Series Paper 29.) Ottawa: National Museums of Canada.
Beland, Jean Pierre. 1978. *Atikamekw morphology and lexicon*. Berkeley, CA: University of California–Berkeley dissertation.
Berman, Howard. 1982. Two phonological innovations in Ritwan. *International Journal of American Linguistics* 48. 412–420.
Berman, Howard. 2003. An archaic pattern of initial change in Yurok. *International Journal of American Linguistics* 69. 229–231.
Berman, Howard. 2006. Studies in Blackfoot prehistory. *International Journal of American Linguistics* 72. 264–284.
Biedny, Jerome, Andrea Cudworth, Sarah Holmstrom, Monica Macaulay, Gabrielle Mistretta, Joseph Salmons, Charlotte Vanhecke & Bo Zhan. 2019. Comparative Algonquian metrical phonology. Paper presented at MidPhon 24, Milwaukee, October.
Blain, Eleanor. 1992. A prosodic look at Ojibwa reduplication. In William Cowan (ed.), *Papers of the 23rd Algonquian Conference*, 22–44. Ottawa: Carlton University.
Bloomfield, Leonard. 1925. On the sound-system of Central Algonquian. *Language* 1. 130–156.
Bloomfield, Leonard. 1946. Algonquian. In *Linguistic structures of Native America*, 85–129. Viking Fund Publications in Anthropology 6. New York: Viking Fund.
Bloomfield, Leonard. 1962. *The Menomini language.* Edited by Charles F. Hockett. New Haven: Yale University Press.
Bloomfield, Leonard. 1975. *Menomini lexicon*. Milwaukee Public Museum Publications in Anthropology and History 3. Milwaukee: Milwaukee Public Museum.
Comrie, Bernard. 1989. *Language universals and linguistic typology: Syntax and morphology*, 2nd edn. Chicago: University of Chicago Press.

Conathan, Lisa & Esther Wood. 2003. Repetitive reduplication in Yurok and Karuk: Semantic effects of contact. In H. C. Wolfart (ed.), *Papers of the 34th Algonquian Conference*, 19–33. Winnipeg: University of Manitoba.

Costa, David J. 1996. Reconstructing initial change in Algonquian. *Anthropological Linguistics* 38. 39–72.

Cowan, William. 1972. Reduplicated bird names in Algonquian. *International Journal of American Linguistics* 38. 229–230.

Dahlstrom, Amy. 1997. Fox reduplication. *International Journal of American Linguistics* 63. 205–226.

Drapeau, Lynn. 2014. *Grammaire de la langue Innue*. Québec: Presses de l'Université du Québec.

Fougeron, Cécile & Patricia Keating. 1997. Articulatory strengthening at edges of prosodic domains. *Journal of the Acoustic Society of America* 101. 3728–3740.

Gafos, Adamantios. 2002. A grammar of gestural coordination. *Natural Language and Linguistic Theory* 20. 269–337.

Garrett, Andrew. 2001. Reduplication and infixation in Yurok: Morphology, semantics and diachrony. *International Journal of American Linguistics* 67. 264–312.

Goddard, Ives. 1979a. *Delaware verbal morphology: A descriptive and comparative study*. New York: Garland.

Goddard, Ives. 1979b. Comparative Algonquian. In Lyle Campbell & Marianne Mithun (eds.), *The languages of Native America*, 70–132. Austin: University of Texas Press.

Goddard, Ives. 2001. Contraction in Fox (Meskwaki). In John D. Nichols (ed.), *Papers of the 32nd Algonquian Conference*, 164–230. Winnipeg: University of Manitoba.

Goddard, Ives. 2010. Reduplication in the Delaware languages. In J. Randolph Valentine & Monica Macaulay (eds.), *Papers of the 42nd Algonquian Conference*, 134–158. Albany: SUNY Press.

Guekguezian, Peter Ara. 2017. Templates as the interaction of recursive word structure and prosodic well-formedness. *Phonology* 34. 81–120.

Haas, Mary R. 1958. Algonkian-Ritwan: The end of a controversy. *International Journal of American Linguistics* 24. 159–173.

Haas, Mary R. 1966. Vowels and semivowels in Algonkian. *Language* 42. 479–488.

Hayes, Bruce. 1995. *Metrical stress theory: Principles and case studies*. Chicago: University of Chicago Press.

Heath, Jeffrey. 1987. *Ablaut and ambiguity: Phonology of a Moroccan Arabic dialect*. Albany: State University of New York Press.

Hewson, John. 1993. *A computer-generated dictionary of Proto-Algonquian*. (Canadian Ethnology Service, Mercury Series Paper 25.) Hull: Canadian Museum of Civilization. https://protoalgonquian.atlas-ling.ca (accessed 3 February 2019).

Hockett, Charles F. 1948. Potawatomi I–IV. *International Journal of American Linguistics* 14. 1–10, 63–73, 139–149, 213–225.

Hockett, Charles F. 1981. The phonological history of Menominee. *Anthropological Linguistics* 23. 51–87.

Junker, Marie-Odile & Louise Blacksmith. 1994. Reduplication in East Cree. In William Cowan (ed.), *Papers of the 25th Algonquian Conference*, 264–273. Ottawa: Carlton University.

Macaulay, Monica. 2018. Notes on reduplication in Menominee. *Anthropological Linguistics* 60. 30–43.

Macken, Marlys & Joseph C. Salmons. 1997. Prosodic templates in sound change. *Diachronica* 14. 33–66.
McCarthy, John J. 1999. A prosodic theory of nonconcatenative morphology. In John A. Goldsmith (ed.), *Phonological theory: The essential readings*, 162–184. Malden, MA: Blackwell.
McCarthy, John J. & Alan S. Prince. 1999. Prosodic morphology. In John A. Goldsmith (ed.), *Phonological theory: The essential readings*, 238–288. Malden, MA: Blackwell.
Mielke, Jeff & Elizabeth Hume. 2001. Consequences of word recognition for metathesis. In Elizabeth Hume, Norval Smith & Jeroen Maarten van de Weijer (eds.), *Surface syllable structure and segment sequencing*, 135–158. Leiden: Holland Institute of Generative Linguistics.
Milligan, Marianne. 2000. A new look at Menominee vowel harmony. In John D. Nichols (ed.), *Papers of the 31st Algonquian Conference*, 237–254. Winnipeg: University of Manitoba.
Milligan, Marianne. 2005. *Menominee prosodic structure*. Madison, WI: University of Wisconsin–Madison dissertation.
Montler, Timothy R. 1989. Infixation, reduplication, and metathesis in the Saanich actual aspect. *Southwest Journal of Linguistics* 9. 92–107.
Murray, Robert W. & Theo Vennemann. 1983. Sound change and syllable structure in Germanic phonology. *Language* 59. 514–528.
Nichols, John David. 1980. *Ojibwe morphology*. Cambridge, MA: Harvard University dissertation.
Niepokuj, Mary. 1997. *The development of verbal reduplication in Indo-European*. Washington: Institute for the Study of Man.
Oxford, Will. 2015. Patterns of contrast in phonological change: Evidence from Algonquian vowel systems. *Language* 91. 308–358.
Page, B. Richard. 1999. The Germanic *Verschärfung* and prosodic change. *Diachronica* 19. 297–334.
Pearson, Bruce L. 1985. Initial change as a natural process. *International Journal of American Linguistics* 51. 531–534.
Pentland, David. 1979. *Algonquian historical phonology*. Toronto: University of Toronto dissertation.
Salmons, Joseph & Huibin Zhuang. 2018. The diachrony of East Asian prosodic templates. *Linguistics* 56. 549–580.
Schaefer, Carl. 2019. Alford's Shawnee translation of the Gospels. In Monica Macaulay & Margaret Noodin (eds.), *Papers of the 48th Algonquian Conference*, 221–238. East Lansing: Michigan State University Press.
Siebert, Frank T. 1967. The original home of the Proto-Algonquian people. In A. D. DeBlois (ed.), *Contributions to Anthropology: Linguistics I (Algonquian)* (National Museum of Canada, Bulletin, 214, Anthropological Series 78), 48–59. Ottawa: National Museum of Canada.
Sluijter, Agatha M. C. 1995. *Phonetic correlates of stress and accent*. The Hague: Holland Academic Graphics.
Smith, Laura Catharine. 2004. *Cross-level interactions in West Germanic phonology and morphology*. Madison, WI: University of Wisconsin–Madison dissertation.
Smith, Laura Catharine & Adam Ussishkin. 2015. The role of prosodic templates in diachrony. In Patrick Honeybone & Joseph Salmons (eds.), *The Oxford handbook of historical phonology*, 262–285. Oxford: Oxford University Press.

Todd, Evelyn Mary. 1970. *A grammar of the Ojibwa language: The Severn dialect.* Chapel Hill, NC: University of North Carolina at Chapel Hill dissertation.

Valentine, J. Randolph. 2001. *Nishnaabemwin reference grammar.* Toronto: University of Toronto Press.

Vennemann, Theo. 1988. *Preference laws for syllable structure and the explanation of sound change: With special reference to German, Germanic, Italian, and Latin.* Berlin: de Gruyter.

Wedel, Andrew, Adam Ussishkin & Adam King. 2019. Crosslinguistic evidence for a strong statistical universal: Phonological neutralization targets word-ends over beginnings. *Language* 95. e428–e446.

Wiese, Richard. 2001. Regular morphology vs. prosodic morphology? The case of truncations in German. *Journal of Germanic Linguistics* 13. 131–177.

Wilbur, Ronnie B. 1973. *The phonology of reduplication.* Bloomington: Indiana University Linguistics Club.

Wolfart, H. Christoph. 1969. *An outline of Plains Cree morphology.* New Haven, CT: Yale University dissertation.

Yip, Moira. 1988. Template morphology and the direction of association. *Natural Language and Linguistic Theory* 6. 551–577.

Yu, Alan C. L. 2007. *A natural history of infixation.* Oxford: Oxford University Press.

Robert Mailhammer
Amurdak intersyllabic phonotactics and morphophonemic alternations as motivated by the Contact Law

Abstract: This contribution examines the intersyllabic phonotactics and morphophonemic alternations of the northern Australian language Amurdak. It argues that they are motivated by the preferences formulated in the Contact Law (Vennemann 1988). Amurdak goes beyond the general tendency of Australian languages to have word-medial clusters that conform to the Contact Law (Baker 2014, Hamilton 1996). Moreover, diachronic patterns of morphophonemic alternations find a natural explanation if the Contact Law as a constraint is assumed (see Baker 2014). What is interesting, however, is how the Contact Law is implemented, because processes of fortition go against the preferences of the Strength Assimilation Law. It is suggested that the fact that these changes occur exclusively at morpheme boundaries may be an important factor in the history of Amurdak phonotactics and morphophonemics.

1 Introduction

One interesting feature of the phonologies of Australian languages is that their phonotactic patterns cannot be elegantly captured within a model that operates with the syllable as the primary prosodic unit (Baker 2014: 143). Instead, the usual

---

Acknowledgements: It is with much joy I offer this contribution to my teacher and mentor, Prof. Theo Vennemann. As a young graduate student, I narrowly missed out on making a contribution to the first festschrift, and I am all the happier for being able to contribute to the second. Thank you, Prof. Vennemann, for being the kindest and best Doktorvater and role model I could have hoped for.
  Parts of this paper was presented as a co-authored paper together with Stephen Laker at a symposium to celebrate Theo Vennemann's 80th birthday in 2017. Afterwards we decided to write up our parts of that paper as separate contributions to this festschrift. I'd like to gratefully acknowledge Stephen Laker's input in discussions of our co-authored paper. I also thank the audience, the editors Laura Catharine Smith and Patrizia Noel Aziz Hanna for valuable comments, and Richard Page for a careful review and great suggestions. Thanks also go to Brett Baker and Mark Harvey, who commented on an earlier version of this contribution. All remaining errors are my own.

Robert Mailhammer, School of Humanities and Communication Arts, Western Sydney University, Sydney/Australia

https://doi.org/10.1515/9783110721461-003

way to describe phonotactics in Australian languages is to use templates; see (1), adapted from Baker (2014: 143).

(1) C_{init} V (C_{inter} V) (C_{fin})

The C_{inter} position can be filled with a single consonant or a cluster. Most languages allow only two consonants as part of a cluster, but some, including Amurdak, the language investigated here, allow up to three, even though such clusters are rare (see Hamilton 1996 for the data). Interestingly, the C_{inter} position typically allows the largest range of consonants, though the second consonant in a cluster is subject to more restrictions. This includes a high number of intervocalic heterorganic consonant clusters, especially nasals plus stops (Baker 2014: 144). By contrast the C_{init} and C_{fin} positions are much more restricted. Many Australian languages do not allow word-final consonants at all (Baker 2014: 144). In initial position, many languages limit the range of liquids that can occur, whereas generally stops, glides, and nasals are permitted (Baker 2014: 144). One key observation that is relevant to this paper is that typically the last consonant in a cluster is more consonantal (less sonorous) than the preceding consonant (Hamilton 1996: 76).

Another feature of Australian languages is that they show alternations between continuants, usually approximants, and stops (Baker 2014: 171–175). Typically, the stops occur after consonants and the approximants after vowels and liquids. Positionally, these alternations usually affect morpheme-initial consonants or word-medial consonants. In some cases, word-initial consonants are affected across word-boundaries, though this is rare. Root- and word-final consonants do not normally take part in these alternations. The following partial paradigm from Iwaidjan language Amurdak illustrates the general distribution.[1]

The processes that produced this type of alternations are not fully clear, but they seem to involve both lenition and fortition. For example, the paradigm for *-bu* 'hit, kill' in the related language Iwaidja shows a similar alternation to that of Amurdak *-wurlka* 'dance' in Table 1. However, the continuant-initial stem

---

[1] This paper uses Leipzig Glossing Rules. In addition, there are the following abbreviations: IPFV = imperfective, NSG = non-singular, DU = dual, TRI = trial, MAL = malefactive, ATT = attenuative, PRON = pronominal. NON-SINGULAR is used in languages that differentiate several number categories apart from the singular, as a cover term for all number categories outside the singular. In Amurdak, NON-SINGULAR comprises dual (2), trial (3) and plural (4+).

Table 1: Partial paradigm for Amurdak -*wurlka* 'dance'. Stop-initial allomorphs are marked in bold.

-*wurlka* 'dance'	Perfective	Imperfective	Future
1SG	am-**b**urlka	angam-**b**urlka	aman-**b**urlka
1NSG.INCL	am-**b**urlka	angam-**b**urlka	aman-**b**urlka
1NSG.EXCL	am-**b**urlka	angam-**b**urlka	arrman-**b**urlka
2SG	anum-**b**urlka	anu-wurlka	uman-**b**urlka
2NSG	awun-**b**urlka	awun-**b**urlka	urrman-**b**urlka
3SG	wara-wurlka	wanu-wurlka	wan-**b**urlka
3NSG	wandu-wurlka	wandu-wurlka	irran-**b**urlka

allomorphs in the case of -*bu* are the product of lenition, on account of Proto-Iwaidjan *-*bu* 'hit' and extra-Iwaidjan cognates (Mailhammer and Harvey 2018). By contrast, in the case of -*wurlka*, they are likely to have resulted from fortition, as suggested by cognates in other languages without this alternation (Mailhammer and Harvey 2018).

Baker (2014: 171) suggests that these processes of fortition could be explained by the Contact Law (Murray and Vennemann 1983, Vennemann 1988; see Section 3 below), as they result in better syllable contacts, because they produce a cluster that ends in a less sonorous segment. It would thus appear that the Contact Law could explain some aspects of the unusual phonotactics of Australian languages and at least one kind of typical stop-continuant alternations.

This paper explores the potential of this tentative explanation by taking a wider perspective, investigating the word-medial phonotactics and the morphophonemic alternations of the Australian Aboriginal language Amurdak. Amurdak is a good test case, as it is one of the few Australian languages with a reconstructed proto-phoneme system that is based on the Comparative Method (Mailhammer and Harvey 2018). I will argue that the Contact Law is indeed able to explain a number of morphophonemic alternations in Amurdak and that it also accounts for intervocalic clusters. However, it cannot account for stop-approximant alternations that are the outcome of lenition. Lenition, however, is a very complex phenomenon in Australian languages that is currently not fully understood, so this is probably not a fatal problem.

This paper is structured as follows. Section 2 gives relevant background information on Amurdak and presents the data. Section 3 evaluates the data in the light of the Preference Laws for syllable structure, especially the Contact Law. Section 4 presents a summary and conclusions.

2 Amurdak: Phonotactics, alternations and processes

2.1 Basic linguistic type and context

Amurdak is an Australian Aboriginal language of the Iwaidjan language family (Evans 2000, Mailhammer and Harvey 2018), traditionally spoken in Northwestern Arnhem Land in the Northern Territory; see Map 1. It is critically endangered, with only three known proficient speakers in Darwin and on Croker Island. No children acquire Amurdak presently, and as all speakers are elderly, the prognosis is that Amurdak will become extinct within the next ten years. Amurdak has not been spoken much for perhaps 30 to 40 years, and it is currently not used for daily communication. All speakers have been using mainly other languages for this purpose, so language attrition and crosslinguistic influence need to be considered as factors.

In spite of this situation, Amurdak is reasonably well documented. There are around 100–150 hours of partially annotated text and elicitation materials collected from the late 1960s to the present, and there is a published text collection (Mailhammer and Handelsmann 2009). In terms of grammatical analysis Amurdak has a draft grammatical description (Handelsmann 1991), a draft dictionary (Handelsmann 1998), a typological sketch (Evans 2000) and descriptions of various aspects of the verb system (Mailhammer 2009, 2014), as well as reconstructions of parts of its history (Mailhammer 2017, Harvey and Mailhammer 2017, Mailhammer and Harvey 2018).

Amurdak is a Non-Pama-Nyungan language. It is head marking – though non-subject arguments are not always expressed – and it uses prefixes as well as suffixes. Verb roots are generally bound morphemes, and so are a number of nominal roots comprising body parts. At the juncture of affixes and stems, Amurdak – like other Iwaidjan languages, such as Iwaidja and Mawng – exhibits significant morphophonemic alternations. The phoneme system of Amurdak comprises the vowels /i, u, a/ as well as the following consonants, see Table 2.[2]

The status of the velar approximant /ɰ/ is not clear, but it is likely that this is not actually a phoneme of Amurdak for two reasons. First, it occurs in only one word, *wahay* 'sugar glider', and since this word is also found in neighbouring Iwaidja with identical meaning and form, it is possible that this is either an

---

[2] Like in Iwaidja (Shaw et al. 2020), stops in Amurdak are generally voiced (own fieldwork).

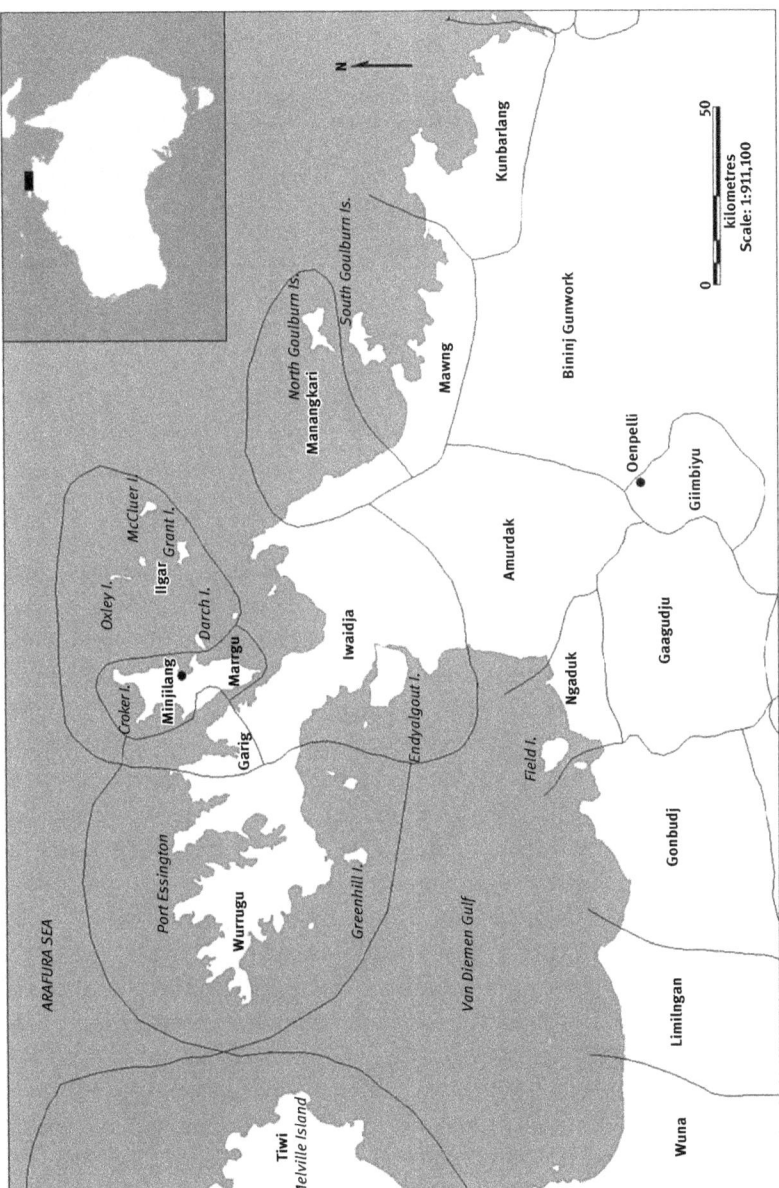

Map 1: Amurdak in its traditional location in Northwestern Arnhem Land (Mailhammer and Harvey 2018: 330).

Table 2: Consonant inventory of Amurdak (practical orthography in brackets).

Consonants	Bilabial	Alveolar	Retroflex	Palatal	Velar
Stop	b <b>	d <d>	ɖ <rt>	ɟ <j>	g <k>
Nasal		n <n>	ɳ <rn>	ɲ <ny>	ŋ <ng>
Tap		r <rr>	ɽ <rd>		
Approximant	w <w>		ɻ <r>	j <y>	ʔɰ <h>
Lateral		l <l>	ɭ <rl>		
Flapped lateral		lʳ <ld>	ɭʳ <rld>		

Iwaidja loanword or a *bona fide* Iwaidja word.³ Second, as the velar approximant in Iwaidja is not a phoneme anyway, but an allophone of /k/ (Shaw et al. 2020), it is likely that this is also the case in Amurdak, as both languages have a very similar phonological system. However, lacking a targeted investigation, the velar approximant is included as a tentative phoneme in Table 2.

The flapped laterals are crosslinguistically rare, though not areally so (e.g. in neighbouring Gaagudju; see Harvey 2002: 31–33). These segments have been proposed for Amurdak, Iwaidja, and Ilgar/Garig. Their phonetic structure and their phonological status are not currently resolved. Phonologically, they could be analysed as either a single complex segment (i.e. a lateral flap) or alternatively a cluster of two homorganic consonants (i.e. lateral + stop). There is no confirmed minimal pair differentiating a putative lateral flap from a cluster of the corresponding lateral and stop in Amurdak or any of the other languages for which flapped laterals have been proposed. The phonetic evidence is inconclusive, mainly because there is a high degree in variability of phonetic realisation (Butcher et al. 2007; see Mailhammer and Harvey 2018: 333, fn. 3 for a discussion of the phonetic evidence). Further instrumental research is required to ascertain the status of the flapped laterals in Amurdak and in Ilgar/Garig and Iwaidja.

The nominal morphology of the Iwaidjan languages generally is far less complex than the verbal morphology. The nominal morphology of Amurdak is even more restricted than in the other Iwaidjan languages on which there is reliable data (Mawng, Iwaidja, Ilgar/Garig). It is basically confined to a subset of body parts, which are obligatorily prefixed for possession, a few inflecting adjectives, and prepositions. For example, 'head' is expressed as a bound morpheme taking a possessor prefix, e.g. *nga-wulya* 'my head' vs. *yi-wulya* 'her/his/its

---

3 That Amurdak speakers would use an Iwaidja word is not unusual. Amurdak has not been used for everyday communication in decades, and its speakers have not lived in their ancestral homeland for at least forty years. Consequently, lexical knowledge and general attrition are factors.

head'. Adjectives can inflect for person and number, e.g. *kalajarr-karrurlu* 'they are deaf' vs. *kalajarr-ngarlu* 'I'm deaf', and so do prepositions, e.g. *urdan-nganu* 'I'm from' vs. *urdan-birra* 'they are from'. The basic morphological elements of the verb system are person-number-TAM prefixes, object-suffixes and enclitics and further suffixed/enclitic morphology. In contrast to the other main Iwaidjan languages Mawng, Iwaidja, and Ilgar/Garig, Amurdak does not have transitive vs. intransitive prefixes and a composite TAM system with prefixed and suffixed components. Generally, prefixes and suffixes express distinct meanings.

(2) a. *warr-yilkin-burduk*
3NSG.PFV-full-DU
'they (2) were full up'
b. *wandu-yilkin-ularr*
3NSG.IPFV-full-PL
'they (>3) were/are still full up'
c. *ala-yilkin*
1SG.NEG.full
'I am/was not full.'
d. *aman-mun-kurrurlu-wurduk*
1SG.FUT-hit, kill-3NSG.O-DU
'I'm going to kill [those] 2.'
e. *wal-mun-kunurlu-murlunu*
3SG.HYP-hit, kill-2SG.O-2SG.MAL
'He might hit you with negative consequences for you.'

[own fieldnotes]

2.2 Phonotactics and syllable structure

In terms of its phonotactics, Amurdak conforms to the general Australian type. In terms of syllable structure, the maximum licit syllable is CVCC. This maximal type occurs more frequently word-finally, e.g. *abidarrk* 'strong, hard', but also medially, e.g. *arrmbu* 'goanna'. The template mentioned in (1) applies also to Amurdak, as the word-initial onset and the word-final coda are more restricted than word-medial onsets and codas in terms of which consonants are allowed. For the purposes of this paper, the C_{inter} position is the most relevant, given that the focus is on intersyllabic relations. Table 3 shows the range of possible medial heterosyllabic consonant clusters.

In addition, C_{inter} can also consist of a single consonant, which forms the onset of the following syllable. This consonant can be any of the following: /l, r,

Table 3: Heterosyllabic consonant clusters in Amurdak.

C1=stop	C1=nasal	C1=lateral	C1=rhotic
/db/	/nb/	/lg/	/rg/
/ɖb/	/mb/	/ḷb/	/rm/
/ʈg/	/nd/	/ḷʈ/	/ɾm/
/ʈb/	/ng/	/ḷm/	/rɲ/
/gb/	/ɳd/	/lm/	/ɾɟ/
/ɖb/	/ɳb/	/ḷɲ/	/rj/
	/ɲʈ/	/ḷn/	/ɾw/
	/ɲg/	/lw/	/rw/
	/ɲb/	/lj/	
	/ɲʈ/		
	/ŋb/		
	/ŋg/		
	/nm/		
	/nŋ/		
	/ɲm/		

b, ɟ, m, ŋ, ɲ, g, ʈ, n, ɭ, d, j, w, ḷ, ɳ, ɖ, lʳ, ḷʳ, ɰ/. It is interesting to note that the most frequently occurring consonant in this position is /m/, followed by /w/, /g/, and /ɾ/. Of the remaining stops /ɟ/ is the most frequent.

2.3 Morphophonemic alternations

Like other Iwaidjan languages, Amurdak shows a number of morphophonemic alternations at both synchronic and historical morpheme boundaries.[4] The first two sets of morphophonemic alternations show an alternation between a stop and an approximant, /b/ vs. /w/ and /ɟ/ vs. /j/. The first alternation (/b/ vs. /w/) is conditioned by preceding obstruents and nasals, i.e. the stop appears after these segments and the continuant after everything else. Examples for this alternation

---

[4] This section updates the description in Handelsmann (1991: 42–44). In some cases, the conditioning factors are generalised hypothetically, even though examples are not attested due to a lack of suitable morphology. For example, the stop-continuant alternation discussed first in the main text is attested for a limited amount of stops and nasals only, and this is because relevant morphology ends in these sounds. However, on comparative evidence from other Iwaidjan and Australian languages, it can be inferred that the stop-continuant alternation is conditioned by all stops and nasals (see Evans 1998, 2000, 2009, Mailhammer and Harvey 2018; for further details, see Baker 2014).

are found in verb morphology (Table 1), possessor affixes to body part nouns (3a), pronominal elements (3b, c), inflected adjectives (3d), derivations, and (historical) compounds (3e).

(3) /b/ vs. /w/ alternations
    a. *arrkany-**b**u*   vs.   *warli-**w**u*
        back-3SG   eye-3SG
        'her/his/its back'   'her/his/its eye'
    b. *wara-maØ-**b**u* (<**wara-mak-**b**u*)⁵   vs.   *wa-muna-**w**u*
        3SG.PFV-get-3SG.OBL   3SG.PFV-say, do-3SG.OBL
        'he got her for himself' [Irrwartbart story]   'he/she said to him/her/it'
    c. *irrambaØ-**b**urduk* (< *irrambak-burduk) vs. *ngarra-**w**urduk*
        3NSG.PRON-DU   1NSG.PRON-DU
        'the two of them'   'the two of us'
        *kurljaØ-**b**udarr* (< **kurljak-**b**udarr*)   vs. *malwa-**w**udarr*
        good-ATT   long-ATT
        'a little bit good'   'a little bit long'
    d. *-riyiØ**b**un*   (< **riyik-**b**u-n*)⁶   vs. (<**-riyi-**w**u-n*)
        'rub between palms'   'vomit'

The second set of stop-continuant alternations involves /ɟ/ vs. /j/ and is also conditioned by a preceding stop or nasal. Examples come from similar areas, as in the case of /b/ vs. /w/, see (4).

(4) /ɟ/ vs. /j/
    jan-jaØ-jurru (< *janjak-jurru)   vs. *jan-mari-yurru*
    1SG.PROX.FUT-go-after   1SG.PROX.FUT run-after
    'I'll follow'   'I'll run after'
    -riØjin (< *rik-jin)   *-aldiyin* (< **-aldi-yin*)
    'count'   'show, point'

---

5 See fn. 6 on the details of the deletion of *-k*.
6 The root-final nasal is a frozen tense suffix that is synchronically part of the root (Mailhammer and Harvey 2018: 335). The */g/ preceding *-bu* is reconstructed on the basis of regular deletion. At any rate, it is uncontroversial that *-bu* is historically identical with *-wu*. Proto-Iwaidjan **-bu* 'hit, kill' has both *-wu* and *-bu* as allomorphs in all daughter languages, and it is used as a word formation element in all Iwaidjan languages, cf. Iwaidja and Mawng *-binbu* 'wash' (the dictionary form and spelling used in Mawng is *-winypu*, but this is just a notational difference). Though probably not cognate, Amurdak *-rijbun* 'wash' is structurally identical to these Iwaidja and Mawng words (see Teo 2007 for further details).

Table 4: Partial paradigm of -*yi* 'stand' with stop alternants bolded.

-*yi* 'stand'	Perfective	Imperfective	Future
1sg	*a-yi*	*anga-yi*	*an-**j**i*
1nsgincl	*a-yi*	*a-yi*	*aban-**j**i*
1nsgexcl	*arr-yi*	*angarr-yi*	*arran-**j**i*
2sg	*anu-yi*	*anu-yi*	*wan-**j**i*
2nsg	*awurr-yi*	*anurwurr-yi*	*urran-**j**i*
3sg	*wa-yi*	*wanu-yi*	*wan-**j**i*
3nsg	*warr-yi*	*wandu-yi*	*irran-**j**i*

The next pattern of alternation involves consonants alternating with zero following or preceding other consonants. In the first set /g/ surfaces as Ø if followed by a stop or liquid. Examples for this alternation are found in (3) and (4); (5) provides a case with a following liquid.

(5) *irrambaØ-laburduk* (< **irrambak-laburduk*)
 3NSG.PRON-TRI
 'the three of them'

This set of alternations is interesting, as it eliminates the conditioning factor for the alternation between stops and continuants (/b/ vs. /w/ and /ɟ/ vs. /j/) discussed above (see Baker 2014: 174–175 for a similar case in the Gunwinyguan language Wubuy). It follows that in cases showing both alternations, the process that caused the stop-continuant alternation must precede the deletion of /g/.

The next pattern where a segment alternates with zero involves /ɻ/, which alternates with Ø if preceded by alveolars /d/ or /n/. This is particularly frequent in verb paradigms, see Table 5.

Two related cases are deletions of /n/ and /ŋ/. The former occurs following /ɲ/ and /n/, the latter following /ŋ/.

(6) a. *a-ldikiny-Øu* vs. *a-muna-nu*
 1.SG.PFV-listen-2SG.OBL 1SG.PFV.-say, do-2SG.OBL
 'I listened to you.' 'I said to you.'
 b. *anu-ldikiny-Øanu* vs. *anu-muna-nganu*
 2.SG.PFV.listen-1SG.OBL 2SG.PFV.-say, do-1SG.OBL
 'You listened to me.' 'You said to me.'

Table 5: Partial paradigm for -rakan 'see, look' with deletions marked by bolded Ø.

-rakan 'see, look'	Perfective	Imperfective	Future
1sg	a-rakan	anga-rakan	an-Øakan
1nsgincl	a-rakan	a-rakan	aban-Øakan
1nsgexcl	ad-Øakan	angad-Øakan	arran-Øakan
2sg	anu-rakan	anu-rakan	wan-Øakan
2nsg	awud-Øakan	anuwud-Øakan	urran-Øakan
3sg	wa-rakan	wanu-rakan	wan-Øakan
3nsg	wad-akan	wandurakan	irran-Øakan

The next set of alternations involve a nasal and a stop. On comparative evidence, the conditioning factor for the appearance of the stop is probably any preceding stop though the attested cases are typically confined to one stop. Like the stop vs. continuant alternations, this pattern is also found in the related languages Iwaidja and Mawng, although it is much more frequent there (see Capell and Hinch 1970, Pym and Larrimore 1979 for details).

(7) /b/ vs. /m/
    a. *urrambalØ=bardan* (*urrambalk* 'house', *mardan* 'small, little')
       house=small, little
       'little house'   (Handelsmann 1998: 44)
    b. *-murranymin* (< **murrany-min*)[7] vs. *-rijbin* (> **-rij-bin*)

(8) /d/ vs. /n/
    aman-maØ-du (< **aman-mak-nu*)
    1sg.fut-get-2SG.OBL
    'I will get it for you'

(9) /g/ vs. /ŋ/
    wandu-maØ-kanu (< **wandu-mak-nganu*)
    3NSG.PFV-get-1SG.OBL
    'they got it for me'

---

[7] *-mi* is a common suffix in Iwaidjan languages to form inchoatives (Teo 2007). In Iwaidja, this suffix is productive, hence *-murranymi* 'grow' from *-murrang* 'big' and *-wurrlulanymi* 'get better' from *-wurruli* 'good'.

Finally, there is a different pattern that is to be considered in connection with the alternation in Table 5. This is the alternation between /ɾ/ and /d/ before /ɻ/. Examples can be obtained from the verb paradigms mentioned. For instance, in *ad-akan* 'we (excl.) see/saw' (Table 5) *ad-* derives from *arr-*, as see e.g. *arr-yi* 'we (excl.) stand/stood'. Similarly, to the /g/ vs. Ø alternation, the change from *arr-* > *ad-* must have happened before the deletion of the root-initial /ɻ/.

3 Amurdak phonotactics and morphophonemic alternations and the Preference Laws

As mentioned in Section 1, Baker (2014) suggests that in certain cases stop-continuant alternations in Australian languages can be explained in the light of the Contact Law. This section investigates this proposition using the morphophonemic processes in Amurdak, and, extending from this, also the possible intersyllabic clusters.

3.1 Amurdak phonotactics and the Contact Law

The Contact Law in its most recent form (Vennemann 1988: 40; see also Murray and Vennemann 1983) is formulated as follows:

(10)   The Contact Law
A syllable contact $A^\$B$ is the more preferred, the less the Consonantal Strength of the offset A and the greater the Consonantal Strength of the onset B; more precisely – the greater the characteristic difference CS(B)-CS(A) between the Consonantal Strength of B and that of A.

Consonantal strength is – in simplified terms – the inverse of sonority, that is speech sounds are ordered according to their "degree of deviation from unimpeded (voiced) airflow" (Vennemann 1988: 8; see Murray 1988 for a history and a discussion of the concept of consonantal strength more generally), see (11) taken from Mailhammer, Restle, and Vennemann (2015: 453).

(11)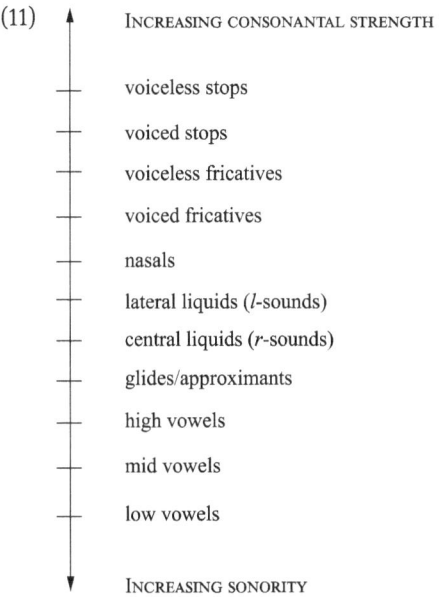

The Contact Law basically says that in a CVC₁.C₂V sequence the consonantal strength of the onset of the second syllable (C₂) should be higher than that of the coda of the preceding syllable (C₁), and the bigger the difference, the better. Consequently, a hypothetical contact between *d* and *l* in German *Adler* 'eagle' is not as good as that in German *Alter* 'age'. This is supported by the fact that *dl* in *Adler* is frequently tautosyllabified by speakers, i.e. /ˈa.dlɐ/, which can be seen from the fact that *d* is not devoiced in these cases, as it should be if *dl* were heterosyllabified, i.e. /ˈat.lɐ/.

Intersyllabic consonant clusters in Amurdak by and large conform to this preference. In the vast majority of licit clusters, the second consonant has a higher consonantal strength than the first. There are two kinds of deviations. First, there are five clusters with no significant difference in consonantal strength, and these are all stop plus stop clusters. Second, there are six clusters in which the consonantal strength decreases from the first to the second consonant: /lj/, /lw/, /ʈj/, /ʈw/, /ɾj/, and /ɾw/, in e.g. *barnalya* 'brain', *malwa* 'long', *-mirdyadban* 'be sticky', *urdwiny* 'shame', *irryarla* 'red bush apple', and *irrwartbart* 'taipan'. In all of these the second consonant is an approximant, the weakest consonant. The first consonant is either a liquid or a tap. Though taps phonetically contain a total obstruction of airflow, just like stops, they seem weaker than stops (published rankings of consonantal strength generally do not contain taps). Amurdak provides an indication that they are also weaker than nasals and that they are of the same strength as *r*-sounds, i.e. that they form part of a class that is commonly called *rhotic*. To understand why this supports that the taps belong to the class of *r*-sounds in (11), Vennemann's Synchronic Maxim has to be considered:

(12) Synchronic Maxim (Vennemann 1988: 3)
A language system will in general not contain a structure on a given parameter without containing those structures constructible with the means of the system that are more preferred in terms of the relevant preference law.

Amurdak has no nasal plus approximant clusters, and these would be less preferred than liquids plus approximant clusters, which do exist in Amurdak. Thus, if the taps are classified as rhotics, then the respective clusters with following approximants are easily understood as the second worst of the syllable contacts in the language (/l/ plus approximant being the worst). And this is in line with the Synchronic Maxim, as there are no "gaps" in the ranking.[8] By contrast, if the taps were considered a kind of stop, then this would be at odds with the Synchronic Maxim. This, together with a more general pattern of alveolar and retroflex taps as rhotics (though often not in Australian languages, see McGregor 1988), suggests that taps belong to the *r*-sounds in (11). Crosslinguistically, taps often are phonetic realisations of other rhotics, especially trills (Ladefoged and Maddieson 1996, Carne et al. 2019).

To sum up, the phonotactics of heterosyllabic consonant clusters in Amurdak largely conform to the preferences expressed by the Contact Law, and cases that do not conform do not violate the Synchronic Maxim, i.e. they are the best of the dispreferred contacts.[9]

---

[8] There is one gap: there are no lateral plus rhotic clusters, but it is not clear where they would fit in terms of their relative degree of preference. If an arbitrary numerical scale is fitted to the consonantal strength hierarchy as in e.g. Mailhammer, Restle, and Vennemann (2015), then lateral plus rhotic clusters are about as bad as rhotic plus approximant clusters. And the Synchronic Maxim does not say that all variants of structural positions must be covered, hence this is unproblematic.

[9] There are two apparent exceptions to these generalisations, *yadyad* 'right hand, straight' and *jalurtjalurt* 'bird species' However, both are reduplicated structures, and this may trump syllabic preferences. In fact, *jalurlurt* is potentially a loanword from Iwaidja (the Iwaidja word is the same), and *yadyad* appears to be a reduplication of **yad*, which may mean '(right) hand' originally, cf. *-yadbin* 'work' (**yad-bin*, i.e. **yad-min* 'hand+inchoative').

3.2 Morphophonemics and the Preference Laws

This section considers the morphophonemic alternations in light of the phonotactics just discussed and the Preference Laws, focusing on the Contact Law and the Strength Assimilation Law. In the first group of alternations, stops alternate with approximants or with zero. In the stop vs. approximant alternations in (3) and (4), the stops are conditioned by a preceding stop or nasal. In the stop vs. zero pattern, which only affects /g/, by contrast, the stop only surfaces if preceded by a stop or if it is followed by a vowel. The effect is that the relevant stops always occur in clusters that are either neutral (stop plus stop) or actually preferred in terms of the Contact Law, because the stop occurs in second position preceded by a nasal or because there is actually only one consonant.

The second group of alternations features nasals that alternate with stops. Unlike the stop vs. approximant alternations, the conditioning factor for the appearance of the stop is a preceding stop but not a preceding nasal. The result is similar to that in the first group: all syllable contacts are either neutral or good.

The third group of alternations involves zero alternating with either one of the two nasals /n/ and /ŋ/ or with the retroflex approximant. The conditioning factors are slightly different, however. In the first case, the nasals do not show up when preceded by a palatal nasal /ɲ/. In the second case, the approximant does not show up if preceded by an alveolar nasal /n/. In both cases, there is an improved syllable contact in the zero variant.

Consequently, the idea that the Contact Law can explain all these seemingly disparate alternations seems sound enough. Such an explanation would mean that the processes involved are not sound changes but rather prosodic changes, i.e. changes that are motivated by syllable structure rather than changes motivated by, e.g., coarticulation.

An alternative hypothesis would be that all these changes are in fact unrelated and that the outcome just looks like it is motivated by the Contact Law. For example, the nasal vs. stop alternation could be a case of assimilatory fortition (Evans 2009: 163), or the stop vs. approximant alternation could be the result of lenition. The result would be similar, with the difference being that independent sound changes did away with syllable structures that are not found in contemporary Amurdak.

At this point it is important to consider more closely what processes were in fact involved in producing these alternations. The reconstruction of the historical phonology of the Iwaidjan languages is a work in progress, but the cases under consideration are relatively clear (Mailhammer and Harvey 2018). The three processes are lenition, fortition, and deletion.

First, in some cases a stop-approximant alternation can actually be described as the result of a process of lenition. This is clearest in cases like Amurdak -*bun* 'hit', which shows *w*-initial forms like the paradigm of -*burlka* 'dance' in Table 1. This is one of the few verb roots that can be reconstructed to the protolanguage of all Australian languages, Proto-Australian, as *bu (Harvey and Mailhammer Ms.). Thus, it is safe to assume that the *w*-initial form is the result of lenition operating intervocalically. However, it is unlikely that lenition is a classical sound change here. The reason is that it operates consistently only at morpheme boundaries but only sporadically morpheme-internally. That is, there is a considerable number of words in all Iwaidjan languages in which a stop occurs morpheme-internally between vowels or sonorants, exactly in the conditioning environment of the approximants in the stop vs. approximant alternations. The Amurdak verb -*rakan* 'see, look' in Table 5 is a case in point, and there is a significant number of similar cases that can be reconstructed for Proto-Iwiadjan (see Mailhammer and Harvey 2018: 341–347 for further details).[10] If this is not a general sound change, motivated e.g. by assimilation to a more sonorous environment in line with the Strength Assimilation Law (Vennemann 1988: 35; see also below), as it is done generally for this very common change (Kümmel 2007), why does it operate only at morpheme boundaries?

Second, in other cases, the stop-alternants are the result of fortition. This is evident from cognates showing the *m*-initial form. For instance, the frequent word-formation element -*ma* goes back to an independent verb *ma that can be reconstructed to Proto-Australian (Harvey and Mailhammer Ms.). Similarly, cases like Amurdak -*jirrka* 'sting' (Iwaidja -*djirrka* 'spear', Mawng -*irrka* 'spear fish', and the Amurdak 2nsg.pron element -*nu* (8) acquired their stop-initial forms by fortition. In other Iwaidjan languages, this is only the case for stop vs. nasal alternations, but in Amurdak fortition can also be the cause for a stop vs. approximant alternation, as Amurdak has generalised the stop vs. approximant alternation at all morpheme boundaries (but not morpheme-internally). For instance, the ancestor of Amurdak -*burlka* 'dance' (Table 1) probably did not have stop-initial forms. The likely cognates in Iwaidja and Mawng have *w*-initial forms that alternate with zero (Mailhammer and Harvey 2018). Consequently, Amurdak has two processes of fortition that are distinct in terms of their conditioning environment. The fortition of approximants is conditioned by preceding stops and nasals, whereas the fortition of nasals is conditioned by preceding stops only.

---

10 The reconstruction of lenition as a sound change assumes that intervocalic stops in modern Iwaidjan languages are the result of either cluster simplification or degemination (see e.g. Evans 2009: 162). However, this is an unproven assumption; existing reconstructions do not confirm this hypothesis (Mailhammer and Harvey 2018: 341–347).

As far as fortition in Amurdak is concerned, we may ask whether we are dealing with regular sound change similarly to what Evans (2009: 165) thinks happened to stop plus nasal clusters in the Iwaidjan languages. For Amurdak such an analysis seems possible, as Amurdak has no stop-nasal clusters or stop-approximant clusters at all.[11] However, (7a) and similar cases in which freely occurring words (in this case *mardan* 'small') show fortition suggest that we are dealing with an ongoing phonological process on a different prosodic level, perhaps in addition to a historical change. There is another reason for why the assumption of a sound change is not convincing. Such a sound change would be at odds with the Strength Assimilation Law in Vennemann (1988: 35):

(13) Strength Assimilation Law
 If Consonantal Strength is assimilated in a syllable contact, the Consonantal Strength of the stronger consonant decreases.

This law predicts that clusters of stop plus nasal should result in a weakened stop, e.g. *k.m > m.m, but in Amurdak and other Iwaidjan languages the opposite happens: the nasal is strengthened to a stop, i.e. *k.m > *kb.

An analysis that views all cases of nasal fortition as improvements of the syllable contact can explain why the Strength Assimilation Law is violated and why these changes occur on all prosodic levels. Fortition in these cases is not motivated by assimilation; it is not a phonetically motivated change; it is prosodically motivated, i.e. by syllable structure, and thus applies to the prosodic word and hence also to cases like in (7a).

Third, some alternations discussed here involve deletions. Deletions are commonly seen as a type of lenition (Shaw et al. 2020), but in the cases discussed here, we are clearly not dealing with weakening in the classical sense. The reason is that segments are deleted in prosodically strong rather than weak positions, i.e. post-consonantally, in syllable-onset position and not e.g. intervocalically in coda position. Again, an explanation based on the Contact Law is able to accommodate these facts. In all cases the syllable contact before deletion is dispreferred.

Firstly, Amurdak does not have any clusters in which a stop is paired up with anything but a stop. What is more, native Amurdak vocabulary does not have any cluster with /g/ as first element. The only three words in the dictionary with /gb/ clusters have an identical form in Iwaidja and could well be loans. If it is assumed that /g/ is the most consonantal stop in Amurdak (see Tsunoda 2008 for such an

---

11 It would not work for Iwaidja or Mawng, as both languages in fact have stop plus nasal clusters, cf. Iwaidja *kudnayanjing* 'look (pl.)!' and Mawng *mijmij* 'sandfly' (*pace* Evans 2009: 165).

analysis of Warrongo), then its elimination as first element of a cluster is straightforward because it would always produce dispreferred clusters.

Secondly, Amurdak does not have nasal plus approximant clusters. Interestingly, in the cases of the two other approximants /j/ and /w/, the syllable contact was improved by fortition (see above), whereas in the case of the retroflex approximant, it was improved by deletion.

Thirdly, Amurdak has only nasal plus nasal clusters with a minimal distance in terms of place of articulation. There are no nasal plus nasal clusters in which the nasals are directly adjacent in terms of place of articulation, and consequently clusters of palatal and alveolar and palatal and velar nasals are eliminated. Arguably, this could be motivated articulatorily rather than on the basis of syllable contact.

From this discussion of morphophonemic alternations in Amurdak we can draw the following conclusions.

First, the processes of fortition and deletion underlying some of these alternations can be convincingly explained by assuming that they aim at improving the syllable contact in line with the Diachronic Maxim:

(14) Diachronic Maxim (Vennemann 1988: 2)
Linguistic change on a given parameter does not affect a language structure as long as there exist structures in the language system that are less preferred in terms of the relevant preference law.

The fortition of /w/ and /j/ eliminates the worst clusters, and the fortition of nasals the next worst clusters (there are no stop-liquid clusters at all in Amurdak).

Second, the processes of lenition producing the stop vs. approximant alternations cannot be easily motivated by the Contact Law, as they worsen the syllable contact. However, they can be motivated by the Strength Assimilation Law. That is, they are not changes that aim at the improvement of syllable structure, but they are assimilatory changes. It is noteworthy that their applicative domain is sensitive to morphological structure, as the change occurs regularly only at morpheme boundaries.

Third, all three processes that produce the morphophonemic alternations in Amurdak operate above word-level. That is, they are not classical sound changes operating on the segmental level. The deletion and fortition processes target bad syllable contacts (with the possible exception of the deletion of /n/ and /ŋ/). The fortition processes also operate beyond the word level, and lenition is sensitive to morphological structure. The fact that lenition is much more inconsistent on an intra-morpheme level than at morpheme boundaries suggests that there may be different levels of applications for Preference Laws.

Fourth, as in other cases, it is interesting to observe different solutions to achieve the same overarching goal. For example, */kl/ is eliminated by deletion of /k/ while */km/ is eliminated by the fortition of /m/.

4 Conclusion

This paper reviewed the phonotactics of Amurdak, an Iwaidjan language from Northern Australia, in light of the Preference Laws for syllable structure, especially the Contact Law. One key finding was that the Contact Law is a strong determinant of intersyllabic clusters in Amurdak. This plays out on the one hand in the language's phonotactics and in the processes that result in morphophonemic alternations on the other. Several changes converge on improving syllable contacts by various, seemingly unrelated changes, so that almost all contacts with a stronger first consonant or no strength difference between first and second consonants are eliminated. It is interesting that among these processes there is little agreement about the way these structures are improved.

In addition to fortition, Amurdak, like all Iwaidjan languages, also shows evidence of lenition, and this could potentially be explained by the Strength Assimilation Law. However, the fact that all of these processes occur mainly at morpheme boundaries introduces an additional complication, which possibly suggests that the historical origin of these alternations are sandhi processes and cliticisation. Such an origin is consistent with a more general reconstruction of the history of Australian languages assuming recurring processes of cliticisation (Harvey and Mailhammer 2017: 475, Harvey and Mailhammer Ms.). Further investigation of languages with similar processes, especially other Iwaidjan languages, may shed more light on the role of the Preference Laws in the development of the phonology of Australian languages. In particular, it might become clearer if different levels or domains of applicability of Preference Laws, e.g. below vs. above word level, have to be assumed.

References

Baker, Brett. 2014. Word structure in Australian languages. In Harold Koch & Rachel Nordlinger (eds.), *The languages and linguistics of Australia*, 139–213. Berlin: de Gruyter.

Butcher, Andy, Bruce Birch, Nicholas Evans & Janet Fletcher. 2007. Stopped laterals (?) in Iwaidja. Paper presented at OzPhon 2007, La Trobe University, 16–18 March.

Capell, Arthur & Heather Hinch. 1970. *Maung grammar, texts and vocabulary*. The Hague: Mouton.
Carne, Michael, Juqiang Chen, Luk Ellison, Sydney Strangways, Clara Stockigt, Robert Mailhammer & Mark Harvey. 2019. Rhotic contrasts in Arabana. In *Proceedings of the 19th International Congress of the Phonetic Sciences, Melbourne, Australia 2019*, 1278–1282. Canberra: Australasian Speech Science and Technology Association Inc.
Evans, Nicholas. 1998. Iwaidja mutation and its origins. In Anna Siewierska & Jae Jung Song (eds.), *Case, typology and grammar: In honor of Barry Blake*. Amsterdam: John Benjamins.
Evans, Nicholas. 2000. Iwaidjan, a very un-Australian language family. *Linguistic Typology* 4. 91–142.
Evans, Nicholas. 2009. Doubled up all over again: Borrowing, sound change and reduplication in Iwaidja. *Morphology* 10. 159–176.
Hamilton, Philip James. 1996. *Constraints and markedness in the phonotactics of Australian Aboriginal languages*. Toronto: University of Toronto dissertation.
Handelsmann, Robert. 1991. *Towards a description of Amurdak: A language of Northern Australia*. Melbourne: The University of Melbourne.
Handelsmann, Robert. 1998. *A draft dictionary of Amurdag*. Melbourne: Parks Australia North.
Harvey, Mark. 2002. *A grammar of Gaagudju*. Berlin: de Gruyter.
Harvey, Mark & Robert Mailhammer. 2017. Reconstructing remote relationships: Proto-Australian noun class prefixation. *Diachronica* 34. 470–515.
Harvey, Mark & Robert Mailhammer. Ms. under review. Proto-Australian. University of Newcastle, Western Sydney University.
Kümmel, Martin. 2007. *Konsonantenwandel*. Wiesbaden: Dr. Ludwig Reichert.
Ladefoged, Peter & Ian Maddieson. 1996. *The sounds of the world's languages*. Malden, MA: Blackwell.
Mailhammer, Robert. 2009. Towards an aspect-based analysis of the verb categories of Amurdak. *Australian Journal of Linguistics* 29. 349–391.
Mailhammer, Robert. 2014. Some answers and more puzzles: Newly discovered modal categories and the history of the Iwaidjan verb system. In Aicha Belkadi, Kakia Chatsiou & Kirsty Rowan (eds.), *Proceedings of Conference on Languge Documentation and Linguistic Theory 4*. London: SOAS.
Mailhammer, Robert. 2017. Zur Rekonstruktion der Verbalpräfixe im Amurdak. *International Journal of Diachronic Linguistics and Linguistic Reconstruction* 14. 1–30.
Mailhammer, Robert & Robert Handelsmann. 2009. *Amurdak Inyman: Six stories in Amurdak told by Bill Neidje and Nelson Mulurinj*. Jabiru: Iwaidja Inyman.
Mailhammer, Robert & Mark Harvey. 2018. A reconstruction of the Proto-Iwaidjan phoneme system. *Australian Journal of Linguistics* 38. 329–359.
Mailhammer, Robert, David Restle & Theo Vennemann. 2015. Preference laws in phonological change. In Patrick Honeybone & Joseph Salmons (eds.), *The Oxford handbook of historical phonology*, 450–466. Oxford: Oxford University Press.
McGregor, William. 1988. On the status of the feature rhotic in some languages of the north-west of Australia. *Aboriginal Linguistics* 1. 166–187.
Murray, Robert. 1988. *Phonological strength and early Germanic syllable structure*. Munich: Fink.
Murray, Robert & Theo Vennemann. 1983. Sound change and syllable structure in Germanic phonology. *Language* 59. 514–528.
Pym, Noreen & Bonnie Larrimore. 1979. *Papers on Iwaidja phonology and grammar*. Darwin: SIL.

Shaw, Jason, Christopher Carignan, Tonya Agostini, Robert Mailhammer, Mark Harvey & Donald Derrick. 2020. Phonological contrast and phonetic variation: The case of velars in Iwaidja. *Language* 96. 578–617.
Teo, Amos. 2007. *Breaking up is hard to do: Teasing apart mophological complexity in Iwaidja and Maung*. Melbourne: The University of Melbourne Honours thesis.
Tsunoda, Tasaku. 2008. Sonority hierarchy in Warrongo (Australia). *Gengo Kenkyu* 133. 147–161.
Vennemann, Theo. 1988. *Preference laws for syllable structure and the explanation of sound change*. Berlin: de Gruyter.

Renate Raffelsiefen
Shortening as a window on phonological grammar

Abstract: Words originating from shortening, including acronyms and clippings, constitute a treasure trove of insight into phonological grammar. In particular, they serve as an ideal testing ground for Optimality Theory (OT) and its view of grammar as an interaction of markedness constraints, which express (dis-) preferences regarding phonological structure in output forms, and faithfulness constraints, which require output forms to correspond to input structure (Prince and Smolensky 1993). This is because shortenings are characterised by a sharply diminished role of faithfulness, allowing for markedness constraints to make their force felt ("The Emergence of the Unmarked").

This article aims to demonstrate the heuristic value of shortening data for testing the OT model and for shedding light on various controversies in German phonology. A particular concern is to draw attention to the need for properly sorting the shortening data, to identify influences on phonological structure due to internal domain boundaries or to special correspondence effects potentially obscuring the view on the maximally unmarked patterns.

1 Introduction

Shortenings which form a single phonological word (i.e. a single domain for syllabification and foot formation) exhibit limits on phonological form often violated in the ordinary vocabulary.[1] Such limits are illustrated with the consistent initial stress observed in CVCV-shortenings as in (1), all of which are composed based on the underlined fragments of the respective source expressions given

---

Acknowledgements: I thank the editors and the anonymous reviewers for their very helpful feedback. I'm also grateful to Marco Gierke, Marc van Oostendorp, and Bianca Weißinger for commenting on earlier drafts.

[1] Reference to prosodic constituents is in accordance with the theory of Prosodic Phonology (Nespor and Vogel 2007). An early study noting the relevance of acronyms for insight into unmarked phonology is Bat-El (1994).

Renate Raffelsiefen, Leibniz-Institut für Deutsche Sprache, Mannheim/Germany, and Institute for English Language and Literature, Freie Universität Berlin, Berlin/Germany

https://doi.org/10.1515/9783110721461-004

to their right (ω = phonological word). Stress always falls on the first syllable, whether the words are based on separate initials as in (1a) (*Initialkurzwörter* in German), on stem-initial strings encompassing the first vowel as in (1b) (*Silbenkurzwörter*), or indicate a mix of those two types as in (1c) (*Mischkurzwörter*).[2]

(1) a. ('bafu)_ω   BAFU   <u>B</u>undes#<u>a</u>mt <u>f</u>ür <u>U</u>mwelt
       ('lufa)_ω   LUFA   <u>L</u>andwirtschaftliche <u>U</u>ntersuchungs-
                           und <u>F</u>orschungs#<u>a</u>nstalt
    b. ('nabu)_ω   NABU   <u>N</u>aturschutz#<u>b</u>und
       ('ʃiʀi)_ω   Schiri <u>Sch</u>ieds#<u>r</u>ichter
    c. ('kyfa)_ω   Küfa   <u>Kü</u>che <u>f</u>ür <u>a</u>lle
       ('fama)_ω   FAMA   <u>F</u>achverband <u>M</u>essen und <u>A</u>usstellungen

The uniformity observed in the CVCV-shortenings distinguishes them from comparable ordinary words, where final stress is rather common (cf. 2).

(2)   /ta'bu/ <Tabu> 'taboo', /ʒe'ni/ <Genie> 'genius', /by'ʀo/ <Büro> 'office'

The extent of the regularity in question is indicated in the table in (3), which compares relevant ordinary C_0VC_0V-words extracted from the German CELEX corpus (i.e. words ending in a full vowel classified as "monomorphemic") to C_0VC_0V-shortenings from a database called *SDS-corpus*[3] ("Single-Domain-Shortening corpus").

(3)   a. Ordinary words (CELEX)   b. Shortenings (SDS-corpus)
     Initial stress   177   75,6 %   606   99,5 %
     Final stress   57   24,4 %   3   0,5 %
     Total   234   100 %   609   100 %

Below I will argue that even the rare cases of final stress in German C_0VC_0V-shortenings are not sporadic exceptions to the sort of uniformity indicated in (3b) but rather indicate special conditions separating them from the regular cases

---

[2] The terminology used here is consistent with Kobler-Trill (1994).
[3] The SDS-corpus (Raffelsiefen in progress) currently includes roughly 1200 entries and includes translations of the full forms into English, which for reasons of space are mostly omitted in the data referred to in this article. The criteria for sorting data are explained further in Section 4. While it is easy to find lists of written abbreviations (e.g. Steinhauer 2005), it is often exceedingly hard to find reliable information on pronunciation. I thank assistants and interns, in particular Alina Behr, Vanessa Dengel, and Bianca Weißinger, for their help with gathering relevant information (finding videos, contacting informants).

(see Section 5).[4] The uniformity of stress patterns in the shortenings is then arguably absolute, in accordance with the intuition that final stress in for instance the shortening (bɑfu)_ω <BAFU> in (1a) would be simply impossible in German.[5] Linguists accordingly need to explain both the (near-)uniformity of the prosodic structure of shortenings in (3) vis-à-vis the potential contrast found in ordinary words and the particular shape of that uniformity (i.e. the occurrence of initial rather than final stress in German C_0VC_0V-shortenings).

Optimality Theory meets this challenge by modelling the relevant conditions in terms of an interaction between correspondence constraints (also known as faithfulness constraints), which preserve (aspects of) input structure, and markedness constraints, which favour phonologically unmarked output structure. The theory thus predicts that irrelevance of faithfulness gives way to unmarkedness, a claim known as TETU ("The Emergence of the Unmarked").

To assess the adequacy of this model, consider first the issue of markedness pertaining to stress. A possible representation of the contrasting stress patterns observed in German minimal pairs such as (ˈetɑ) 'eta' (Greek letter name) versus (eˈtɑ) <Etat> 'budget' in accordance with Prosodic Phonology (Nespor and Vogel 2007) is shown in (4) (ω = "phonological word", Σ = "foot", σ = "syllable", O = "onset", N = "nucleus", Hd = "head", ↓_L = subphonemic lengthening).

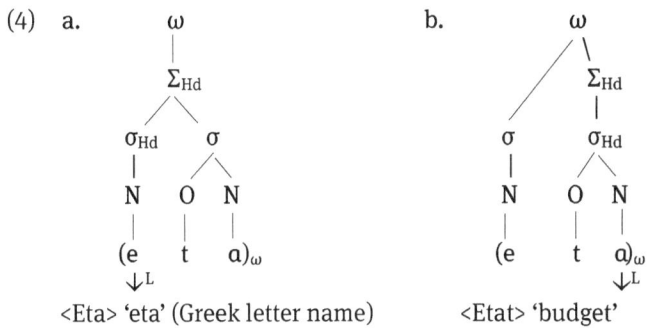

(4) a. <Eta> 'eta' (Greek letter name)   b. <Etat> 'budget'

The well-formedness conditions on prosodic organisations as in (4) can be stated in terms of constraints, some of which are assumed to be universally inviolable (Selkirk 1996). So-called alignment constraints require edges of various

---

[4] The three exceptions are *Ergee* (see [36]), *atü* and *BaWü*, for which stress varies ((bɑˈvy)_ω ~ (ˈbɑvy)_ω, see [44]).
[5] German differs then from English, where /u/ is never tolerated in the weak syllable of the foot but consistently attracts stress (e.g. main stress in /snæˈfu/ <snafu> [< _situation normal: all fucked up_] or secondary stress as in /ˈzɑˌnu/ <ZANU> [< _Zimbabwe African National Union_]).

constituents to coincide, capturing the observation that the domains for the prosodic organisation of phonemes necessarily align with morphological boundaries (cf. 5a, b[6]). They further capture the edge-orientation of stress, including the consistent location of the prominent syllable in foot-initial position in languages like English or German. Independent evidence for the specific organisations in (4) comes from contextual conditions on phonetic vowel lengthening indicated by the downward arrow. That is, reference to the trees in (4) allows for lengthening to be associated with vowels in open head syllables in accordance with well-known restrictions on phonetic implementation (i.e. enhancement in a prominent position). Assuming the adequacy of the representations in (4), the preference for initial stress observed in (3) is then captured straightforwardly in terms of universal markedness constraints. Only the trochaic foot structure as in (4a) satisfies the constraints PARSE-SYLL (cf. 5d) and FOOT-BIN (at the syllabic level, cf. 5e[7]) (Prince and Smolensky 1993).

(5) a. ALIGN (Stem, E; Phonological Word, E): The (left, right) edge of every stem coincides with the corresponding edge of a phonological word.
  b. ALIGN (Phonological Word, E; Stem, E): The (left, right) edge of every phonological word coincides with the corresponding edge of a stem.
  c. ALIGN (Foot, Left; Head of the Foot, Left): Feet are left-headed.
  d. PARSE-SYLL: Syllables are parsed into feet.
  e. FOOT-BIN: Feet consist of either two syllables or of one heavy syllable.

Assuming that the particular stress pattern seen in shortenings indicates an active role of one or both of the constraints in (5d, e), the potential contrasts seen in ordinary words could be captured in terms of faithfulness preserving structure specified in the input.[8] This assumption is motivated independently by the adaptation of loan words such as English /tæˈbu/ <taboo> versus /ˈvuˌdu/ <voodoo> into German, where the relative prominence observed in English is preserved

---

[6] The observation that certain morphemes (e.g. vowel-initial suffixes) integrate into the phonological word of the stem (Dixon 1977) indicates that (5a) is violable. The mirror-image constraint in (5b) is universally inviolable.
[7] The question of the weight of monosyllabic feet in German is addressed in Sections 3 and 4.
[8] In OT it is generally assumed that there are no restrictions on input forms (ROTB (< *Richness of the Base*)). The idea is that for any hypothetical input, the grammar selects the corresponding optimal output. The effect described here is perhaps best conceived of in terms of output-output correspondence, where one type of output (i.e. actual forms encountered by speakers) is associated with another (respective forms produced by the speaker). For a discussion of this question in connection with Spanish truncation, see Piñeros (2000: 65).

in German. The representation of stress in the input forms seems plausible as German speakers can be assumed to be sensitive to perceiving main stress in different positions of a word and moreover can be assumed to have access to the English pronunciations. Once the stress is represented in the input, its preservation can be modelled in terms of a high-ranking correspondence constraint requiring stress patterns in input and output forms to match.

The observation that in general none of the prominence patterns associated with full forms are preserved in shortenings, even when speakers are fully aware of them, indicates some sort of inaccessibility of the structures in question. That inaccessibility is represented informally by the small font in (6c). There surely is a difference between the cases modelled in (6a, b), where prosodic structure is directly associated with a given contiguous phoneme string in the input, and the case involving shortening in (6c), where the material associated with full forms standing in correspondence is often non-contiguous and the formation moreover involves some sort of intermediate representation consisting of mere graphemes (i.e. <BAFU>). Inaccessibility of input structure will forestall any faithfulness effects, with the result that the prosodic organisation of the relevant phoneme strings is shaped by markedness constraints alone. (The segmental structure of the relevant candidates is determined by a faithfulness constraint not indicated in tableau (6), which concerns grapheme-phoneme correspondence conventions based on the grapheme string <BAFU> see Section 3.)

(6)	a.	/tæˈbu/ ~ /təˈbu/[9] <taboo>	FAITH(Stress)	FOOT-BIN
		((ˈtabu)$_\Sigma$)$_\omega$	*!	
		☞ (ta(ˈbu)$_\Sigma$)$_\omega$		*
	b.	/ ˈvuˌdu / <voodoo>		
		☞ ((ˈvudu)$_\Sigma$)$_\omega$		
		(vu(ˈdu)$_\Sigma$)$_\omega$	*!	*
	c.	/bʊn.dəs.amt.fyʀ.ˈʊm.vɛlt/ <Bundesamt für Umwelt>		
		<BAFU>		
		(ba(ˈfu)$_\Sigma$)$_\omega$		*!
		☞ ((ˈbafu)$_\Sigma$)$_\omega$		

---

[9] The word is typically pronounced with /æ/ in American English and with /ə/ in British English. The quality /ɑ/ chosen in the German adaptation is presumably due to spelling.

Once established, the trochaic organisation of a shortening becomes part of the input and is entirely stable, since both faithfulness and markedness favour the same structure.[10]

While highlighting the role of input structure for the emergence of the unmarked stress pattern in the shortening, the parallel treatment of the cases in (6) is evidently in need of elaboration. The cases in (6a, b) concern loan word adaptation, pertaining to existing words encountered in acquisition, while the case in (6c) illustrates a special case of word-formation, involving a base (the source expression), from which a new word exhibiting a novel composition of segmental material is derived. The comparison in (6) then concerns only one aspect of the relevant word-formation rule, namely the prosodic organisation of the segmental material.[11] Indeed, there are two additional aspects under which shortenings are relevant to learning about the role of phonological markedness in grammar: the selection of material from source forms and the alignment of that material with prosodic domains. As for selection, consider the representation of the initial of the function word *für* in (7a, b), which appears to be motivated by a constraint against hiatus. This is because function words, marked by a small font in (7), are typically passed over when forming acronyms. The preference for representing content words only is manifest in (7c). Here the hiatus is avoided by organising the correspondent of the grapheme <I>, the vowel /i/, in onset position, rendering the inclusion of /f/ superfluous. (The icon "☹" is meant to indicate that the form is not used, despite being phonologically well-formed and similar to existing acronyms.)

(7) a. Deutsches Institut für   DIFE   ('di.fə)_ω   (☹ ('di.ə)_ω)
        Ernährungs#forschung
    b. Institut für Umwelt#informatik IFU   ('i.fu)_ω   (☹ ('iu.i)_ω)

---

10 The grammar in (6) accordingly predicts the unidirectionality of stress shifts. A word borrowed with an unmarked pattern is expected to keep that pattern, resulting in a stable form (cf. *voodoo* in [6b]). A word borrowed with final stress is susceptible to variance, ultimately favouring the less marked form. This development is seen in /kɑ'nu/ <Kanu> (from English /kə'nu/ <canoe>), which varies with more and more preferred /'kɑnu/. Unidirectionality is predicted because the impact of stress-preserving FAITH(stress) hinges upon speakers' attention to the marked pronunciation, whereas the unmarked form emerges by default. Future changes in the phonological grammar may of course lead to destabilisation of currently unmarked structure.

11 The term "prosodic organization" subsumes all aspects of grouping items into prosodic constituents, including the association of phonemes with syllable positions, the association of syllables with feet, the determination of prominence relations among syllables within feet (i.e. the determination of the head syllable), and prominence relations among feet (i.e. the determination of the head foot).

c. Institut für Umwelt#physik IUP[12] (iʊp)_ω (☺ ('i.fu)_ω)
d. Universitäts#klinikum UKE ((u)_ω(ka)_ω(e)_ωHd)_CC (☹ ('u.kə)_ω
   Hamburg-Eppendorf

Yet another way in which shortenings shed light on phonological markedness concerns their mapping into prosodic domains. For shortenings consisting of initials, there is always a grammatical candidate, namely a copulative compound (CC) consisting of the respective letter names (see Section 2). The choice between that particular candidate and its single-domain competitor, whose phonemic content is determined by grapheme-phoneme correspondence, appears to be largely governed by phonological markedness. For instance, in German the organisation as a single phonological word is quite regularly preferred to an alternative letter compound if the string can be parsed into two well-formed syllables, at least one of which has an onset (cf. 7a, b). An exception is seen in (7d), where the relevant single domain candidate ('u.kə)_ω <UKE> ends in the grapheme <E>, which licenses the phoneme schwa. The presence of that schwa together with the absence of a word-initial onset render the candidate ('u.kə)_ω unacceptable. The alternative pronunciation of the acronym as a letter compound results, indicating the active constraints *SCHWA (No schwa) and ONSET (A syllable needs an onset) in the phonology of German.

The few glimpses caught here indicate an extraordinarily complex overall picture, where the selection of material from source forms, the mapping into prosodic domains, and the organisation of phonemes within single domains are strongly influenced by phonological markedness constraints. The dependence of the selection and the domain formation on the phonological shape of the respective output forms argues against modelling shortenings in some sort of flow chart, starting with the selection of material from full forms and ending with its prosodic organisation. Instead the respective dependencies call for a highly complex grammar where inputs consist of full source forms and candidates are evaluated in parallel, mapping every word, including compounds and phrases, to their optimal shortenings.

It is beyond the scope of this article to tackle the concrete modelling of such a shortening grammar; instead its focus is on the prosodic organisation of segmental material forming a single phonological word. This specific choice is motivated by the relative ease with which the relevant generalisations can be delimited along with the particular degree of regularity observed in the patterns in ques-

---

[12] The word *IUP* (part of Heidelberg University) is homophonous to *Jupp* (a regional variant of the name *Josef*).

tion. For instance, the selection of a consonant as a hiatus buffer as in (7a, b) is common but by no means entirely systematic.[13] Strict regularity concerns its organisation: an intervocalic single consonant regularly forms an onset, whether that consonant corresponds to a regular initial in a content word as in (ˈlufɑ)$_\omega$ LUFA (see 1a) or to a segment in a function word as in (ˈdi.fə)$_\omega$ DIFE (see 7a) (cf. also the regularity shown in 3).

Returning to the analysis in tableau (6), one might consider implementing the idea to model specifically prosodic organisation by simply omitting reference to the full source form from the input, thereby targeting the mapping of the grapheme string <BAFU> to the prosodified optimal output (ˈbɑfu)$_\omega$. In this particular case, this would indeed be unproblematic. However, under certain conditions we find that phonological properties pertaining to spoken source forms do affect the prosodic organisation of the shortening (see below). At least those aspects of the phonology of source forms need to be included in input forms then, an observation to be accommodated in full-fledged formal modelling.

The article is organised as follows. Section 2 discusses two competing ideas regarding the phonology of novel words. Section 3 illustrates various generalisations pertaining to the prosodic organisation of single-domain shortenings and discusses more general insights to be drawn from those cases for the phonology of German. Section 4 briefly reviews various shortening types in German and their respective potential to shed light on unmarked phonological structure. Section 5 examines further criteria for sorting the shortening data, emphasising the need to identify all internal phonological word boundaries and likely prosodic correspondence effects. This is to ensure that the cases in question are treated separately and do not "clog up" the window on unmarked structure. Section 6 concludes.

2 Competing proposals

It has been proposed that the prosodic organisation of novel words follows that of comparable familiar words deemed to be sufficiently similar where analogical influences might be enhanced by the token and/or type frequencies of those known words (Schindler 1994). Based on that view it would be entirely

---

13 Consider the selection of the hiatus buffer in (i), but not in (ii), which may serve to increase the distance between the identical consonant graphemes but could also be more or less random.

(i) <u>D</u>eutsches <u>I</u>nstitut <u>f</u>ür <u>a</u>ngewandte <u>D</u>atenverarbeitung DIFAD (ˈdi.fat)$_\omega$
(ii) <u>B</u>remer <u>I</u>nstitut <u>f</u>ür <u>a</u>ngewandte <u>S</u>trahlentechnik BIAS (ˈbi.as)$_\omega$

possible for the shortening NABU (see 1b) to exhibit final stress in analogy with an existing word such as *Tabu*, especially if that word were particularly frequent or part of a larger group of words ending in stressed /u/. Such an idea could in principle be integrated into the model in (6), by associating inputs with "clouds" of comparable words familiar to the speaker, where this enriched input then serves as a base for faithfulness constraints. However, the ratio in (3) argues against such enriched input structures. Indeed there is scant evidence for analogy to existing words in the prosodic organisation of shortenings in German.

Interestingly, Schindler's claims concerning the prosodic organisation of novel words are based not on shortening data but rather partly on stress variation in loan words (with no regard for the directionality of possible shifts) and partly on a survey where students were asked to pronounce written nonce words spelled with all caps such as <USPIK>. The lack of variation in the pronunciation of genuine acronym data calls into question the value of that particular elicitation technique, where responses might be guided by a concern for producing "correct" answers, and analogy with the known may indeed be a significant factor.[14] The sort of uniformity observed in the shortening data vis-à-vis experimental data is then significant in itself, presumably indicating a lessened role of orthoepic concerns or of deliberate reflection on how to pronounce shortenings.[15] Hence the particular value of shortening data for studies of phonological grammar.

While shortenings do not lend themselves to analyses based on similarity to individual existing words, they also fail to support the opposing view of preferences cultivated specifically in that type of word-formation (Ronneberger-Sibold 1992). Examples for alleged differences among preferences pertaining to shortenings (based on her corpus of ca. 150 items to be described further below) vis-à-vis the ordinary vocabulary in German stated by Ronneberger-Sibold (1992: 123) are cited in (8):

---

14 In connection with a study of the preferred position for main stress in three-syllable nonce words, Janßen (2004: 65) reports that some subjects chose either consistently initial or consistently final main stress for each of the test items, regardless of syllable structure. This indicates certain more or less arbitrary speculations about phonological rules, which appear to not affect the pronunciations of shortenings. See also footnote 21.

15 Let me share an anecdote here. When noting the initials MEK on a museum in Berlin (*Museum Europäischer Kulturen* 'Museum of European cultures'), I asked the staff how they pronounce this word. One woman responded, "*Wir nennen das einfach* /mɛk/" ('We just call it /mɛk/'), which set off an amused chuckle among her fellow workers. The source of the humor may have been that they had never before consciously reflected on the question of how to pronounce this acronym (?/mek/, ?/mɛk/), yet they were in perfect agreement about the outcome.

(8) Preferences in shortenings   Preferences in the "normal" vocabulary
a.   open syllables   closed syllables
b.   closed syllables in word-initial   closed syllables in word-final position
     position
c.   initial stress   penult stress in words with three syllables
d.   (almost) no schwa   Schwa ("most frequent vowel")
e.   vowels: o - i - a   vowels (in stressed syllables): e - i - a
f.   equal preference for short and   short vowels
     long vowels

The juxtaposition in (8) does not express the remarkable difference concerning the uniformity of shortenings vis-à-vis the more varied patterns found in ordinary words observed in (3). What is the reason for this? An inspection of the corpus compiled by Ronneberger-Sibold shows indeed many apparent counterexamples to the claim that C_0VC_0V-shortenings are regularly organised as trochees, including her examples in (9):

(9) /beˈhɑ/ BH < Büsten#halter 'bra' /ɑˈde/ a.D. < außer Dienst 'retired', /tˢeˈte/ c.t. < cum tempore 'academic quarter', /ɑˈge/ AG < Arbeits#gemeinschaft 'working group'

It turns out that almost all of Ronneberger-Sibold's examples of word-final main stress are letter compounds in which each of the graphemes included in the written form of the shortening is associated with a stem form representing the conventional German letter name (<A> = /ɑ/, <B> = /be/, <C> = /tˢe/, etc.). Significantly, there is clear evidence that these stems form separate phonological words (cf. the alignment constraint in 5a). The classification of the relevant compounds as copulative follows from the equal morphological and semantic status of the respective constituent members.[16]

(10)   <BH> ⇨ [[be]$_{STM}$[hɑ]$_{STM}$]$_{CC}$ ⇨ ((be)$_ω$(hɑ)$_{ωHd}$)$_{CC}$

The prosodic organisation of letter words as copulative compounds shown in (10) is manifest in systematic correlations between syllable structure and stress. First, final consonants in letter names form codas even when a vowel follows

---

[16] This condition also captures final main stress in compounds consisting of phonologically similar meaningless syllables such as ((pi)$_ω$(pɑ)$_ω$(po)$_{ωHd}$)$_{COP\text{-}COMP}$ *Pipapo*, English ((tɪk)$_ω$(tæk)$_ω$(təʊ)$_{ωHd}$)$_{COP\text{-}COMP}$ *tic-tac-toe*. The relevant stress rules for copulative compounds in German and English appear to be the same.

(e.g. /ɛs.ɛm.fau/, see (11)), which clearly indicates intervening phonological word boundaries (i.e. ((ɛs)_ω(ɛm)_ω(fau)_ωHd)_CC). Second, the consistent placement of main stress on the final letter name is in accordance with the regular head finality characteristic of copulative compounds. This is illustrated in (11b), where the rightmost member of a copulative compound always forms its prosodic head and attracts main stress, regardless of how many members there are in total.

(11) a. B̲üsten#h̲alter 'bra'   b. ((be)_ω(**ha**)_ωHd)_CC *BH*
          S̲chüler#m̲it#v̲erwaltung   ((ɛs)_ω(ɛm)_ω(**fau**)_ωHd)_CC *SMV*
          'student representation'
          Ö̲ffentlicher P̲ersonen#n̲ah#v̲erkehr   ((ø)_ω(pe)_ω(ɛn)_ω(**fau**)_ωHd)_CC
          'public transportation'   *ÖPNV*

Ronneberger-Sibold's non-consideration of internal prosodic domain boundaries is then a serious shortcoming, which leads to results of little or no significance (e.g. the ratio of final stress basically indicates the ratio of letter compounds in the relevant corpus) and moreover obscures relevant generalisations (e.g. the absolute regularity of initial stress in C_0VC_0V-shortenings seen in 3).

There is a second reason for why the sort of remarkable regularity seen in (3) does not manifest in Ronneberger-Sibold's juxtaposition of phonological properties in (8). This is the lack of discrimination between aspects of structure determined by the *prosodic organisation* of given phonemic material versus those concerning the *selection* of segmental material from full forms. Consider the distribution of open versus closed syllables in the *Initialkurzwörter* illustrated in (12):

(12) a. ('daː.pi)_ω   DAPI   D̲eutsches A̲rznei#p̲rüfungs#i̲nstitut
          ('aː.ɢʁa)_ω   Agra   A̲rbeits#g̲emeinschaft der R̲edakteur#a̲usschüsse
      b. ('al.fu)_ω   Alfu   A̲rbeits#l̲osen#f̲ürsorge#u̲ntersuchung
          ('at.go)_ω   Adgo   A̲llgemeine D̲eutsche G̲ebühren#o̲rdnung

The syllable boundaries indicated in (12) are supported by the evidence from phonetic vowel lengthening: the long pronunciation of stressed /a/ in (12a) indicates open head syllables while vowel shortness despite the initial main stress in (12b) indicates closed syllables. Syllable structure is then plausibly determined by sonority (see Section 3), such that single intervocalic consonants or clusters exhibiting a sharp increase in sonority form onsets (see 12a), while other clusters are heterosyllabic (see 12b). While these generalisations concerning the prosodic organisation of given phonemic material are without exception, the respective distribution among open versus closed syllables depends on the material in the respective full forms. Here faithfulness (including grapheme-phoneme correspondence constraints) comes into play, where resulting structures ultimately reflect the distribution of graphemes in stem-initial positions in full forms (cf. the underlined graphemes in 12). That distribution is hardly of interest to linguists and neither is the resulting ratio of closed versus open syllables in shortenings.

It is of course conceivable that the selection of segmental material from source forms is affected by phonological markedness constraints, and as noted earlier, there is indeed clear evidence for that kind of impact. The extent of this impact is arguably best captured in an OT grammar, where markedness constraints interact with faithfulness aiming to preserve the segmental structure of full forms. An investigation of the SDS-corpus mentioned above has yielded no conclusive evidence for a specific avoidance of consonants whose presence would result in closed syllables (cf. Raffelsiefen in progress).[17] Even when markedness can be shown to influence the selection of segmental material, the effects are not as regular as those associated with the prosodic organisation of that material. For instance, it is true that there is a tendency to avoid schwa in shortenings (cf. Ronneberger-Sibold's claim in 8), in that the grapheme <E> in full forms is often not selected when its correspondent phoneme in the shortening were to be located at the end of the phonological word and therefore, by regular grapheme-phoneme correspondence, associated with /ə/ rather than the full vowel /e/ (cf. *JuZ* < *Jugend#zentrum* 'youth center' versus *JuPo* < *Jugend#posaunenchor* 'youth trombone choir').[18] Significantly, the phonological

---

[17] Specifically, it is shown that the distribution of open versus closed syllables in German shortenings can be captured in terms of interacting faithfulness and markedness constraints, where shortening itself is driven by the markedness constraint *STRUC (No Structure), which bans structure altogether (see Prince and Smolensky (1993: 25), who credit Cheryl Zoll for proposing that constraint). The prevalence of open syllables in German shortenings is then due to the absence of markedness constraints favouring coda segments (as opposed to those favouring segments in the nucleus). There simply is no evidence for an active role of the constraint NOCODA mitigating against closed syllables in the phonological grammar of German shortenings.

This result challenges Ronneberger-Sibold's idea that special phonological preferences linked specifically to shortenings can be established by way of counting occurrences of various segments or syllables (open versus closed) and then comparing the relevant counts in shortenings versus ordinary words. The validity of that approach, along with her criteria for categorising shortening data, has largely eluded scrutiny. Nübling (2001: 185) praises the *sound statistical results* ("fundierte statistische Ergebnisse") in Ronneberger-Sibold (1992), whose methodology has been adopted in various studies (Leuschner 2008, Lux 2016). (See also footnotes 37, 42 below.)

[18] The association of the grapheme <E> with schwa in word-final position or before word-final {R,l,n} blocks its regular correspondence with full vowels. The tendency to pass over the grapheme <E> when selecting material for shortenings pertains only to these narrow contexts, evidently motivated by the avoidance of the highly marked vowel /ə/ itself (see footnotes 19, 45). Data from the SDS corpus hence do not corroborate Ronneberger-Sibold's claim that /e/ and /ɛ/ are generally avoided in unstressed syllables (2007: 286). For instance, among the trochaic shortenings ending in

preference in question can be overridden by other constraints, including the need to represent the initial of salient words (cf. the inclusion of <E> in ('difə)_ω <DIFE> in 7a). The current count of schwa-final words among the C_0VC_0V-shortenings in the SDS-corpus is 22, after all amounting to 3.4% of those cases. It is true that the ratio of schwa-final trochees in the ordinary vocabulary is far higher, but this does not prove distinct preferences for schwa in the relevant data sets but may reflect on distinct (historical) origins of that vowel.[19] Indeed, one may doubt all of the opposing preferences in (8) claimed by Ronneberger-Sibold: the observed asymmetries may well be consistent with a single phonological grammar for German (i.e. a single ranking of constraints), where shortenings exhibit less marked structure due to the absence of prosodic faithfulness effects along with access to alternative organisations such as letter compounds (cf. 7d).

3 Unmarked prosodic organisation of single-domain shortenings

The empirical validity of the model outlined in the preceding section hinges both on the determination of prosodic organisation by segmental structure only (mediated by grapheme-phoneme correspondence) and on the analysability of the relevant patterns in terms of independently motivated markedness constraints. Some examples for restrictions on prosodic organisation observed in the SDS-corpus are listed in (13). The names are added merely for ease of reference:

(13) a. 2σ-RULE: Disyllabic phonological words not ending in one of the sonorants {R,l,n} have initial stress, regardless of whether their syllables are open or closed.
   b. 3σC-RULE: Trisyllabic phonological words with an open penult ending in a consonant other than {R,l,n} have initial main stress and secondary stress on the final syllable.

---

a closed syllable, there are 32 cases with unstressed /ɛ/ (e.g. ('vivɛp)_ω WIWeB (< _We_hrwissenschaftliches _I_nstitut für _We_rk- und _Be_triebsstoffe)), compared to 16 cases with unstressed /ɔ/ (e.g. ('buvɔk)_ω BUWOG (< _Bu_ndes_wo_hnungs_ge_sellschaft)). This ratio also casts doubt on Ronneberger-Sibold's claim concerning the distribution of full vowels in shortenings cited in (8).

[19] An active role in the history of German of the markedness constraint *SCHWA (No schwa), which has caused the loss of all schwas not needed to satisfy higher-ranking constraints, is motivated in Raffelsiefen (1995, 2000). There is then no "preference" for schwa in the regular vocabulary.

c. 3σV-RULE: Trisyllabic phonological words with an open penult and ending in a vowel have penult main stress by default (see below).

d. σ$^{op/clos}$-RULE: The nuclei of open syllables are restricted to peripheral vowels; the nuclei of closed syllables are restricted to centralised vowels.

The feature [±peripheral] (Lindau 1978), motivated by the more peripheral tongue position associated with the vowels in the upper row compared to the respective vowels listed underneath, is meant to represent a proportional vowel quality opposition shown in (14):

(14)	high			mid			low	
[+peripheral]	/i/	/y/	/u/	/e/	/ø/	/o/	/ɑ/	(/æ/)[20]
[-peripheral]	/ɪ/	/ʏ/	/ʊ/	/ɛ/	/œ/	/ɔ/	/a/	-

The generalisations in (13) are illustrated by the prosodic representations in (15). (Apparent exceptions will be discussed below.)

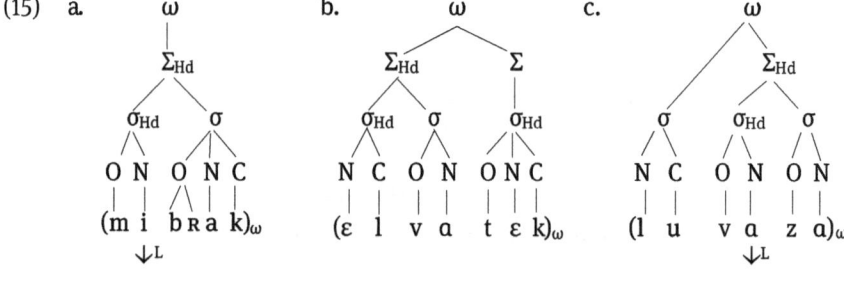

('mi.bʀak)$_ω$	MIBRAG	Mitteldeutsche Braunkohlengesellschaft mbH
('ɛl.va‚tɛk)$_ω$	Elwatec	Elektrolyse- und Wassertechnik GmbH
(lu'va.za)$_ω$	Luwasa	Luft Wasser Sand

---

[20] The vowel /æ/ is parenthesised because contrasts like /tˢæ/ <zäh> 'tough' vs. /tˢe/ <Zeh> 'toe' exist for only roughly half of German speakers, mostly located in western areas and in Switzerland. The fact that /æ/ is the only vowel lacking an opposition member in (14) is presumably due to its markedness, as it is both low and front. (The phonological lowness of the vowel in words like /tˢæ/ <zäh> 'tough' is often overlooked, perhaps due to an unfortunate convention to transcribe that vowel with the symbol /ɛː/. See Raffelsiefen (2018) for discussion of the historical origin of that convention as well as its empirical inadequacy).

The trochaic organisation of the disyllabic tree in (15a) illustrates the dominance of the constraints Foot-BINARITY (specifically the branching of the foot into two syllables) and PARSE-SYLLABLE (see 5d, e). The fact that not both of these constraints can be fully satisfied in trisyllabic words yields special insight into constraints on foot formation and syllable weight in German. Specifically, the relevance of the closedness of the final syllable for the regular occurrence of initial main stress in trisyllabic words indicates that that syllable forms a separate foot (cf. 15b).[21] The preceding two syllables are then organised into a trochee functioning as the head foot, resulting in main prominence on the initial syllable. This pattern is in accordance with independent evidence for the assumption that only closed syllables are heavy in German, which also fits with the depiction of vowel length as a purely phonetic property (Vennemann 1991a, 1991b).[22] The observation that such a monosyllabic final foot, unlike disyllabic feet, does not attract main stress within the phonological word indicates an overall preference ranking among feet as follows (Σ/σ^L = a foot dominating a single light [i.e. open] syllable, Σ/σ^H = a foot dominating a single heavy [i.e. closed] syllable, $\Sigma/\sigma\sigma$ = a foot dominating two syllables).

(16)   worse feet $\Sigma/\sigma^L \gg \Sigma/\sigma^H \gg \Sigma/\sigma\sigma$ better feet

The generalisation is then that a final closed syllable regularly licenses a separate foot but is not "good enough" to form a head foot. This is what leads to initial main stress in shortenings like *Elwatec*. In vowel-final trisyllabic words such as

---

[21] These patterns are obscured not only by the stress variety found in ordinary words (e.g. (kleˈmɑtɪs)_ω <Klematis> 'clematis', (kɑzɑˈtʃɔk)_ω <Kasatschok> 'Kozachok') but also by the variation found in experimental studies with nonce words. Janßen (2004: 70) finds a mere preference for initial main stress in the relevant trisyllabic nonce words (i.e. *Binsakaf* and *Fekomot*), not the near-categorical pattern observed in shortenings:

nonce word	ˈσ σ σ		σ ˈσ σ		σ σ ˈσ	
Bin.sa.kaf	107	51,2%	48	23%	54	25,8%
Fe.ko.mot	99	42,3%	46	19,7%	89	38%

[22] Vennemann's argument against the analysis of vowel length in German as a phonological property concerns the instability of penult stress on phonetically long vowels (e.g. Alˈt[oː]na ~ ˈAlt[o]na) versus the stability of penult stress on short vowels (e.g. Maˈd[ɔ]na (*ˈMadonna)) (Vennemann 1991a, 1991b, 1998). This indeed robust pattern shows that vowel length is not a phonological property that attracts stress but rather a subphonemic process affecting vowels in stressed open syllables. The stability of penult stress in words like *Madonna* corresponds to that seen in closed penult syllables in words such as *Veranda*, suggesting that the stress stability in *Madonna* is due to (ambisyllabic) syllable closure as well (i.e. the /n/ closing the syllable; cf. the discussion of the contrast in German *Koma* versus *Komma* in [18] below). Evidence that closed syllables count as heavy while open syllables count as light has also been noted for Dutch (Visch and Kager 1984).

Luwasa, this parsing is not available as the final syllable is open and light; the (default) rule here is to group the last two syllables into a trochee and leave the initial syllable unparsed as in (15c).

Consider next the generalisation concerning the distribution of peripheral versus centralised vowels in (13d), which corresponds directly to the independently motivated markedness constraints in (17).[23]

(17) a. *σ^{open}/N$^{[-per]}$: No centralised vowel in the nucleus of an open syllable.
   b. *σ^{closed}/N$^{[+per]}$: No peripheral vowel in the nucleus of a closed syllable.

Both constraints are consistently obeyed in shortenings, including the cases illustrated in (15). They are arguably obeyed in the ordinary vocabulary as well, assuming that for instance contrasts such as ('komɑ)$_ω$ <Koma> 'coma' versus ('kɔmɑ)$_ω$ <Komma> 'comma' are represented as follows:

(18)

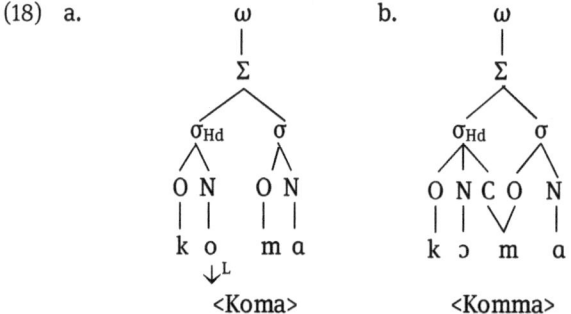

The vowel contrast as in (18a, b) can be modelled by assuming a high-ranking faithfulness constraint FAITH([±peripheral]), which preserves the value for this feature encountered in the relevant input forms. Assuming the inviolability of the markedness constraints in (17), the association of the intervocalic single consonant with the coda and the concomitant violation of the markedness constraint (*AMBISYLLABICITY ["No ambisyllabicity"]) is the "price" paid in the phonological grammar

---

[23] The markedness constraints in (17) appear to manifest in neutralisation patterns concerning certain vowel quality differences in open versus closed syllables in various languages, including French. While the quality differences in question are referred to by various labels (e.g. [±tense], [±ATR]), even height in French (low-mid : high-mid), there is a consistent affinity between more centralised vowels and closed syllables (e.g. /ɛ/, not */e/, in closed syllables in French /tɛt/ <tête> 'head') versus more peripheral vowel in open syllables (e.g. /o/, /ø/, not */ɔ/,*/œ/, in open syllables in French /bo/ <beau> 'beautiful' or /fø/ <feu> 'fire'). The relevant distribution makes no reference to vowel length, only to vowel quality.

of German for the increase of the contrastive potential manifest in minimal pairs such *Koma* versus *Komma*.[24] The absence of this type of contrast in shortenings, where the unmarked organisation as in (18a) prevails, can again be explained with reference to the relevant input forms. Assuming that not the phonemes in the full forms but rather the graphemes representing the shortenings are accessed, the unmarked organisation emerges as a TETU-effect. This is because every German vowel grapheme corresponds to both a peripheral vowel phoneme and its centralised opposition member, the choice among which is determined by the respective position of the corresponding phoneme in an open versus closed syllable along with markedness (i.e. the constraints in 17). Some graphemes, including <E>, correspond to additional phonemes whose distribution is also governed by context.[25]

(19)   <A> : {/ɑ/[+per], /a/[-per]}
       <E> : {/e/[+per], /ɛ/[-per], /ə/}

The availability of these choices, and the particular ways in which they are resolved, depending on context, contributes to making single domain shortenings such a rich source of insight into phonological grammar.[26] The observed patterns support the high ranking of the constraints in (17) in German, thereby also indicating the relevance of syllable structure (open versus closed) and associated markedness constraints.[27] Here sonority plays a key role, as has been noted already with regard to the syllabification of intervocalic consonant clusters in (12). The idea, originating with Whitney (1861),[28] is that there is correlation between inherent articulatory

---

[24] The relevant fragment of the phonological grammar of German, which forces a single intervocalic consonant to close the syllable when a centralised vowel precedes, is expressed in the ranking below (cf. Raffelsiefen 2016). The subscript "$_{PROM}$" links the effect to vowels in prominent (e.g. stressed) position, a case of so-called "Positional Faithfulness" (Beckman 1998).

   *σ^{open}/N[-per] >> FAITH([±peripheral])$_{PROM}$ >> *AMBISYLLABICITY

[25] Correspondences involving grapheme clusters such as <EI> or <IE> take precedence over simple graphemes via the *Elsewhere Principle* (cf. Section 5).
[26] By the same token the absence of choices pertaining to the association between graphemes and corresponding letter names (e.g. <A> = /ɑ/, <E> = /e/, <Y> = /ʏpsilɔn/, etc.) renders letter compounds as in (11b) much less interesting to phonologists. Still, these cases shed light on phonological constraints affecting copulative compounding (see Raffelsiefen in progress).
[27] Reference to vowel length in Ronneberger-Sibold's study (cf. [8f]) is of questionable value, as it essentially compares the distribution of stressed open syllables to that of all remaining syllables.
[28] Although his original ranking shown in (i) (Whitney 1861, 1874) has gained wide recognition, Whitney is rarely credited with the idea. (The ranking "*M/R >> *M/l" in [20] matches a

properties of speech sounds (their sonority) and their associability with syllable positions. Specifically, Whitney claims that speech sounds are ordered based on their openness, where those exhibiting maximal openness, i.e. low vowels, are the best occupants of the syllable nucleus whereas those exhibiting maximal closedness, plosives, are the best occupants of the margin. All other sounds occupy ranked intermediate positions. This idea can be expressed in terms of so-called anti-association constraints, which prohibit the association of phonemes with syllable positions (*M/R ["No /R/ in the margin"] [Prince and Smolensky 1993]). Parts of the specific ranking supported by German data is stated in (20).

(20) *M/ɑ >> ... >> *M/i >> *M/R >> *M/l >> *M/n >> *M/m >> ... >> *M/*plosives*

The extreme status attributed to /R/ as the worst consonant to occupy the margin is supported by the fact that plosive + /R/ is the only cluster consistently syllabified in the onset (cf. ('mi.bRak)$_\omega$ in 15a), due to the maximal sonority distance between the respective phonemes (cf. Vennemann's Head Law [1988: 13]).[29] The status of /n/ as the most sonorous nasal is supported by its common association with liquids in German word prosody (cf. reference to the set {R,l,n} in 13). Consider the distribution of peripheral versus centralised vowels in C_0VC-shortenings ending in a sonorant illustrated in (21). Here systematic differences prevail as final /m/ consistently patterns with obstruents in that only centralised vowels precede (cf. 21a), whereas final /R/ is preceded only by peripheral vowels (cf. 21d). The sonorants /l/ and /n/ take an intermediate position in that both types of vowels precede (21b, c).

(21) a. (bɪm)$_\omega$ / *(bim)$_\omega$ BIM   <u>B</u>onner <u>I</u>nstitut für <u>M</u>igrationsforschung und Interkulturelles Lernen
     b. (vɪn)$_\omega$ WIN   <u>W</u>irtschafts-<u>I</u>dentifikations#<u>n</u>ummer
        (din)$_\omega$ DIN   <u>D</u>eutsches <u>I</u>nstitut für <u>N</u>ormung

---

differentiation among liquids proposed in subsequent work, to the effect that rhotics are more sonorous than laterals [Sievers 1876: 112]).

(i)   preferred nuclei   preferred margins
      <--->
      low vowels   mid vowels   high vowels   liquids   nasals   fricatives   plosives

[29] Note also the initial main stress and the peripheral /i/ in the pronunciation ('agi͵sRɑ)$_\omega$ <Agisra> (< <u>A</u>rbeitsgemeinschaft gegen <u>i</u>nternationale <u>s</u>exuelle und <u>r</u>assistische <u>A</u>usbeutung), which indicates the organisation of the cluster /sR/ as a complex onset, which in that position also licenses a separate (weak) foot (cf. ('vilɑ͵pRy)$_\omega$ <WiLaPrü> (< <u>Wi</u>ssenschaftliches <u>La</u>ndes<u>prü</u>fungsamt)). Possibly the presence of the high vowel, for which [+peripheral] is the unmarked value, is a factor in this syllabification of /sR/ (cf. ('i.sRɑ͵ɛl)$_\omega$ <Israel>).

c. (iyl)_ω   JüL   Jahrgangs#übergreifendes Lernen
    (dɪl)_ω   DIL   Deutsches Institut für Lebensmitteltechnik
d. (mir)_ω / *(mɪr)_ω   MiR   Musiktheater im Revier

Assuming the inviolability of the markedness constraints in (17), the distribution among peripheral and centralised vowels shown in (21) entails that final /m/, like final obstruents, always closes the syllable (22a), whereas the most sonorous consonant, /R/, resists association with the coda and forms an onset instead (22d).[30] Final /n/ (and /l/) can associate with either margin position (22b, c), allowing for both types of vowels to precede.[31] The association of this effect with the word-final position only is due to a restriction on empty nuclei to the effect that they are banned from occurring word-internally (cf. Harris and Gussman 2002).

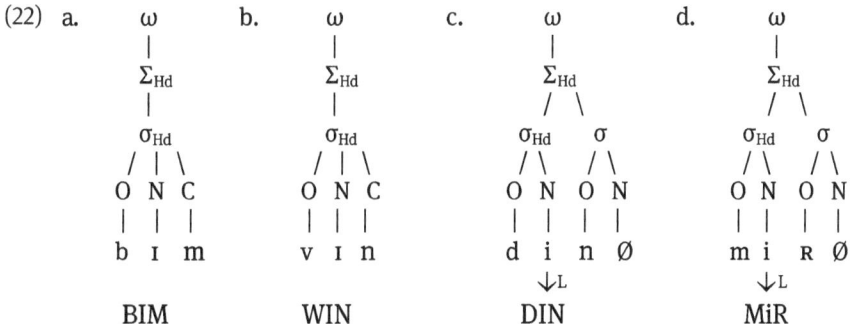

The shortening data then provide significant support for the ranking among the sonorants in (20), which is obscured in ordinary words, where peripheral and centralised vowels contrast before both /R/ and /m/ (e.g. (heR)_ω <Heer> 'army' versus (hɛR)_ω <Herr> 'mister', (lɑm)_ω <lahm> 'lame' versus (lam)_ω <Lamm> 'lamb').[32] The inviolability of the constraints in (17) and the consequent representation of final

---

30 The phonetic implementation of the phoneme /R/ in this particular onset position is conducive to articulatory weakening, manifest in vocalisation in German (see Schiller and Mooshammer 1995). Vocalisation also affects /R/ in the coda, though to a lesser degree.
31 The conditions on syllabification shown in (22a) can be expressed in OT in terms of local constraint conjunctions (Smolensky 1997), such that the ranked anti-association constraints are conjoined with the constraint NoCoda.
32 The potential for this contrast in the ordinary vocabulary can again be linked to the accessibility of the relevant feature values in the input. That potential indicates that Faith([±peripheral]) dominates the markedness constraint *N/∅ (No empty nuclei) as well, such that /R/ is forced to close the syllable in cases like (hɛR)_ω <Herr>, where a centralised vowel precedes. Word-final /m/, on the other hand, is forced to form the onset of a syllable with an empty nucleus in cases

/R/ as an onset of a syllable with an empty nucleus as in (22d) is supported by stress. Specifically, such a representation accounts for the potential presence of main stress on vowels preceding one of the sonorants {R,l,n} in word-final position, thereby accounting for the difference in stress in the shortenings illustrated in (23):

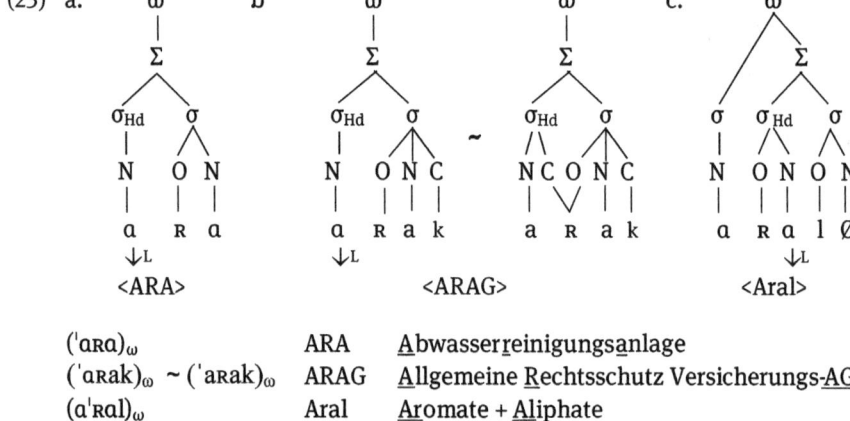

('aRa)_ω   ARA   Abwasserreinigungsanlage
('aRak)_ω ~ ('aRak)_ω ARAG   Allgemeine Rechtsschutz Versicherungs-AG
(a'Ral)_ω   Aral   Aromate + Aliphate

In all cases in (23) the last two syllables form a disyllabic foot whose leftmost syllable functions as the head. The words differ in the structure of the word-final syllable, in particular the presence of an empty nucleus licensed by the presence of stem-final /l/. The openness of the syllable preceding /l/ in (23c) is indicated by the lengthening of the vowel in the nucleus.[33]

---

like (lam)_ω <lahm>, as a stressed peripheral vowel precedes (cf. Raffelsiefen 2016). The relevant ranking is stated below (cf. footnote 24):

*σ^closed/N^[+per] >> Faith([±peripheral])_PROM >> *N/Ø

33 Interestingly this pattern of head foot formation is far more regular in shortenings with three (non-catalectic) syllables (e.g. (ʃtyRo'poR)_ω Styropor (< Polystyrol + porös), (alu'zil)_ω Alusil < Aluminium + Silicium) than in shortenings with two (non-catalectic) syllables (e.g. ('zial)_ω (< Silicium + Aluminium)). Here we find that word-final {R,l,n} exhibit regular onset behavior only when a high vowel precedes, manifest in the peripherality of that vowel (e.g. ('eˌkiR)_ω, not *('ekIR)_ω) EKiR (< Evangelische Kirche im Rheinland)). Even peripheral vowels in that particular context (i.e. a single syllable precedes, word-final {R,l,n} follows) often associate with secondary rather than primary stress (e.g. ('eˌkiR)_ω, not *(e'kiR)_ω).

The observation that the stressed vowel in ARAG may resist lengthening, as opposed to the stressed vowels in the other two words in (23), is of particular interest here as it sheds light on the phonological status of vowel quality, length, and syllable structure. The possible pronunciation of the stressed syllable with a short vowel is linked to the presence of a following unstressed closed syllable, where both syllables include vowels sharing the features for height, backness, and roundedness. This indicates an active vowel harmony constraint applying within feet, whereby a centralised vowel causes the vowel in the preceding stressed syllable to be centralised as well, especially when this harmony results in identical vowels.[34] (The stressed centralised vowel then conditions the association of the following consonant with the coda, to satisfy the constraint in (17a). Hence the ambisyllabicity and lack of phonetic lengthening.) Evidence for the activity of this harmony constraint in German strongly supports the assumption of a vowel quality opposition [±peripheral] as in (14). This is because harmony is known to refer to segmental quality features but never to length (i.e. moraic structure) or syllable structure.

Insights to be gained from the shortening data accordingly include generalisations pertaining not only to unmarked prosodic organisation but also to notorious controversies in German phonology including syllable weight, vowel length, and abstractness of representation. Evidence for sonority rankings comes not only from syllable structure and the respective distribution of peripheral and centralised vowels but also from foot formation, as can be illustrated by certain systematic exceptions to the "default" pattern of penult stress in vowel-final trisyllabic shortenings shown in (24a).

(24) a. ('haʀi̯bo)_ω Haribo < Hans Riegel, Bonn   b. *(ha'ʀibo)_ω
     ('**dimi**i̯do)_ω Dimido < Dienstag, Mittwoch, Donnerstag   *(di'mido)_ω
     ('**mali**i̯mo)_ω Malimo < Mauersberger aus Limbach-   *(ma'limo)_ω
                                 Oberfrohna, Molton
     ('ʀomi̯ka)_ω Romika < Rollmann, Michael & Kaufmann   *(ʀo'mika)_ω

---

[34] The harmony constraint can be observed in ordinary words as well, accounting for the occurrence of short centralised stressed vowels in cases like ('tabak)_ω *Tabak* 'tobacco', ('nʊbʊk)_ω *Nubuk* 'nubuck' versus (gopak)_ω *Gopak* 'Russian dance', or the city names ('bɔxɔlt)_ω *Bocholt* versus ('boxʊm)_ω *Bochum*. The constraint is not equally pervasive in all contexts and for all speakers, but many will likely agree that for instance the vowels in the stressed syllables in the names ('zaʀa)_ω *Sarah*, ('tilo)_ω *Tilo* are necessarily peripheral, subject to lengthening, whereas the corresponding vowels in the names *Harald*, *Philipp* can be centralised and short (i.e. ('haʀald)_ω ~ ('haʀald)_ω, ('filɪp)_ω ~ ('filɪp)_ω). (Cf. the variation noted in the shortening in [23a, b].)

The fact that the potential final trochees shown in (24b) typically exhibit a sonorant in foot-initial position along with the vowel /i/ in the nucleus of the head syllable indicates the relevance of sonority constraints (Kenstowicz 1997). Reference to /i/ in the head syllable supports the ranking of /i/ as the least sonorous vowel and therefore worst vocalic nucleus in a prominent syllable,[35] reference to sonorants in foot-initial position supports their ranking as the most sonorous consonants and therefore least preferred occupants of the syllable margin. In conjunction the relevant constraint violations lead to the elimination of the relevant foot parsings (see 24b).[36] A final trochee afflicted with only one of these problems (only a marked foot-initial onset as in 25a or only /i/ in the head syllable as in 25b), is accepted.[37]

(25) a. (zoˈlavi)_ω   SoLaWi   Solidarische Landwirtschaft
        (haˈnuta)_ω   Hanuta   Haselnusstafel
    b. (meˈdima)_ω   Medima   Medizin in Maschen
        (geˈziba)_ω   GESIBA   Gemeinnützige Siedlungs- und Bauaktiengesellschaft

The picture that emerges is that prosodic organisation of phonemic material is fundamentally determined by phonemic content and domain boundaries. Phonemic content determines not only syllable structure (open or closed) but also the organisation of syllables into feet and the concomitant relative prominence relations, which in turn determine the phonetic implementation, causing strengthening of the articulation in prominent positions (e.g. vowel lengthening in open head syllables). Shortenings provide an ideal window for studying markedness constraints, as their effects are minimally obscured by faithfulness constraints.

---

[35] That status is confirmed by the fact that /i/ is the only vowel that can form an onset in German (cf. the shortening (iʊp)_ω <IUP> in [7c]).
[36] Here again we see the value of shortenings as a window on unmarkedness, as the relevant stress regularities are obscured by a preference for word-final trochees in feminine proper names (e.g. Karína, Maríta, Elísa; cf. also María, Sofía versus (ˈbebʀi‿a)_ω BEBRIA (< Berliner Briefmarken-Ausstellung), (ˈvidi‿a)_ω Widia (< Wie Diamant)). The effect of constraint conjunction was also seen in connection with the data in (7a, b) versus (7d).
[37] These correlations between sonority and stress argue against Ronneberger-Sibold's claim that penult stress as in (25) is due to a special Romance stress rule in German (2015: 489). Her idea of multiple stress rules in German associated with specific subsets of the vocabulary has been criticised by Vennemann (1998: 236).

4 Shortening types and prosodic domains

This section gives a brief overview of the major shortening types in German, mainly to motivate the particular restrictions on the single-domain shortening corpus on which the generalisations illustrated in the preceding section (see 3, 8) were based.[38]

Before reviewing the main types of single domain shortenings below, I will briefly illustrate the two main types of multi-domain shortenings, both of which are compounds with internal morphological structure. The first type consists of copulative compounds, typically letter compounds as in (26a), which are characterised by the equal status of all members and main stress on the final member. The second type consists of determinative compounds (DC), where the final stem in the source form is fully retained and functions as the morphological head of the compound. The preceding part of the source form is shortened, represented for instance by a letter name as in (26b), which then forms a separate phonological word constituting the prosodic head of the compound.

(26)   source form   spelling and morphology   prosodic organisation
  a.   <u>D</u>eutsche <u>B</u>ahn   [[de][be]]_CC <DB>   ((de)_ω(be)_ωHd)_CC
  b.   <u>S</u>tadt<u>bahn</u>   [[ɛs][ban]]_DC <S-Bahn>   ((ɛs)_ωHd(ban)_ω)_DC

Apart from a few cases of so-called hidden compounds (see Section 5), both types in (26) are easily identified and all relevant diagnostics consistently support the respective separate prosodic domains for syllabification and foot formation.

The first three of the single domain shortenings in (27) have already been mentioned. They are characterised by correspondences to graphemes located at the left edge of multiple morphemes in the source form. Additional material can be included, as in (27b, c), but only when forming a contiguous string, typically up to and including the first syllabic vowel.

(27)   shortening type   source form   spelling and   prosodic
                                                  morphology   organisation
  a.   Initialkurzwort   <u>U</u>mwelt#<u>b</u>undes#<u>a</u>mt   [UBA]_N-NEUT   (ˈuba)_ω
  b.   Silbenkurzwort   <u>Ki</u>nder#<u>ta</u>ges#stätte   [Kita]_N-FEM   (ˈkita)_ω
  c.   Mischkurzwort   <u>Ju</u>gend#<u>k</u>ultur#<u>z</u>entrum   [Jukuz]_N-NEUT   (ˈjʊkʊtˢ)_ω
  d.   Clipping   <u>Info</u>rmation   [Info]_N-FEM   (ˈɪnfo)_ω

---

[38] The classification is adapted from Bergstrøm-Nielsen (1952) and Kobler-Trill (1994).

Necessary reference to a morpheme-initial segment and contiguity of all additional material standing in correspondence is also characteristic for clippings illustrated in (27d). Clippings differ from other shortenings in that they correspond to a single contiguous string, which may allow for source forms to be recovered more easily by hearers. Clippings also differ in that they appear to require less reference to written forms.

There is a question then of whether to merge all of the different types of single domain shortenings shown in (27) into a single corpus or whether to treat them separately. This is ultimately an empirical question, answered by an examination of the relevant patterns. The approach is to establish a baseline by examining a clearly defined subset upon which to base the comparison with additional types of data. Assuming then the patterns observed in the first three types of shortenings in (27) as a basis for comparison, it may first appear that clippings conform to the relevant generalisations. The prosodic shape of the clippings in (28) entirely matches that of the shortenings studied so far: disyllabic strings are organised as trochees, regardless of the stress patterns and prosodic boundaries given in source forms. Intervocalic single consonants yield two open syllables, and vowels in open head syllables are phonetically lengthened. (The relevant portion of source forms is represented phonologically.)

(28) ('geʃi)_ω   Geschi   (gə)_σ('ʃıçts)_ω...   Ge#schichts#unterricht
      ('tˢula)_ω   Zula   ('tˢu)_ω('lasʊŋs)_ω...   Zu#lassungs#arbeit
      ('tˢivi)_ω   Zivi   (tˢi'vil)_ω...   Zivil#dienst#leistender
      ('ʃpetˢi)_ω   Spezi   (ʃpe'tˢial)_ω...   Spezial#freund

As for the last generalisation mentioned above, a systematic difference is, however, seen in many other clippings, which favour centralised vowels in head syllables, even when only one consonant follows (see 29b), where parentheses in the source forms indicate phonological word boundaries). They therefore contrast with *Silben-*, *Misch-*, and *Initialkurzwörter* as in (29a), which exhibit peripheral vowels:[39]

---

[39] Clippings containing only mid vowels constitute a systematic exception as they favour peripheral vowels instead (cf. [i]). This pattern is reminiscent of evidence for ATR-harmony restricted to specific vowel heights (Archangeli and Pulleyblank 1989). If indeed systematic and indicative of a constraint requiring harmony, this would further support the assumption of a vowel quality opposition (see the discussion of *ARAG* in [23b]).

(i)   /'ʃoko/   Schoko   (Schokoláde)   /'deko/   Deko   (Dekoratión)
      /'kʀoko/   Kroko   (Krokodíl)   /'velo/   Velo   (Velozipéd)
      /'øko/   Öko   (Ökologíe)   /'memo/   Memo   (Memorándum)

(29) a.

(ˈtˢeli)_ω	ZeLi	Zehlendorfer Lichtspiele	b.	(ˈʀɛli)_ω	Reli	(Religións)unterricht
(ˈʃtabi)_ω	Stabi	Staats#bibliothek		(ˈabi)_ω	Abi	(Abitúr)
(ˈʃtino)_ω	Stino	stink#normaler Mann		(ˈlɪmo)_ω	Limo	(Limonáde)
(ˈbema)_ω	Bema	Bewertungs#maßstab		(ˈkʀɪmi)_ω	Krimi	(Kriminál)roman
(ˈbuna)_ω	Buna	Butadien mit Natrium		(ˈʊni)_ω	Uni	(Universität)
(ˈzovi)_ω	SoWi	Sozial#wissenschaften		(ˈnavi)_ω	Navi	(Navigatións)gerät
(ˈmoma)_ω	Moma	Morgen-Magazin		(ˈpʀɔmi)_ω	Promi	(prominénte) Person

The assumption that the peripheral vowels in (29a) represent unmarkedness whereas the centralised vowels in (29b) indicate correspondence (i.e. faithfulness to input structure) is supported by the contingency of the latter on a narrow prosodic context. The strings affected by correspondence in the relevant source forms, underlined in (29b), consist of two contiguous syllables, located at the left periphery of the source form where they precede the syllable carrying main stress. This context favours rhythmic accent on the initial syllable, where the association of prominence with phonetic vowel shortness is prone to be interpreted as indicative of a centralised vowel[40] (cf. Vennemann 1991a: 236, Becker 1998: 95). This (re)analysis leads to the occurrence of a centralised vowel in the clipped forms in (29b) via correspondence. The contrast between the unmarked organisation of a *Silbenkurzwort* such as (ˈtˢeli)_ω *ZeLi* in (29a) and the organisation resulting from correspondence in a clipping such as (ˈʀɛli)_ω *Reli* in (29b) can then be represented analogous to the contrast between (ˈkoma)_ω *Koma* and (ˈkɔma)_ω *Komma* shown in (18a, b).

The relevance of the presence of a contiguous disyllabic string for this sort of correspondence effect can be demonstrated with *Silbenkurzwörter* as in (30), which are characterised by noncontiguity of the relevant syllables in the source form. Here the peripherality value of the vowel in the source form, regardless of its prominence, is not regularly preserved in the shortening.

---

40 This is because peripheral vowels are phonetically lengthened under stress whereas centralised vowels remain short.

(30) a. (ˈkɪʀʃ)_ω ...   Kirsch-Banane-Saft   b. (ˈki.bɑ)_ω   Kiba
       (mɔlkəˈʀai)_ω ...   Molkerei#produkte   (ˈmo.pʀo)_ω   Mopro
       (ioˈhanɪs)_ω ...   Johannis#beeren,   (ˈiɔs.tɑ)_ω   Josta
                           Stachel#beeren
       (ˈybəʀ)_ω ...   Überlandwerke und   (ˈʏs.tʀɑ)_ω   Üstra
                           Straßenbahnen Hannover AG

The claim that vowel correspondence in clippings requires a matching disyllabic string is supported by the monosyllabic clippings, which are indistinguishable from *Initial-* or *Mischkurzwörter*. Before final obstruents or /m/ only centralised vowels precede as in (31a); before /l/ or /n/ both types of vowels are possible (cf. 31b).

(31)   Clippings   *Initial-* or *Mischkurzwörter*
a.   (ˈbɪp)_ω   Bib   (Bibliothék)   (ˈpɪp)_ω   PiB   Pflegekinder in Bremen
       (ˈtʊt)_ω   Tut   (Tutórium)   (ˈbɔp)_ω   BOB   Bayerische Oberlandbahn
b.   (ˈgel)_ω   Gel   (Gelatíne)   (ˈdin)_ω   DIN   Deutsches Institut für
                                                               Normung
       (ˈfɪl)_ω   Phil (Philosophíe)   (ˈtɪl)_ω   TiL   Talent im Land

Recall that the correspondence effect in question requires not only a contiguous disyllabic string in the source form but also the containment of that string in a single phonological word where the first syllable is more prominent than the second (cf. 29b versus 28). The effect presupposes then the correspondence of entire trochees. This is the type of condition on systematic correspondence necessarily referring to spoken source forms alluded to in Section 1. Importantly, such cases influenced by correspondence need to be treated separately so as not to distort the insight that the type of organisation seen in (18a) is unmarked in German.[41]

As for sorting the data consider finally the question of how to treat so-called *Kunstwörter* illustrated in (32):

---

[41] The view of the open syllables as in *Koma* (see [18a]) as unmarked prosody in German is challenged by the fact that the ambisyllabic structure as in *Komma* (see 18b) dominates in certain contexts (e.g. expressions such as (ˈmamɑ)_ω *Mama*, (ˈpɪpi)_ω *Pipi* in children's speech) and appears to be linked to a more casual register. Here another markedness constraint known as Prokosch's Law, which requires stressed syllables to be heavy (i.e, closed in German), may come into play. This may account for variation in a few shortenings (e.g. (ˈʃtukɑ)_ω ~ (ˈʃtʊkɑ)_ω *Stuka* (< *Sturzkampfflugzeug*)).

(32) Elsa Tesmer ('tezɑ)_ω Tesa (adhesive tape)
    Emil Pauly (mi'lupɑ)_ω Milupa (baby food)
    Bizer Balingen (bi'tˢɛʀ.bɑ)_ω Bizerba (scales)
    Hermann Tietze ('hɛʀ.ti)_ω Hertie (department store)
    Adi Dassler ('adi̯das)_ω Adidas (sportswear)
    Wie Diamant ('vidi̯ɑ)_ω Widia (steel tools)
    Perborat & Silikat (pɛʀ'zil)_ω Persil (laundry detergent)

Kunstwörter stand apart from all remaining shortening types in that they are not necessarily coreferential with respect to their source form nor is their gender determined by that form. (The name *Elsa Tesmer* refers to a female individual, whereas *Tesa* is a neuter noun referring to a brand of adhesive tape.) Unlike regular shortenings, which aim to provide an alternative expression of an independently existing source form, the formation of a *Kunstwort* aims to create a novel expression, typically a trademark. This difference in function correlates with frequent violations of rules determining the formation of regular shortenings: there is no necessary reference to the left edge of morphemes, no necessary preservation of the linear order of the material as given in source forms, and no need to select contiguous material or to obey the limits on segments to be represented. For instance, none of the boldface segments in (32) would be included in a regular *Silbenkurzwort*.

Although it seems plausible to separate all *Kunstwörter* due to these rather striking differences in function and form, the comparison of the relevant patterns to the baseline established with reference to *Initial-*, *Silben-*, and *Mischkurzwörter* indicates that the patterns are largely alike. A few examples comparing the *Kunstwörter* introduced above in the lefthand column to regular shortenings to their right are given in (33).

(33) ('tezɑ)_ω   ≈ ('gezɑ)_ω   Gesa   Gefangenen#sammelstelle
    (mi'lupɑ)_ω   ≈ (zo'lavi)_ω   SoLaWi   Solidarische Landwirtschaft
    (bi'tˢɛʀ.bɑ)_ω ≈ (ge'dɛlfi)_ω   Gedelfi Großeinkauf Deutscher
                                              Lebensmittelfilialbetriebe
    ('hɛʀti)_ω   ≈ ('ɛlfi)_ω   Elphi   Elbphilharmonie
    ('adi̯das)_ω   ≈ ('asfi̯nak)_ω   ASFINAG Autobahnen- und
                                              Schnellstraßen-Finanzierung-
                                              Aktiengesellschaft
    ('vidi̯ɑ)_ω   ≈ ('bebʀi̯ɑ)_ω   BEBRIA   Berliner Briefmarken-
                                              Ausstellung
    (pɛʀ'zil)_ω   ≈ (hɑ'bil)_ω   Habil   Habilitationsschrift

Kunstwörter are therefore included in the SDS-corpus, as long as they are indeed formed by shortening. Other novel words used for brand names, including so-called fantasy words, which have no recognisable source form, are not included due to their likely origin in intended shapes in the minds of speakers, to which they are then molded. Indeed, fantasy words often violate constraints on prosodic organisation not violated in any shortenings (e.g. final main stress in /bɑlɑˈhe/ <Balahé>, a brand name for perfume).[42]

5 Screening the shortening data for potential interferences

All claims regarding the regularity of the prosodic organisation of given phoneme sequences presuppose both single phonological word domains and the lack of prosodic correspondence effects. The purpose of this section is to further clarify these two prerequisites and explain apparent counter-examples as a consequence of non-adherence to one or the other.

5.1 Cases of non-obvious internal phonological word boundaries

In this section I will draw attention to a few cases of likely internal phonological word boundaries motivating the exclusion of shortenings from the SDS-corpus.

Consider the shortening *Meckpomm* in (34a), where final stress seemingly violates the 2σ-RULE stated in (13a). The closed syllables deviate from the selection patterns characteristic of German *Silbenkurzwörter*. They indicate the presence of two consecutive shortenings [mɛk] and [pɔm], organised as a copulative compound (cf. 34a) in analogy with the source expression, a two-member copulative compound consisting of the names of two states. The output to be expected from a more typical shortening of the source compound, two open syllables organised as a trochee within a single phonological word, is illustrated in (34b).

---

[42] Ronneberger-Sibold separates all product names from her main corpus, based on her claim that their phonological shape is characterised by the intent to attract attention, leading to deliberate deviations from the prosody of other shortenings (1992: 116). Plausible though this idea may seem, it is not corroborated by the data.

(34) a. Me̲ck̲lenburg-Vorpo̲mmern ((mɛk)_ω(pɔm)_ωHd)_CC *Meckpomm*
     b. Me̲cklenburg-V̲orpommern ('mefo)_ω   *MEVO*⁴³

Another violation of the generalisations likely to result from internal phonological word boundaries concerns the word-final stress in the shortening *rororo* (trade name for a publishing company) shown in (35a). While indicating the selectional patterns of a regular *Silbenkurzwort*, that word is special in that it consists of three identical syllables, thereby inviting a reanalysis as a copulative compound [[ʀo][ʀo][ʀo]]. This organisation results in final main stress (cf. 35b).

(35) a. /ʀoʀo'ʀo/ *rororo* R̲owohlt R̲otations R̲omane b. ((ʀo)_ω(ʀo)_ω(ʀo)_ωHd)_CC

Final stress in the trade names in (36) is associated with written representations likely to conceal letter compounds, as these shortenings are parsable into consecutive stems associated with the boldfaced initials in the source forms. Final stress then again follows from the regular head status of the rightmost member of a copulative compound.

(36) /ɛlbe'o/ Elbeo   L̲ouis B̲ahner O̲berlungwitz (tights)   ((ɛl)_ω(be)_ω(o)_ωHd)_CC⁴⁴
     /ɛs'tˢɛt/ Eszet   S̲taengel & Z̲iller (chocolate)   ((ɛs)_ω(tˢɛt)_ωHd)_CC
     /tˢe've/ CEWE   C̲arl W̲öltje (photo technology)   ((tˢe)_ω(ve)_ωHd)_CC
     /fau'de/ Vaude   Albrecht v̲on D̲ewitz (sportswear)   ((fau)_ω(de)_ωHd)_CC
     /ɛʀ'ge/ Ergee   E̲dwin R̲össler, G̲elenau/E̲rzgebirge   ((ɛʀ)_ω(ge)_ωHd)_CC⁴⁵
                        (tights)

---

43 This particular shortening is uncommon as it is blocked by the common abbreviation in (34a). Significantly, it can be pronounced only with peripheral vowels and initial stress.

44 It goes without saying that concealed letter compounds invite "mispronunciations" as a single phonological word, which would destabilise final main stress and, for this phoneme sequence, allow for a shift to penult stress (cf. ('ʀode,o_ω) ~ (ʀo'deo)_ω <Rodeo> 'rodeo'). The originally intended copulative compound structure of *Elbeo* can be verified by examining commercials for this product, where the final main stress along with the glottalisation of the vowel /o/, due to its phonological word-initial position, is unmistakably heard.

45 The doubling of the final vowel in the written form might be intended to forestall GP-CORR constraints, which would map a single final <E> (as in <Erge>) to schwa. The alleged motivation of <Ergee> as an acronym based on the graphemes underlined in *E̲dwin R̲össler, G̲elenau/ E̲rzgebirge* is then possibly a case of backronymy. *CEWE* and *Vaude* are not included in the set of apparent counter-examples in (3) because their status as concealed letter compounds is not in question.

An additional case of somewhat hidden internal domain boundaries concerns (quasi)prefixes, which in German are not integrated into the phonological word of the stem. Consider the shortening /deˈstatɪs/ in (37a), where violations of both the σ^op/clos-RULE in (13d), which requires a centralised vowel in a closed syllable (cf. (mɛsˈtitˢə)_ω <Mestize> 'mestizo', (tɛsˈtikəl)_ω <Testikel> 'testicle') and the 3σC-RULE in (13b), which predicts word-initial main stress, indicate the recognition of a quasi-prefix *de-*. The relevant prosodic organisation as a Composite Group (CG) is shown in (37b) (Nespor and Vogel 2007: xvii). A few related cases of quasi-prefixes and their effect on prosodic organisation are listed below.

(37) a. /deˈstatɪs/   Destatis   Deutsches Statistik-   b. (de(ˈstatɪs)_ω)_CG
                                  Informationssystem
     /geˈstɑpo/   Gestapo   Geheime   (ge(ˈstɑpo)_ω)_CG
                                  Staatspolizei
     /pʀoˈmedɔs/   Promedos   Programmierte   (pʀo(ˈmedɔs)_ω)_CG
                                  Medikamenten-
                                  Dosierung

Yet another case of potential internal domain boundaries concerns (quasi)compounds, where the recurrence of sound and meaning at the right periphery as in (38a, b) ([pol] matches the beginning of the word [poliˈtˢai] <Polizei> 'police' and refers to police organisations, [mɪl] matches the beginning of the word [mɪlç] <Milch> 'milk' and refers to milk products marketed as baby food) invite an analysis as determinative compounds (e.g. [[ɔiʀo][pol]], [[milu][mɪl]]). The respective prosodic organisations are shown in the righthand column. The examples in (38c) show the distinct stress patterns resulting from the organisation of a three-syllable shortening ending in /l/ as a single phonological word:

(38) a. /ˈɔiʀoˌpol/   Europol   Europäisches   ((ˈɔiʀo)_ωHd(pol)_ω) END-COMP
                                  Polizeiamt
     /ˈɪntəʀˌpol/   Interpol   Internationale   ((ˈɪntəʀ)_ωHd(pol)_ω) END-COMP
                                  Kriminal-
                                  polizeiliche
                                  Organisation
     b. /ˈaptɑˌmɪl/   Aptamil   Adaptierte -a- Milch   ((ˈaptɑ)_ωHd(mɪl)_ω)_END-COMP
        /ˈmiluˌmɪl/   Milumil   Milupa Milch   ((ˈmilu)_ωHd(mɪl)_ω)_END-COMP
     c. /penɑˈzol/   Penasol   Penaten + Latin   (penɑˈzol)_ω
                                  sol 'sun'
        /vitɑˈmol/   Vitamol   Vitamin + Oleum   (vitɑˈmol)_ω
                                  morrhuae

While it could be argued that the shortenings in (38c) are also morphologically complex and contain a (pseudo)suffix *-ol,* it holds in general that vowel-initial suffixes form a single phonological word with the preceding stem (Raffelsiefen forthc.). The phonological word structure shown in (38c) is therefore adequate, regardless of whether a suffix *-ol* is recognised.

5.2 Cases of potential interference from correspondence with prosodic structure

Some evidence for systematic prosodic correspondence effects has already been noted in connection with clippings (see Section 4). Here I wish to draw attention to further cases illustrating the potential distortion of unmarked prosody resulting from such influences.

The perhaps most obvious case of prosodic correspondence concerns borrowed shortenings with their original stress pattern preserved, such as Greek (pa'sɔk)_ω PASOK. Here final stress simply corresponds to the pattern in the Greek source expressions. The problem raised by some of the stress-preservation cases lies in their subsequent association with reconstructed source forms based on German words, which may give them the appearance of having been coined natively. Examples are shown in (39):

(39)   Source forms: Reconstructed full forms?
    (dia'mat)_ω   DIAMAT   Russian dia**mát**   (Dialektischer Materialismus)
    (bi'onɪk)_ω   Bionik   English biónics   (Biologie + Technik)

If the stress patterns in (39) are borrowed they do not count as counterexamples to the claim that trisyllabic words ending in a closed syllable are regularly organised with initial main stress (see 13b).[46]

---

[46] There is no need to treat separately all shortenings of foreign origin. Especially those showing signs of assimilation to the phonology of German, most notably cases where letter compounds in the source language are reorganised as single-domain acronyms in German, are included in the SDS-corpus.

Source	Acronym	Source language (English)	German
Factory-Outlet-Center	FOC	((ɛf)_ω(əu)_ω(si)_ωHd)_COP-COMP	(fɔk)_ω
free on board	fob	((ɛf)_ω(əu)_ω(bi)_ωHd)_COP-COMP	(fɔp)_ω

Certain shortenings originating in Swiss German are, however, to be treated separately due to the preference for initial stress in that variety of German (e.g. ('ʀiko‚la)_ω Ricola (< Richterich & Compagnie, Laufen) (candy)).

Consider now various cases of prosodic correspondence effects seen in shortenings originating in German. Such an effect may underlie the initial main stress in the shortening *Edeka* shown in (40a), which contrasts with the expected stress on the penult in trisyllabic words ending in an open syllable shown in (40b).

(40) a. (ˈede̩ˌka)_ω *Edeka*   E̲inkaufsgenossenschaft d̲er K̲olonialwarenhändler
     b. (teˈgeva)_ω *TEGEWA* Verband der T̲e̲xtilhilfsmittel-, Lederhilfsmittel-, G̲e̲rbstoff- und W̲a̲schrohstoff-Industrie

The stress variation is explained by the distinct conditions under which the shortenings came about. Whereas *TEGEWA* is a regular *Silbenkurzwort* whose prosodic organisation is organised from scratch, the word *Edeka* comes from a letter compound *EDK*, which constitutes the original shortening based on the full form (see 41a). Three-letter compounds exhibit a prominence pattern marked by rhythmic accent on the initial member, caused by the main stress on the final prosodic head (the different font sizes in 41a are intended to mimic different degrees of phonetic prominence). The organisation of the first two syllables as a trochaic foot, followed by a monosyllabic foot, preserves the original prominence profile in the prosodically fused variant (see 41b). (The reversal of relative prominence indicates the domain of a single phonological word, where monosyllabic final feet are prone to lose their head status to a preceding trochee, cf. 13b). Stress correspondence then forestalls the regular organisation of the last two open syllables as a trochaic foot seen in (teˈge.va)_ω *TEGEWA*. Fused letter compounds such as *EDEKA* are therefore to be treated separately.

(41) a. ((**e**)_ω(de)_ω(**ka**)_ωHd)_CC   b. ((ˈ**ede**)_ΣHd(ka)_Σ)_ω

Stress preservation in the disyllabic contiguous strings is reminiscent of the correspondence effect in clippings discussed above (see 29b). Consider also the trade names in (42a), where matching disyllabic foot structure (underlined) goes hand in hand with matching peripherality values for the stressed vowels. The occurrence of this correspondence effect is forestalled in (42b), where the relevant vowels are not embedded in matching trochees. Here intervocalic single consonants form simple onsets, manifest in the peripherality of the preceding vowel.[47]

---

[47] The centralised stressed vowel in the brand name for pain medication (koˈnaʃu)_ω *Konaschu* (<K̲o̲pf, N̲a̲cken, S̲chultern) is no exception as /ʃ/, (even more so /s/), prefers an ambisyllabic organisation, causing a restriction to centralised vowels in the preceding nucleus (e.g. (ˈtaʃə)_ω *Tasche* 'bag', (ˈɛʃə)_ω *Esche* 'ash tree'). Only high vowels exhibit a peripherality contrast before /ʃ/ (e.g. (ˈniʃə)_ω *Nische* 'niche' vs. (ˈfʀɪʃə)_ω *Frische* 'freshness' (ˈʀyʃə)_ω *Rüsche* 'frill' vs. (ˈbʏʃə)_ω *Büsche*

(42) a. No Motte -a (...('mɔtə)_ω ...)   (no'mɔta)_ω Nomotta (moth repellent)
        Sanne & Ella (...('ɛla)_ω)   (za'nɛla)_ω Sanella (margarine)
        nicht knitternd -a
        (...('knɪtəRnd)_ω ...)   (ni'knɪta)_ω Niknitta (fabric)
     b. Adressiermaschine
        ((adRɛ'siR)_ω ...)   (a'dRema)_ω Adrema (mailing machine)
        Metallbohrdreher ((me'tal)_ω ...) (me'tabo)_ω Metabo (metal drill)
        Haselnusstafel (...('nʊs)_ω ...) (ha'nuta)_ω Hanuta (candy)

Similar effects connected to phonological salience are seen in (43a), where the most prominent foot, when located at the right periphery in the source form, is preserved in the shortening, leading to deviations from the generalisations in (13) (i.e. 2σ-RULE, 3σ-RULE). Those conditions do not obtain in (43b) and the shortenings fully conform to the generalisations in (13):

(43) a. Bacteri Trimetoprím (...(tRimeto'pRim)_ω)   (bak'tRim)_ω Bactrim
        Rifampicin Trimetoprím (...(tRimeto'pRim)_ω)   (Rifa'pRim)_ω Rifaprim
        lavare + Automat (...(auto'mat)_ω)   (lava'mat)_ω Lavamat
     b. durare + Cefadroxil (...(tˢefadRɔk'sil)_ω)   ('duRa͡tˢɛf)_ω Duracef
        Flores Europa(e) (...(ɔi'Rɔpa)_ω)   ('flɔiRɔp)_ω Fleurop
        Milchrahm (('mɪlç)_ωHd('Ram)_ω)_DC   ('mɪlRam)_ω Milram

A possible highly restricted condition on prosodic correspondence presupposes vowel markedness associated with foremost prominence in the source form. Relevant cases are shown in (44):

(44) a. Atmosphären#über#druck   atü   (a'ty)_ω
        Baden-Württemberg   BaWü (ba'vy)_ω ~ ('ba.vy)_ω
     b. Regen#über#lauf#becken ('ybəR) RÜB (Ryb)_ω [48]

'bushes'). This presumably relates to the fact that only among high vowels are peripheral vowels unmarked vis-à-vis centralised vowels (see footnote 29).

48 The assumption of a voiced obstruent here is motivated by the organisation of that obstruent in onset position due to the preceding peripheral vowel. In onset position, the relevant GP-CORR convention associates the grapheme <B> with the phoneme /b/, as opposed to the coda position in cases like *PfÜB* in (45b), where that grapheme links to /p/ instead. (De)voicing is then relegated to phonetic implementation, affecting obstruents preceding a word-final empty nucleus (a process of articulatory weakening akin to the vocalisation of /R/ in final onset position, see footnote 30). Evidence for the need to discern such cases of phonetic Final Devoicing from a markedness constraint restricting all coda obstruents to voiceless phonemes is discussed in Raffelsiefen (2016).

Here correspondence leads to violations of σ$^{op/clos}$-RULE and 2σ-RULE in the shortenings, where final main stress in the shortenings mimics the main prominence of the corresponding syllable in the source form. The relevance of the conjoined conditions in question is supported by the absence of a correspondence effect when only one (or none) of the conditions is met. A source form whose main stressed syllable contains an unmarked vowel (cf. 45a) or a marked vowel that fails to carry main stress (cf. 45b) yields shortenings which conform to the generalisations in (13).

(45) a. Bundes**gár**tenschau   BUGA (ˈbugɑ)$_ω$
   Karl-**Jó**sef   Kajo (ˈkɑio)$_ω$
   Bayerische **Ó**berland#bahn (...(ˈobəʀ)...)   BOB (bɔp)$_ω$
  b. Technischer **Ü**berw**á**chungs-Verein (...(ˈybəʀ)...)   TÜV (tʏf)$_ω$
   Pfändungs- und **Ü**berw**éi**sungs#bescheid   PfÜB (pfʏp)$_ω$
   (...(ˈybəʀ)...)
   Neue **Ö**konomische Pol**ití**k (...(ˈøko...)...)   NÖP (nœp)$_ω$

Consider next the possible explanation for the violation of regular prosody (i.e. σ$^{op/clos}$-RULE) in (46) due to so-called apronymy, a term referring to the deliberate modelling of shortenings on existing words.

(46)   Kaffee-**H**andels-**A**ktiengesellschaft   Kaffee   Kaffee
                  HAG   (hɑg)$_ω$
   Staatliche **E**rfassungsgesellschaft für öffentliches **G**ut   STEG   (ʃteg)$_ω$

The idea that the brand name *Kaffee HAG* is intended to evoke the positive connotations associated with the stem *hag* (cf. *be*(hɑg)$_ω$*lich* 'content', *Be*(hɑgən)$_ω$ 'contentment') is supported by the odd shortening pattern leaving the first word of the source form intact (instead of forming a *Silbenkurzwort* "Kaha" or a *Mischkurzwort* "Kahag").[49] Also in STEG, the representation of the content word *öffentlich* is skipped, apparently to achieve homophony with the existing word (ʃteg)$_ω$ *Steg* 'footbridge'.

---

[49] A rare case of a regular shortening exhibiting a deviation from unmarked phonology likely motivated by analogy is (ˈkvabi)$_ω$ *Quabi* (< *Qualifizierter beruflicher Bildungsabschluss*), which appears to be modelled directly on *Quali* (also a degree in the Bavarian school system), and perhaps *Abi*. Both *Quali* and *Abi* are clippings (< *qualifizierender Abschluss der Mittelschule*, < *Abitúr*)), characterised by a centralised stressed vowel. Such influences may require similarity regarding both form and meaning.

One could consider an alternative explanation of the highly exceptional phonological shapes of the shortenings in (46) as some sort of spelling pronunciation, due to the strong association of graphemes linked to voiced plosives with a preceding peripheral vowel in the ordinary vocabulary (e.g. (lid)$_\omega$ *Lid* 'eyelid'). However, among the 26 C$_0$VC shortenings spelled with a final <B>, <D>, or <G> in the current SDS-corpus, only *RÜB* (see 44b), *Kaffee HAG*, and *STEG* (see 46) are pronounced with a peripheral vowel. Spelling pronunciations are indeed generally absent in this context. For instance, the presence of a single grapheme <z>, systematically associated with a preceding peripheral vowel in the ordinary vocabulary (e.g. *Flöz* 'lode'), has similarly no effect: the unmarked choice persists, that is, a centralised vowel in a closed syllable (cf. 47a). Also word-final grapheme combinations typically associated with stress, including vowel and consonant geminates (*Armée* 'army', *Prográmm* 'program'), the digraph <ie> (*Partíe* 'game'), final <H> (*Felláh* 'fellah') never seem to yield violations of unmarked stress patterns in shortenings (cf. the regular trochees in 47b).

(47) a. (kœp)$_\omega$ Kö**B**   **K**atholische **ö**ffentliche **B**ücherei
          (plɪp)$_\omega$ PLI**B**   **P**ädagogisches **L**andes**i**nstitut **B**randenburg
          (fat^s)$_\omega$ FA**Z**   **F**rankfurter **A**llgemeine **Z**eitung
      b. (ˈbafa)$_\omega$ BAf**AA**   **B**undes**a**nstalt für **A**rbeitsvermittlung und **A**rbeitslosenversicherung
          (ˈveʀa)$_\omega$ VER**AH**   **V**ersorgungs**a**ssistentin in der **H**ausarztpraxis
          (ˈhɛʀti)$_\omega$ Hert**ie**   **H**ermann **T**ietze
          (ˈdikɔm)$_\omega$ diko**mm**   **Z**ukunft **D**igitale **Kom**mune
          (ˈefɪʃ)$_\omega$ EFI**FF**   **E**uropäisches **F**ortbildungs**i**nstitut für **F**ilm und **F**ernsehen

Indeed there are only two contexts where I have noticed deviations from expected prosodic organisation of shortenings due to spelling, both involving geminate spellings. In (48a) geminate consonants appear to yield ambisyllabicity via the Elsewhere Principle (the applicability of a specific rule blocks the application of the more general rule), but only in contexts where ambisyllabicity is licensed in regular German prosody: foot-internally between a stressed and an unstressed vowel (cf. 18b). This accounts for the unexpected occurrence of the centralised vowel in the shortening in (48a).

(48) a. **I**nternationale **F**leischerei-   IFFA   (ˈɪfa)$_\omega$
          Fach**a**usstellung
      b. **D**eutscher **A**kademischer   DAAD   ((de)$_\omega$(a)$_\omega$(a)$_\omega$(de)$_{\omega Hd}$)$_{CC}$
          Austausch**d**ienst

The vowel geminate in (48a), by contrast, induces an organisation as a letter compound. This somewhat cumbersome structure resolves the dilemma between a pronunciation (dat)$_\omega$, with inadequate grapheme-phoneme correspondence in the head syllable, and (dɑd)$_\omega$/(dɑt)$_\omega$, which violate the constraint against (word-final) empty nuclei or against peripheral vowels in closed syllables. Here we see an interesting asymmetry and gain insight into the relation between written and spoken language, where shortenings again provide a unique window.

6 Conclusion and outlook

This article aims to draw attention to the unique potential of shortenings to serve as a window on unmarked phonological structure. To fully explore this potential, it is necessary to properly sort the shortening data, to ensure the presence of proper domains (single phonological words) and the absence of prosodic correspondence effects. It is further necessary to refer to a specific degree of abstractness of phonological representation. When executed with care, this approach can be shown to reveal remarkably regular sound patterns, which can then be further explored by phonologists aiming to model phonological grammar. The patterns appear to lend themselves to an analysis in terms of independently motivated phonological markedness constraints in accordance with Optimality Theory.

In view of the regularity and consistency observed in the properly sorted SDS-corpus, one could argue that despite its relatively small size (currently roughly 1200 items) it is more valuable to phonologists than vast corpora of unsorted speech. The extraction of statistical patterns based on raw phonetic data, regardless of the size of the corpus, is indeed of dubious interest to linguists interested in phonology at the word level. Even careful and consistent annotations, which are hard to find, will not help discern the inherited and imitated from the unmarked patterns to be identified in a phonological grammar aiming at explanatory adequacy.

References

Archangeli, Diana & Douglas Pulleyblank. 1989. Yoruba vowel harmony. *Linguistic Inquiry* 20. 173–217.
Bat-El, Outi. 1994. The optimal acronym word in Hebrew. In Päivi Koskinen (ed.), *Proceedings of the 1994 Annual Conference of the Canadian Linguistic Association*, 23–37. Toronto: Toronto Working Papers in Linguistics.

Becker, Thomas. 1998. *Das Vokalsystem der deutschen Standardsprache.* Frankfurt am Main: Lang.
Beckman, Jill. 1998. *Positional faithfulness.* Amherst, MA: University of Massachusetts Amherst dissertation.
Bergstrøm-Nielsen, Henrik. 1952. Die Kurzwörter im heutigen Deutsch. *Moderna Språk* 46. 2–22.
Dixon, Robert Malcolm Ward. 1997. Some phonological rules in Yidiny. *Linguistic Inquiry* 8. 1–34.
Harris, John & Edmund Gussman. 2002. Word-final onsets. UCL *Working Papers in Linguistics* 14. 1–42.
Janßen, Ulrike. 2004. *Untersuchungen zum Wortakzent im Deutschen und Niederländischen.* Düsseldorf: University of Düsseldorf dissertation.
Kenstowicz, Michael. 1997. Quality-sensitive stress. *Rivista di Linguistica* 9. 157–188.
Kobler-Trill, Dorothea. 1994. *Das Kurzwort im Deutschen: Eine Untersuchung zu Definition, Typologie und Entwicklung.* Tübingen: Max Niemeyer.
Leuschner, Torsten. 2008. Kurzwortbildung im Deutschen und Niederländischen: Grundlagen und Ergebnisse eines prototypischen Vergleichs. *Germanistische Mitteilungen* 57. 247–261.
Lindau, Mona. 1978. Vowel features. *Language* 54. 541–563.
Lux, Barbara. 2016. *Kurzwortbildung im Deutschen und Schwedischen: Eine kontrastive Untersuchung phonologischer und grammatischer Aspekte.* Tübingen: Narr Francke Attempto Verlag.
Nespor, Marina & Irene Vogel. 2007. *Prosodic phonology.* Berlin: de Gruyter.
Nübling, Damaris. 2001. *Auto – bil, Reha – rehab, Mikro – mick, Alki – alkis*: Kurzwörter im Deutschen und Schwedischen. *Skandinavistik* 31. 167–199.
Piñeros, Carlos-Eduardo. 2000. Prosodic and segmental unmarkedness in Spanish truncation. *Linguistics* 38. 63–98.
Prince, Alan & Paul Smolensky. 1993. *Optimality theory: Constraint interaction in generative grammar.* New Brunswick, NJ: Rutgers University Center for Cognitive Science.
Raffelsiefen, Renate. 1995. Conditions for stability. *Arbeiten des Sonderforschungsbereich* 282 (69).
Raffelsiefen, Renate. 2000. Constraints on schwa apocope in Middle High German. In Aditi Lahiri (ed.), *Analogy, levelling, markedness*, 125–170. Berlin: de Gruyter.
Raffelsiefen, Renate. 2016. Allomorphy and the question of abstractness: Evidence from German. *Morphology* 26. 235–267.
Raffelsiefen, Renate. 2018. Phonologische Abstraktheit und symbolische Repräsentation. In Angelika Wöllstein, Peter Gallmann, Mechthild Habermann & Manfred Krifka (eds.), *Grammatiktheorie und Empirie in der germanistischen Linguistik*, 549–586. Berlin: de Gruyter.
Raffelsiefen, Renate. Forthc. Morpho-phonological asymmetries in affixation. In Peter Ackema, Sabrina Bendjaballah, Eulalia Bonet & Antonio Fábregas (eds.), *The Wiley Blackwell Companion to Morphology.* New York: John Wiley & Sons.
Raffelsiefen, Renate. In progress. The grammar of shortening in German (including the SDS-corpus). Mannheim: Leibniz-Institut für Deutsche Sprache.
Ronneberger-Sibold, Elke. 1992. *Die Lautgestalt neuer Wurzeln: Kürzungen und Kunstwörter im Deutschen und Französischen.* Freiburg: Albert-Ludwigs-Universität Freiburg im Breisgau Habilitationsschrift.

Ronneberger-Sibold, Elke. 2007. Zur Grammatik von Kurzwörtern. In Jochen Bär, Thorsten Roelcke & Anja Steinhauer (eds.), *Sprachliche Kürze*, 276–291. Berlin: de Gruyter.

Ronneberger-Sibold, Elke. 2015. Word creation. In Peter Müller, Ingeborg Ohnheiser, Susan Olsen & Franz Rainer (eds.), *Word formation: An international handbook of the languages of Europe*, 485–499. Vol. 1. Berlin: de Gruyter.

Schiller, Niels & Christine Mooshammer. 1995. The character of /r/-sounds: Articulatory evidence for different reduction processes with special reference to German. In Kjell Elenius & Peter Branderud (eds.), *Proceedings of the XIIIth International Congress of Phonetic Sciences, Stockholm 1995*, 452–455. Vol. 3. Stockholm: the Congress organisers at KTH and Stockholm University.

Schindler, Wolfgang. 1994. Analogische Wortakzentvergabe im Deutschen. *Sprachtypologie und Universalienforschung* 47. 355–370.

Selkirk, Elisabeth. 1996. The prosodic structure of function words. In James Morgan & Katherine Demuth (eds.), *Signal to syntax: Bootstrapping from speech to grammar in early acquisition*, 187–213. Mahwah/NJ: Lawrence Erlbaum Associates.

Sievers, Eduard. 1876. *Grundzüge der Lautphysiologie zur Einführung in das Studium der Lautlehre der indogermanischen Sprachen*. Leipzig: Breitkopf und Härtel.

Smolensky, Paul. 1997. Constraint interaction in generative grammar II: Local conjunction. Talk presented at the Hopkins Optimality Theory Conference.

Steinhauer, Anja. 2005. *Duden: Das Wörterbuch der Abkürzungen*. 5th ed. Mannheim: Dudenverlag.

Vennemann, Theo. 1988. *Preference laws for syllable structure and the explanation of sound change*. Berlin: de Gruyter.

Vennemann, Theo. 1991a. Syllable structure and syllable cut prosodies in Modern Standard German. In Pier Marco Bertinetto, Michael Kenstowicz & Michele Loporcaro (eds.), *Certamen Phonologicum II: Papers from the 1990 Cortona Phonology Meeting*, 211–243. Turin: Rosenberg & Sellier.

Vennemann, Theo. 1991b. Skizze der deutschen Wortprosodie. *Zeitschrift für Sprachwissenschaft* 10. 86–111.

Vennemann, Theo. 1998. Prosodie und Wortgewinnung. In Matthias Butt & Nanna Fuhrhop (eds.), *Variation und Stabilität in der Wortstruktur: Untersuchungen zu Entwicklung, Erwerb und Varietäten des Deutschen und anderer Sprachen*, 225–244. Hildesheim: Georg Olms Verlag.

Visch, Ellis & René Kager. 1984. Syllable weight and Dutch word stress. In Hans Bennis & Wus van Lessen Kloeke (eds.), *Linguistics in the Netherlands*, 197–205. Amsterdam: Benjamins.

Whitney, William Dwight. 1861. On Lepsius's standard alphabet. *Journal of the American Oriental Society* 7. 299–332.

Whitney, William Dwight. 1874. *Oriental and linguistic studies*. Second series. New York: Scribner, Armstrong, and Company.

Laura Catharine Smith
Moving from syllables to feet in the prosodic hierarchy: How foot-based templates reflect prosodic preferences

Abstract: Building on Vennemann's (1988) treatise on the Preference Laws for syllable structure, this paper shifts the focus up the prosodic hierarchy from syllables to feet formed by sequences of syllables, demonstrating that some languages show a clear preference for particular foot types in driving language change and organisation. I demonstrate how the foot has been shown in more recent years since Vennemann's proposal to drive sound change and shape lexical and phonological patterns. Drawing primarily on language data from the history of the West Germanic languages, e.g. Old Saxon *i*-stem nouns, Old High German *jan*-verbs, and Old Frisian vowel balance, the trochaic foot is shown to have shaped the loss or reduction of vowels based on their mapping to a trochaic foot. Likewise, plural formation in both Modern German and Dutch illustrates the preference for plurals to adhere to a syllabic trochee (for German: Eisenberg 1991, Wiese 2000, 2001; for Dutch: Booij 1998, 2002, van der Hulst and Kooij 1998), a claim substantiated by experimental evidence (e.g. Smith, Schuhmann, and Champenois

---

Acknowledgements: It is a distinct pleasure to celebrate the contributions of Theo Vennemann to linguistics in this thematic volume. I count myself fortunate to have had the opportunity to study with him in Munich not just once, but twice, with the help of DAAD grants as a graduate student. Indeed some of the work in this paper, notably my analysis of Old Saxon, was initially carried out and presented at an Oberseminar during my second time in Munich. The generous feedback I received from Professor Vennemann then and through the years has helped shape my thinking about language change and continues to do so today. His generosity of spirit, kindness and support cannot be understated. It is an honour to dedicate this paper to him.

I would be remiss if I did not thank my MA advisor, Robert Murray (Calgary), for having the forethought to send me to Munich to work with his *Doktorvater* and then to Wisconsin to work with Joseph Salmons who encouraged me to build on what the Preference Laws started. I have been blessed and humbled to stand on the shoulders of these exemplary scholars and mentors.

And a special thanks to Patrizia Noel Aziz Hanna and Dietmar Zaefferer for organising the Symposium on Preferences that brought Professor Vennemann's students and colleagues together to celebrate his contributions and served as the catalyst for this dedicated volume. And lastly, many thanks to Patrizia Noel Aziz Hanna and Katharina Schuhmann for their feedback on drafts of this chapter. Any remaining errors are nevertheless my own.

Laura Catharine Smith, Department of German and Russian, Brigham Young University, Provo, UT/USA

https://doi.org/10.1515/9783110721461-005

2016). The paper is intended to invite scholars to consider what role prosody may play in shaping phonological and morphological patterns not only in terms of the syllable but also in terms of sequences of syllables, namely prosodic feet, to account for sound changes and lexical developments in a broader range of languages and language families.

1 Introduction

Although syllables had long figured into explanations of sound changes and phonological patterns in terms of identifying the phonetic environment of those changes, it was not until Murray and Vennemann's (1983) seminal article followed by Vennemann's (1988) treatise on the Preference Laws for syllables that scholars began to see the syllable as a motivating factor guiding sound change. This shift in thinking stemmed from the ability of the Preference Laws to show that phenomena that had up to that point been viewed as divergent and unrelated were actually remarkably more similar across the world's languages than previously thought. By drawing attention to the role of prosody via syllables, including syllable weight, the Preference Laws invited scholars to explore the role of prosody in sound change, not only in terms of the phonetic environment as had been the case, but indeed as a motivating force behind the changes themselves.

In the last three plus decades since this ground-breaking work was initially published, increasing research has implicated the role of another prosodic unit, namely the foot, in driving additional changes and patterns in both the phonology and morphophonology of a wide variety of unrelated language families, including Semitic (e.g. Arabic and Hebrew; cf. McCarthy and Prince 1995, Ussishkin 2005, Smith and Ussishkin 2015), Germanic (e.g. German, Dutch, and Frisian; cf. Holsinger 2000, 2001, Wiese 2001, Smith 2004, 2020), and Mixtec (Macken and Salmons 1997), among many others (see also Macaulay and Salmons in this volume). This shift in focus up the prosodic hierarchy from syllables to feet (formed by sequences of syllables), reflected in Vennemann's own (1995) analysis of i-stem nouns in Old High German (OHG) and Old Saxon and further spurred on in part by McCarthy and Prince's (1995) work on Prosodic Morphology, has likewise demonstrated a broader role for prosody to drive sound change and shape lexical and phonological patterns. I follow Macken and Salmons' (1997) work on Mixtec to argue that the foot's ability to account for such divergent patterns highlights its preferential shape in these languages and thus its ability to serve as a fundamental template for language change. These templates are preferences rather than absolutes, such that different preferences come into conflict at times, where sometimes prosody wins out, while at other times, phonotactic or morphological requirements take precedence. By drawing on data from both the older and more modern West Germanic languages, this paper shows how some of the principles underpinning Vennemann's (1988) Preference Laws, e.g. the Diachronic and Synchronic Maxims, are also reflected in foot-based change.

To this end, the paper is organised as follows. First, I begin with an overview of some of the pertinent aspects of Vennemann's (1988) Preference Laws which play a role in language change beyond just syllable-based change. From there I move to a discussion of the trochaic foot at work in the data presented in this chapter followed by a brief introduction to foot-based templates. Next, I highlight data from the Germanic languages, beginning with two approaches to the Old Saxon *i*-stem nouns, including Vennemann's own (1995) analysis. I then apply the notion of foot-based preferences outlined for the Old Saxon data to the Old High German *jan*-verbs to show the push and pull of competing phonetic, prosodic, and even morphological preferences that come into conflict. This discussion sets the stage for an analysis of Old Frisian vowel balance, before I turn to a discussion of Modern German and Dutch plurals, which are likewise preferentially trochaic. These data, which have been discussed elsewhere, are revisited here to explore the lessons they teach us about prosodic preferences at the foot level. With this in mind, I now turn to an overview of the Preference Laws and foot structure.

2 Background

Although the *Preference laws for syllable structure* emphasised the role of the syllable in shaping language change, the specific syllable laws for individual syllables, e.g. Head Law or Coda Law, or sequences of syllables, e.g. the Contact Law, drew on a broader and more fundamental notion regarding preferences in language. Since I argue in this chapter that these fundamentals, embodied in the Diachronic (and to a lesser extent the Synchronic) Maxim, can be adduced for foot-based preferences shaping language, I begin this section with an overview of Vennemann's (1988) concept of preferences before providing an introduction to foot formation in the history of Germanic and prosodic templates.

2.1 Preference laws

In his 1988 treatise, Vennemann introduced his notion of "a graded concept of linguistic quality relative to a given parameter" (1988: 1). This new perspective meant that structures were not viewed according to a binary classification, e.g. in terms of "good or bad (natural or unnatural, unmarked or marked)" (Vennemann 1988: 1) as was common in the theoretical discussion at the time, but were viewed instead in terms of a graded continuum. This shift in thinking was founded on the notion that a particular structure could be more or less preferred to another structure in terms of a specific parameter. Consequently, for Vennemann (1988: 1) every change in a language system was seen as a local improvement relative to the parameter in question.

By being able to evaluate different structures in terms of whether they were more or less preferred according to a parameter, Vennemann theorised that remedial measures and/or language change would first impact the less preferred structures before the more preferred structures. This hypothesis was embodied in Vennemann's Diachronic Maxim (1988: 2):

(1) *Diachronic Maxim:* Linguistic change on a given parameter does not affect a language structure as long as there exist structures in the language system that are less preferred in terms of the relevant preference law.

In other words, the least preferred structures would be targeted first for language change.

This hypothesis was argued to also have consequences for synchronic analyses since viewing a language at one slice of time allows us to not only analyse it synchronically, but to see it as one stage in the history and evolution of that language as well. As such we would also not expect to see less preferable structures relative to a parameter without also seeing more preferable structures for that parameter. For instance, if we were to find syllables not footed within the minimal bimoraic foot or CCVCC (V=vowel, C=consonant) syllables (both less preferred structures), we would also expect to find the more preferred structures, namely syllables footed within the bimoraic minimal foot and CV syllables respectively, in that language. This hypothesis is captured in Vennemann's Synchronic Maxim (1988: 3):

(2) *Synchronic Maxim:* A language system will in general not contain a structure on a given parameter without containing those structures constructible with the means of the system that are more preferential in terms of the relevant preference law.

When these maxims are combined, we would expect that over time, repairs would first impact the less preferable structures to help bring them more in alignment with the more preferred structures for a given parameter, e.g. a more preferential syllable or foot. The same structure could be repaired in a variety of ways, and as

I would argue, differences in the specific repair strategies could further reinforce dialect differences, which could in turn lead to divergent sister languages over time.

The data in this chapter highlight the universality of these maxims beyond Vennemann's primarily syllabic application of preferences. Moreover, moving up the prosodic hierarchy to foot-based changes and patterns, these data also provide evidence for how conflicts are resolved between competing parameter preferences, where, for instance, phonotactic or syllable-based parameters at times take precedence over foot-based parameters. As Vennemann reminds us, "improvement on one parameter can entail deterioration on another" making it "impossible to optimise a language system on all parameters at once; there can exist no 'optimal' language system as such, but only systems that are optimised on some parameters" (1988: 65).

With this in mind, I now turn to a brief overview of the relevant foot types for the data in this chapter, namely the moraic and syllabic trochees.

2.2 Moraic and syllabic trochees

Since this chapter aims to demonstrate that Vennemann's notion of preferences can be found at work in foot-based language changes, this shift in perspective moves our gaze one step up the prosodic hierarchy presented in (3) below, from the syllable to the foot:

(3) Prosodic hierarchy (cf. McCarthy and Prince 1995)

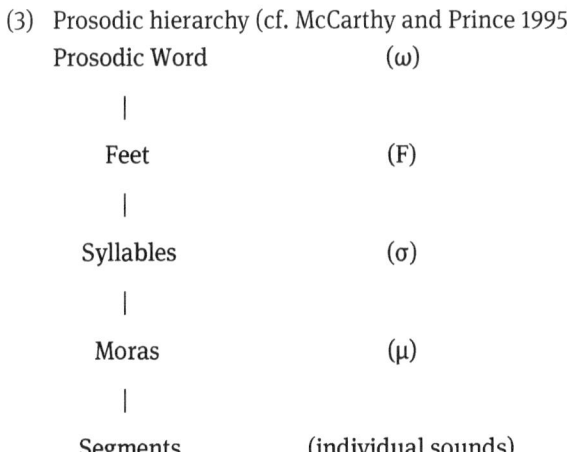

Just as the Preference Laws for syllable structure addressed syllables and the building blocks thereof, e.g. moras and segments, foot-based changes likewise reflect combinations of the lower-level units on the hierarchy, namely syllables and moras, and even at times reflect the interaction of individual segments with those higher levels in the hierarchy.

To discuss the foot-based phenomena presented in this chapter, it is important to define the specific foot types behind these data, namely moraic and syllabic trochees. Historically, the early foot type at work in the West Germanic languages was the moraic trochee, but as shifts in quantity arose, so did a shift to the syllabic trochee predominantly found in the standard varieties of Modern German and Dutch.

2.2.1 The moraic trochee of West Germanic

As noted, the moraic trochee was the foot type found during the weight-sensitive stages of the West Germanic languages (as well as many other Germanic languages). This moraic trochee was formed based on a minimum of bimoricity, where both moras could be found within a single heavy syllable as in (4) or across two syllables as in (5).

As the examples in (4) from Old Saxon illustrate, a single heavy syllable consisting of either a long vowel (V:) or a closed syllable with a short vowel followed by a consonant (VC) could build a foot on its own. (Foot boundaries are indicated by square brackets [ ]. H represents a heavy syllable, while L is for a light syllable.)

(4) a. Moraic trochee: single heavy syllable (cf. Smith 2004, 2020)

    F   Foot level
  ['H] L   Syllable level
  [μμ] μ   Moraic level
  OS gas ti 'guest' (VC) Segmental level
  OS thra: di 'thread' (V:)

 b. Syllable and moraic structure of a heavy syllable moraic trochee with a following light syllable

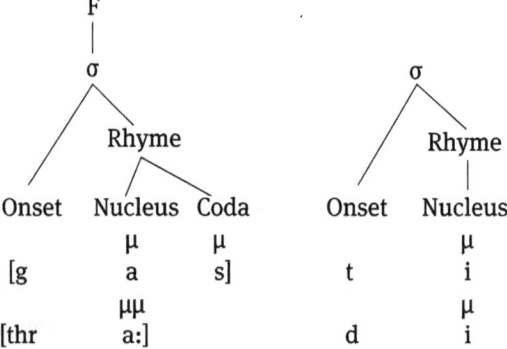

In these Old Saxon (OS) examples, the stressed heavy syllable is composed of two moras, each one assigned to the segments under the rhyme, with long vowels having two moras and short vowels just one. Thus, the initial syllable *gas* in *gasti* derives one mora from the short vowel and one from the coda *s*, while the initial syllable *thrā* in *thradi* derives both moras from the long vowel. These heavy initial syllables consequently form a foot on their own as indicated by the square brackets. In these examples, the following light syllable (L) is considered unfooted (cf. Smith 2020) or, following Vennemann's (1995) analysis, not footed with the minimal bimoraic foot and instead attached directly to the foot.

However, both moras required to build the foot can be spread across two syllables. This happens when the initial syllable is light ending in a single short vowel as in (5). Although this monomoraic, i.e. light (L), syllable cannot form a foot on its own, it does so in combination with a following adjacent syllable of any weight (Fulk 2018: 41).

(5) a. Moraic trochee: light + light syllables (cf. Smith 2004, 2020)

b.

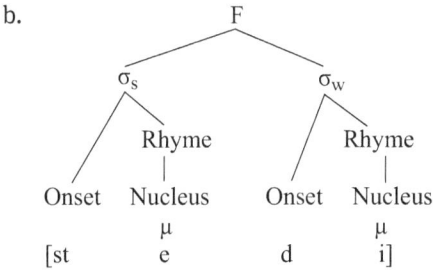

The equivalence of the [H] and [LL] moraic trochee types found in early Germanic can also be understood in terms of Prokosch's Law. According to Prokosch, languages with stress accent have a preference for bimoraic stressed syllables (Vennemann 1995, Fulk 2018), namely a heavy syllable, which as noted, can form a foot on its own. Conversely, a single light syllable would be dispreferred according to Prokosch's Law and would thus attract a following syllable to it to form a foot. Whether in combination of a [LL] or even at times [LH] sequence,[1]

---

1 As Vennemann (1988: 30) notes in his discussion of his Weight Law: "The optimal stressed syllable is bimoric, the optimal unstressed syllable is unimoric." In the event that shortening does

these two syllables together form a minimally bimoraic foot equivalent to one formed by a single heavy syllable [H] via a process known as resolution (cf. Fulk 2018: 41). In the resulting bisyllabic foot, the first syllable attracts stress and is marked as "strong" (subscript "s" in 5) while the second syllable is weak (subscript "w") and unstressed.

2.2.2 Syllabic trochees

While the moraic trochee was the common foot type found in the early Germanic languages, it was replaced by the syllabic trochee following quantity shifts in many Germanic languages and dialects. Cross-linguistically, this foot type is simply the sequence of a stressed-unstressed syllable [σ́. σ] where syllable weight is irrelevant. Consider the German word *Winter*:

(6) Syllabic trochees
    F   Foot level
  [σ́. σ] Syllabic level
  Wín.ter Segmental level

Although the initial syllable in this example could be classified as bimoraic, its weight is irrelevant in syllabic trochees. Instead, what matters is that the initial syllable is stressed and is followed by an unstressed syllable.

2.3 Prosodic templates

Since prosodic templates based on the foot play a role in the analyses presented for the data below, it is worth providing a brief introduction to the concept before discussing the data below. McCarthy and Prince (1995) demonstrated that authentic prosodic units, such as the syllable or foot, could be adduced to account for either the stems or outputs of a variety of morphological operations, such as croppings,

---

not impact a following heavy syllable, e.g. when a light stem noun has a heavy ending as in Old Saxon *huges, -ies, -ias* 'mind, gen. sg.', the heavy final syllable in the [LH] foot contributes the final mora necessary to met the bimoraic minimum necessary to form the trochee. In sum, once the bimoraic requirement is met, the foot is closed. For an initial H syllable, the bimoraic requirement is met within that single syllable. However, in the case of an initial L syllable, the additional mora is attracted to the L syllable from the following syllable to meet the bimoraic requirement (cf. Fulk 2018: 41). As shown in Section 3.1, Vennemann refers to this as the minimal foot.

reduplication, and affixation. As they demonstrated, the canonical shapes of either the stems or outputs aligned with prosodic constituents. According to Downing (2006), the canonical stem shape of lexical morphemes is one prosodic constituent in particular, namely the foot.

However, as analyses of other languages have shown, these templates have not just shaped stems and morphological outputs (e.g. Holsinger 2000, 2001, Smith 2007a, 2020). Indeed, the foot has been shown to licence segments and segmental features just as Itô (1986) and others have shown to be the case for the syllable. For instance, in his study of lenition of medial consonants across German and Dutch dialects, Holsinger (2001) demonstrated that some phonological processes target specific foot positions. These processes, he noted, could not otherwise be explained in terms of the syllable alone.

Following Smith (2020), I demonstrate in this chapter the varied ways that foot-based templates shape language. In some data, such as the Old High German *jan*-verbs, the template will provide the input for suffixation. In other data, e.g. plural formation, the template will constrain the outcome of a morphological operation. Meanwhile, in other data, phonological processes will be shaped by the foot, be it maintenance or loss of segments, the appearance of full versus reduced vowels, or even licencing of features. What the data below have in common is that the changes are driven by a foot-based template stipulating preferences.

Having defined the two foot types featured in the data in this chapter as well as having introduced the notion of foot-based templates, I now turn to the data to highlight how Vennemann's notion of preferences can help us better understand foot-driven phenomena. I begin by discussing historical data in West Germanic before demonstrating the trochee's role in Modern German and Dutch plurals.

3 Evidence for the role of the trochaic foot in West Germanic

Vowel loss and reduction in the history of the West Germanic languages provide evidence not only for the role of the moraic trochee but also for its interaction with different competing preferences and factors such as phonotactics and even morphological transparency. In this section, I begin by discussing and comparing two approaches to high vowel loss in Old Saxon *i*-stem nouns, namely my own outlined in Smith (2004, 2007b) and Vennemann's (1995) approach in which he highlights the application of the Diachronic Maxim. This discussion lays the groundwork for further accounts of *i*-loss in Old High German *jan*-verbs,

Old Frisian vowel balance, and plural formation in Modern German and Dutch. Experimental evidence supporting the role of the foot in the grammar of native speakers is also provided.

3.1 Old Saxon *i*-stem nouns

In Old Saxon, *i*-apocope impacted *i*-stem nouns based on the size or weight of the noun stem. After a heavy[2] stem ending in either a VCC or V:CC, *i* was lost as in ⁺*gasti* → *gast* 'guest' or ⁺*thra:di* → *thra:d* 'thread' (see 7 below). Conversely, *i* was retained (at least initially during Old Saxon before being lost in later stages of the language) following a light stem ending in a VC sequence, e.g. *stedi* 'place, city' as in (7).

(7) Old Saxon long vs. short stems (nom./acc. forms from Sehrt 1925; cf. also Vennemann 1995, Smith 2004, 2007b)

Heavy (long) stems		Light (short) stems
VCC	V:C	VC
gast (m.) 'guest'	*thrād* (m.) 'thread'	*stedi* (f.) 'city'
fard (f.) 'journey'	*quān* (f.) 'woman'	*uuini* (m.) 'friend'
burg (f.) 'town, city'	*wāg* (m.) 'wave'	*seli* (m.) 'room'
uurm (m.) 'worm'	*brūd* (f.) 'woman'	*friundskepi* (m.) 'friendship'

Vennemann (1995) and Fulk (2018) alike attribute this development to Prokosch's law, which stipulates a preference for stressed syllables to be bimoraic. Recall that a single heavy syllable can form a foot on its own. Conversely, a single light syllable would be considered dispreferred and would thus attract a following syllable to it to form a foot. A simple foot-based analysis accounts for the loss versus maintenance of the *i* following these nouns in terms of whether the vowel was footed or not as in (8) (cf. Smith 2004, 2007b). In these examples, the foot

---

[2] Language grammars often refer to the contrast between long and short syllable nouns in terms of heavy and light stems, respectively (cf. Braune and Eggers 1987 for Old High German; Gallée and Lochner 1910 for Old Saxon; Wright 1917). Although they generally omit any explicit reference to stress, they refer to the size of the *Wurzelsilbe*, or root syllable. Vennemann (1995: 192) clarifies the distinction by referring to the stress of the relevant stems in his analysis: "In (9) ist illustriert, wie im Altsächsischen und Althochdeutschen nach schwerer Akzentsilbe der hohe Stammvokal abfällt, nach leichter Akzentsilbe nicht." [(9) illustrates how the high stem vowel is lost after a heavy accented syllable in Old Saxon and Old High German, but not after a light accented syllable.]

structure of the original form with *i* is depicted alongside the output of *i*-loss where appropriate, namely after heavy stems.

(8) Foot structure before and after Old Saxon *i*-loss[3]

Heavy (Long)						Light (Short)		
VCC			V:CC			VC		
[H]	L	[H]	[H]	L	[H]	[L	L]	[L L]
[μμ]	μ	μμμ	[μμ]	μ	μμμ	[μ	μ]	μ μ
C_0VC.	Ci		C_0V:.	Ci		C_0V.	Ci	
f a r	di →	fard	ti:	di →	ti:d	se	li →	seli

In the examples in (8), the initial heavy syllable forms a foot on its own, leaving the following light syllable unfooted. This light syllable could then be attached directly to the prosodic word. Such an analysis argues that when the *i* is unfooted with the stem syllable, e.g. as is the case for the heavy stems, the unfooted *i* underwent apocope. In this case, the stem's heavy syllable is able to form a trochee on its own, leaving the final syllable containing the *i* unfooted and susceptible to loss. However, when the stem was light, the initial light syllable was unable to form a trochee on its own. Consequently, the syllable containing the *i* was footed with the previous light syllable via resolution, thereby protecting it from deletion during this stage of the language.[4] From a templatic perspective, if the *i* cannot be mapped onto the trochaic template, then it is lost, as is the case for the heavy stems. However, when *i* can be mapped onto the trochee as seen for the light stems, then it is retained.

In contrast to this analysis, Vennemann's (1995) foot-based approach for both Old Saxon and Old High German integrates more intimately the notion of preferences, drawing on a distinct preference for a minimal foot (F_{min}) in early West Germanic consisting of two moras. Thus, in the case of a heavy stem as in (9), the initial syllable would already satisfy the minimal bimoraic foot on its own. The subsequent light syllable containing the *i* would thus be outside the minimal foot and attached to the expanded foot, making the entire orig-

---

[3] Following apocope in the heavy (long) stems, the stem-final consonant is resyllabified into the coda of the preceding syllable. Since the question as to whether the resulting coda has two or three moras is not relevant for the analysis per se, I set it aside to retain focus on the role of the foot in shaping this language change.

[4] It is worth noting that *i* was not lost in all endings. In the Old Saxon plural *wurmi* 'worm, nom./ acc. pl.', the *i* was retained. In this case, the plural ending was long, i.e. [i:]. Consequently, it was able to form a foot on its own, meaning that it was not subject to reduction. Only short [i] in the singular forms was thus a target of apocope in these nouns.

inal expanded foot prior to apocope trimoraic, or as Vennemann (1995: 194) notes, "*mehr-als-zweimorig*" [more than bimoraic]. This preference for a bimoraic minimal foot coincides with a preference for words at this stage of the language(s) to reduce and become shorter, especially through the loss and reduction of inflectional endings (cf. Vennemann 1995; see also Salmons 2012 for discussion of reduction and loss of inflectional endings as well as footbased changes). Apocope thus serves to eliminate the additional mora in the unstressed final syllable, i.e. the syllable containing the *i* that does not fall within the bimoraic minimal foot. When the onset *t* of this now eliminated syllable is integrated into the preceding heavy syllable, i.e. the minimal foot, it does so without adding to moraic count.

(9) Vennemann's (1995: 193) analysis of apocope in Old Saxon/Old High German heavy *i*-stem nouns

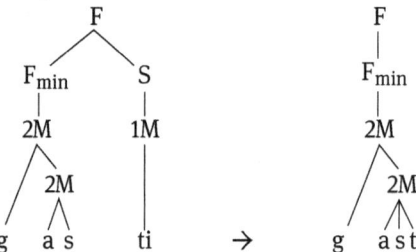

The reduction of the number of moras in the word is critical for Vennemann's approach. It is not just the shortening of the word at play in terms of segment count, but rather the eliminating of the excess mora attached to the extended foot. Vennemann (1995: 194) describes this sound change as follows: "Es hat eine echte Wortkürzung stattgefunden: Wo vor dem Lautwandel eine dreimorige Wortstruktur vorlag, die einen erweiterten Fuß ausmachte, liegt nach dem Lautwandel eine zweimorige Struktur, ein minimaler Fuß vor." [A real word shortening took place: where there had been a trimoraic word structure that built an extended foot before the sound change, there was now after the sound change a bimoraic structure, a minimal foot. Translated by author.]

So what does this mean for the light stem words, like *wini* 'friend' or *stedi* 'city'? According to Vennemann's analysis, there is no purpose to shortening words of this shape. As illustrated in (10), the initial structure containing the *i* already forms a minimal foot, i.e. it is bimoraic, with a single mora assigned to both light syllables. With the *i* already within the minimal foot, there is no need for it to undergo reduction. In other words, there is no excess mora to eliminate, and loss of *i* would simply result in another bimoraic foot yielding no prosodic improvement. In short, apocope was used not so much to shorten words per se in terms of segmental count, but rather to eliminate additional moras beyond the minimal foot.

(10) Vennemann's (1995: 193) analysis of apocope in Old Saxon/Old High German light *i*-stem nouns

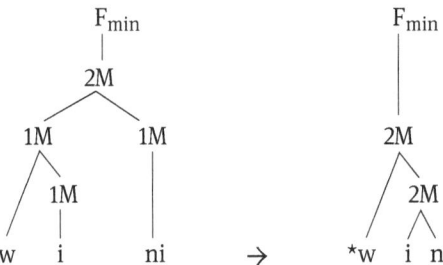

As noted, Vennemann describes the application of apocope in Old High German and Old Saxon *i*-stem nouns in terms of preferences, noting that all language changes are language improvements along a given local parameter (1995: 195). Thus, shortening of words in languages that prioritise bimoraic feet took place only when the shortening resulted in the elimination of excess moras. In sum, the drive to shorten words was not simply to create segmentally shorter words; instead, it was driven at this time by a prosodic preference to reduce excess moras.

Despite the slight differences between the analyses by both Smith (2004, 2007b) and Vennemann (1995), both analyses correctly predict the order of *i*-loss in the data from a preference-standpoint. For instance, *i* was first lost after heavy stems where the *i* would have been unfooted à la Smith, namely when *i* was least preferred to occur. However, even the more preferred footed *i* is eventually targeted for apocope. From Vennemann's perspective, *i* is first lost when it appears in the extended foot (less preferred position) rather than in the minimal foot (more preferred position) to bring the moraic count closer to two before being lost later in the languages' history after light stems where the *i* was footed within the bimoraic (minimal) foot. In terms of preferences, this means that apocope did indeed first impact less preferential structures, while initially leaving alone structures that already aligned with the bimoraic minimal foot. This is illustrated in the continuum in (11) below:

(11) *i*-loss in Old High German and Old Saxon: a preference-based perspective:

	Less preferred ←―――――――――――――――――――→ *More preferred*	
Smith (2004, 2007b)	unfooted −*i*	footed −*i*
Vennemann (1995)	foot of 3+ moras	foot = 2 moras

In sum, this initial stage of apocope, which created the distinction between the light and heavy stems, i.e. the retention and loss of *i* respectively within this lexical class, served to create a more preferred structure prosodically, as Vennemann rightly argues. In this case, we see the role of the foot in shaping this specific morphological class. It will be this approach to preferences for prosodically driven change that will guide the discussion of the remaining sets of data, whether the data are tied to a particular lexical class or morphological function (i.e. *i*-syncope in *jan*-verbs and plural formation) or a more general phonological process (i.e. Old Frisian vowel balance).

3.2 *i*-syncope in Old High German *jan*-verbs

Historically the preterite of Germanic weak verbs was formed from three parts: a verb stem, followed by a linking vowel that indicated the verb class to which the verb belonged, and finally the dental preterite ending. For the Class 1 weak verbs, or *jan*-verbs as they are also known, the intervening *i* reconstructed in Germanic between the verb stem and preterite ending arose from the vocalisation of the *j* in the *jan*-verb ending. However, by the time Old High German was documented in the mid-8th century, this vowel had been retained only following light stems, e.g. *nerita* 'saved, 1st and 3rd sg.'.[5]

Syncope of *i* in Old High German *jan*-verbs shares much in common with *i*-apocope just discussed in Old Saxon (and Old High German) in two important ways. First, both types of *i*-loss are associated with a particular lexical class, making any changes local to this morphological class. And second, *i*- is retained after so-called light stems, e.g. *knusi+ta* 'crushed, pounded, 1st and 3rd sg.' (where "+" represents the morpheme boundary between the verb stem and the dental preterite ending), but lost after heavy or polysyllabic verb stems, e.g. *teil+ta* 'divided, 1st and 3rd sg.' and *nidar+ta* 'lowered, 1st and 3rd sg.', respectively. A larger sample of words is found in (12):

---

[5] Other West Germanic languages such as Old Saxon and Old English (see 12b) had similar patterns of retention versus loss but with some additional changes beyond the scope of this chapter.

(12) a. Old High German *jan*-verbs (based on Braune and Eggers 1987; cf. Smith 2004)

Stem Type	Infinitive	Preterite	Glosses
Light	knussen	knusita	'to crush, pound'
	frummen	frumita	'to promote, encourage'
Heavy	teilen	teilta	'to divide'
	wānen	wānta	'to mean'
	hengen	hancta, hangta	'to hang'
Polysyllabic	nidaren	nidarta	'to lower'
	heilazen	heilazta	'to greet, hail'
	anazen	anazta	'to urge, drive on'

b. Behaviour of *i* based on weight of stem (Smith 2004)[6]

i. Light	⁺ner-i-da	→ OHG *nerita*, OS *nerida*, OE *nerede* 'saved, 1ˢᵗ/3ʳᵈ sg.'
ii. Heavy	⁺hōr-i-da	→ OHG *hōrta*, OS *hōrda*, OE *hiērda* 'heard, 1ˢᵗ/3ʳᵈ sg.'
	⁺drank-i-da	→ OHG *drankta*, OE *drencte* 'watered, soaked, 1ˢᵗ/3ʳᵈ sg.'
iii. Polysyll.	⁺mahal-i-ta	→ OHG *mahalta* 'vowed, pledged, 1ˢᵗ/3ʳᵈ sg.'

A foot-based analysis similar to that proposed for the Old Saxon *i*-stem nouns can account for the loss versus maintenance of the thematic vowel, but with one caveat: the *i* is retained when it can be footed with the verb stem prior to affixation of the preterite ending as in (13) below. However, when the *i* is not footed with the verbal stem, it undergoes syncope as in the heavy (13b) and polysyllabic (13c) verbal stems (from Smith 2004).

(13) a. Retention after light verb stems (ending in VC)

LL → No change		
[L	L] + ta	
[μ	μ]	
C₀V.	Ci + ta	
[ne	ri] + ta	→ nerita

---

6 A raised "⁺" before a form denotes a reconstructed form.

b. Loss after heavy verb stems (ending in VCC and V:CC)

Heavy: HL→H		
F		
[H]	L	+ta
[μμ]	μ	
C₀VC.	Ci	+ta
C₀VV.	Ci	+ta
[tr an]	ki	+ta → trancta
[h ō]	ri	+ta → hōrta

c. Loss after polysyllabic verb stems

Polysyllabic: LLL→ LH				Polysyllabic HHL→ HH			
[L	L]	L	+ ta	[H]	[H]	L	
[μ	μ]	μ		[μμ]	μμ	μ	
C₀V.	CV	Ci	+ ta	C₀VC.	C₀VC		
[ni	da]	ri	+ ta → nidarta	[am]	[bah]	ti	+ta → ambahta

As seen in the example in (13a), when *i* is mapped to a foot, then it is retained as with the light stems. However, following a heavy or polysyllabic stem as in (13b) and (13c), the *i* is lost. Now, the reader may ask, why is the syllable containing the *i* not simply footed with the dental preterite ending, e.g. [ni.da] [ri+ta]? The answer is simple: the dental preterite ending of the *jan*-verbs prefers attaching to the right edge of a foot. Thus the +*ta* cannot be in the middle of a foot, but rather must attach to the end of a foot, e.g. [ni.dar] + *ta*. In other words, the end of the verb stem must align with the end of a foot. Thus, the preference for retaining *i* in these verbs does not apply across the whole word as it did for the *i*-stem nouns but rather applies to the verb stem itself:

(14) *i*-loss in Old High German *jan*-verbs: a preference-based perspective

Less preferred   *More preferred*
◄───►

preterite suffix does not   preterite suffix attaches to
attach to right edge of foot   right edge of foot

OR: right edge of verb stem   OR: right edge of verb stem
does not align with right edge   aligns with right edge of foot
of foot

In Smith (2004), I refer to this prosodically-defined stem shape, namely one in which the right edge of the verb stem aligns with the right edge of the foot, in terms of a template needed for suffixation of the dental preterite ending. In this way, mapping the verb stem to this foot-shaped template serves to drive sound change by imposing the preference(s) outlined above. Drawing on Vennemann's (1995) analysis for *i*-stem nouns, *i*-loss in *jan*-verbs can then be argued to be another instance where the shortening of words is done less in terms of losing segments and more in terms of eliminating excess moras that do not fit the template for the verb stem. Since the [LL] stem shape would include the footed *i*, the vowel is retained longer in this position and the dental preterite ending is affixed directly to the right edge of the verbal stem with the *i* intact. Indeed, no repair is needed to eliminate *i* since its loss would neither change nor improve the moraic structure of the stem. In short, there is no excess moraic material intervening between the stem and the preterite suffix needing to be eliminated. However, in the case of heavy and polysyllabic verbs, the unfooted *i* is removed, ensuring that the preterite suffix is able to attach directly to the right edge of the foot containing the verbal stem with no intervening segmental or prosodic material. In this way, the preference for the alignment of the verb stem with the foot edge is not merely a phonological phenomenon but rather a necessary precursor for a morphological process, namely suffixation. This alone distinguishes the foot-based preferences from those outlined for syllables since the foot level appears to be where phonological preferences intersect with morphological preferences, such as the phonological shape of stems needed for suffixation to occur. This interaction, however, also highlights places were preferences come into conflict.

As Vennemann (1988) rightfully notes, language improvement along one parameter can nevertheless result in worsening along a different parameter. In the natural tendency toward shortening words by eliminating high vowels that are either unfooted or outside of the minimal foot (depending on the theoretical approach), such loss can create conflict with two other preferences: 1) the preference for morphological transparency between stems and suffixes or 2) more fundamentally, the preference for words to adhere to a language's phonotactics. Consider the examples below in (15) and (16):

(15) Retention of *i* after heavy or polysyllabic stems in *t* or *d* (Smith 2004)
      Exception   OHG Manuscript
      chundita   Frg. 51. 53
      cunditun, cunditi Tatian
      ahtitun   Tatian
      zundeta   Mcp.
      baldita   F

As the examples in (15) illustrate, when the verb root ends in a *d* or *t*, *i* is retained even for heavy stem verbs. It could be argued that this retention preserves morphological transparency between the verb and the preterite suffix, thereby ensuring the past-tense meaning remains clear. Thus, instead of the expected *chundta* or *cundti* in the indicative and optative forms, respectively, the *i* is retained: *chundita* and *cunditi*. In this way, the preference for morphological transparency has a higher priority than a preference for the suffix to be added to the right edge of a (minimal) foot. This higher priority for morphological transparency is particularly interesting in light of the fact that suffixation of the preterite itself plays a key role in driving syncope, ensuring the suffix attaches to the edge of a (minimal) foot. However, prosodic preferences are sacrificed here to ensure morphological transparency and therewith clarity of communication.

This leaves us with the conflict between prosodic preferences and phonotactics. When loss of *i* would violate the phonotactics and therewith the pronunciation of a given word, two potential "repairs" can be found in the data. Either an anaptyctic vowel, typically *a* or *e*, is inserted to break up the difficult cluster as (16a) or syncope is blocked altogether as in (16b).

(16)   Addressing phonotactic violations with *i*-syncope (Smith 2004)

	a. Anaptyxis	b. *i*-loss blocked
+bauhnjan	pauhh*a*nta	bauhn*i*da
	pouch*e*nta	gabauhn*i*ta

While anaptyxis and blocking of *i*-loss preserve the phonotactics and therewith the pronounceability of the verbs, both processes also conversely work against the tendency (if not preference) to shorten the words from a segmental perspective. Yet despite this superficial similarity, each process has a different prosodic consequence as illustrated in (17):

(17)   Prosodic outputs of phonotactic "repair" strategies with *i*-loss

a. Anaptyctic Vowel				b. *i*-loss blocking			
[H]	[H]	+ ta		[H]	L	+da	
[μμ]	[μμ]			[μμμ]	μ		
C₀VV.	C₀VC]	+ ta		C₀VVC.	C₀V	+da	
[pau]	[chan]	+ ta	pauchanta	[bauh]	ni	+da	bauhnida

As a means of ensuring both transparency of morphemes and phonotactics, anaptyxis breaks up the [xnt] cluster in (17a) arising from syncope by inserting the vowel within the verb stem itself. The result is the alignment of the right edge of the verb stem with the right edge of a foot. This in turn allows the dental preterite suffix to attach, as is preferred, directly to the right edge of the foot with no intervening segmental or prosodic material. This is notable because the alternative solution shown in (17b), namely the failure to delete *i* in examples like *bauhnida*, may preserve phonotactics but does so by sacrificing the prosodic preference, i.e. template, for suffixation of the preterite ending to the end of a foot. Although anaptyxis results in a prosodically preferred structure and one that would adhere to the foot-based template used for preterite formation of *jan*-verbs, both anaptyxis and blocking of *i*-loss nevertheless co-exist as "repair" solutions in Old High German. Yet despite the prosodic differences between the two processes, the choice of the specific strategy appears to be manuscript dependent.

As the *jan*-verb data illustrate, the prosodic preferences associated with foot-based phenomena may potentially interact not only with preferences from other levels of the prosodic hierarchy, e.g. phonotactics (i.e. syllable level), but also with morphological preferences. When this happens, it appears, at least from the phenomena detailed thus far, that preferences related to phonotactics and morphological transparency may be more highly prioritised than prosodic preferences. And thus, language improvements in terms of prosody can be blocked if they were to negatively impact those phonotactic (i.e. pronounceability) and morphological preferences. In this way, prosodic improvements are checked against these more highly prioritised preferences before proceeding. And these preferences, rather than being inviolable constraints, are indeed violable and interactive with other language preferences guiding language change and improvement.

3.3 Old Frisian vowel balance

To this point, the data discussed have focussed on vowel loss within specific lexical classes based on the footing of the vowel. Old Frisian vowel balance offers a slight variation on this theme. Unlike other Old West Germanic languages whose first written documents date from much earlier, e.g. roughly mid-7th century for Old English, mid-8th century for Old High German, and 9th century for Old Saxon, the earliest Old Frisian texts we have date back to just the 1200s. Consequently, Old Frisian texts were written during the middle periods of the other West Germanic sister languages. Despite the time discrepancy, remnants of a contrast between heavy and light stems nevertheless exist in the East Frisian Riustringer manuscripts dating back to about 1300, with traces in some later dialects. Unlike *i*-syncope and apocope, vowel balance was a general phonological process rather than one tied to one lexical class or morphological process.

As illustrated in (18), full vowels *i* and *u* were found following light or short stems ending in a VC sequence, e.g. *godi* 'God, dat.sg.' and *sunu* 'son, nom./acc. sg.'. However, following long (or heavy) stems as well as polysyllabic stems, *e* and *o* respectively appear instead. These vowels have been argued to be reduced vowels corresponding to *i* and *u*.

(18) Old Frisian vowel balance (Smith 2007a, 2020)
Full vowels *i* and *u* appear after short stems (VC)

i *u*

god<u>i</u> 'God, dat. sg.' *sun<u>u</u>* 'son, nom./acc. sg.'
cum<u>i</u> 'come, 3rd pers. sg. pres. opt.' *skip<u>u</u>* 'ship, nom. pl.'
wet<u>i</u>r 'water, nom./acc. sg., nom. pl.' *skil<u>u</u>n* 'should, must, 3rd pers. pl. pres. indic.'
ekim<u>i</u>n 'come, past participle' *sik<u>u</u>r* 'not guilty, predicative'
to sem<u>i</u>ne 'together' *him<u>u</u>le* 'heaven, dat. sg.'

Reduced vowels *e* and *o* appear after long (V:C and VCC) and polysyllabic stems

e *o*

hus<u>e</u> 'house, dat. sg.' *ag<u>o</u>n* 'eye, nom./acc. pl.
liod<u>e</u> 'people, nom. pl.' *bok<u>o</u>n* 'book, dat. pl.'
drocht<u>e</u>n 'Lord, nom. sg.' *gers<u>o</u>* 'grass, nom. pl.'
wrald<u>e</u> 'world, dat./gen. sg.' *angl<u>o</u>n* 'angel, dat. pl.'
himul<u>e</u> 'heaven, dat. sg.' *wetir<u>o</u>n* 'water, dat. pl.'
tholad<u>e</u> 'endure, 3rd sg., pret. indic.' *helig<u>o</u>n* 'holy, dat. pl.'

The result of vowel balance is a series of contrasts highlighting the full and reduced vowels as in (19):

(19) Word pairs showing the effects of vowel balance in Old Frisian (Smith 2007a)

Full Vowels Reduced Vowels

god<u>i</u>s 'God, gen. sg.' *god<u>e</u>s* 'good, gen. sg.'
far<u>i</u> 'travel, 3rd sg., pres. opt.' *for<u>e</u>* 'travel, 3rd sg., pret. opt.
for<u>i</u> 'before' *for<u>e</u>* 'travel, 3rd sg., pret. opt.
skil<u>u</u> 'should, must, 1st pl. pres. indic.' *skill<u>e</u>* 'should, must, 1st sg. pres. opt.'

The contrast between *godis* 'God, gen. sg.', with its short stem vowel, and *godes* 'good, gen. sg.', with its long stem vowel and the full versus reduced vowels that follow each stem respectively highlight the effects of vowel balance nicely. In both cases, the genitive singular ending is underlyingly -*is*. While it could be argued that the assumption of vowel length here is circular, i.e. assuming vowel length based on the appearance of *i* versus *e*, the verb contrasts support such an assertion. Compare *fari* and *fore* for a moment. Although the contrast here is based in part on vowel quality, Class VI strong verbs also differ between singular present and preterite stems in terms of vowel length, with a short *a* in the present stem and long *ō* in the preterite forms. This contrast in vowel length can thus account for the differential behaviour of the inflectional endings. Likewise, the single *l* in *skilu* 'should/must, 1ˢᵗ pers. pl. indic.' indicates a light stem and is accompanied by the full vowel *i*, while a couple of factors suggest that the optative form *skille* is heavy, namely the geminate *ll* and the reduced vowel *e* in the ending.

So what does this mean for a foot-based analysis? When the vowels *i* and *u* were footed as in (20a), they appeared as full vowels. Conversely, when unfooted in the Riustring dialect of Old Frisian as in (20b), they appeared as their reduced counterparts.

(20) Old Frisian vowel balance: a foot-based analysis (cf. Smith 2020)

a. Foot structure in light stems: full vowels		b. Foot structure in heavy stems: reduced vowels	
F	Foot level	F	Foot level
[L L]	Syllabic level	[H] L	Syllabic level
μ μ	Moraic level	μμ μ	Moraic level
[sti.di]	Segmental level	[wral] de	Segmental level

Simply put, the foot preserved the high vowels from reduction and eventual loss as seen in some modern Frisian dialects:

(21) Vowel loss, reduction, or maintenance in Modern Frisian dialects (Smith 2020)

Dialect	Light first syllable (Level-stress)	Heavy first syllable
Wursten Frisian (Smith and van Leyden 2007)	/(hood)-mikiir/ 'hat maker' /nukuude/ 'naked'	/(kon)-jootər/ 'pot moulder'
Wangeroog Frisian (Kock 1904)	hunə 'chicken' (OFr. hona) stidi 'stead' (OFr. stidi) sxypu 'ship' (OFr. skipu)	móᵘn 'moon' (OFr. môna) þûm 'thumb' (OFr. thûma)

In Wursten Frisian, the contrast between the light and heavy weight of the first syllable continues to impact some contrasts between full and reduced vowels, respectively, while in other dialects, such as Wangeroog as recorded by Kock in 1904, the vowels after many heavy first syllables have undergone full reduction, i.e. apocope, but are retained after an initial light stem.

Examining these changes from a syllabic perspective fails to account for the changes or the location of the changes within the word. But when examined from the perspective of the foot, these developments have a unified explanation, namely adherance to the preferences of the foot-based template. In sum, the foot appears to preserve vowels against loss or reduction in Old Frisian vowel balance as it did in the Old Saxon and Old High German data. While Old Frisian vowel balance reflects a trend towards vowel reduction (rather than word shortening), the preference is for full vowels to appear within the bimoraic foot. Indeed, the appearance of full high vowels reinforces the boundaries of the foot as well as the contrast between heavy and light word stems, with full vowels within the foot and reduced vowels outside of the initial foot. Seen from a templatic perspective, the minimally bimoraic foot is the prosodic unit that ensures the maintenance of full vowels:

(22) Preference for high vowels in Old Frisian vowel balance
Less preferred *More preferred*

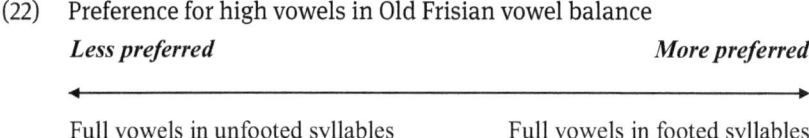

Full vowels in unfooted syllables   Full vowels in footed syllables

The Diachronic Maxim correctly predicts that the less preferred structures will be targeted for change before the more preferred structures since both reduction and apocope have been evidenced for the less preferred structure, namely the unfooted full vowels.

To this point, the discussion has reflected the Diachronic Maxim, where language change first impacts those structures that are less preferred before they impact those that are more preferred. Likewise, we have seen the importance of the foot in shaping these changes. But can we ascribe a synchronic function to the foot in shaping language? Is the trochee, for example, an active part of a speaker's grammar, shaping the way the speaker produces words? If so, such evidence would reinforce the notion that the trochee in general, and the trochaic template in particular, is capable of shaping language and can thus be argued to have played an active role in the West Germanic languages over their recorded history. These questions guide the remaining discussion.

3.4 Plural formation in Modern German: Experimental evidence for the trochee

In contrast to the weight-sensitive moraic trochaic at work in the early West Germanic languages, the trochee of Modern German and Dutch tends towards a bisyllabic trochee.⁷ This trochee has been argued to account for divergent changes and patterns in the modern languages ranging from lenition in onsets of weak syllables and deletion in consonant clusters (Holsinger 2000, 2001; see also Smith 2020 for an overview of these and more changes) to shaping lexical classes and morphological processes such as plural formation in German and Dutch and even Dutch diminutive formation. In this section, I outline the foot's role in shaping plurals in German and Dutch before presenting experimental data supporting the existence of the foot in the grammar of native speakers.

3.4.1 Prosodically-driven plural formation in Dutch and German

Despite differences in the plural suffixes at work in Standard German and Dutch, plural formation in both languages is driven by the bisyllabic trochee. In Dutch, if the singular already ends in a trochee, then the plural ending -s is typically affixed so as to maintain the trochee as in (23a). However, when the noun does not end in a trochee in the singular as in (23b), -en (pronounced as [ə]) is typically added to align the end of the plural with a trochee.⁸

(23) Plural formation in Standard Dutch (cf. Smith 2020)

a. Stem is syllabic trochee: add -s [όσ] → [όσ]	b. Stem is not a syllabic trochee: add -en [ό] → [όσ]
moeder – moeders 'mother – mothers'	*boek – boeken* 'book – books'
natie – naties 'nation – nations'	*vrou – vrouwen* 'woman – women'
lepel – lepels 'spoon – spoons'	*man – mannen* 'man – men'

---

7 In truth, many German and Dutch dialects continue to show evidence of weight-sensitive trochees shaping the languages, such as in plurals and diminutive formation (cf. Smith 2004, 2007b, 2020), although the standard languages reflect a shift towards the bisyllabic trochee. It appears that if a language has a moraic trochee where a single heavy syllable and two light syllables can both form a foot, it can also have a bisyllabic foot.

8 Dutch plural formation admittedly has additional rules that appear to contradict these generalisations. For instance, in nouns derived from adjectives that already end in schwa, the -en ending is used instead of -s regardless of stress position, e.g. *werkende – werkenden* 'working person – working people', *gepensioneerde – gepensioneerden* 'retiree – retirees' (examples from https://www.dutchgrammar.com/en/?n=NounsAndArticles.11-Draft). On the other hand, -s is the commonly used ending for foreign words, acronyms, etc. Moreover, it could be argued that (extra) heavy final suffixes build their own foot, thus accounting for use of -s, e.g. [micro][foon] – [micro][foons] 'microphone – microphones'. Despite this additional complexity in plural formation rules, the overall tendency is for the choice of plural ending in Standard Dutch to be driven by the prosodic shape of the singular noun stem.

A similar tendency exists in German, where syllabic endings, i.e. *-e*, *-en*, and *-er*, are used with nouns not ending in a trochee, e.g. *Frau+en* 'women', *Männ+er* 'men', while the non-syllabic *–n* or zero endings are typically used with nouns already ending in a trochee, e.g. *Tafel+n* 'tables', *Lehrer+Ø* 'teacher'. This larger pattern is illustrated in (24) below:

(24) Plural formation in High German (cf. Smith 2020)

Stem is already a syllabic trochee: ['σσ] → ['σσ]			Stem is not a syllabic trochee: ['σ] → ['σσ]		
Ta feln	'tables'	*-n*	*Uh ren*	'clocks'	*-en*
Tan ten	'aunts'		*Frau en*	'women'	
Nich ten	'nieces'		*Tü ren*	'doors'	
Leh rer	'teachers'	No ending	*Freun de*	'friends'	*-e*
Fen ster	'windows'		*Stif te*	'pencils'	
On kel	'uncles'		*Jah re*	'years'	
Vä ter	'fathers'	No ending	*Bü cher*	'books'	*-er* (with or
Brü der	'brothers'	(With umlaut)	*Wör ter*	'words'	without
Vö gel	'birds'		*Kin der*	'children'	umlaut)

In both the Dutch and German data, the choice of plural ending helps align the end of the plural with a bisyllabic trochee. Thus, if nouns already end in a trochee in the singular, the non-syllabic plural ending ensures that the plural remains trochaic. However, for nouns not ending in a trochee, the syllabic plural endings add the extra unstressed syllable to fit the plural to the trochaic template illustrated below in (25).

(25) Template for German and Dutch plurals
    [Ft]#   Word-final foot
    ['σσ]   Bisyllabic trochee
    |
    ə   Preference for schwa syllable

This template shows the preference for aligning the right edge of plurals with the right edge of a trochee, or in other words, a preference for plurals to end in a trochee. Consequently the preferences embodied in this template reflect a phonological or prosodic preference for word-final trochees that relate to a specific morphological class/process, i.e. plural forms. As noted above, this association of prosodic preferences with specific morphological classes and processes sets foot-based preferences apart from Vennemann's syllabic preferences, which were focussed on phonetic (or phonological) environment regardless of morphological or lexical classes. Added to this prosodic-morphological interaction is a tendency for these plurals to also reflect a segmental preference: plurals tend to (but do not always) end in a schwa syllable, namely one ending in a schwa, [ɐ], or syllabic liquid or nasal. In other words, the weak branch of the trochee, i.e. the second syllable, preferentially contains a weak vowel or syllabic sonorant. This tendency is helped along by a more general tendency for bisyllabic nouns in German and Dutch to already end in schwa syllables, e.g. German *Vater* 'father', *Tafel* 'table, tablet', *Artikel* 'article', *Boden* 'ground, floor', *Freude* 'joy'; Dutch *vader* 'father', *bodem* 'ground, floor', *haven* 'harbour', *schande* 'shame', and even *letsel* 'injury, harm' and *overblijfsel* 'remainder, remains'. This means that when the non-syllabic plural endings are added, the final syllable remains a schwa syllable. For the non-trochaic singulars, however, like German *Buch – Bücher* or Dutch *boek – boeken* 'book – books', the plural ending provides the final unstressed schwa syllable that builds the word-final trochee. This additional preference for schwa syllables, or schwallables (cf. Booij 2002), means an additional cross-level interaction at the morphology-prosody interface involving a segmental preference.

This then leads us to ask two subsequent questions. First, was this prosodic tendency for plurals to be trochaic inherited from earlier stages of the language history? And second, even if this tendency is the result of the language history, does it also exist as a psychological reality in the grammars of actual native speakers today?

3.4.2 The historical development of plurals in German

To answer the first question, we can compare noun plurals from Old High German and Middle High German (MHG). As the data in (26) illustrate, the weakening of word-final vowels and syllables from Old High German to Middle High German resulted in plurals that appeared to become more trochaic. The polysyllabic genitive (and dative) plural endings found in Old High German were not trochaic but did frequently reduce to single syllables by MHG, e.g. OHG *lemb+i.ro* → MHG *lemb+er* 'lambs, g.pl.' and OHG *lemb+i.rum* → MHG *lemb+ern* 'lambs, d.pl.' The result was a plural ending in Middle High German that appears to be more trochaic in many cases.

(26) Plurals in Old High German and Middle High German (Wright 1917)
'lamb', strong neuter noun   'tongue', weak feminine noun

	OHG		MHG		OHG		MHG
N Sg.	lamb	N Sg.	lamp	N Sg.	zunga	N Sg.	zunge
N.Pl.	lembir	N Pl.	lember	N Pl.	zungūn	N Pl.	zungen
A Pl.	lembir	A Pl.	lember	A Pl.	zungūn	A Pl.	zungen
G Pl.	lembĭro	G Pl.	lember	G Pl.	zungōno	G Pl.	zungen
D Pl.	lembirum	D Pl.	lembern	D Pl.	zungōm	D Pl.	zungen

Despite this trend, however, some nouns and noun classes had forms that reflected the suffixation of plural endings without regard for the non-trochaic plurals that resulted:

(27) Middle High German plurals, strong masculine first declension (Wright, 1917)

tac 'day'		*kil* 'quill'		*engel* 'angel'	
N Sg.	tac	N Sg.	kil	N Sg.	engel
NAG Pl.	tage	NAG Pl.	kil(e)	NAG Pl.	engel(e)
D Pl.	tagen	D Pl.	kil(e)n	D Pl.	engel(e)n

As Wright (1917: 38) notes, "masculine polysyllabic nouns ending in *-el, -em, -en, -er*, when their stem-syllable is long" are declined like *engel* in (27). These are the nouns that lack any ending in Modern German plurals, thereby ensuring their trochaic shape, e.g. *der Vogel – die Vögel* 'bird – birds', *Boden – die Böden* 'floor/ground-floors', and *der Sommer – die Sommer* 'summer – summers'. And yet during Middle High German, they were not yet uniformly trochaic. Indeed, as Wright (1917: 38) continues, "those ending in *-em, -en* generally retain the *e* in the dative plural" and "polysyllabic nouns with short stem-syllables fluctuate between the retention or loss of the *e*, as gen. sing. *vogeles* or *vogels*, dat. sing. and nom. acc. pl. *vogele* or *vogel*". In other words, during this time period, the loss of *e* had not yet been completed and the tendency for plurals to become trochaic was likewise not yet complete. Nevertheless, tracking these developments highlights that the trochaic preference for German (and likely also Dutch) plurals arose as a result of the weakening of final vowels and therewith the reduction of polysyllabic plural endings to a single syllable. Another final consequence of the vowel and syllable reduction is worth noting. This reduction of stem-final vowels to schwa in polysyllabic nouns, as well as the reduction of the full vowels in the Old High German plural suffixes to schwa syllables, accounts for the plural template combining the trochaic preference with the preference for the trochee ending in a schwa syllable.

But one final question remains: Is the plural pattern observed in Modern German (and Dutch) merely a byproduct of this vocalic and syllabic reduction in the history of German (and Dutch)? Or is the trochaic preference for plural formation an active part of a speaker's grammar? To answer this question, I turn to a brief discussion of experimental evidence testing native speakers' plural intuitions.

3.4.3 Experimental evidence for trochaic plurals

The first set of evidence demonstrating that the trochee is a part of a native speaker's grammar for plurals comes from Kauschke, Renner, and Domahs' (2013) study testing the formation of German plurals by native German speaking children with and without language learning impairments. This study built on a claim found in the literature regarding the relationship between prosody and morphological acquisition. According to Demuth (2009), the acquisition of grammatical morphemes appears to be closely tied to children's development of prosodic representations. From this it follows that "morphological acquisition cannot be viewed independently of the acquisition of prosody" (Kauschke, Renner, and Domahs 2013: 576). Previous research had already highlighted the mismatch between general prosodic acquisition and morphological acquisition of plural endings: while typically developing native German speaking children generally master the primary aspects of German word stress and foot structure by the age of 2.6 years (Grimm 2010, Penner 2000), their acquisition of the morphological complexity of German plural suffixes has been shown to lag further behind for much longer (Kauschke, Renner, and Domahs 2013). Thus, to test the prosody-morphology relationship for German plural acquisition, Kauschke, Renner, and Domahs used a plural-elicitation task consisting of 60 real words and 20 pseudowords to compare the plural production by typically developing children and those with speech delays. What they found was that typically developing children showed a clear bias for producing trochaic plurals while the speech-language-impaired children did not. Moreover, even when the typically developing children produced incorrect plural forms, their productions tended towards bisyllabic trochees. These results underscore the tendency for children to detect the prosodic preference for plurals even while they have not yet worked out the correct plural suffix required for the words.

A similar preference for trochaic plural forms was seen in a recent study by Smith, Schuhmann, and Champenois (2016). A total of 54 adult native German speakers completed two tasks. For the production task, subjects were asked to produce plurals of nonsense words, e.g. *Zaupen*, *Wenfel*, in a plural-elicitation task. For the perception task, they were asked to rate how good or bad correct and incorrect plurals, e.g. *Schlüssel, Schlüssels*, or *Schlüsselen*, sounded. In this last task, the incorrect plurals included both trochaic and non-trochaic forms. The results showed a bias for trochaic plurals similar to that found by Kauschke, Renner, and Domahs (2013). For the production task, the native German speakers overwhelmingly produced plurals that were trochaic in shape (91.6%), even when they did not necessarily agree on the specific plural suffix to use. For the plural rating perception task, native speakers not surprisingly gave correct plurals a more favourable rating than the incorrect plurals. But more to the point, trochaic plurals were more preferred than their non-trochaic counterparts whether the plural forms were correct or not.

What the experimental evidence demonstrates is that native speakers, beginning already as children, have a clear preference for plurals that adhere to the bisyllabic trochee. In this way, the trochee serves as a template to guide the formation of the plurals. In sum, the trochaic template is indeed an active part of a native speakers' grammar and intuition. Thus, the trochaic plurals in German, and we might assume Dutch as well, are not only an accidental outcome of vowel reduction in the language's history but are also part of the active grammar of speakers.

4 Conclusion

At the outset of this chapter, I noted that the data would allow us to apply Vennemann's notion of preferences to foot-based changes and patterns. However, drawing on the foot is not simply moving our gaze one level up the prosodic hierarchy. While syllable-based preferences and changes tended to be associated with phonological changes without reference to lexical classes or morphological operations, foot-based preferences as have been shown can either impact the phonological patterns of languages and dialects, e.g. Old Frisian vowel balance, or be tied to specific lexical or morphological classes, e.g. *i*-stem nouns and *jan*-verbs in Old High German and Old Saxon or plural formation in Modern German and Dutch.

As a template, the foot can licence which features are permitted in which foot positions, e.g. Old Frisian vowel balance, or it can delimit the length of words based less on segmental count and more on the prosodic shape of the word. Indeed, as the *i*-stem nouns and *jan*-verbs illustrate, loss of segmental material in these data is better understood in terms of reducing excess moras rather than just shortening stems and words to make them shorter. In this way, light stems retain *i* because there is no motivation to eliminate a vowel that is already footed and thus is not adding excess moraic structure. These data help us rethink word shortening: it is not always about reducing the number of segments.

The template can also reflect the intersection of not only prosodic preferences but also morphological and segmental preferences. The morphological preferences stipulate, e.g., that a stem needs to align with a prosodic boundary as in the suffixation of the dental preterite to the *jan*-verbs, or it can stipulate the output of some morphological operation as seen in the German and Dutch plurals. However, this intersection of morphological and prosodic preferences can also result in a conflict between preferences. When morphological transparency is negatively impacted or where pronounceability is threatened, prosodic preferences can be set aside. Indeed, the interaction and conflict between preferences help us better understand the complex nature of language in general and the complexity of the foot's role in shaping language via prosodic templates.

What is apparent from the data discussed is a clear role for the foot where the syllable alone fails to explain what is happening. And yet many of the same principles championed and proposed as part of the Preference Laws for syllable structure can be applied to analyses drawing on the foot. For instance, changes may manifest themselves in terms of preferences for vowels to be footed, for fully articulated consonants to appear in strong branches of feet, for words to conform to the foot of the language in question, etc. Likewise, Vennemann's maxims, which he initially developed as part of his work on understanding syllable-based sound change, help us better comprehend the direction of language change, where the less preferred structures undergo changes and repairs first.

As Macken and Salmons (1997) rightfully state, Vennemann's work on preferences shifted the landscape of our understanding of language change, providing a mechanism to explain motivations at the syllable level. As we continue to examine language data, my hope is that more linguists will consider the role of the foot in shaping language change and examine ways that the Diachronic Maxim can explain the "messy middle" of language change in progress, where those first structures in flux are those that are less preferred than others. The contrast between long and short stems during the earlier stages of language change highlights the middle before all such vowels are ultimately lost. Similarly, it could explain differences within and between dialects as manifest in cluster simplification in medial onsets (e.g. Holsinger 2000, see also Smith 2020), Dutch diminutives (cf. Smith 2007b), and even Frisian dialects with and without signs of vowel balance.

What is clear is that none of this research into the foot would have been possible without Vennemann's work on the Preference Laws, which brought to light the role that prosody could play in motivating language change, rather than relegating prosodic structures to being merely phonetic environments described by linguists to account for where language change occurs. While the role of the foot may not be as critical in some languages as it has been in Germanic, I invite other scholars to revisit the language families they work on to see if the foot or foot-based preferences might help tie seemingly divergent language phenomena together. As the small set of data from West Germanic illustrate, even vastly different language data find a common structure and source: the trochaic foot.

References

Booij, Geert. 1998. Phonological output constraints in morphology. In Wolfgang Kehrein & Richard Wiese (eds.), *Phonology and morphology of the Germanic languages*, 143–163. Tübingen: Max Niemeyer.

Booij, Geert. 2002. Prosodic restrictions on affixation in Dutch. In Geert Booij & Jaap van Marle (eds.), *Yearbook of morphology 2001*, 183–201. Dordrecht: Springer.

Braune, Wilhelm & Hans Eggers. 1987. *Althochdeutsche Grammatik*. 14th edn. Tübingen: Max Niemeyer.

Demuth, Katherine. 2009. The prosody of syllables, words and morphemes. In Edith Bavin (ed.), *Cambridge handbook of child language*, 183–198. Cambridge: Cambridge University Press.

Downing, Laura. 2006. *Canonical forms in prosodic morphology*. Oxford: Oxford University Press.

Eisenberg, Peter. 1991. Syllabische Struktur und Wortakzent: Prinzipien der Prosodik deutscher Wörter. *Zeitschrift für Sprachwissenschaft* 10. 37–64.

Fulk, Robert D. 2018. *A comparative grammar of early Germanic languages*. Amsterdam: John Benjamins.

Gallée, Johan Hendrik & Johannes Lochner. 1910. *Altsächsische Grammatik*. Halle: Max Niemeyer.

Grimm, Angela. 2010. *The development of early prosodic word structure in child German: Simplex words and compounds*. Potsdam: University of Potsdam dissertation.

Holsinger, David. 2000. *Lenition in Germanic: Prosodic templates in sound change*. Madison, WI: University of Wisconsin–Madison dissertation.

Holsinger, David. 2001. Weak position constraints: The role of prosodic templates in contrast distribution. *Zentrum für Allgemeine Sprachwissenschaft Papers in Linguistics* 19. 91–118.

Hulst, Harry van der & Jan G. Kooij. 1998. Prosodic choices and the Dutch nominal plural. In Wolfgang Kehrein & Richard Wiese (eds.), *Phonology and morphology of the Germanic languages*, 187–197. Tübingen: Max Niemeyer.

Itô, Junko. 1986. *Syllable theory in prosodic phonology*. Amherst, MA: University of Massachusetts Amherst dissertation.

Kauschke, Christina, Lena Renner & Ulrike Domahs. 2013. Prosodic constraints on inflected words: An area of difficulty for German-speaking children with specific language impairment? *Clinical Linguistics & Phonetics* 27. 574–593.

Kock, Axel. 1904. Vocalbalance im Altfriesischen. *Beiträge zur Geschichte der deutschen Sprache und Literatur* 29. 175–193.

Macken, Marlys & Joseph Salmons. 1997. Prosodic templates in sound change. *Diachronica* 14. 33–66.

McCarthy, John & Alan Prince. 1995. Prosodic morphology. In John Goldsmith (ed.), *The handbook of phonological theory*, 318–366. Cambridge, MA: Blackwell.

Murray, Robert & Vennemann, Theo. 1983. Sound change and syllabic structure in Germanic phonology. *Language* 59. 514–528.

Penner, Zvi. 2000. Phonologische Entwicklung: Eine Übersicht. In Hannelore Grimm (ed.), *Sprachentwicklung*, 41–103. Göttingen: Hogrefe.
Salmons, Joseph. 2012. *A history of German: What the past reveals about today's language*. Oxford: Oxford University Press.
Sehrt, Edward H. 1925. *Vollständiges Wörterbuch zum* Heliand *und zur altsächsischen* Genesis. Göttingen: Vandenhoeck & Ruprecht; Baltimore: Johns Hopkins Press.
Smith, Laura Catharine. 2004. *Cross-level interactions in West Germanic phonology and morphology*. Madison, WI: University of Wisconsin–Madison dissertation.
Smith, Laura Catharine. 2007a. Old Frisian vowel balance and its relationship to West Germanic apocope and syncope. In Rolf Bremmer Jr., Stephen Laker & Oebele Vries (eds.), *Advances in Old Frisian philology*, 379–410. Amsterdam: Rodopi.
Smith, Laura Catharine. 2007b. The resilience of prosodic templates in the history of West Germanic. In Joseph Salmons & Shannon Dubenion-Smith (eds.), *Historical linguistics 2005: Selected papers from the 17th International Conference on Historical Linguistics, Madison, 31 July–5 August 2005*, 351–365. Amsterdam: John Benjamins.
Smith, Laura Catharine. 2020. The role of foot structure in Germanic. In Richard Page & Michael Putnam (eds.), *Cambridge handbook of Germanic linguistics*, 49–72. Cambridge: Cambridge University Press.
Smith, Laura Catharine, Katharina Schuhmann & Charlotte Champenois. 2016. The role of prosody in shaping German plurals: A study. Paper presented at GLAC 2016, Iceland, May 20–22, 2016.
Smith, Laura Catharine & Adam Ussishkin. 2015. The role of prosodic templates in diachrony and dialects: Prosodically-driven language change. In Patrick Honeybone & Joseph Salmons (eds.), *The Oxford handbook of historical phonology*, 262–288. Oxford: Oxford University Press. https://doi.org/10.1093/oxfordhb/9780199232819.013.028
Smith, Norval & Klaske van Leyden. 2007. The unusual outcome of a level-stress situation: In the case of Wursten Frisian. *The North-Western European Language Evolution* 52. 31–66.
Ussishkin, Adam. 2005. A fixed prosodic theory of nonconcatenative templatic morphology. *Natural Language and Linguistic Theory* 23. 169–218.
Vennemann, Theo 1988. *Preference laws for syllable structure and the explanation of sound change: With special reference to German, Germanic, Italian, and Latin*. Berlin: de Gruyter.
Vennemann, Theo. 1995. Der Zusammenbruch der Quantität im Spätmittelalter und sein Einfluß auf die Metrik. In Hans Fix (ed.), *Quantätsproblematik und Metrik: Greifswalder Symposion zur germanischen Grammatik*, 195–223. Amsterdam: Rodopi.
Wiese, Richard. 2000. *The phonology of German*. Oxford: Oxford University Press.
Wiese, Richard 2001. How prosody shapes German words and morphemes. *Interdisciplinary Journal for Germanic Linguistics and Semiotic Analysis* 6. 155–184.
Wright, Joseph. 1917. *A Middle High German primer: With grammar, notes, and glossary*, 3rd edn. Oxford: Clarendon Press.

Part II: **Prioritisation and the inferring of preferences from observed choices**

Hans Basbøll
Danish Stød in the light of morae, the Weight Law and sonority (strength): A personal view

Abstract: My point of departure is Theo Vennemann's classic *Preference laws for syllable structure and the explanation of sound change* (1988), in particular the concept of syllable weight expressed in terms of morae, the relation to stress accent and vowel length expressed in the Weight Law, and the importance of a strength or sonority hierarchy. I present my own analysis of the Danish stød, notably its phonological aspects, in terms of these concepts, and finally I include a proposal by the late Jørgen Rischel (2001) on areal and chronological variation of stød in the discussion.

1 Introduction: Danish stød and Vennemann's (1988) principles

1.1 Danish stød

According to Louis Hjelmslev, every language has a particularly difficult descriptive problem around which the whole linguistic analysis must center, viz. for Danish: the stød (Hjelmslev 1951). Stød is a laryngeal syllable rhyme prosody with a very complicated grammatical and lexical distribution. The absence or presence of a stød can be the only difference that distinguishes words with otherwise identical pronunciations, e.g. *ven, vend!* 'friend', 'turn!' [vɛn vɛnˀ]; *musen, musen* 'the muse', 'the mouse' [ˈmuːsən ˈmuːˀsən]; *vandet, vandet* 'watery', 'the water' [ˈvanəð ˈvanˀəð].[1] Diachronic aspects are emphasized in Sections 5–7.

Acknowledgement: The present paper to a large degree consists of revised parts of earlier publications of mine, in particular Basbøll (2001), (2005), (2008), (2014), (2017), and (2018). I am indebted to Nina Grønnum, an anonymous reviewer, and the editors for numerous useful remarks on the manuscript.

---

1 Fischer-Jørgensen (1987, 1989) and Aage Hansen (1943) have given standard treatments of the Danish stød.

Hans Basbøll, Department of Language and Communication, University of Southern Denmark, Odense/Denmark

https://doi.org/10.1515/9783110721461-006

1.2 The Non-Stød Model

The Non-Stød Model (Basbøll 2008) gives the following account for stød: Stød is a signal for bimoraic (heavy) syllables, located in the second mora (see further Section 3). What must be accounted for, then, is *the absence of stød in bimoraic syllables*: "Non-Stød". This is a crucial difference to other treatments which all attempt to give rules for the occurrence of stød, and this approach has radically changed the whole stød-picture. There are two kinds of principles of Non-Stød, viz. *Lexical Non-Stød* and *Word-structure Non-Stød*.[2] Word-structure Non-Stød is not discussed in this paper, except for the diachronic perspective given in Section 6.

1.3 Vennemann (1988) on Danish stød and vowel length

Vennemann (1988: 5) says: "The prosodic function π is the conjunct of several functions – possibly empty in part – which assign each syllable its *nuclear, moric, tonal,* and *cut* (or *ballistic*) *properties* [note 9] as well as others, e.g. the presence or absence of the stød in Danish".

In note 9 (1988: 70), he states,

> [...] Chief among the moric properties of syllables is nuclear length in languages such as Old English, Latin, and Japanese. For example, the first syllable of the Latin words *malum* 'evil' and *malum* 'apple' [...] have the same base, /ma/, but π assigns the former nuclear shortness, the latter nuclear length. [...] Syllable cut properties are recognized for Standard German unreduced syllables, viz. *smooth cut* and *abrupt cut*. Smoothly cut syllables have tense vowels (long when accented) and may be closed or open. Abruptly cut syllables have lax vowels (always short) and must be closed [...], namely by ambisyllabicity [...].[3]

1.4 Vennemann (1988) on the Weight Law, morae, and vowel length

Vennemann (1988: 30) formulates the Weight Law as follows: "In stress accent languages an accented syllable is the more preferred, the closer its syllable weight is to two moras, and an unaccented syllable is the more preferred the closer its weight is to one mora. (The optimal stressed syllable is bimoric, the optimal unstressed syllable is unimoric.)"

---

[2] The presentation of the Non-Stød Model here is largely built upon my earlier work, in particular Basbøll (2005, 2008, 2014 and 2018).
[3] I do not use Vennemann's technical notations in this paper.

He ends this section (1988: 32) by saying: "Open syllable lengthening of nuclei is, of course, a widespread phenomenon. It occurs only in stress accent languages, and there only in stressed syllables. The Weight Law thus explains why the combination of contrastive nuclear length and a stress accent are universally disfavored, whereas in pitch accent languages and tone languages contrastive nuclear length is commonplace".

Danish is a stress accent language with a contrastive nuclear length. All attempts to interpret Danish vowel length phonetically and/or phonologically in terms of a tense:lax opposition have in my view failed;[4] this is true also for the rather recent attempt by Herslund (2002: 4–8), cf. Basbøll (2006).

1.5 Vennemann (1988) on consonantal strength

Vennemann (1988: 9) presents the hierarchy of Consonantal Strength that is crucial for his whole approach. He gives a ten-step hierarchy of consonantal strength as follows (I have added numbers to the steps); I give that hierarchy here, following Vennemann, with the highest values of strength being at the top, i.e. strength increases as we move upwards:

(10) voiceless plosives
(9) voiced plosives
(8) voiceless fricatives
(7) voiced fricatives
(6) nasals
(5) lateral liquids (*l*-sounds)
(4) central liquids (*r*-sounds)
(3) high vowels
(2) mid vowels
(1) low vowels

I have several reservations about this strength hierarchy – which can also be called a sonority hierarchy, with high sonority corresponding, by definition, to low consonantal strength, and vice versa:

---

[4] Essentially, the feature tense/lax for vowels (as seen in German and – less clearly – in English, for example) involves both qualitative and quantitative aspects. Such a distinction is not found in Danish, and, to my knowledge, no specialist of Danish phonetics has claimed that, cf., for example, Fischer-Jørgensen (1985: 89) and Grønnum (2005: 96–98).

(i)   I do not find the internal order within obstruents convincing, in particular I disagree that voiced plosives (9) should be stronger than voiceless fricatives (8). An order syllable-initially of voiced plosive–voiceless fricative is highly unnatural phonetically, whereas an order of voiceless fricative–voiceless plosive is both natural and frequently occurring; importantly, the latter order agrees with my Sonority Syllable Model where [–spread glottis] is the outermost sonority-hierarchical feature.[5]
(ii) The category *liquids* is, in my view, not well-defined phonetically and phonologically, see Section 2.4.
(iii) The ten steps are not "equidistant" (this is no criticism of Vennemann, of course), whereas the order *obstruents – sonorant contoids – vocoids* – to use the terminology of Pike (1943) – is very well established: first 10-through-7, then 6-through-4, last 3-through-1, see Section 2.

My own proposal for a sonority – or strength – hierarchy will be briefly presented in the next section. The purpose of my model is not to predict all possible phonotactic patterns motivated by "sonority" or "strength".[6] Rather, I derive my Sonority Syllable Model from as few and as basic observations as possible, taking *Occam's razor principle* as far as I can. From this perspective, my approach is completely different from Steve Parker's impressive *Quantifying the sonority hierarchy* (2002).

2 A sonority (or strength) hierarchy based upon general phonetics

2.1 The vocoid is the prototypical peak of a syllable

All languages have vocoids as peaks, but only some have non-vocoids = contoids as peaks (as in the Czech word for 'wolf' *vlk*); all languages have contoids as non-peaks, but only some have vocoids ("glides, semivowels"); thus, *vocoids are*

---

[5] The implication is that [spread glottis]-segments would be at the absolute margin of the Sonority Syllable which agrees well, I think, with the fact that the rest position of glottis is widely open. The relation between voiceless fricatives and voiced plosives is discussed by Parker (2002: 68–70, 226–228 and 235–242).
[6] It is also well known that there are principles lying behind phonotactics that cannot be derived from "sonority" or "strength", e.g. involving place features; this is of no concern in this paper.

prototypical peaks. Since the peak-function is central in the notion of the syllable, the point of departure here is the vocoid, not the vowel in a functional sense, including the peak-function of a syllable: this latter starting point would be circular (cf. Ohala 1992, 2008, Ohala and Kawasaki-Fukumori 1997).

Ladefoged (1971: 91) aptly says about his feature *Consonantal*: "This feature has a different status from all other features in that it can be *defined* only in terms of the intersection of classes already defined by other features. Thus nonconsonantal sounds are nonlateral and sonorant [and also oral/HB]. They correspond largely to what Pike (1943) called vocoids, which he defined as central resonant orals".

In my view, *cover features* (as Ladefoged calls them) *are preferable* to independently defined features, other things being equal, *since we adhere to Occam's razor principle of simplicity*; this is particularly true for Major class features.

2.2 Definition of the vocoid

The definition of the feature Vocoid is the cornerstone of my approach:

[vocoid] = $_{DEF}$ [sonorant, –stop, –lateral]

The features used here are all strictly binary, with no use of "ambiguous zeroes". The marked – i.e. phonetically homogeneous[7] – member of the opposition has no '+', i.e. the '+' is implied. Thus [vocoid] means exactly the same as [+vocoid] here. In the following, I write feature names – regardless of their specification with plus or minus – without square brackets but starting with a capital letter (e.g. Vocoid).

Sonorants are defined acoustically, following Ladefoged (1971: 58): "a comparatively large amount of acoustic energy within a clearly defined formant structure", cf. p. 93: "greater acoustic energy in the formants"; they are – as their complementary class (obstruents), by the way – phonetically homogeneous.

---

[7] Vocoids constitute a phonetically homogeneous class; their opposite member – contoids in Pike's (1943) terminology – do not constitute a similarly homogeneous class, since they include plosives and fricatives as well as sonorant laterals, for example.

2.3 A fundamental logical relation between segment types: sonority-hierarchical features

1) The point of departure is the prototypical syllabic peak, which is a vocoid, i.e. a phonetic – as opposed to a "functional" – vowel, to avoid circularity (Section 2.1).
2) All vocoids are, necessarily, sonorant: this follows from the definition.
3) But some sonorants are not vocoids, viz. prototypical (sonorant) laterals, which are [sonorant, lateral], and nasal contoids – in Pike's (1943) terminology, i.e. phonetic consonants – which are [sonorant, stop].
ERGO: *[vocoid] IMPLIES [sonorant] (and not the other way round)*

All features that can enter into an implication chain starting with [vocoid], are, *by definition, sonority-hierarchical features*.

2.4 Major classes defined by the definition of [vocoid]

As said, I depart from Basbøll's definition (e.g. 2001, but in fact already 1973):

[vocoid] = $_{DEF}$ [sonorant, –lateral, –stop]

This definition, as noted in Section 2.2, is inspired by Ladefoged's use of *cover features* (1971: 91, cf. 58, 93) drawing upon Pike's (1943) definition of *vocoids*.

Departing *only* – cf. Occam's razor – from this definition of vocoids, one can derive the five Major classes in Table 1 by means of only the three features Vocoid, Sonorant and Stop. The remaining three logical possibilities (2^3 minus 5) from these three binary features are excluded by the very definition which is a considerable simplification according to Occam's razor principle.

Table 1: Major classes defined by the features Vocoid, Sonorant and Stop. Redundant feature values, given the definition of [vocoid], are parenthesized (from Basbøll 2001: 89).

	V	L	N	F	P	*	*	*
Vocoid	+	–	(–)	(–)	(–)	+	+	+
Sonorant	(+)	+	+	–	–	+	–	–
Stop	(–)	–	+	–	+	+	–	+

Note that the classes (segment types) L and N encompass only sonorant members – even though voiceless nasals and laterals do occur – which are those occupying a well defined position in sonority hierarchies.

The category "liquids" is a difficult category to define. *l*-sounds and *r*-sounds may be widely different with respect to "sonority": *r*-sounds can phonetically be voiceless or voiced fricatives, trills, flaps, or glides, and *l*-sounds can be voiceless or voiced fricatives, for example, in addition to the – prototypical – sonorant laterals.[8] One should therefore be suspicious towards claims that "liquids" constitute a natural class phonetically, in particular in articulatory terms. Perceptually, partly acoustically, as well as phonologically, I do not want to exclude that liquids can form a natural class, however.

2.5 Modeling Major classes in a two-dimensional plane

Figure 1 illustrates how the three features Vocoid, Sonorant and Stop define five possible areas for the Major classes (segment types) of Table 1:

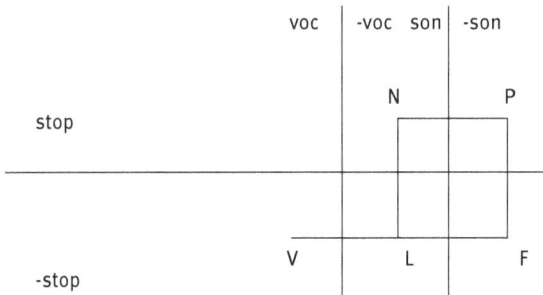

Figure 1: The five Major classes of Table 1 depicted in a two-dimensional graph with [vocoid] segments in the left-hand column, [–vocoid, sonorant] segments in the middle column, and [– sonorant] segments (obstruents) in the righthand column. [stop] segments occur in the upper row and [–stop] segments in the lower row (from Basbøll 2001: 91).

Sonority-hierarchical features are [vocoid] and [sonorant] as employed here; the only further sonority-hierarchical features are [voiced] and [–spread glottis].[9]

---

8 Cf. Parker (2002: 232–234).
9 I have earlier (e.g. Basbøl 2005: 195) proposed a complete (maximal) sonority hierarchy: [voc] > [son] > [voi] > [–spr glott]. The weakest point in this chain – which by its very logic excludes the combination *[voi, spr glott] – is [voi], due to the existence of voiced aspirated plosives. I here use

Sonority-hierarchical features are horizontal, other features – here only Stop – are vertical.

The modeling departs from the [vocoid] in the bottom left corner. The figure is fully determined by the principles stated. Table 2 is a notational variant of Figure 1.

Table 2: A notational variant of Figure 1. Redundant feature values are parenthesized (all features are fully specified); furthermore [–stop] is redundant for V; all redundancies follow from the definition of [vocoid] (from Basbøll 2017: 75).

	+ vocoid	– vocoid	(– vocoid)
	(+ sonorant)	+ sonorant	– sonorant
+ stop		N	P
– stop	V	L	F

2.6 Measuring distances between Major classes

In the Sonority Syllable Model (e.g. Basbøll 2017), Stop is different from the two other features in that it cannot enter into any unidirectional implication chain with [vocoid] in the centre – i.e. [vocoid] implies [sonorant] implies [voiced]; or [vocoid] implies [sonorant] implies [–spread glottis] – since it is not true, e.g., that [sonorant] segments are necessarily [stop] (e.g. sonorant laterals), nor that [stop] segments are necessarily sonorants (e.g. plosives).

The distances are measured in a "binary" way, i.e. a Major class – segment type – is either in a particular field, or it is not, *tertium non datur*. Departing from our point of departure, viz. the *vocoid*, distances – as seen in Figure 1 – can in principle be calculated in two different ways, viz. (i) in the horizontal dimension only, or (ii) paying attention to both the horizontal and the vertical dimension, cf. also Table 2. This "double" way to count is illustrated in Table 3.
(i) Sonority-steps strictly speaking is the horizontal dimension in Figure 1;
(ii) Distance from V should be counted both horizontally and vertically since N (nasals) and P (plosives) – both [stop] – are clearly more distant from V than L (laterals) or F (fricatives), respectively, because V (vocoids), by definition, is [–stop].

---

the (reduced) sonority hierarchy [voc] > [son] > [–spr glott] which predicts [spr glott]-segments being at the margin of the sonority syllable, cf. note 5. For discussion, see Basbøll (2017, 2018: 223–231).

The *sum of these two measures of distance* seems to capture an intuitive notion of "strength" as often employed in the literature – as well as the notion of "sonority", whose values are inversely proportional to those of "strength".

Table 3: Calculations of sonority-steps and distance-from-V, and of their sum, for the five Major classes of Table 1 (and Figure 1 and Table 2) (from Basbøll 2001: 91).

Major class in Table 1, Figure 1 and Table 2	V	L	N	F	P
Sonority-step (only horizontally)	0	1	1	2	2
Distance from V (both horizontally and vertically)	0	1	2	2	3
Their sum	0	2	3	4	5

3 A typology of syllable weight in Scandinavian, and markedness of stød in Danish

3.1 Phonological weight and morae in Scandinavian

Table 4 gives the central information on the moraic typology used in this paper, but only in so far as Scandinavian languages are concerned; μ and σ symbolise "mora" and "syllable", respectively, and < > indicates an extraprosodic segment or prosody, here vowel length, see Section 4.

Table 4 is here interpreted as stating a set of *well-formedness restrictions on syllable structure* in Scandinavian languages: Stressed syllables in Old Norse can be either mono-, bi- or trimoraic, in Modern Scandinavian except Danish they are always bimoraic; in modern Danish they are either mono- or bimoraic. Unstressed syllables in Old Norse are likewise mono-, bi- or trimoraic, whereas in Modern Scandinavian they are always monomoraic. In Danish, only sonorant consonants can be moraic, no such restriction applies in other Scandinavian languages. The last two rows of Table 4 indicates that Danish is particular by allowing Extra-Prosodicity in word-final syllables, see Section 4. Such a moraic analysis is a great methodological advantage – according to Occam's razor – when compared to alternatives interpreting syllable weight as a gradual phenomenon.

Table 4: Moraic and syllabic structure in Scandinavian languages. Only the main forms of the modern languages are included; excluded are Danish dialects with tonal word accents – in Southern Jutland and in southern parts of the Funish area – or without stød; likewise excluded are Swedish and Norwegian dialects without tonal word accents, or with different quantity systems, cf. Kristoffersen (1999, 2011) and Gårding (1977). The figure is taken from a part of table 10.1 in Basbøll (2005: 292), which is based upon the final table of Basbøll (1989).

	Old Norse	(Modern) Icelandic/ Swedish/Norwegian	(Modern) Danish
μ in stressed (primary or secondary) σ	1 or 2 or 3	2	1 or 2
μ in unstressed σ	1 or 2 or 3	1	1
Which types of C can be moraic?	all	all	only sonorants
Word-final moraic C?	yes	yes	only in stød-syllables
Length of word-final V under stress	only /V:/	only /V:/	mostly /V:/ (in some "small" and/or foreign words /V<:>/, e.g. *vi* 'we' [vi])

3.2 Building up moraic structure in Danish

Leaving aside Extra-Prosodicity for the moment (see Section 4), the principles that specify which elements in a syllable are moraic and which are not, are:
(i)   Any pre-V segment is non-moraic.
(ii) Any V is moraic.
(iii) A non-V after a short full V is either moraic (if it is ':' or a sonorant C) or non-moraic (if it is a non-sonorant C, viz. an obstruent)
(iv) Any subsequent C is non-moraic (since trimoraic syllables are excluded in Danish, cf. Table 4).

The crucial difference between (Modern) Danish and the other (modern) Scandinavian languages is the role of sonority: only sonorants can be moraic in Danish, whereas obstruents can be moraic in the other Scandinavian languages (e.g. in words like Swedish *hoppa* 'hop, verb' with a geminate – and ambisyllabic – /p/). The difference between Old Norse and the modern Scandinavian languages can be seen as a parallel to the difference between Latin and Italian, for example, as amply illustrated in Vennemann's work.

3.3 Markedness of stød phonetically

There is no doubt that stød is phonetically "something extra" (a kind of creaky voice, i.e. laryngealisation), cf. Fischer-Jørgensen (1987), Grønnum and Basbøll (2007). The phonetic realisation of stød can be highly variable phonetically, and the difference between stød and no stød can sometimes be extremely slight acoustically, as emphasized by Grønnum and Basbøll (2007, cf. 2012, and Grønnum, Vázquez-Larruscáin, and Basbøll 2013). However, I have never seen – and cannot imagine – any phonetic argument for the opposite position, viz. that syllables without stød should be phonetically more marked; thus *stød is marked phonetically*.

3.4 Markedness of stød phonologically

Syllables with stød must have a long-sonority rhyme and have either primary or secondary stress. Following the Non-Stød Model, a syllable with stød is bimoraic, stød being evidence of the second mora. There are no phonological restrictions for syllables without stød, i.e. all types of syllables, with or without long-sonority rhyme, with or without stress, with or without full vowel peak, etc., can occur without stød. Thus stød is phonologically marked in the sense that there are heavy phonological conditions on which syllables can have stød, but no phonological conditions on which kind of syllables can occur without stød, i.e. *stød is marked phonologically*.

3.5 Markedness of non-stød lexically

Non-Stød can be a property of lexical items (*Lexical Non-Stød*), both in native words like *ven* 'friend' (without stød, but with stød in definite *vennen* [ˈvɛnˀən]) and in French loans like *balkon* 'balcony' [b̥alˈkʰʌn] (without stød, but stød in def. *balkonen* [b̥alˈkʰʌnˀən]). In the nativelike part of the vocabulary, Non-Stød is *marked*, but in the non-nativelike part, Non-Stød applies *generally*.

According to the Non-Stød Model, Lexical Non-Stød is a mechanism of wide applicability throughout the language, in particular in the non-native vocabulary – e.g. non-integrated English and French loans – but also for a range of native lexemes.[10] For the native – and nativelike, including established

---

[10] A lexical specification [stød] is not excluded within the framework of the Non-Stød Model, since a certain phonetic or phonological feature, if it occurs in all forms of a given lexeme, will be

German, Greek and Latin loans – vocabulary, the default case is that heavy = bimoraic syllables have stød (Section 1.2). According to the Non-Stød Model, Non-Stød – i.e. lack of stød in such syllables (i.e. with stød-basis) – is thus lexically marked, i.e. *stød is lexically unmarked*.

4 Extra-Prosodicity and Lexical specification [–stød]: the two mechanisms of Lexical Non-Stød

4.1 Extra-Prosodicity (on a lexeme)

Extra-Prosodicity means that the final consonant of the lexeme is disregarded when the moraic structure is being decided,[11] cf. Section 3.2. I shall here limit myself, for expository reasons, to indicating *Extra-Prosodicity* by *angled brackets* as follows: if a lexeme is specified for Lexical Non-Stød, the consonant in the first non-V position after a short full V in the final syllable of the lexeme will be indicated as extra-prosodic, and surrounded by '< >', if it is a sonorant and is lexeme-final (no conditions on stress are needed). Moraic segments are underlined in the phonemic description, indicated by / /.

This may sound complicated, but it follows from the logic of Extra-Prosodicity: if a lexeme is specified for Lexical Non-Stød, the lexeme-final consonant is extra-prosodic, but this can only make a difference for a sonorant C immediately following a short full V, and only in this case will Extra-Prosodicity be indicated in the phonemic notation here. Thus Extra-Prosodicity is relevant in cases like *ven* 'friend', *hul* 'hole', *mad* 'food' [vɛn hɔl mað] /vɛ<n> hɔ<l> ma<ð>/ (cf. cases like *pen* 'pen', *hal* 'hall' [pʰɛn² halˀ] /pɛn hal/). On the other hand, the final consonant in *hals* 'neck', *pæn* 'nice' [halˀs pʰɛːˀn] will be extra-prosodic and thus non-moraic in any case, hence no indication is called for: /hals pɛːn/. When Extra-Prosodicity is indicated as done here, the total moraic structure follows.

---

part of the lexical make-up of that lexeme, phonetic details (and stress reduction, cf. Section 4.2) left aside. This is, in my view, the psycholinguistically most plausible assumption (Basbøll 2005: 385–387).

11 On the build-up of syllabic-moraic structure, see Basbøll (2005: 283–291 and 388–395).

4.2 Lexical specification [–stød]

There are cases of aberrant Non-Stød in lexemes that cannot be accounted for by Extra-Prosodicity since the syllables in question are unambiguously bimoraic, e.g. the English loan word *spleen* [sb̥liːn] /sbliːn/. Since stød, according to the Non-Stød Model, is evidence of the second mora of its syllable, I propose to indicate the aberrant behaviour of such lexemes by the lexical feature [–stød] which will be associated with the second mora (the locus for stød, phonologically speaking). According to my general framework on lexical specifications, it follows that lexemes thus specified will not participate in (non-suppletive) morphological stød-alternations, except as a consequence of stress reduction (when bimoraic syllables become monomoraic). *Spleen* is not an isolated example of Lexical specification [–stød]: not fully integrated loans from English and French, and many loans and names from other foreign languages – except German and the classical languages Latin and Greek – are thus specified. In other words, such a Lexical specification [–stød] will take effect through a lexical redundancy rule systematically covering large parts of the vocabulary, e.g. English loans, etc., as mentioned.

Lexical specification [–stød] is not limited to such "foreign words and names", however. Native words like *tørst* 'thirst', *torsk* 'cod' and *barsk* 'harsh' [tˢœɐ̯sd̥ tˢɒːsg̊ b̥ɑːsg̊] are also unambiguously bimoraic but they lack stød, due to their evolution from short vowels followed by a voiceless and thus obstruent /r/ (in the 19th century, cf. Section 5.1), i.e. they have only become eligible for stød – bimoraic – quite recently. The lexemes in this group can thus be defined historically.[12] That they are given a Lexical specification [–stød] here agrees with their behaviour, in the sense that the development of increasing stød occurrences would correspond to a lexical specification – aberrant, or at least highly marked – being lost in an increasing number of lexemes.

4.3 Extra-Prosodicity takes priority over Lexical specification [–stød]

Thus most foreign words and names – such as *spleen, balkon* – as well as some native lexemes – such as *torsk, ven*, for example – are specified as Lexical Non-Stød. It must then be decided how Extra-Prosodicity and Lexical specifica-

---

[12] This is not to be taken as a synchronic explanation, but is an example of how diachrony influences the contemporary language structure.

tion [–stød] take effect. According to the logic of the system, there is no choice: *Extra-Prosodicity must take priority over Lexical specification [–stød]* since Extra-Prosodicity is a precondition for establishing the moraic structure, whereas Lexical specification [–stød] presupposes exactly the moraic structure (since it affects the second mora). Thus, for lexemes specified for Lexical Non-Stød: *if Extra-Prosodicity (symbolized by '/< >/') applies, i.e. if the lexeme-final consonant is a sonorant in '< >' immediately following a short full V, Lexical specification [–stød] does not apply to the final syllable; in all other cases – i.e. for all non-final syllables and for all final syllables not marked for Extra-Prosodicity – Lexical specification [–stød] applies.* I find it satisfying from a methodological point of view that the model enforces a priority, rather than leaving the possibility open for an (in principle) arbitrary decision. Furthermore, the priority inherent in the system is in accord with general linguistic arguments, since Extra-Prosodicity (sometimes called extra-metricality) is a well-known phenomenon of wide applicability,[13] whereas Lexical specification [–stød] is a straightforward treatment of exceptions.[14]

4.4 How Extra-Prosodicity and Lexical specification [–stød] work together in the lexicon

I shall now give a few examples illustrating how Lexical Non-Stød works. Notice that this part of the Non-Stød Model is highly restricted in that it makes only a bipartite distinction in the vocabulary concerning stød, and that it makes very specific predictions on the distribution of stød and of possible stød-alternations in the non-native vocabulary. |^{NS}| is an arbitrary lexical indication for (Lexical) Non-Stød; it applies to morphophonemic transcriptions, indicated by | |.

In *spleen* [sb̥liːn] |sbliːn ^{NS}|, the lexeme-final C is a sonorant but it does not immediately follow a short full V. It is thus not extra-prosodic in the relevant sense (indicated by '/< >/'); this gives a bimoraic syllable with Lexical specification [–stød], and thus it has no stød whether as a monosyllable, or in any other context, such as *spleenen* (definite form) ['sb̥liːnən].[15] Other English loans, such as *boom, mail*, are also – quite regularly – always stød-less. A French name like *de Gaulle* [d̥øˈg̊ɔːl] |d̥øˈgɔːl ^{NS}| will likewise, in all contexts, be without stød, just like

---

[13] For the use, diachronically, in Danish according to the Non-Stød Model, see Basbøll (2005: 388–395) and (2008).
[14] This is still making predictions according to my framework, however, viz. the non-participation in morphological stød-alternations of the lexemes involved (apart from effects of stress reduction, cf. footnote 10).
[15] Schwa-assimilation is generally not indicated in this paper.

e.g. the city name *Beaune*. The same applies to native lexemes like *torsk, tørst* (cf. Section 4.2): these lexemes do not participate in morphological stød-alternations, but are stød-less everywhere.

ven 'friend' [vɛn] |vɛn ᴺˢ|: the lexeme-final C is a sonorant immediately following a short full V, it is thus extra-prosodic in the relevant sense: /vɛ<n>/; this gives a monomoraic syllable: /vɛ̱n/. Thus it has no stød when it occurs as a monosyllable: [vɛn]; but it can participate in stød-alternations, e.g. definite *vennen* ['vɛn²ən], since the lexeme-final C is not word-final in this form and therefore not extra-prosodic. *Clinton* ['k̬lentˢʌn] |klentɔn ᴺˢ| likewise has an extra-prosodic final /n/ (/klentɔ<n>/); but in a(n ad hoc) plural form (for Hillary and Bill) it would be pronounced ['k̬len̩tˢʌn²ɐ], with stød. Also a French loan word like *balkon* 'balcony' [b̥al'kʰʌŋ] |bal'kɔŋ ᴺˢ| is pronounced without stød due to the extra-prosodic final sonorant C (/bal'kɔ<ŋ>/); in inflected forms the lexeme-final C will no longer be extra-prosodic – since it is no longer word-final – hence there is stød in e.g. plural *balkoner* [b̥al'kʰʌŋ²ɐ].

4.5 Extra-prosodic vowel length /<:>/

According to the Non-Stød Model, vowel length is indicated in the underlying form (as ":"), and resulting from the build-up of syllabic-moraic structures a long vowel "V:" ends up as adjoined to two morae, a short V just to one (Basbøll 2005: 283–288). In cases of mora-drop – e.g. in pretonal syllables, as a consequence of stress reduction – a long vowel is automatically shortened, since the realization of vowel length presupposes a second mora in the syllable (this follows from the model). As a consequence, a sequence V plus /<:>/, when it occurs in the final syllable of a word, will, necessarily, end up as short, according to the model. Thus, without introducing any additional machinery, Extra-Prosodicity can account for a number of vowel length alternations in examples of the type *pate* (French *pâté*) [pʰa'tˢe] |pa'te: ᴺˢ| which will lead to Extra-Prosodicity /pa'te<:>/; its definite singular form will be *pateen* [pʰa'tˢe:²ən] where vowel length will be manifested since it is no longer word-final and therefore not extra-prosodic either. By a similar approach aberrant monosyllables with a final short vowel phonetically can be accounted for, e.g. *nu* 'now', [nu] |nu: ᴺˢ| which will lead to extra-prosodic vowel length /nu<:>/, a length that will be manifested e.g. in the definite *nuet* 'the present moment' ['nu:²əð].[16] In both of these cases, the definite form will, regularly, have stød.

---

[16] Before a pause, words with extra-prosodic vowel length are often pronounced with strong aspiration (e.g. *nu* [nuh], *vi* 'we' [vih], just like *ven* [vɛnh]), which Jørgen Rischel sees as "demorification" (p.c., Basbøll 2005: 391, note 10).

The analysis of extra-prosodic vowel length allows the – also from a diachronic point of view –tempting generalisation that *a full vowel in a final open syllable is invariably long phonologically*; in some words, however, this length is extra-prosodic and therefore the syllable, when not followed by a suffix, has no stød. Accordingly, the implication of the Non-Stød Model is that *no words will end in a long stød-less vowel*: there is only one theoretically possible way, according to the Non-Stød Model, how a long vowel could end up without stød in this position – where Word-structure Non-Stød cannot apply, cf. Basbøll (2008) – viz. by Lexical Non-Stød. But neither Extra-Prosodicity nor Lexical specification [–stød], the only two mechanisms of Lexical Non-Stød, can provide a long stød-less final vowel: Extra-Prosodicity is relevant – cf. *nu* just above – thus Lexical specification [–stød] is not allowed to apply; but Extra-Prosodicity will give a short vowel (the case of *nu*). This prediction is interesting since the banning of long stød-less final vowels is a robust observation, but it has not been accounted for in any principled way, to my knowledge (it is different from cases like *spleen*). The whole approach of Extra-Prosodicity does not depend on its also being accepted with respect to vowel length, but I find it a very promising analysis, and I shall follow it throughout this paper.[17]

5 The Non-Stød Model and sound changes in the 19th and 20th century: *r*-vocalisation, Extra-Prosodicity, and developments of vowel length

5.1 The evolution of postvocalic /r/

As noted in Section 4.2, native words like *tørst* 'thirst', *torsk* 'cod' and *barsk* 'harsh' [tˢœɐ̯sd̥ tˢɒːsg̊ b̥ɑːsg̊] are unambiguously bimoraic but lack stød, due to their evolution in the 19th century from short vowels followed by a voiceless and thus obstruent /r/. They became eligible for stød – bimoraic – only when the postvocalic /r/ vocalized to become a glide, i.e. the second component of a diphthong (in *tørst*), or fused with the vowel completely (in *torsk, barsk*). Stød is gradually spreading in such forms, with imperatives – like *spark!* 'kick!' [sb̥ɑːˀg̊] – and certain derivatives – like *tyrkisk* 'Turkish', *færdsel* 'traffic' ['tˢyɐ̯ˀg̊isg̊ 'fæɐ̯ˀsl̩] – in

---

17 As I did in Basbøll (2008), but in disagreement with Basbøll (2005: 391), cf. Liberman (2007: 105–107).

the lead, with a tendency now towards generalising such forms with stød. Earlier in the twentieth century, these words were pronounced [sba̯:ɠ̊ ˈtˢyɹ̝̊ɠ̊isɠ̊ ˈfæɹ̝̊səl], and before that something like [sba̯ɹ̥kʰ ˈtʰøɹ̥kʰiskʰ ˈfɛɹ̥səl] (cf. Brink and Lund 1975: 261–284). The lexemes in this group can thus be defined historically, as those departing from the sequence short vowel plus /r/ plus a further voiceless consonant – with spread glottis – that devoices the preceding /r/. The decisive point in the evolution, seen from the perspective of the Non-Stød Model, comes when the post-V /r/ becomes a sonorant and thereby qualifies for moraicity; this state of affairs ensues with its vocalization ending up with a glide or ':'. That they are, in my model, provided with a Lexical specification [−stød], makes the prediction that their [−stød] can be lost – whereby they get stød – and will be expected to disappear over time, by being lost – since such a lexical marking is exceptional, or at least highly marked – in an increasing number of lexemes, perhaps organized in lexical subgroups.

r-vocalization has also struck monosyllables with a short vowel and a word-final /r/, such as *bær* 'berry', *smør* 'berry', 'butter', to-day pronounced [b̥æɐ̯ smœɐ̯] with a final glide. To take a famous example, the writer Karen Blixen (Isak Dinesen) (1885–1962), who had a very conservative language for her age, pronounced this word-final /r/ after a short stressed vowel before pause as a strongly aspirated fricative, just as /ð/ could be pronounced as an aspirated or even affricated fricative, e.g. in examples like *tør, gud* 'dare(s)', 'god' [tʰœʁh/tˢœʁh ɠ̊uθh].[18] From the point of view of the Non-Stød Model, the important change comes, as mentioned above, when these word-final obstruents occurring after short stressed vowels become sonorants and thereby qualify for moraicity. This is a precondition for stød, but stød will not occur unless or until they have been lifted from the ban of Non-Stød, so to speak.

5.2 Glides, Extra-Prosodicity and vowel length

The crucial question within my framework is the status of Extra-Prosodicity. As far as the glides are concerned – and the approximant /ð/ [ð̞] in Modern Danish belongs in this group too – the most simple chronology is that Extra-Prosodicity was the general principle[19] over a long period of time. This period ends when an ongoing vowel shortening before glides and approximants has been carried

---

[18] Several taped interviews with Karen Blixen exist, and her pronunciation, as approximately given above, i.e. with aspiration and affrication, is clearly audible.
[19] I.e. the default case; this also seems to be Rischel's position for Danish more generally, see Section 7.

through, a phenomenon that is happening now (see Basbøll 2005: 392–395): *ud* 'out', *bog* 'book', *bag* 'behind', *bord* 'table' are no longer pronounced [u:ˀð b̥ɔ:ˀw b̥æ:ˀɪ̯ b̥o:ˀɐ̯] but [uð² b̥ɔw² b̥æɪ̯²/b̥æ:² b̥oɐ̯²]. We thereby proceed from general to lexically specified Extra-Prosodicity, e.g. *vid* 'wit' [við], which before this change would be covered by general Extra-Prosodicity, but after this change will have to be lexically specified for Extra-Prosodicity, since the vowel of the type *hvid* 'white' is no longer a phonologically long vowel: old [vi:ˀð] new [við²]. When this vowel shortening becomes lexicalised, the stød system is restructured with far ranging consequences.[20] The change of words like *syd* 'south', *spyd* 'spear', *stød* 'push' from [sy:ˀð sb̥y:ˀð sd̥ø:ˀð] (19th century) to [syð sb̥yð sd̥øð] is, primarily, a case of *mora-drop*, and only secondarily drop of stød, just like drop of stød in pretonal position which, according to the Non-Stød Model, is mora-drop with the automatic consequence that stød is lost (e.g. *gå!* (fully stressed) 'go!', *gå hjem!* 'go home!' [ɡ̊ɔ:ˀ ɡ̊ɔˈjɛm²]).

5.3 Stød, morae and quantity

Eli Fischer-Jørgensen states in the summary of her large scale instrumental study of the stød (1987: 129) that "long vowels with stød were found to be significantly shorter than long vowels without stød (but only in distinct speech), whereas sonorant consonants with stød were significantly longer than sonorant consonants without stød".

That long vowels with stød are shorter than long vowels without stød in distinct speech, but not in natural non-distinct speech, agrees very well with the phonetic proposal by Grønnum and Basbøll (2007) involving a ballistic gesture. This would make us predict that both vowels and consonants with stød would not be prolonged in positions or situations – be they stylistic or dependent on position – where similar segments without stød could well be prolonged (this would also apply to Eli Fischer-Jørgensen's material). This might account for the length patterns one finds at high levels of formality, in utterance final position, or in child-directed speech: segments without stød are expected, according to this proposal, to be extendable in time more or less freely, as opposed to segments with stød.

---

20 This restructuring also involves the sonorant consonants, i.e. nasals and /l/ – Rischel's sonority type VS, cf. Section 7.1 – which are proceeding from lexical specification of moraicity to being unspecified.

The situation of *utterance medial sonorant consonants* with or without stød is quite a different matter. Grønnum and Basbøll (2001) found that consonants with stød are not generally longer acoustically than consonants without stød across all positions (cf. Grønnum and Basbøll 2007: 199). For my original proposal on moraic consonants (Basbøll 1988, 1998) I had built, regarding phonetic matters, on Fischer-Jørgensen (1987), who was in agreement, as far as consonant length is concerned, with Riber Petersen (1973) and Brink et al. (1991: 88). The decisive type of phonetic counterevidence against this early version of my moraic analysis was examples like *vinder* 'win(s)', *vinder* 'winner' [ˈvenˀɐ ˈvenɐ] where Grønnum and I found no significant difference in length of the intervocalic consonant (as against Fischer-Jørgensen's and others' statements). But this was an early version of my model, without the now crucial concept of Extra-Prosodicity. I will here present the strongest possible claims, for reasons of methodology, of the Non-Stød Model as presented in this paper. The predictions of length of sonorant consonants with or without stød are as follows:

(i) *moraic consonants are longer than* similar (also with respect to position) *non-moraic consonants*, or, in other words: *mora is a unit of quantity also for consonants* (not only for vowels); this is a stronger, and a more general, position than the one presented in Basbøll (2005: 305): now *mora is a unit of quantity*, like segment and syllable;

(ii) it follows that *word-medial sonorant consonants* (after a short full vowel) *with and without stød are not expected to differ (significantly) in length* since Extra-Prosodicity is excluded in this position, thus all the consonants involved are moraic;

(iii) it also follows that (utterance-medial) *word-final sonorant consonants* – after a short full vowel – *with and without stød are expected to differ (significantly) in length* since Extra-Prosodicity will make a difference here, the consonant without stød being extra-prosodic and thus non-moraic and the consonant with stød being moraic. Grønnum and Basbøll (2001: 239) found that in word-final position utterance-medially, "the tendency is for the stød consonant to be slightly longer, and there are 13 instances (from a total of 20) where the stød consonant is significantly longer than the stød-less consonant, by 0.8–3.1 cs (table 2)." There is still an exciting story to be told, in my view, concerning the relations between moraicity, length and stød of sonorant consonants, diachronically and geographically.

6 The Non-Stød Model and the recent expansion of stød

Grønnum and Basbøll (2007: 203–205) give the following examples (with no indication of secondary stress), based upon Grønnum's observations, mainly from Danish radio broadcasts, through many years (cf. Grønnum 2007: 80–81, Grønnum 2005 [1998]: 239–241):

<u>Simple nouns in the plural</u>
[ˈfoːmuːˀɐ] *formuer* 'fortunes' but [ˈfoːmuːu] *formue* is always without stød in the singular;
[ˈʌmʁɔːˀðɐ] *områder* 'areas' but [ˈʌmʁɔːðə] *område* is always without stød in the singular. (Grønnum and Basbøll 2007: 203).

<u>Compound nouns in the plural</u>
[ˈviːnnɑwˀnə] *vinnavne* 'wine names' but [ˈnɑwnə] *navne* alone is always without stød in isolation;
[ˈsyːyhuːˀsə] *sygehuse* 'sickhouses (i.e. hospitals)' but [ˈhuːsə] *huse* alone is always without stød in isolation. (Grønnum and Basbøll 2007: 204).

Grønnum and Basbøll (2007: 204) suggest that a generalisation, along the following lines, of part of the principles of word-structure Non-Stød, is underway:[21] "[B]efore any syllabic suffix only monosyllabic stems have no stød." We continue to give the following example: "[ˈviːnˌɡɔmˀi] *vingummi* 'wine gum' but [ˈɡɔmi] *gummi* alone is always without stød". And we suggest a further generalisation (2007: 205): "in any word which phonetically resembles a stem + a syllabic suffix, only monosyllabic stems have no stød."

Seen from the point of view of the Non-Stød Model, such a generalisation would not affect the phonological part of the model: bimoraic syllables will still have stød. Also the lexical part: Lexical Non-Stød, encompassing Extra-Prosodicity and Lexical specification [–stød], will still apply as before (but cf. Section 5.1 on *r*-vocalisation). Only the principle of Word-structure Non-Stød will have to be modified more or less radically depending on which tendencies will become prevailing stød-changes.[22]

---

[21] Only syllables with stød-basis are considered in this and the following formulation about 'without stød/no stød' (= Non-Stød here), and first parts of compounds are not covered.
[22] Grønnum, Pharao, and Basbøll (2020) have recently been experimentally investigating these tendencies.

7 Morae and sonority: Rischel's (2001) hypothesis on a dialect specific distribution of stød in monosyllables, and a comparison with the Non-Stød Model

7.1 Rischel's sonority types and the Sonority Syllable Model

In his small but important semi-published paper (in Danish) on the origin of stød (2001), Jørgen Rischel presents (in his Section 3) a specific hypothesis on how the interaction of the sonority hierarchy – loosely speaking, see below – and a moraic analysis of stød can account for some decisive differences in laryngealisation between different Danish dialects.[23] In the present section, I shall present some of Rischel's views mainly by translating central passages from the not very accessible "grey paper" (Rischel 2001), which at a general level I endorse, and discuss them in relation to my own models of syllable structure and stød, viz. the Sonority Syllable Model and the Non-Stød Model. Rischel (2001: 21–22) says:[24]

> One can operate with a sonority hierarchy where V = vowel is most sonorous, then comes G = glide (2nd component of [falling] diphthongs), then S = postvocalic consonantal sonorant, and last, O = final obstruent ('+ENCL' is meant to symbolize enclitically added sonorous material):[25]
>
> | I | II | III | IV |
> |---|----|----|-----|
> | V: | VG | VS | V** |
> | VSS | VSO | | VO |
> | VG/VS+ENCL* | | | |
>
> (* expansions of type II and type III)
> (** only 'small words' with vowel shortening and the type *vindu* 'window')[26]

---

23 See Rischel (2008) for his general "Unified Theory of Nordic *i*-Umlaut, Syncope, and Stød" in which morae play a crucial role.
24 In my translation, all emphasis is in the original; I have used '?' as symbol for the stød. This also applies to the following quotations from Rischel (2001). Rischel's examples are orthographic, but with a stød symbol added.
25 Rischel's original: Man kan operere med et klangstavelseshierarki, hvor V = vokal er mest sonor, så kommer G = glide (2. diftongkomponent), så S = postvokalisk konsonantisk sonorant, og sidst O = final obstruent ("+ENKL" skal symbolisere enklitisk tilføjet sonort materiale).
26 Rischel's original: * udvidelser af type II og type III; ** kun "småord" med vokalforkortelse og typen *vindu*.

As examples, the following words can be mentioned:

I	II	III	IV
V: *bo²*, *lå²s* ['live', 'lock']	VG *vej²*, *tov* ['road', 'rope']	VS *(et) hul*, *skud* ['(a) hole', 'shot, sb.']	V *vi* (pron.) ['we']
VSS *hal²m* ['straw']	VSO *kal²k* ['chalk']		VO *kat* ['cat']
VG/VS+ENCL *vej²en*, *hul²let* ['the road', 'the hole']			

Type I–II may be called "sonority-heavy" [heavy with respect to sonority], type III–IV "sonority-light".[27]

This categorization is very interesting, and from a general phonological point of view, I shall interpret these two tables as follows: Rischel uses, as he says, the sonority hierarchy to define the segments in the formula of the tables. The categories used (V, G, S, O) can be defined as syllabic vocoids, non-syllabic vocoids, sonorant non-vocoids, and non-sonorant segments = obstruents (which are redundantly non-vocoid), respectively (cf. Basbøll 2005: 173–187), see Section 2. But the four types I–IV cannot be defined solely by reference to the sonority hierarchy which attributes inherent sonority to individual segments. Even Rischel's main distinction between types I–II together (as "sonority-heavy") versus III–IV together (as "sonority-light") seems blurred, from a pure sonority hierarchy point of view, by the fact that VSS (as type I) and VS (as type III) have, strictly speaking, the same sequence of (inherent) sonority.

But this only appears to be a problem. In fact, Rischel's types are in my view adequate, insightful and well defined, but we need to invoke *sonority length of the rhyme* (pre-V consonants being irrelevant here, cf. Section 3.2) and not just degree of sonority of the individual segments. It is obvious that the rhyme has longer sonority in type I (which has longer sonority than in a short V followed by a single non-syllabic sonorant) than in both type II and type III. In both type II and type III the sonority length of the rhyme is longer than in type IV whose sonority is just in the short V. Concerning the distinction between type II and type III, G has higher inherent sonority than S – as a vocoid (sonorant) versus a non-vocoid sonorant – so this difference can account for the distinction between VG and VS.[28]

---

[27] Rischel's original: Type I–II kan man kalde "klangtunge", type III–IV kan man kalde "klanglette".
[28] But if we wanted to use only a common criterion it would have to be sonority rhyme length; the question then would be whether a glide is inherently longer than a sonorant consonant (I do not know the answer).

Finally, concerning the subtype (of II) VSO, its rhyme length, but not sonority rhyme length, distinguishes it from VS (III).[29] I conclude that Rischel's (2001) sonority types use three criteria: (i) the sonority hierarchy (sonority sequencing); (ii) sonority rhyme length; and (iii) rhyme length. All three criteria are phonological, with length being measured in number of phonological segments, i.e. (morpho)phonemes. What unites the criteria is the relation between sonority and mora counting, a relation that varies geographically and diachronically, according to Rischel's typology.

7.2 Rischel's hypothesis on the areal and chronological distribution of stød, and its relation to the Non-Stød Model

Rischel continues his argument as follows:

> Now, in the different regional variants [or dialects/HB] the threshold for laryngealisation applies to different steps of the sonority hierarchy (according to modern linguistic jargon, this is a question of "parameter setting") (Rischel 2001):[30]

Southern Danish (and Scandinavian more generally):	no laryngealisation
Northern West Danish:	laryngealisation in type I
Northern East Danish:	laryngealisation in type I and II, but variation in the type VG (*vej?*, *tov* ['street, rope'])

[...]

> In type II a plosive is assimilated to a sonorant: *land* > *[lan?]*; long obstruent > short (*takk* > *tak*); the difference long : short survives in sonorants as a difference in number of morae. The stød is now distinctive [contrastive] at the surface for non-declined nouns: *ven* 'friend' [vɛn] ctr. *mæn?d* 'men' [mɛn?], *(det almene) vel* ['(the common) good' [vɛl]] ctr. *væl?d* ['flood, torrent' [vɛl?]].[31]

> The normal case is that type III has not in itself got any stød, because an unchecked sonorant [i.e. a sonorant not followed by a tautosyllabic consonant/HB] did not count as a mora and thus did not have the word-final falling tone. Nor did type IV get the stød. But stød as a rule occurred in three situations where the number of morae increased, viz. before *enclisis*

---

29 Extra-Prosodicity may be relevant here (cf. Section 4).
30 Rischel's original: Man kan nu sige at i de forskellige regionale varianter befinder tærskelværdien for laryngalisering sig forskellige steder i klangstavelseshierarkiet (iflg. moderne lingvistjargon er det et spørgsmål om forskellig "parameter setting").
31 Rischel's original: I type II assimileres klusil til sonorant [. . .] lang obstruent > kort [. . .]; forskellen lang:kort overlever som en forskel i moralet. Stødet er nu overfladedistinktivt i ubøjede substantiver: *ven* ctr. *mæn'd*, *(det almene) vel* ctr. *væl'd*.

(see type I) with the result *(et) tal*, but *tal?let* ['number, indef. and def.']; in *hiatus* in the type *vindu?et* ['the window']; and in *imperative* with the result *tæl?!* ['count!']. Within the framework of my hypothesis, the most plausible explanation would be that, in exactly these three situations, the total word contour with a strongly falling tone has been concentrated in a syllable that would otherwise be too light [to receive the stød/HB]; the function is as if the sonorant occurred in checked position finally in the syllable.[32]

Rischel's generalisation in the table above shows an interesting regional distribution of "laryngealisation" depending on sonority type of the syllables. The cases that demand a specific account, according to Rischel, are the syllables with the structure VS that do get stød, and he lists three types of those syllables. He takes lack of stød to be the unmarked situation in his type III "because an unchecked sonorant did not count as a mora". This corresponds very well to Extra-Prosodicity in the Non-Stød Model (cf. Section 4). The three situations to be accounted for specifically "where the number of morae increased" and where we get stød, will here be analysed according to the Non-Stød Model (modern standard pronunciation):
(i) *enclisis*, i.e. stød in *tallet* 'the number' ['tˢalˀəð], cf. sg. indef. *tal* 'number' [tˢal] without stød. The final /l/ in *tal* is extra-prosodic, i.e. /<l>/ (since *tal* has Lexical Non-Stød), but when the def. ending is added, /l/ is no longer extra-prosodic, the syllable is therefore bimoraic, hence stød;
(ii) *hiatus*, i.e. stød in *vinduet* 'the window' ['ven̩ˌdu:ˀəð], cf. sg. indef. *vindu* ['vend̥u] without stød. There is, as for all other word-final full vowels, a final vowel length marker /:/ in *vindu*. The final syllable being unstressed in the base form (sg. indef.), this /:/ must be extra-prosodic (i.e. /<:>/, see Section 4.5). When the def. ending is added, /:/ can no longer be extra-prosodic, the syllable is therefore bimoraic, hence stød (and secondary stress);
(iii) *imperative*, i.e. stød in *tæl!* 'count!' [tˢɛlˀ], cf. infinitive *tælle* ['tˢɛlə]. The verb is the only word class where the stem is not always a basic word,[33] therefore the imperative cannot have an extra-prosodic last segment, hence an imperative cannot be a VS-syllable with no stød. The imperatives *spil!, skod!* [sb̥elˀ

---

32 Rischel's original: Type III har normalt ikke i sig selv fået stød, fordi en udækket sonorant ikke talte som mora og ikke fik den ordfinale faldende tone. Type IV fik heller ikke stød. Men stød indtraf regelmæssigt i tre stillinger, hvor moratallet blev øget, nemlig foran *enklise* (se type I), så man får *(et) tal*, men *tal?let*, ved *hiat* i typen *vindu?et* og i *imperativ*, så man får *tæl?!*. Inden for rammerne af min hypotese ville den mest plausible forklaring være at man netop i de tre stillinger har fået den totale ordkontur med stærkt faldende tone koncentreret på en stavelse der ellers er for let; det har altså her fungeret som om sonoranten stod i dækket stilling sidst i stavelsen.
33 Cf. an imperative like *hækl!* from *hækle* '(to) crochet' which deviates from principles for both word structure and syllable structure, see Basbøll (2018).

sg̊ʌð²], from infinitive *spille, skodde* 'play', 'butt (a cigarette)' [ˈsb̥elə ˈsg̊ʌðə], illustrate this when compared to the corresponding nouns *spil, skod* 'play', 'butt' [sb̥el sg̊ʌð] which do not have stød; in the Non-Stød Model this is due to Extra-Prosodicity.

Thus all three specific cases of stød in VS-monosyllables mentioned by Rischel (2001) have a unitary account according to the Non-Stød Model, viz. Extra-Prosodicity, in full agreement with Rischel's suggestions in the text. Rischel (2001: 22) says further,

> The stød in imperatives is one reason why there is in Danish *distinctive [contrastive] stød also in monosyllabic word forms*. There is a further, collateral, reason, also concerning types II/III, namely the set of sound changes that strike some words of type II (the subcategory VSO), whereby, first, the combination sonorant + plosive was assimilated to sonorant, as in *land* > [*lan²*] ['country'], and, second, the earlier difference in length between long and short consonant disappeared, so that we ended up by having total or partial segmental identity between the *n*s in *ven* and *vend* [the latter with stød and "mute d"/HB]. Thereby stød has become distinctive [contrastive] at the surface also in non-declined nouns, even though this opposition can be interpreted, structurally, as a difference in number of morae.³⁴ [cf. the quotation above starting with "In type II"/HB]

Rischel (2001: 23–24) concludes his discussion as follows, with formulations I wholeheartedly endorse:

> One can also change the point of departure for the description of Nordic accentuation and say – perhaps more à la Basbøll – that *lack of stød, respectively accent 2, in polysyllables with heavy (in Danish: sonority-heavy) full syllables indicates that phonologically, the words concerned are prototypical, completely streamlined polysyllabic words which also morphologically-lexically are perceived as well integrated unified wholes*. Then we just have to add a paragraph about why we lack stød in Danish also in monosyllables of the type *ven*.³⁵

---

34 Rischel's original: Imperativstødet er én grund til at vi i dansk har fået *distinktivt stød også i enstavede ordformer*. Der er en samvirkende grund, også vedrørende type II/III, nemlig det sæt lydudviklinger der ramte en del ord af type II (underkategorien VSO), hvorved for det første sonorant + klusil blev assimileret til sonorant, som i *land* > *[lan²]*, og for det andet den tidligere længdeforskel mellem lang og kort konsonant svandt, så vi helt eller delvis fik segmental identitet mellem *n*'erne i *ven* og *vend*. Derved er stødet blevet overfladedistinktivt også i ubøjede substantiver, selv om modsætningen strukturelt kan tolkes som en forskel i moratal.

35 Rischel's original: Man kan også skifte udgangspunkt for beskrivelsen af nordisk accentuation og – måske mere Basbøllsk – sige at *stødløshed, henholdsvis akcent 2, i flerstavelsesord med tunge (i dansk: klangtunge) fuldstavelser markerer at der fonologisk er tale om prototypiske, helt strømlinjede flerstavelsesord der samtidig morfologisk-leksikalsk opleves som velintegrerede helheder*. – Så skal der blot tilføjes en særlig paragraf om hvorfor stødløsheden i dansk også findes i enstavelsesord af typen *ven*.

The last paragraph Rischel (2001) calls for is easily formulated in terms of Extra-Prosodicity within my framework (Section 4.4). It gives a coherent overall description, and even though there are many complexities in the stød-system, and many dialect speakers do not have any systematic use of stød in their language (cf. Ejskjær 1990), there is no tendency at all towards general loss of stød: The language evolution seems to take quite another direction (cf. Section 6).

8 Envoi

For many decades, Theo Vennemann has been a pioneer in scrutinizing syllable structure, weight phenomena and hierarchies in phonology. He has generalised the concept of Preference Laws to apply to other linguistic domains in addition to phonology. He has scientifically explored the relation between diachrony and synchrony in linguistics in a very insightful and most original way. It is therefore a pleasure to dedicate the present paper to the truly *Great Master of Linguistics Theo Vennemann!*

References

Basbøll, Hans. 1973. Notes on Danish consonant combinations. *Annual Report of the Institute of Phonetics. University of Copenhagen* 7. 103–142.
Basbøll, Hans. 1988. The Modern Danish stød and phonological weight. In Pier Marco Bertinetto & Michele Loporcaro (eds.), *Certamen Phonologicum: Papers from the 1987 Cortona Phonology Meeting*. 119–152. Torino: Rosenberg & Sellier.
Basbøll, Hans. 1989. Phonological weight and Italian radoppiamento fonosintattico. *Rivista di linguistica (= Italian Journal of Linguistics)* 1. 5–31.
Basbøll, Hans. 1998. Nyt om stødet i moderne rigsdansk – om samspillet mellem lydstruktur og ordgrammatik [News concerning the stød in modern standard Danish – on the interaction between sound structure and word grammar (morphology)]. *Danske Studier* 1998. 33–86.
Basbøll, Hans. 2001. What can be derived from just three binary features? Occam's razor and Major Classes for phonotactics. In Nina Grønnum & Jørgen Rischel (eds.), *To honour Eli Fischer-Jørgensen: Festschrift on the occasion of her 90th birthday, February 11th, 2001*. 74–99. Copenhagen: C. A. Reitzel.
Basbøll, Hans. 2005. *The phonology of Danish*. Oxford: Oxford University Press.
Basbøll, Hans. 2006. French and Danish syllables and their peaks: A typological perspective. In Henning Nølke, Irène Baron, Hanne Korzen, Iørn Korzen & Henrik Müller (eds.), *Grammatica: Festschrift in honour of Michael Herslund*, 19–31. Bern: Peter Lang.
Basbøll, Hans. 2008. Stød, diachrony and the Non-Stød Model. *North-Western European Language Evolution* 54/55. 147–189.

Basbøll, Hans. 2014. Danish stød as evidence for grammaticalization of suffixal positions in word structure. *Acta Linguistica Hafniensia* 46. 137–158.
Basbøll, Hans. 2017. The Sonority Syllable Model reconsidered: Two challenges and their solution. In Elena Babatsouli (ed.), *Proceedings of the International Symposium on Monolingual and Bilingual Speech 2017*, 71–77. Chania: Institute of Monolingual and Bilingual Speech.
Basbøll, Hans. 2018. Danish imperative formation: A problem for the phonology/morphology interface. *Scandinavian Philology* 16. 219–244.
Brink, Lars & Jørn Lund. 1975. *Dansk Rigsmål 1–2*. Copenhagen: Gyldendal.
Brink, Lars, Jørn Lund, Steffen Heger & Lars Normann Jørgensen. 1991. *Den store danske udtaleordbog* [The comprehensive dictionary of Danish pronunciation]. Copenhagen: Munksgaard.
Ejskjær, Inger. 1990. Stød and pitch accents in the Danish dialects. *Acta Linguistica Hafniensia* 22. 49–76.
Fischer-Jørgensen, Eli. 1985. Some basic vowel features, their acoustic correlates and their explanatory power. In Victoria Fromkin (ed.), *Phonetic linguistics: Essays in honor of Peter Ladefoged*, 79–99. Orlando: Academic Press.
Fischer-Jørgensen, Eli. 1987. A phonetic study of the stød in standard Danish. *Annual Report of the Institute of Phonetics, University of Copenhagen* 21. 55–265. [Slightly revised version published as monograph, Turku 1989.]
Fischer-Jørgensen, Eli. 1989. Phonetic analysis of the stød in standard Danish. *Phonetica* 46. 1–59.
Grønnum, Nina. 2005 [1998]. *Fonetik og fonologi – Almen og Dansk* [Phonetics and phonology – General and Danish]. Copenhagen: Akademisk Forlag [1st edn. 1998, 2d edn. 2001, 3d edn. 2005].
Grønnum, Nina. 2007. *Rødgrød med fløde – En lille bog om dansk fonetik* [Red berry compote with cream[36] – A little book on Danish phonetics]. Copenhagen: Akademisk Forlag [e-book 2010].
Grønnum, Nina & Hans Basbøll. 2001. Consonant length, stød and morae in Standard Danish. *Phonetica* 58. 230–53.
Grønnum, Nina & Hans Basbøll. 2007. Danish stød: Phonological and cognitive issues. In Marie-José Solé, Patricia Beddor & Manjari Ohala (eds.), *Experimental approaches to phonology*, 192–206. Oxford: Oxford University Press.
Grønnum, Nina & Hans Basbøll. 2012. Danish stød: Towards simpler structural principles? In Oliver Niebuhr (ed.), *Understanding Prosody: The role of context, function, and communication*, 27–46. Berlin: de Gruyter.
Grønnum, Nina, Miguel Vázquez-Larruscáin & Hans Basbøll. 2013. Danish stød: Laryngealization or tone. *Phonetica* 70. 66–92.
Grønnum, Nina, Nicolai Pharao & Hans Basbøll. 2020. Stød in unexpected morphological contexts in Standard Danish – an experimental approach to sound change in progress. *Nordic Journal of Linguistics* 43. 147–180. DOI:10.1017/S0332586520000074.
Gårding, Eva. 1977. *The Scandinavian word accents*. Lund: Gleerup.
Hansen, Aage. 1943. *Stødet i dansk* [The stød in Danish]. Copenhagen: Munksgaard.
Herslund, Michael. 2002. *Danish*. Munich: LINCOM Europa.

---

[36] A traditional Danish dish that is famous for being very difficult to pronounce for foreigners.

Hjelmslev, Louis. 1951. Grundtræk af det danske udtrykssystem med særligt henblik på stødet. *Selskab for Nordisk Filologi: Årsberetning for 1948–49–50*. 14–24. Copenhagen. [Translated as "Outline of the Danish expression system with special reference to the stød" in Louis Hjelmslev. 1973. *Essais linguistiques* II, 247–266. Copenhagen: Nordisk Sprog-og Kulturforlag.]

Kristoffersen, Gjert. 1999. Quantity in Norwegian syllable structure. In Harry van der Hulst & Nancy Ritter (eds.), *The syllable: Views and facts*, 631–650. Berlin: de Gruyter.

Kristoffersen, Gjert. 2011. Quantity in Old Norse and modern peninsular North Germanic. *Journal of Comparative Germanic Linguistics* 14. 47–80.

Ladefoged, Peter. 1971. *Preliminaries to linguistic phonetics*. Chicago: Chicago University Press.

Liberman, Anatoly. 2007. Review article of Basbøll 2005. *North-Western European Language Evolution* 52. 101–111.

Ohala, John 1992. Alternatives to the sonority hierarchy for explaining segmental sequential constraints. *Papers from the parasession on the syllable*, 319–338. Chicago: Chicago Linguistic Society.

Ohala, John 2008. The emergent syllable. In Barbara Davis & Krisztina Zajdo (eds.), *The syllable in speech production*, 179–186. London: Francis & Taylor.

Ohala, John & Haruko Kawasaki-Fukumori. 1997. Explaining sequential segmental constraints. In Stig Eliasson & Ernst Håkon Jahr (eds.), *Language and its ecology: Essays in memory of Einar Haugen*, 343–365. Berlin: de Gruyter.

Parker, Stephen. 2002. *Quantifying the sonority hierarchy*. Amherst, MA: University of Massachusetts Amherst dissertation. https://www.diu.edu/documents/Parker%20 dissertation.pdf (accessed 29 July, 2021).

Pike, Kenneth. 1943. *Phonetics: A critical analysis of phonetic theory and a technic for the practical description of sounds*. Ann Arbor, MI: The University of Michigan Press.

Riber Petersen, Pia. 1973. An instrumental investigation of the Danish Stød. *Annual Report of the Institute of Phonetics, University of Copenhagen* 7. 195–234.

Rischel, Jørgen. 2001. Om stødets opkomst [On the origin of the stød]. In Jørgen Rischel & Hans Basbøll (eds.), *Tre indlæg om stødet* [Three contributions on the stød]. *Pluridicta* 38. 16–25. Odense: Institut for Sprog og Kommunikation, Syddansk Universitet.

Rischel, Jørgen. 2008. A unified theory of Nordic i-umlaut, syncope, and stød. *North-Western European Language Evolution* 54/55. 191–235. Also in Rischel 2009: 272–311.

Rischel, Jørgen. 2009. *Sound structure in language*. Edited and with an introduction by Nina Grønnum, Frans Gregersen & Hans Basbøll. Oxford: Oxford University Press.

Vennemann, Theo. 1988. *Preference laws for syllable structure and the explanation of sound change*. Berlin: de Gruyter.

Philip Hoole
Towards phonetic explanations for preferred sound patterns

Abstract: We focus here on consonant clusters as a test-bed for an examination of the phonetic forces shaping the structure of sound systems, taking as point of departure the hypothesis of Chitoran, Goldstein, and Byrd (2002) that preferred clusters may represent a good compromise between parallel transmission of segmental information, i.e. large overlap (efficient for the speaker), and clear modulation of the acoustic signal (efficient for the listener). We look firstly at clusters involving obstruent plus nasal, lateral, or rhotic, since these are well known to differ widely in their diachronic stability (Vennemann 2000). Articulatory measurements of German and French speakers (using electromagnetic articulography) were supplemented by articulatory synthesis to simulate the aerodynamic conditions in these clusters. Results for obstruent plus nasal (low overlap) vs. obstruent plus lateral (higher overlap) matched the hypothesis in a simple way. Obstruent plus rhotic also showed a low-overlap pattern, which in the light of the hypothesis was unexpected given their relatively preferred status. But good aerodynamic reasons for the low-overlap pattern were uncovered, and a potentially very close link between rhotic and vowel is discussed.

Two further sections present, firstly, an articulatory analysis of syllabic consonants in Slovak. The patterns of gestural coordination (consonant-consonant and consonant-vowel) turn out to provide insight into why these sounds are overall dispreferred (and perhaps also into why they may nonetheless become well-established in specific languages). Finally, the diachronic preference for vowel nasalisation to occur more readily in the context of following nasal plus voiceless obstruent (vs. nasal plus voiced obstruent) is examined synchronically by comparing temporal patterns of velum movement (using real-time magnetic resonance imaging) in German word-pairs such as *Panda* 'panda' and *Panther* 'panther'. Clear differences in velar movement were found, consistent with stronger forces in the voiceless case towards a shift of the velar movement from the nasal onto the vowel.

Philip Hoole, Institute of Phonetics and Speech Processing, Ludwig-Maximilians-Universität München, Munich/Germany

https://doi.org/10.1515/9783110721461-007

1 Introduction

A long-standing concern at the interface between phonetics and phonology is to improve our understanding of the phonetic forces shaping the structure of sound systems. This paper will review here some of our recent work in this field, concentrating in particular on consonant clusters for which many important regularities have been observed (e.g. Vennemann 2000, 2012). We will mainly be concerned with articulatory analysis of consonant clusters in German and French (in Section 2), but will also widen the perspective somewhat to take in syllabic consonants in Slovak (in Section 3) and also possible links between phonological vowel nasalisation and properties of post-vocalic consonants, based on a real-time magnetic resonance imaging study of German (in Section 4). Within the context of the present paper, we take preferred sound patterns to mean those clusters that are widely attested in the languages of the world and/or show diachronic stability. The overall hypothesis guiding our work (set out in more detail in Section 2) is that preferred patterns are those that allow a good compromise between efficiency for the speaker (by allowing parallel transmission of segmental information) and efficiency for the listener (i.e. robust recoverability in perception of the sounds intended by the speaker).

1.1 Preliminary examples

To set the scene we will first look briefly at two examples from the literature to illustrate what we mean by phonetic forces shaping sound structure. Both these examples will turn out to be relevant as background for some of the explanations offered for the more detailed findings discussed in subsequent sections.

1.1.1 The case of missing /g/

Ohala (1983) has provided very cogent evidence that an understanding of the aerodynamic processes involved in speech production can be necessary for an understanding of some classes of regularities and preferences in sound patterns. We would like to exemplify this here with the observation that if one of the voiced consonants in the standard /b, d, g/ series is missing, then it is typically /g/. Based on the survey of Sherman quoted by Ohala, 40 languages (of over 500 surveyed) had a gap at the velar place but only two at the labial place.

The relevant aerodynamic background is that vocal fold vibration needs an air-flow through the glottis. This in turn requires a pressure-drop across the glottis, and this pressure-drop is more difficult to maintain in some sounds than others. Specifically, in the case of voiced plosives there is less volume behind the constriction for /g/ than for /d/ or /b/. This leads to quicker equalisation of the transglottal pressure difference and thus to devoicing.[1]

1.1.2 Clusters in Georgian

Here we briefly summarise some of the interesting results of Chitoran, Goldstein, and Byrd (2002). In their articulatory study of Georgian, they observed less articulatory overlap between C1 (Consonant 1) and C2 (Consonant 2) in /gb/ than /bg/ sequences, i.e. the order of place of articulation in the cluster is relevant. For the back-front order (/gb/), there is more danger of the acoustic properties of C1 being masked by C2 than in the front-back order (/bg/) (see Figure 2 below for an example of articulatory overlap measurements in consonant sequences). Thus these results illustrate the important but perhaps not inherently surprising point that articulatory planning may be constrained by the necessity for the resulting acoustic output to provide enough information for listeners to be able to recover the underlying articulations from the acoustic signal. However, perhaps more intriguingly, the results also illustrate how articulatory constraints can be reflected in relationships between apparently distinct parts of the sound system.

There is in Georgian an interesting interaction between the articulatory regularity we have just outlined (often referred to as the place-order effect) and the laryngeal specification of consonant sequences. Specifically, only the low-overlap back-front order allows laryngeally complex onsets such as /tʰ b/.

High-overlap front-back clusters such as /bg/ are laryngeally homogenous (traditionally referred to as "harmonic" clusters). From the point of view of the articulatory/aerodynamic constraints, these patterns seem quite natural: the realisation of a laryngeally complex onset quite simply requires time. In the example just given of a laryngeally complex onset, the glottal configuration must change from open to adducted, and probably also the increased intra-oral air-pressure in the first part of the cluster /t/ must decline sufficiently after the release of the /t/ for initiation of voicing for the following voiced consonant to be possible. These timing constraints in turn require a low-overlap coordination of the oral articulators, which the back-front order for place of articulation fulfils.

---

[1] Strictly speaking, as pointed out by Ohala, it is not just the smaller volume of air per se, but rather the fact that this smaller volume allows less possibility for passive expansion, that would slow the rise in pressure as air flows into the oral cavity behind the articulatory constriction.

2 Articulatory coordination in obstruent-sonorant clusters

We now turn to the first of our more detailed examples. The overall question can be framed as follows: How is linguistic structure reflected in the coordination relations between articulators?

For the present paper, we will be focussing on consonant clusters, leading to a condensed cluster-specific version of the above general question, namely: What makes a good cluster (cf. Bombien 2011)? To turn this rather terse question into a guiding hypothesis for our work, we were much influenced by the approach exemplified in the paper of Chitoran, Goldstein, and Byrd (2002) referred to in Section 1.1.2 above.

Following their work, we hypothesise that a successful cluster should represent a good compromise between efficiency for the speaker and efficiency for the listener. Efficiency for the speaker can be achieved through parallel transmission of segmental information, i.e. substantial articulatory overlap between the elements of the cluster, while efficiency for the listener is assumed to reside in clear modulation of the acoustic signal.

We will approach this overall question in two stages. In the first stage we will compare the articulatory coordination of plosive+lateral and plosive+nasal clusters, basing our findings both on direct articulatory measurements as well as on modelling, i.e. articulatory synthesis. In the second stage we will consider whether the quite neat picture that emerges from the first stage remains intact when we extend the approach to plosive+rhotic clusters.

2.1 Clusters of plosive plus lateral or nasal

The specific question to be addressed here is whether there is a phonetically well-founded sense in which sequences of **plosive + nasal** are less suitable as a complex onset than **plosive + lateral**. Indications that clusters such as /kl/ are more preferred than /kn/ are the more widespread occurrence of the former in a synchronic perspective and the greater tendency of the latter to simplify to a singleton in a diachronic perspective, as exemplified by English *knee* vs. German *Knie* 'knee' (whereas comparable /kl/ clusters have been retained in both languages).

An aerodynamically motivated explanation for why /kn/ may be susceptible to reduction to /n/ is that substantial overlap between /k/ and /n/ in the cluster may compromise the characteristics of the plosive burst (opening of the velum for /n/ may lead to a premature reduction in the intraoral air-pressure necessary for the plosive burst). The counterpart to this line of explanation is that in languages such as German where /kn/ has been retained, then this may come at the price of requiring an articulatory coordination pattern involving low overlap between plosive and nasal.

Even though the account sketched out here may seem plausible a priori, it remains speculative as long as the hypothesised differences in coordination have not been demonstrated by means of articulatory measurements. Accordingly, in the immediately following section, we will present results of articulatory analysis and then supplement the approach in Section 2.1.2 with modelling (articulatory synthesis).

2.1.1 Articulatory analysis

We analysed the movements of the relevant articulators (tongue-tip, tongue-back, lips) by means of electromagnetic articulography (EMA; AG500, Carstens Medizinelektronik, Göttingen). Briefly, EMA measures the movement of small sensors attached to the articulators, based on the signal induced in these sensors by a set of transmitter coils mounted around the head (see Figure 1 and Hoole and Zierdt 2010 for further details).

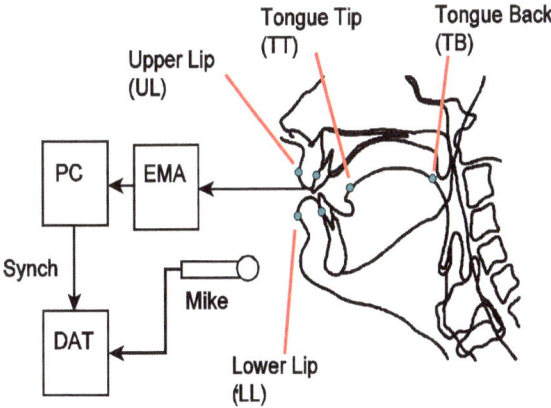

Figure 1: Schematic overview of synchronised acquisition of articulatory and acoustic data. Locations of sensors for the relevant articulators are shown. Additional reference sensors are used to factor out head movements of the speakers.

The measurements made are illustrated in Figure 2 using the onset cluster /kl/ as an example. Various measures have been proposed in the literature for capturing the coordination of two articulators. The measure outlined in Figure 2 is based on the temporal location of the closure phase of the /l/, as identified in the tongue-tip signal, relative to the closure phase of the /k/, as identified in the tongue-back signal. Specifically:

normalised overlap (%) = ((Offset_2 - Onset_4) / (Offset_4 - Onset_2)) * 100

where "Onset_2" and "Offset_2" refer to the temporal location of the left edge and right edge of the phase labelled "2" in the figure (similarly for Phase 4). Note that positive values indicate overlap between Phase 2 and Phase 4 (left edge of Phase 4 occurs earlier than the right edge of phase 2) whereas negative values indicate a lag.

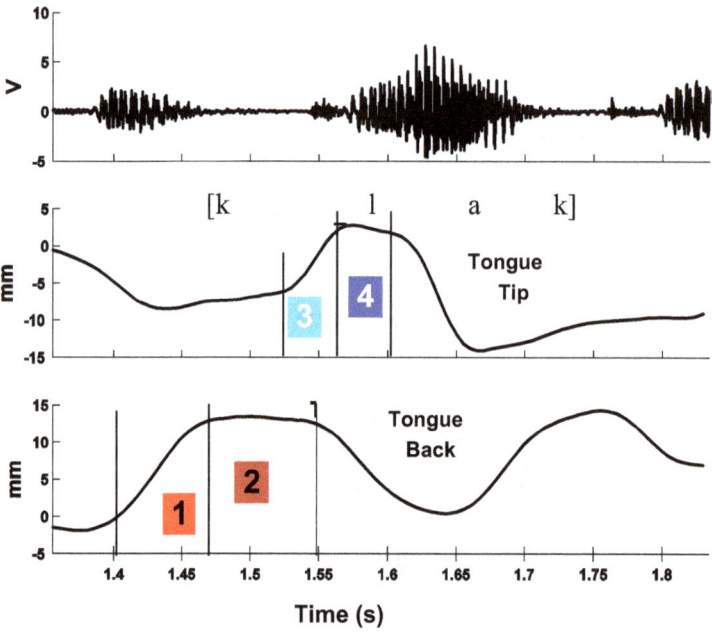

Figure 2: Illustration of measurements made to assess coordination of tongue-tip and tongue-back. The respective panels show the vertical component of the movement of these two articulators. The phases labelled "4" (tongue-tip) and "2" (tongue-back) indicate the closure phases as determined by a velocity threshold.

Figure 3 shows results averaged over five German speakers for three pairs of clusters varying /l/ and /n/ as C2: kl/kn, gl/gn, pl/pn. The clusters were located in onset position of the target words (monosyllables and some trochaic words) and spoken in a constant carrier phrase. Each cluster was embedded in (usually) two different words, each word being repeated ten times in randomised order, i.e. a total of about 100 items per cluster (further details of the recording and analysis procedures for the investigation from which these results are taken can be found e.g. in Bombien, Mooshammer, and Hoole 2013 and Bombien 2011).

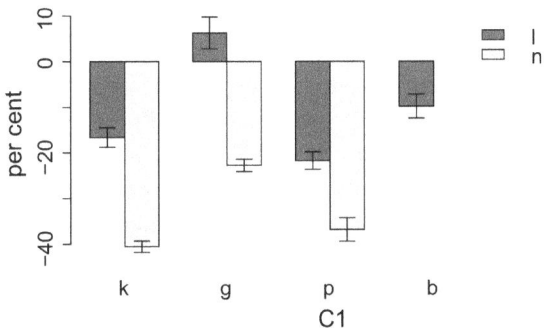

Figure 3: Results for the normalised overlap measure (averaged over 5 speakers of German) for clusters contrasting /l/ and /n/ as C2.

There is a clear pattern that the plosive+n clusters show more negative values of the overlap measure. As defined above, negative values of this measure correspond to a lag between the offset of the closure of C1 (i.e. the right edge of phase 2 in Figure 2) and the onset of the closure of C2 (left edge of phase 4), with more negative values corresponding to a longer lag.

This result appears to represent a robust effect, i.e. it appears to generalise well, beyond the specific material on which Figure 3 is based. It is also found in a separate set of recordings in which the same speakers contrast the kl/kn pair in prosodically more varied conditions, and it has been found for a separate set of German speakers recorded with a different technique, namely electropalatography (see Bombien et al. 2010 and Bombien, Mooshammer, and Hoole 2013 for details). For example, both the latter two papers find equally robust differences in the timing of /kl/ vs. /kn/ regardless of whether they are in the onset of words with a trochaic or iambic stress pattern. The effect has also been found in several more recent experiments in our lab, for example Pastätter (2017), on Polish (see especially fig. 4.2 in chap. 4), and Peters (2015; see especially chap. 5), investigating children as well as adults (as well as in a small amount of earlier data for French in Kühnert, Hoole, and Mooshammer 2006).

2.1.2 Modelling

Having shown in the previous section that speakers may well adopt different coordination patterns for clusters that are very similar in terms of place of articulation (e.g. velar plus alveolar for both /kl/ and /kn/) the scenario could now be made more compelling if we could formally demonstrate that the coordination patterns reflect the speakers' response to the different aerodynamic constraints of the lateral vs. nasal clusters, i.e. give a quantitative basis to the phonetic intuition outlined above.

Articulatory synthesis is an appropriate tool to this end, since it allows us to investigate the aerodynamic, acoustic and perceptual implications of different coordination strategies. For the specific question to be addressed here we used the TADA software package (Nam et al. 2006, Nam, Goldstein, and Saltzman 2009). This is an implementation of the Task Dynamic model of speech production, incorporating the so-called "competitive coupled-oscillator model of speech timing", which, based on insights from the framework of Articulatory Phonology (e.g. Browman and Goldstein 1990), in turn incorporates a theory of gestural timing for correctly coordinating consonant and vowel gestures in complex syllables, i.e. C1 with C2, C1 and C2 with V.

For present purposes we investigated what gestural coordination patterns appeared to be crucial to successfully synthesise the sequence /apna/. The steps are outlined below. Spectrograms of the sound output from the three steps are shown in Figure 4:

> Step 1. The default gestural coordination for C1 and C2 in syllable onsets was used (based on previous work this was known to be appropriate for /pl/). The result was clearly deficient: velar lowering associated with C2 indeed prevented sufficient oral pressure build-up for /p/. This is reflected in the sonagram (left panel of Figure 4) by the absence of a burst at the end of the closure phase.
>
> Step 2. A non-default low-overlap coordination topology that had originally been suggested by Goldstein et al. (2009) was used to model the Georgian non-harmonic, laryngeally heterogeneous clusters discussed above. The result was substantially better since a release burst for /p/ was now present (Figure 4, middle panel).
>
> Step 3. Additional experimentation revealed that a further slight increase in the salience of the burst for /p/ (and the naturalness of the result) could be achieved by increasing the velocity of the velum movement from its default value, giving a sharper transition between closed position of the velum to open position for /n/ (Figure 4, right panel).[2]

---

[2] An interesting feature of this kind of articulatory synthesis is that it generates not only the acoustic output but also the underlying air-pressure and air-flow in the vocal tract. For further discussion and illustration of the present example by means of intraoral air-pressure patterns, see Hoole et al. (2013).

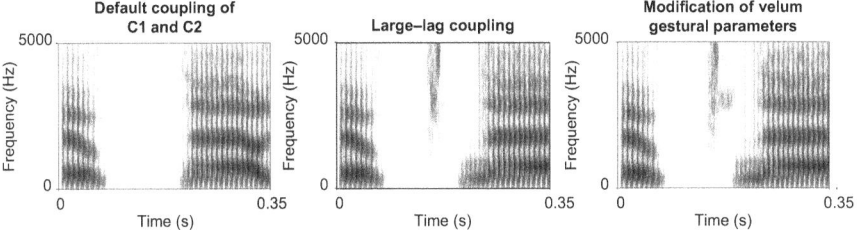

Figure 4: Synthesis of /pn/ with three different gestural specifications.

The result of this exploratory use of articulatory synthesis can ultimately be seen as support for the very general hypothesis inspired by the Articulatory Phonology approach of Browman and Goldstein (1990), namely that gestural coupling topologies capture phonologically relevant aspects of gestural structure.

For the Georgian example above, the phonological relevance is given by the fact that greater laryngeal complexity is allowed in a topology with lower overlap. For the present German example, the different coupling topologies capture the overlap differences between plosive+/l/ and plosive+/n/ clusters, and this is phonologically relevant: because of the different diachronic behaviour of clusters like /kn/ in English and German (and the similar behaviour for /kl/).

To conclude this section, let us refer back to one of the original questions, namely what makes a good cluster (or here rather to its counterpart, namely what makes a cluster synchronically or diachronically unattractive):

The sequence plosive+/n/ may be disfavoured (relative to plosive+/l/) because it is physiologically costly, i.e. a substantial departure from default coordination relations is necessary for acceptable sound production, and would thus represent a relatively poor compromise between efficiency for the speaker and efficiency for the hearer.

2.2 Muddying the waters: How do rhotic clusters fit in?

Following on from the previous section, we now slightly broaden the perspective to ask what is to be expected from a comparison of plosive+lateral and plosive+rhotic. Clusters of plosive+rhotic are not diachronically unstable, at least not in the same way plosive+nasal clusters are. Indeed, following Vennemann (2000), plosive+rhotic appears to be the most favoured of the cluster types considered here and in the previous section. In the spirit of the initial hypotheses of the previous section, this could lead to the expectation that plosive+rhotic clusters are very suitable for "parallel transmission" and thus should show a high degree of overlap between C1 and C2. Figure 5 shows the results of the articulatory measurements for four speakers of German and five of French, comparing overlap patterns for plosive+l and plosive+r.[3]

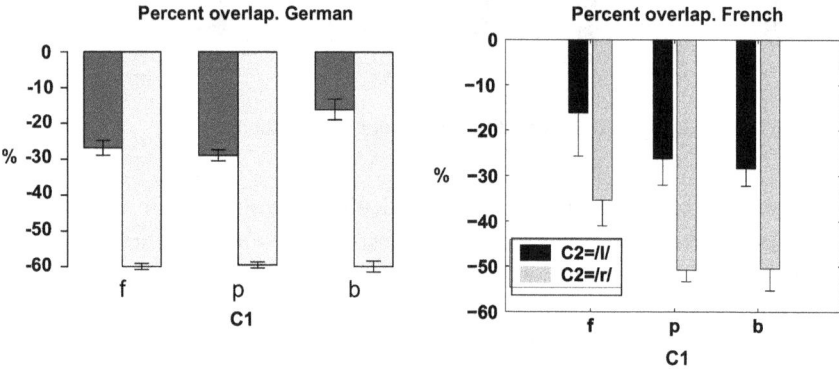

Figure 5: Articulatory overlap in onset clusters /fl, fr, pl, pr, bl, br/ (from left to right in each panel). Overlap computed as illustrated in Figure 2: for /l/-clusters overlap of lip and tongue-tip; for /r/-clusters overlap of lip and dorsum. Averaged over 4 speakers of German and 5 speakers of French. More negative values indicate less overlap. Error bars indicate standard error of mean over speakers.

Clearly, the results show *lower* overlap (i.e. more strongly negative values) for plosive+rhotic than plosive+lateral.

Does this mean that our line of argument for the plosive+nasal clusters is invalid? This would seem to be the case, at least at first sight. However, the clash with the prediction could be resolved if it were possible to show, by taking a wider view of the coordination relations within the syllable, that these (dorsal) rhotics have a specially close coordination relation to the vowel, rather than the preceding consonant. This close link to the vowel might, in turn, have the effect of pulling them away from C1.[4] Such a close link between rhotic and vowel would at least make it easy to account for metathesis of the following kind:

---

[3] All speakers had a dorsal rhotic. We use /r/ here for typographical convenience. The German speakers are the same as those in the previous section, but leaving out one speaker with an apical /r/.

[4] The title for this section was inspired by an off-the-cuff remark of Henning Reetz (p.c.): "r's are like dirt on the vowel (*Dreck auf dem Vokal*)". As we will note briefly below, this kind of phonetic intuition may be supported by evidence from recent real-time MRI films of articulation.

French, standard vs. dialectal:	*premier*: /prœmje/ vs. /permje/ (quoted from Russell Webb & Bradley 2009)
Germanic:	*hross* (Icel.) and *hros* (OHG) vs. *horse* (rhotic Engl. dialects)
English, standard vs. dialectal:	*pretty* vs. *perty*

By extension, the above observations lead to the hypothesis that this kind of metathesis is more common with rhotics than laterals. However, we are not currently aware of any quantitative typological or diachronic information that would allow us to determine whether this prediction is correct. Equally interesting, but perhaps even more difficult to quantify, would be the relative frequency of such metatheses on the one hand and the diachronic instability of plosive+nasal on the other hand.

However, a question of equal importance, and one that is potentially addressable by empirical data, is whether there is indeed any articulatory evidence that low overlap of C1-C2 (when C2 is rhotic) is accompanied by high overlap of C2 and the following vowel. Unfortunately, the corpora of articulatory data on which the above results for patterns of C1 and C2 coordination were based was not explicitly designed to address this question. One would require material where the syllable rhyme (vowel plus coda consonant(s)) is held constant over different onset clusters (e.g. /pl/ vs. /pr/) and over appropriate control contexts with onset singletons (e.g. /pr/ vs. /r/). With material of this kind, it would be possible to relate the timing of the right-most consonant in the onset to a common anchor-point in the coda and thus determine to what extent any shift of the onset consonant over the vowel depends on the complexity and nature of the onset (see Hoole et al. 2013 for further background)[5].

Thus, even though we cannot pursue this issue empirically here, we believe that it would be well worth-while to do so, because even casual inspection of real-time MRI recordings of articulation (currently becoming more and more readily available) makes the close integration of rhotic and vowel movement appear quite compelling. An example is given in the supplementary materials (https://www.degruyter.com/document/isbn/9783110721461/html. videosupplement-1-hoole.mp4): the /r/ in the German word *brannten* is difficult to identify as a specific articulatory target but rather appears to form part of an overall pattern of tongue movement extending from initial /b/ through the vowel to the following /n/ (for

---

[5] It is perhaps interesting to note here that Russell Webb and Bradley (2009) take this line of thought even a step further by simply assuming in their optimality theory account of metathesis that the centre of the rhotic is coordinated with the centre of the vowel.

easier orientation in the movie, the articulatory movements can be linked to a synchronised sonagram: the release of initial /b/ in *brannten* 'burnt, 1/3 pl. ind. pret.' occurs slightly before 1s on the time axis. The post-vocalic /n/ is reached at about 1.2s. For more details of the context in which these recordings were made, please refer to Section 4 below).

If these rather informal observations can be substantiated, then it would indicate that the concept of parallel transmission, which we introduced above and which was initially presented in terms of parallel transmission of consonant information, may need to be re-conceptualised for rhotic clusters in terms of parallel information of consonant and vowel.

In an effort to get back to firmer ground, we can in this section, too, use articulatory synthesis to better understand the driving forces behind the preferred patterns, i.e. here why plosive-rhotic clusters favour low overlap between C1 and C2. For this experiment we used VocalTractLab (Birkholz 2012, Birkholz, Jackèl, and Kröger 2006) to synthesise two versions of the syllable /bra/. Version 1 used normal overlap of /b/ and /r/, i.e. it aimed to reproduce a normal production of this German syllable. Version 2 was based on increased overlap of /b/ and /r/, i.e. the labial gesture for /b/ and the dorsal gesture for /r/ were moved closer together in time. Spectrograms of the two versions are shown in Figure 6.

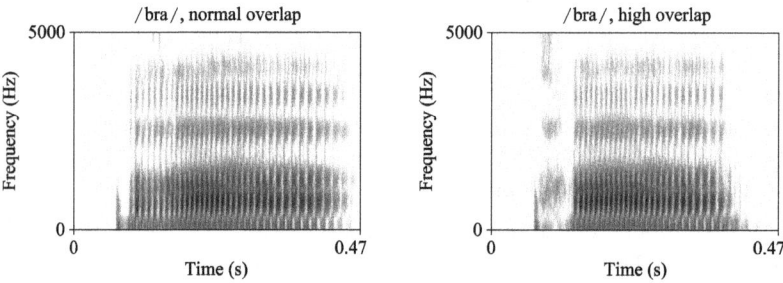

Figure 6: Comparison of acoustic output for onset consonants of syllable /bra/ synthesised with normal overlap (left) and high overlap (right).

The striking finding is that changing the overlap of the oral gestures (for /b/ and /r/) also affects voicing onset: the /r/ is essentially voiceless in the second case. VocalTractLab incorporates a self-oscillating model of the vocal folds, and, because it also simulates air-pressure and air-flow in the vocal tract, vibration of the vocal folds will only occur when appropriate aerodynamic conditions obtain. This takes us back to our preliminary example of "missing g" in Section 1.1.1 above: Dorsals are unfavourable for voicing. Aerodynamic conditions may thus provide a bias against high overlap in voiced obstruents+rhotics, since if there is a strong dorsal constriction already in place at the time of the release of the /b/, then the raised intra-oral air-pressure that has built up during the /b/ closure will not be able to decline very fast and thus re-initiation of vocal-fold vibration will be delayed. This is a problem because the rhotic following a voiceless plosive is most likely voiceless in any case (further examples below), and thus in the high-overlap scenario the distinction between /br/ and /pr/ would tend to collapse.[6]

We hypothesise that the coordination pattern that becomes established for aerodynamic reasons in voiced plosive + rhotics then generalises to voiceless plosives + rhotics.

The more general point that we believe can be derived from observations of this kind is that by taking aerodynamic conditions and articulatory coordination patterns into account, it may be possible to develop more insightful accounts of apparently massive surface variability. To exemplify this we would like to consider a re-interpretation of some of the very interesting observations on vowel epenthesis in French and Spanish provided in Colantoni and Steele (2007).

As a point of departure, consider the spectrogram in Figure 7 contrasting French words with /br/ and /pr/ in the onset. Clearly the rhotics in this French example are radically different at the acoustic surface: voiced in /br/ (also with clear evidence of an epenthetic vowel between /b/ and /r/ in this example) and (extremely) voiceless in /pr/.[7]

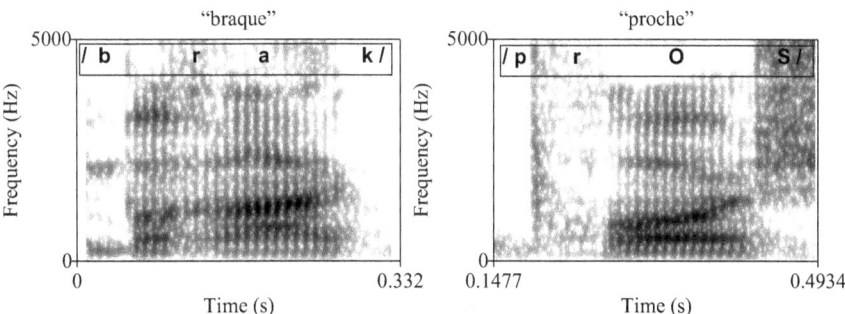

Figure 7: Example of the /br/ vs. /pr/ contrast in onset position for a speaker of French.

---

[6] For this example, based on a German model, the /b/ itself is essentially voiceless in initial position. For a language with pre-voiced /b/ the high overlap scenario will increase the chances of an interruption in voicing (rather than delaying its re-initiation as in the German case).

[7] The source of the substantial voicelessness in /pr/ is actually an interesting point in itself, given that many phonological accounts do not assume an active spread-glottis specification for voiceless plosives in French. This cannot be followed up here, but see Hoole and Bombien (2017) for direct measurements of the relevant laryngeal behaviour and further discussion of the phonological implications.

Colantoni and Steele (2007) assume that radically different cluster simplification ("repair") processes can operate in cases such as /br/ vs. /pr/. In the cases with voiced C1 (e.g. /br/) they see the frequent occurrence of vowel epenthesis as a process of *dissimilation*.[8] On the other hand, in voiceless C1 (e.g. /pr/) they see a process of *assimilation* at work, specifically voicing assimilation (as in the example spectrogram, /r/ in /pr/ is indeed invariably voiceless; further data in Hoole and Bombien 2017).

For the crucial point in this discussion, it is necessary to refer back again to the overlap results shown in Figure 5 above. In addition to showing the clear differences between C2=/l/ (dark bars) vs. C2=/r/ (light bars), which was the point of departure for the present section, Figure 5 also shows *no* difference in overlap between C1 and C2 in /br/ vs. /pr/ (compare adjacent light bars in each panel). This makes the assumption of different epenthetic processes in the two cases much less attractive, i.e. it seems difficult to imagine that a phonological process of vowel insertion is happening in the /br/ case but not in the /pr/ case if the relative timing of C1 and C2 stays the same. Whether epenthesis *appears* to be present or not is, we would claim, just an accidental effect of whether there is continuous voicing or not. Thus, by corollary, epenthesis may be less apparent in German than French /br/ because voicing tends to be interrupted in German /b/, thus making any intrusive vowel less salient, even though the timing patterns for the oral articulators of French and German /br/ are actually quite similar, as Figure 5 also indicates. The (massive) voicelessness of the rhotic in /pr/ simply falls out from the devoicing gesture for the /p/ (which we assume to be present in French just as it is for German, as discussed further in Hoole and Bombien 2017), combined with the very unfavourable conditions for voicing caused by the dorsal constriction for /r/.

To conclude this section, the more general implications are that differences between rhotics like those in /pr/ vs. /br/ in French do not require an account in terms of phonological processes. They emerge from the interplay of general principles of articulatory coordination with aerodynamic conditions. However, what we still need is an understanding of the coordination relations that each language preferentially makes use of. This is an issue that we will briefly look at in the next section.

---

8 Interestingly, they note that the frequency of vowel epenthesis is essentially negligible in cases such as /bl/, which fits in very neatly with the overlap measures we presented above in Figure 5 (right panel): much lower overlap (or much longer lags between C1 and C2) for /Cr/ compared to /Cl/ clusters.

3 Liquids as syllabic nuclei in Slovak

The overall motivation for this work on syllabic nuclei in Slovak[9] was to aim at a better understanding of the phonetic forces that lead to the very restricted occurrence of syllabic consonants. The strategy to achieve this aim was to investigate a language where the occurrence is, in fact, relatively unrestricted. Specifically, /l, r/ in Slovak can occur in onset, nucleus, and coda. Moreover, syllabic consonants are not restricted to weak syllables, can themselves take complex onsets, and are fully integrated into the Slovak morphology of nucleus length alternations. Thus they have a much more central status in the language's phonology than is the case with syllabic consonants in English, for example.

The specific questions to be addressed were:
- How are sounds modified depending on their role in the syllable?
- To what extent do syllabic consonants become more vocalic?
- How does coordination differ, e.g. /kr/ where /r/ is part of the onset vs. /kr/ where /r/ forms the nucleus?
- Does onset-nucleus timing depend on whether the nucleus is vocalic or consonantal?

3.1 Experimental procedures

Basically the same EMA setup was used as for the investigations in Section 2 above (sensors on tongue, lips, and jaw). Five Slovak speakers were recorded. Each speaker spoke approximately 6 repetitions of each target word. Here we will focus on liquids in onset position (lak, lob; rak, raky, rok) vs. liquids in nucleus position (chlp, blb; mrk, krk, krb). Liquids in coda position were also recorded but will not be considered further here.

The target words were embedded in the carrier phrase *Užhovoríme* _____ *hodinu*.

3.2 Analysis and results

Two types of analyses were carried out: (1) Basic kinematic analysis (durations, velocities) and (2) Analysis of articulatory coordination.

---

[9] The work presented in this section is based on the original investigation published in Pouplier and Beňuš (2011) and further discussed in Hoole et al. (2013).

3.2.1 Results: Basic kinematic analysis

The results for the first set of analyses can be summarised very briefly. The aim was to determine whether basic kinematic properties of liquids depend on syllable position, i.e. onset vs. nucleus. If the consonant effectively becomes more vocalic when located in the nucleus, one might expect it to show longer durations and lower velocities in that location, compared to onset position. In fact, no evidence was found for this. We can summarise this by saying that in phonetic terms syllabic consonants are still consonants.

3.2.2 Results: Articulatory coordination

Articulatory coordination will be looked at from two points of view. Firstly, we look at consonant-consonant coordination by measuring the lag between successive consonants, e.g. for /**mr**/ in **mr**ak (onset cluster) vs. /**mr**/ in **mr**k (onset nucleus). In terms of Figure 2 above, we measured the time from the right edge of Phase 2 (end of closure of C1) to the left edge of Phase 4 (start of closure of C2). The average values for this lag measurement are summarised here (as absolute values in ms.):

	/l/	/r/
onset cluster (CC)	50	84
onset nucleus (CL)	64	90

The main finding is thus that there is a longer lag (i.e. less overlap between the two consonants) when the liquid is in the nucleus.[10] These results together show that CLC-syllables have internal structure, just like CVC syllables, i.e. they are not just a simple CCC-concatenation.[11]

The second perspective taken in these analyses is to look at onset-nucleus coordination in CL vs. CV syllables. This is also based on lag measurements between the articulators involved, however, for technical reasons the lag measure

---

[10] Note that here more positive values mean a greater distance between C1 and C2, which is the reverse of the procedure followed in Section 2 above.

[11] As in Section 2 above, there is overall longer lag (less overlap) for rhotics, even though the rhotics are completely different phonetically (dorsal in Fr./Ger., apical in Slovak). Gibson et al. (2018) suggest that the low-overlap pattern for apical rhotics is driven by the need for a preparatory lowering and retraction movement of the dorsum to occur before the actual apical constriction gesture. See Pouplier and Beňuš (2011) for further discussion of the possible role of the dorsal component of liquids within the specific context of syllabic consonants.

is defined as the interval from the time of peak velocity of the closing movement for the onset consonant to the time of peak velocity of the movement towards the target of the nucleus, whether consonantal (e.g. **/blb/**) or vocalic (e.g. **/bib/**).[12]

The mean peak velocity lag values (in ms. with sd in brackets), broken down by nucleus type are as follows:

    vowel   82.5 (23.7)
    /l/   106.4 (16.4)
    /r/   151.9 (10.2)

It will be observed that the lag is shortest for the vowel nucleus. The implication of this is that even though CLC-syllables have internal structure just like CVC-syllables, the coordination patterns for vocalic and consonantal nuclei are not identical. The key issue now is what could be driving this long-lag (low-overlap) pattern for the consonantal nuclei.

Many models (e.g. Articulatory Phonology) assume synchronous initiation of C and V in basic CV(C) syllables (see e.g. Goldstein et al. 2009 and Pouplier 2011 for illustrative gestural scores). Because the vowel is longer/slower than the consonant, it will not be unduly obscured by the consonant (this is typically implemented by lower stiffness for vowels in the underlying dynamic specification in these models). For consonantal nuclei there would be a problem, since we showed that nucleus consonants and onset consonants are very similar in length; hence the syllabic consonant would be potentially obscured by the onset consonant if speakers retained the typical coordination pattern for onset+vowel.

3.3 Implications of the Slovak results

We are now in a position to propose some possible reasons for the typological rarity of syllabic consonants:
- They require a departure from "default" CV coordination patterns.
- They disrupt the basic construction principle often assumed for speech of a slow, continuous vocalic substrate with overlaid consonantal constrictions (an idea that can be traced at least as far back as Öhman 1966).
- They require low overlap of consonantal gestures.

---

[12] This procedure tends to give more reliable results than that used in previous sections when one of the two movements involved can be towards a vocalic target.

As a final comment, we would like to note that wide spacing between consonants seems to be characteristic of Slovak, characteristic in the sense that it is not just a special feature when the liquid forms the syllable nucleus (which is what we have emphasiszed here), but also when it is part of an onset cluster (see Pouplier and Beňuš 2011, Fig. 4, for an illustration of this). Thus, in synchronic terms we can clearly say that the overall coordination settings in Slovak seem to be favourable for successful realisation of syllabic consonants, but we will refrain from any chicken-and-egg diachronic speculation about whether an existing low-overlap pattern allowed the emergence of syllabic consonants or whether syllabic consonants pushed the language towards a more stable low-overlap pattern than had existed before.

4 Interactions between vowel nasalisation and post-vocalic consonants

All the examples in the previous sections looked at articulatory coordination involving consonants in the syllable onset. As a final example, we will look briefly at a case involving post-vocalic consonants. The wider framework is given by the important diachronic process in which a postvocalic nasal has led to phonologisation of nasalisation on the preceding vowel, accompanied by the eventual disappearance of the nasal consonant itself (see Sampson 1999 for extensive treatment of the Romance languages). This in turn is part of an even wider framework that involves looking for the seeds of sound change in coarticulatory processes (Carignan et al. 2021), in other words in understanding how the speaker/listener no longer attributes a coarticulatory effect to its source (in this case a post-vocalic nasal) but rather treats it as an inherent property of the affected segment (see e.g. Ohala 1983 and Beddor 2009 for important work in this vein, albeit from slightly different perspectives). The focus of the present section is thus slightly different from that of the previous sections but remains firmly anchored in the phonetic forces underlying shifts in phonological patterns. Our specific interest is namely in the fact that in cases where the nasal is followed by an occlusive, there is considerable evidence that the diachronic process just outlined occurs preferentially when the occlusive is voiceless rather than voiced (Beddor 2009, Hajek 1997, Sampson 1999). In a synchronic perspective, Beddor (2009) found some acoustic evidence that the timing of the velum opening gesture is earlier in Am. Eng. *sent* than *send*. There is a plausible aerodynamic motivation for this pattern that is, in some sense, a mirror image of the arguments proposed above for avoiding high C1-C2 overlap in /kn/ clusters: Assuming that a salient burst is more important in a voiceless than a voiced plosive, then there is a constraint that raising of the velum should be completed earlier in the voiceless case in order to give more time for intra-oral air-pressure to rise before the release of the articulatory constriction occurs. This could be the seed of a bias in the articulatory system that in diachronic terms slowly shifts the timing of the velar gesture from the postvocalic consonant onto the vowel itself, leaving behind a purely oral consonant. Once again we have a plausible aerodynamically-driven scenario that would, however – as in Section 2.1 – be much more compelling if we could show that the predicted articulatory consequences are observable at the synchronic level. For this, we believed that German would be a particularly suitable language (i.e. potentially more interesting than the original American English example of Beddor) precisely because there is no reason to believe that phonologisation of vowel nasalisation is an ongoing process in Standard German. In other words, the relevant articulatory constraints can be observed as a purely phonetic process that has not yet become part of the phonological grammar (the situation is not so clear in American English, where vowel nasalisation may in some contexts have gone quite a long way down the road of phonologisation). In addition, we were keen to base the analyses on direct articulatory measurements rather than having to infer patterns of velar movement from the acoustic record, which is fraught with difficulties given the highly complex acoustics of nasals. Accordingly, we have carried out extensive recordings of the movements of the velum (and the other articulators) using real-time magnetic resonance imaging in collaboration with the group of J. Frahm at the Max Planck Institute for Biophysical Chemistry, Göttingen. The state-of-the art procedures developed by this group (i.e. 50 frames/s temporal resolution and 1.4 mm spatial resolution) provide an appropriate foundation on which to base analysis of the quite subtle coarticulatory processes of interest here (see example mp4 movie in the supplementary materials: https://www.degruyter.com/document/isbn/9783110721461/html).

Figure 8 shows one of the examples presented in Carignan et al. (2019; see Carignan et al., 2021, for more extensive analysis and discussion).

It shows the velar opening patterns (higher values indicate more open velum) for one selected quasi-minimal pair *Panther* vs. *Panda* in two prosodic conditions averaged over 35 subjects.

In this figure, the trajectories have been time-aligned with the (acoustic) vowel offset, which is denoted by the middle set of symbols (circles and squares) at time zero. The left set of symbols denotes the vowel onset (as determined by the acoustics), and the right set of symbols denotes the offset of the post-vocalic consonant /t/or /d/. Voicing of the oral post-vocalic consonant is denoted by line and symbol (/Vnd/ = solid line + circles, /Vnt/ = dotted line+ squares). Stress is denoted by colour (accentuated = blue, neutral = red). From this figure, it appears that the velum gesture for /Vnt/ is shorter in duration and begins and ends earlier

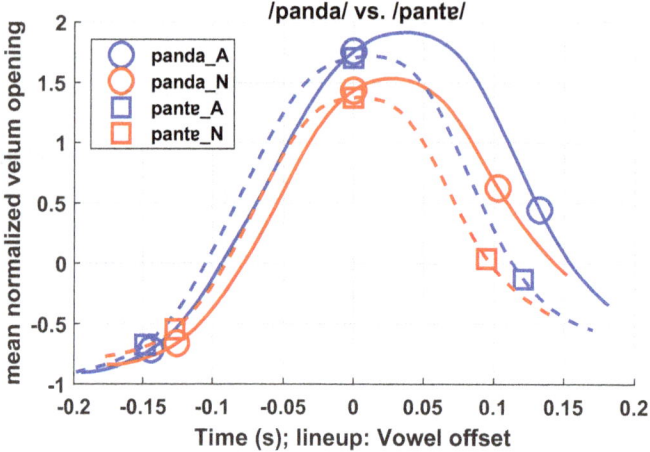

Figure 8: Ensemble averages over 35 speakers of velum movement signals for *Panda* 'panda' vs. *Panther* 'panther'. Higher values indicate more velum opening. See text for details.

compared to /Vnd/. In addition, the amplitude of the movement is smaller in the /Vnt/ case.

Taking the full range of material considered in Carignan et al. (2019, 2021) into account, the most robust aspects of these findings are the earlier timing of the closing movement (coupled with shorter overall duration of the opening-closing movement) and the small amplitude of the velar movement in the /Vnt/ context. Thus important features of the velar movement depend on the phonetic context and are consistent with the aerodynamic hypothesis outlined above that timely closing of the velum is particularly important in the context of the voiceless plosive. What was rather less clear was whether the velar opening movement is initiated earlier in the voiceless context or, in other words, whether in this context the velar opening movement spreads more extensively over the preceding vowel. Nevertheless, the results indicate that there are indeed phonetic forces active that bias the system towards a preference for vowel nasalisation in the voiceless context. The actual shift of the timing of the velar gesture towards an earlier location relative to the vowel may simply be a later stage in this process, which is not (yet) visible in Standard German.

5 Overall conclusions and outlook

In this brief review we have explored how phonetic forces can inform our understanding of characteristic patterns in sound systems, in other words taking into account that sound systems are always implemented in the context of human anatomy and physiology. To be more precise, this means that all sounds involve the use of the speech organs to shape aerodynamic processes, which in turn lead to acoustic events that have to be appropriately salient to human perceptual systems. We have focussed here in particular on patterns found in the structure of syllables because this allows fruitful links to the rich phonological literature exemplified by the work of Vennemann. Moreover, the sound patterns examined here are also particularly appropriate for throwing further light on our overall hypothesis that preferences for sound sequences need to be understood as the interplay between motor efficiency (speaker-oriented) and perceptual recoverability (listener-oriented).

We must concede, however, that we have been treating this hypothesis here in essentially qualitative terms. How might it be operationalised more quantitatively? The key approach in our view would be to make more extensive use of articulatory synthesis to generate stimuli for formal perception experiments (e.g. in which coordination patterns, such as overlap between C1 and C2, are systematically varied). In the examples above, we showed how changes in coordination patterns can result in drastic differences in the acoustic output. We simply assumed that such changes are perceptually salient. However, in general the relationship between properties of the acoustic signal and salience for the listener is highly non-linear and requires empirical investigation. For example, in preliminary perception experiments on nasal coarticulation based on the material discussed above in Section 4, we found that listeners are quite insensitive to the amount of nasalisation on the vowel in a word like *bahnte* 'channelled, 1/3 sg. ind. pret.' if the only change generated by means of the articulatory synthesis is to locate the start of velum opening for the post-vocalic /n/ earlier and earlier in the vowel. But listeners are much more sensitive (by almost an order of magnitude) if the manipulation involves simultaneously decreasing the duration of nasalisation in the post-vocalic /nt/ cluster and increasing the duration of vowel nasalisation. Thus such experiments can give an indication of the conditions that need to obtain for the phonological structure of a lexical item to be reinterpreted across time by the speaker/listener. Overall, a stimulus continuum generated by articulatory synthesis makes it possible to investigate how salience for the listener varies as a function of, for example, articulatory overlap. This salience can even be defined in complementary ways, e.g. by accuracy of identification of lexical items in difficult listening conditions (such as low signal-to-noise ratio) or through judgements of naturalness or prototypicality of the speech items. Further preliminary perception experiments in which overlap patterns of C1 and C2 were systematically varied in /kl/ and /kn/ onset clusters have also indicated ways in which such experiments can even lead to refinements of the overall hypothesis: The reason why /kn/ is disfavoured may not have to do just with the requirement for low overlap per se but also with the fact that perceptually acceptable productions may only be possible within rather a narrow window of overlap values (compared to /kl/). In other words, the speaker may have quite a fine line to tread between timing the /n/ too early (which destroys the burst of /k/) and timing it too late (which destroys the structure of the onset by resulting perceptually in vowel epenthesis). This is just one indication of how a concept such as "efficiency for the speaker" can be further fleshed out. Following up on such ideas systematically actually represents a substantial research programme for the future.

In conclusion, we would, however, like to recall that even beyond the ideas advanced in the previous paragraph there are many further directions that a research programme of this kind can take. To give just two examples: Consonant voicing is well known to be closely implicated in diachronic developments in tone languages, with voiced and voiceless consonants being linked to lower and higher tonal patterns, respectively. See, for example, Hoole and Honda (2011) for discussion and further references of the phonetic mechanisms underlying the link between voicing control and fundamental frequency differences. This example is similar in spirit to those considered in the body of this paper but simply considers a rather different aspect of sound systems. Finally, to take an example that explores the implications of a much more detailed consideration of human anatomy and biomechanics than we have followed in this paper, Blasi et al. (2019) outline a scenario by which changes in human bite, related in turn to changes from hunter-gatherer to agricultural diets, may have favoured the emergence of labiodental sounds.

References

Beddor, Patrice. 2009. A coarticulatory path to sound change. *Language* 85. 785–821.
Birkholz, Peter. 2012. VocalTractLab Version 2.0. www.vocaltractlab.de (accessed 8 January 2021).
Birkholz, Peter, Dietmar Jackèl & Bernd Kröger. 2006. Construction and control of a three-dimensional vocal tract model. *Proceedings of the International Conference on Acoustics, Speech, and Signal Processing* (ICASSP 2006, Toulouse). 873–876. Toulouse: IEEE.
Blasi, Damian, Stephen Moran, Scott Moisik, Paul Widmer, Dan Dediu & Balthasar Bickel. 2019. Human sound systems are shaped by post-Neolithic changes in bite configuration. *Science* 363 (6432). eaav3218. https://doi.org/10.1126/science.aav3218 (accessed 13 June 2019).
Bombien, Lasse. 2011. *Segmental and prosodic aspects in the production of consonant clusters: on the goodness of clusters*. Munich: Ludwig-Maximilians-Universität München dissertation. https://edoc.ub.uni-muenchen.de/12840/ (accessed 13 June 2019).

Bombien, Lasse, Christine Mooshammer, Philip Hoole & Barbara Kühnert. 2010. Prosodic and segmental effects on EPG contact patterns of word-initial German clusters. *Journal of Phonetics* 38. 388–403.

Bombien, Lasse, Christine Mooshammer & Philip Hoole. 2013. Articulatory coordination in word-initial clusters of German. *Journal of Phonetics* 41. 546–561

Browman, Catherine & Louis Goldstein. 1990. Gestural specification using dynamically-defined articulatory structures. *Journal of Phonetics* 18. 299–320.

Carignan, Christopher, Philip Hoole, Esther Kunay, Arun Joseph, Dirk Voit, Jens Frahm & Jonathan Harrington. 2019. The phonetic basis of phonological vowel nasality: Evidence from real-time MRI velum movement in German. In Sasha Calhoun, Paola Escudero, Marija Tabain & Paul Warren (eds.), *Proceedings of the 19th International Congress of Phonetic Sciences, Melbourne, Australia 2019*, 413–417. Canberra, Australia: Australasian Speech Science and Technology Association Inc.

Carignan, Christopher, Stefano Coretta, Jens Frahm, Jonathan Harrington, Philip Hoole, Arun Joseph, Esther Kunay & Dirk Voit. 2021. Planting the seed for sound change: Evidence from real-time MRI of velum kinematics in German. *Language* 97. 333–364.

Chitoran, Ioana, Louis Goldstein & Dani Byrd. 2002. Gestural overlap and recoverability: Articulatory evidence from Georgian. In Carlos Gussenhoven & Natasha Warner (eds.), *Laboratory Phonology 7*, 419–447. Berlin: Mouton de Gruyter.

Colantoni, Laura & Jeffrey Steele. 2007. Voicing-dependent cluster simplification asymmetries in Spanish and French. In Pilar Prieto, Joan Mascaró & Maria-Josep Solé (eds.), *Segmental and prosodic issues in Romance linguistics*, 109–129. Amsterdam: John Benjamins.

Gibson, Mark, Stavroula Sotiropoulou, Stephen Tobin & Adamantios Gafos. 2018. On some temporal properties of Spanish consonant-liquid and consonant-rhotic clusters. In *Proceedings of the conference on phonetics and phonology in German-speaking countries (P&P13)*, 73–76. https://edoc.hu-berlin.de/bitstream/handle/18452/19531/Proceedings_PP13.pdf (accessed 13 June 2019).

Goldstein, Louis, Hosung Nam, Elliot Saltzman & Ioana Chitoran. 2009. Coupled oscillator planning model of speech timing and syllable structure. In Gunnar Fant, Hiroya Fujisaki & Jiaxuen Shen (eds.), *Frontiers in phonetics and speech science. Festschrift for Wu Zongji*, 239–250. Beijing: Commercial Press.

Hajek, John. 1997. *Universals of sound change in nasalization*. Oxford: Blackwell.

Hoole, Philip & Andreas Zierdt. 2010. Five-dimensional articulography. In Ben Maassen & Pascal van Lieshout (eds.), *Speech motor control: New developments in basic and applied research*, 331–349. Oxford: Oxford University Press.

Hoole, Philip & Kiyoshi Honda. 2011. Automaticity vs. feature-enhancement in the control of segmental F0. In G. Nick Clements & Rachid Ridouane (eds.), *Where do phonological features come from? Cognitive, physical and developmental bases of distinctive speech categories*, 131–171. Amsterdam: John Benjamins.

Hoole, Philip & Lasse Bombien. 2017. A cross-language study of laryngeal-oral coordination across varying prosodic and syllable-structure conditions. *Journal of Speech, Language and Hearing Research* 60. 525–539.

Hoole, Philip, Marianne Pouplier, Štefan Beňuš & Lasse Bombien. 2013. Articulatory coordination in obstruent-sonorant clusters and syllabic consonants: Data and modelling. In Lorenzo Spreafico & Alessandro Vietti (eds.), *Proceedings of Ratics 3*, 81–97. Bolzano: Bolzano University Press.

Kühnert, Barbara, Philip Hoole & Christine Mooshammer. 2006. Gestural overlap and C-center in selected French consonant clusters. In Hani Yehia, Didier Demolin & Raphael Laboissière (eds.), *Proceedings of the 7th International Seminar on Speech Production*, 327–334. Belo Horizonte: UFMG.

Nam, Hosung, Louis Goldstein, Catherine Browman, Philip Rubin, Michael Proctor & Elliot Saltzman. 2006. *TADA (TAsk Dynamics Application) manual*. https://sail.usc.edu/~lgoldste/ArtPhon/TADA%20stuff/TADA_manual_v09.pdf (accessed 15 February 2019).

Nam, Hosung, Louis Goldstein & Elliot Saltzman. 2009. Self-organization of syllable structure: A coupled oscillator model. In François Pellegrino, Egidio Marsico, Ioana Chitoran & Christophe Coupé (eds.), *Approaches to phonological complexity*, 299–328. Berlin: Mouton de Gruyter.

Ohala, John. 1983. The origin of sound patterns in vocal tract constraints. In Peter MacNeilage (ed.), *The production of speech*, 189–216. New York: Springer.

Öhman, Sven. 1966. Coarticulation in VCV utterances: Spectrographic measurements. *Journal of the Acoustical Society of America* 39. 151–168.

Pastätter, Manfred. 2017. *The effect of coarticulatory resistance and aerodynamic requirements of consonants on syllable organization in Polish*. Munich: Ludwig-Maximilians-Universität München dissertation. https://edoc.ub.uni-muenchen.de/22584/ (accessed 4 April 2019).

Peters, Sandra. 2015. *The effects of syllable structure on consonantal timing and vowel compression in child and adult speakers of German*. Munich: Ludwig-Maximilians-Universität München dissertation. https://edoc.ub.uni-muenchen.de/19557/ (accessed 4 April 2019).

Pouplier, Marianne. 2011. The atoms of phonological representations. In Marc van Oostendorp, Keren Rice, Beth Hume & Colin Ewen (eds.), *The Blackwell companion to phonology*, 107B129. Oxford: Wiley-Blackwell.

Pouplier, Marianne & Štefan Beňuš. 2011. On the phonetic status of syllabic consonants: Evidence from Slovak. *Journal of Laboratory Phonology* 2. 243–273.

Russell Webb, Eric & Travis G. Bradley. 2009. Rhotic metathesis asymmetries in Romance: Formalizing the effects of articulation and perception on sound change. In Pascual Masullo, Erin O'Rourke & Chia-Hui Huang (eds.), *Romance linguistics 2007: Selected papers from the 37th linguistic symposium on Romance languages (LSRL)*, 321–337. Amsterdam: Benjamins.

Sampson, Rodney. 1999. *Nasal vowel evolution in Romance*. Oxford: Oxford University Press.

Vennemann, Theo. 2000. Triple-cluster reduction in Germanic: Etymology without sound laws? *Historische Sprachforschung (Historical Linguistics)* 113, 239–258.

Vennemann, Theo. 2012. Structural complexity of consonant clusters: A phonologist's view. In Philip Hoole, Lasse Bombien, Marianne Pouplier, Christine Mooshammer & Barbara Kühnert (eds.), *Consonant clusters and structural complexity*, 9–31. Berlin: Mouton de Gruyter.

Larry M. Hyman
The first person singular subject negative portmanteau in Luganda and Lusoga

Abstract: In this paper I present an analysis of a rather common irregularity in the Bantu verb paradigm, concerning the combination of 'first person singular subject' and 'negative'. Although normally realized as a succession of prefixes, this particular combination is often expressed through a single 'portmanteau' morph, e.g. Swahili *si-*. I begin by illustrating the phenomenon in Swahili and then turn to consider the related facts of Luganda *si-* and its closest relative, Lusoga, where the corresponding morph is *ti-*. Interestingly, while Luganda *si-* replaces the otherwise expected *ti-n-* and *n-ta-* sequences in main vs. relative clauses, respectively, Lusoga *ti-* only replaces the former. Despite other possible interpretations of the Lusoga form, e.g. /t-i-/, /ti-i-/, /ti-Ø-/, where *i-* or Ø- would be an allomorph of the more general first person singular prefix *n-*, I demonstrate that *ti-* must be analyzed as a portmanteau morph, as in Swahili and Luganda, despite its likely derivation from historical *ti-i-*. I conclude that this reanalysis by pre-Lusoga speakers reveals a preference for a unitary interpretation over a more abstract derivational analysis.

> Suppletion is undesirable, uniformity of linguistic symbolization is desirable: Both roots and grammatical markers should be unique and constant (Vennemann 1972a: 184).

1 Introduction

One of the basic principles of language structure that I learned as a former student of Theo Vennemann's was what he termed "Humboldt's Universal". Often summarized as "one form, one meaning" (Vennemann 1990: 18), the "ideal human language" would be one where "a single concept is symbolized by a constant sound image" (Vennemann 1972a: 183). Corrupting this ideal or preference are the phonetic changes and other linguistic processes which create allomorphs – especially suppletive allomorphs whose "sound images" may not even intersect. This is particularly true in portmanteau morphology, where two meanings which are usually expressed as independent forms in the general morphology are instead realized as a single suppletive morph when occurring together. A case well-known

Larry M. Hyman, Department of Linguistics, University of California, Berkeley/USA

to Bantuists concerns morphological irregularities in the expression of the first person singular subject marker (SM) in negative paradigms (Kamba Muzenga 1981: 87). The most often cited such irregularity concerns the appearance of *si-* in the following present and past paradigms from Swahili (Ashton 1944: 36, 71):

(1) present

	Affirmative			Negative			
1sg	ni-	na-	tak-a	1sg	si-		tak-i
2sg	u-	na-	tak-a	2sg	h-	u-	tak-i
3sg	a-	na-	tak-a	3sg	h-	a-	tak-i
1pl	tu-	na-	tak-a	1pl	ha-	tu-	tak-i
2pl	m-	na-	tak-a	2pl	ha-	m-	tak-i
3pl	wa-	na-	tak-a	3pl	ha-	wa-	tak-i

past

	Affirmative			Negative			
1sg	ni-	li-	tak-a	1sg	si-		ku-	tak-a
2sg	u-	li-	tak-a	2sg	h-	u-	ku-	tak-a
3sg	a-	li-	tak-a	3sg	h-	a-	ku-	tak-a
1pl	tu-	li-	tak-a	1pl	ha-	tu-	ku-	tak-a
2pl	m-	li-	tak-a	2pl	ha-	m-	ku-	tak-a
3pl	wa-	li-	tak-a	3pl	ha-	wa-	ku-	tak-a

As seen in the affirmative forms, six distinct subject prefixes mark person and number followed by a present (*na-*) or past (*li-*) tense marker, the verb root *-tak-* 'want', and the inflectional final vowel (FV) *-a* form the verb. The corresponding negatives show an initial *ha-* which undergoes vowel elision before *u-* '2sg.' and *a-* '3sg.' (noun class 1), different tense allomorphs in the present (Ø) and past (*ku-*), and a change of the FV from *-a* to *-i* in the present. The first person singular is notably irregular: rather than the expected sequence **ha-ni-*, a single portmanteau form *si-* "conflates" both the negative and 1sg. "slots" (see Stump 2017a,b for a formal approach to such conflation, including Swahili). In the following two sections I discuss the analogous situations in Luganda and Lusoga, two very closely related Bantu languages spoken in Uganda that, however, differ from each other in rather significant ways. I end with some diachronic discussion and a brief conclusion.

2 Luganda

In order to identify the underlying representations of the subject markers (SMs) in Luganda, we begin with the present tense affirmative forms in (2).

(2) Present tense affirmative
    singular   plural
1st ǹ-nímá   tú-lìmá   'I/we cultivate'
2nd ò-límá   mú-lìmá   'you cultivate'
3rd à-límá   bá-lìmá   '(s)he/they cultivate'

Aside from a few sound changes, these resemble those just seen in Swahili, although now we can add tone (as realized with a final H% boundary tone): the singular SMs are underlyingly toneless and realized L(ow), while the plural SMs are H(igh). Since it is the 1sg. prefix that interests us, we take particular note that it consists of a nasal consonant which in the example causes the following /l/ of the verb root /-lim-/ 'cultivate' to become [n] by a process known as Meinhof's Rule (see Katamba and Hyman 1991 for the full Luganda details). Although the 1sg. SM is always a homorganic nasal when followed by a consonant (cf. m̀-bál-á 'I count', ǹ-gúl-á 'I buy'), when it is directly followed by a prefixal vowel, it is realized as [n]. We can thus determine from the following general past affirmative forms that the underlying consonant has to be /n/:

(3) General past affirmative
    singular   plural
1st n-à-lím-à   tw-áá-lìm-á   'I/we cultivated'
2nd w-à-lím-à   mw-áá-lìm-á   'you cultivated'
3rd y-à-lím-à   b-áá-lìm-á   '(s)he/they cultivated'

The above forms show two other things. First, instead of the expected human noun class 1 SM *a-*, the glide *y-* is observed before the tense marker (TM) *-a-*. Parallel to the mid vowel of 2sg. *o-*, I will assume that before a vowel class 1 has an allomorph /e-/, perhaps as a rule of referral to the (animal) class 9 prefix *e-* (cf. è-lím-á 'it (class 9) cultivates', y-à-lím-à 'it (class 9) cultivated'). An equally plausible, slightly more abstract (but historically correct) analysis could recognize 2sg. and class 1 3sg. as /u-/ and /i-/, since these high vowels do not occur word-initially and hence would automatically lower to [o] and [e]. (For further discussion, see Hyman and Katamba 1999 and references cited therein.)

This brings us to the second issue, vowel coalescence. The examples in (3) also show that the singular SMs lose their syllabicity, with /e-/ and /o-/ gliding to [y] and [w], respectively. The plural SMs /tu-/ and /mu-/ also undergo gliding, this time with compensatory lengthening (CL) of the TM *-a-*. In the case of (class 2) 3pl., the /a/ of /bá-/ is deleted by a general rule in the language, again triggering CL of the following (identical) vowel (cf. /bá-el-a/ → b-éèl-á 'they sweep'). In Luganda in general, a CV+V sequence results in a long vowel, while an onsetless

V+V is realized short. Long vowels are obligatorily shortened before a geminate consonant and in clitic group-final position (see Clements 1986 and Hyman and Katamba 1990 for more detail). Whether there is CL or not will turn out to have implications for our analysis of both Luganda and Lusoga.

Before moving on to the negative forms, in order to further establish the expected SM forms, let us consider a third set of affirmative verb forms, the general future affirmative:

(4) General future affirmative

	singular	plural	
1st	ǹ-dí-lìm-á	tú-lì-lìm-á	'I/we will cultivate'
2nd	ò-lí-lìm-á	mú-lì-lìm-á	'you will cultivate'
3rd	à-lí-lìm-á	bá-lì-lìm-á	'(s)he/they will cultivate'

As seen, the same SMs are observed as in the present tense in (2), since they are followed by the consonant-initial TM -lí- 'general future'. The only detail we note is that the /l/ of -lí- becomes [d] after the 1sg. nasal prefix n-. It does not become [n] since it does not meet the conditions of Meinhof's Rule, which strictly targets voiced consonants followed by a nasal within the verb stem (Katamba and Hyman 1991: 188). I also do not follow a detail of Luganda orthography (Ashton et al. 1954), which transcribes /l/ as r after the front vowels /i/ and /e/, hence without tones: ndirima 'I will cultivate'.

With the above established, we now consider the corresponding negative forms of the three tenses we have examined. We start with the present tense negative:

(5) Present tense negative

	singular	plural	
1st	sí-lìm-á	tè-tú-lìm-á	'I/we don't cultivate'
2nd	t-ó-lìm-á	tè-mú-lìm-á	'you don't cultivate'
3rd	t-á-lìm-á	tè-bá-lìm-á	'(s)he/they don't cultivate'

Aside from (irrelevant) tonal differences with the corresponding affirmative forms in (2), we note the following: First, we see from the plural forms that the negative prefix is tè- before a consonant. Second, the (surface) realization of the negative prefix is t- before a vowel, which is realized short: t-ó-, t-á-. (If analyzed as /te-ó-/ and /te-á-/, these inputs would be an exception to CL, as we do not obtain *t-óó-, *t-áá-.) Finally, we see that the 1sg. negative SM is realized as the portmanteau morpheme si-, exactly as in Swahili in (1). Thus, instead of the expected, but ungrammatical *te-n- sequence, si- represents the same conflation of the SM and TM "slots" as in Stump's (2017a: 437–438, 2017b: 122) analysis of Swahili.

The same distribution of si-, t- and te- is observed in the general future negative:

(6) General future negative
   singular plural
 1 sí-lì-lìm-á tè-tú-lì-lìm-á 'I/we won't cultivate'
 2 t-ó-lì-lìm-á tè-mú-lì-lìm-á 'you won't cultivate'
 3 t-á-lì-lìm-á tè-bá-lì-lìm-á '(s)he/they won't cultivate'

Except for 1sg., the general past negative shows the te- allomorph throughout, since it is followed in all forms by a consonantal SM:

(7) General past negative
   singular plural
 1 s-áá-lìm-á tè-tw-áá-lìm-á 'I/we didn't cultivate'
 2 tè-w-á-lìm-á tè-mw-áá-lìm-á 'you didn't cultivate'
 3 tè-y-á-lìm-á tè-b-áá-lìm-á '(s)he/they didn't cultivate'

The 2sg. and 3sg. forms show that /o-/ and /e-/ must first glide to [w] and [y], again without CL, which then allows the negative prefix to be realized te-. Turning to the 1sg. we observe that the vowel of the TM is long, since si-a- involves a CV+V sequence. Other than guaranteeing that the te- vs. t- realizations will be sensitive to the consonantal outputs of /o-a-/ → [wa] and /e-a-/ → [ya] rather than to the vocalic inputs, the only other question is whether these allomorphs should be independent spell-outs of [+neg] or whether the allomorphs are derived from a single underlying representation (UR), either /te-/ via vowel deletion or /t-/ with vowel epenthesis. In either case, if the phonology applied all at once to /te-o-a-/ or /t-o-a-/ and /te-e-a-/ or /t-e-a-/, this would presumably produce the incorrect outputs *tw-aa- and *ty-aa-. Since parallel questions of analysis arise even more centrally in closely related Lusoga, we will further address such issues in the next section.

3 Lusoga

In this section we will consider the realization of the same SMs in the corresponding Lusoga affirmative and negative tenses. Since there are only tonal differences in the affirmative tenses, these are presented together in (8–10).

(8) Present habitual tense affirmative
        singular plural
  1st ǹ-ním-á tù-lìm-á 'I/we cultivate'
  2nd ò-lím-á mù-lìm-á 'you cultivate'
  3rd à-lím-á bà-lìm-á '(s)he/they cultivate'

(9) General past affirmative
        singular plural
  1st n-á-lìm-á tw-áà-lìm-á 'I/we cultivated'
  2nd w-á-lìm-á mw-áà-lìm-á 'you cultivated'
  3rd y-á-lìm-á b-áà-lìm-á '(s)he/they cultivated'

(10) General future affirmative
        singular   plural
  1st ń-dì-lìm-á tù-lì-lìm-á 'I/we will cultivate'
  2nd ó-lì-lìm-á mù-lì-lìm-á 'you will cultivate'
  3rd á-lì-lìm-á bà-lì-lìm-á '(s)he/they will cultivate'

As seen, the same SMs and TMs, root -*lim*-, and inflectional final vowel -*a* are observed as in Luganda in each case – a remarkable illustration of just how close these languages are.

However, such exact segmental equivalence does not occur in the corresponding negatives, as seen in the present habitual forms in (11).

(11) Present habitual tense negative
        singular plural
  1st tí-lím-à tí-tú-lím-à 'I/we don't cultivate'
  2nd t-ó-lím-à tí-mú-lím-à 'you don't cultivate'
  3rd t-á-lím-à tí-bá-lím-à '(s)he/they don't cultivate'

While the same *t*- allomorph of the negative is seen before 2sg. *o*- and 3sg. *e*-, the (pre-consonantal) allomorph in the plural is *ti*- (vs. Luganda *te*-). In addition, the 1sg. + negative form is [ti] vs. the portmanteau *si*- in the Luganda negative paradigm. (The expected *ti-n-* sequence is ungrammatical.) The same facts are observed in the general future negative:

(12) General future negative
        singular   plural
  1 tí-lì-lìm-á tí-tù-lì-lìm-á 'I/we won't cultivate'
  2 t-ó-lì-lìm-á tí-mù-lì-lìm-á 'you won't cultivate'
  3 t-á-lì-lìm-á tí-bà-lì-lìm-á '(s)he/they won't cultivate'

The question that arises from these data is how to analyze what appears to be the 1sg. negative marker *ti-*. There are at least four potential analyses, schematized in (13).

(13)   Negative   1sg. subject
   a.   *ti-*   Ø-
   b.   *t-*   *i-*
   c.   *ti-*   *i-*
   d.   *ti-*   (portmanteau)

In the first analysis in (13a), there is no overt 1sg. subject prefix. Instead, the preconsonantal negative allomorph *ti-* occurs when followed by the verb root *-lim-* or the future prefix *-li-*. Although this was my first hypothesis, we see from the following general past negative forms that this cannot work:

(14)   General past negative
            singular   plural
       1   *tý-áà-lìm-á*   *tì-tw-áà-lìm-á*   'I/we didn't cultivate'
       2   *tì-w-á-lìm-á*   *tì-mw-áà-lìm-á*   'you didn't cultivate'
       3   *tì-y-á-lìm-á*   *tì-b-áà-lìm-á*   '(s)he/they didn't cultivate'

As seen, the negative marker is *ti-* throughout – even in the 1sg. form. If the 1sg. SM is Ø and the negative is directly followed by the past tense prefix *-a-*, we would expect the prevocalic allomorph *t-*, in which case the output should be **t-á-lìm-á*. In other words, if the input is *ti-Ø-a-*, the Ø SM would have to block the *t-* allomorph expected before *-a-*. Note that we cannot propose that the 1sg. is a featureless "ghost" consonant, since we would expect /ti-C-a-/ to have the ungrammatical output *[tia], not [tyaa]. We could stipulate that somehow the negative allomorphy cannot see the *-a-* of the TM through the null subject. However, there are other possible analyses that do not require this stipulation.

In the alternative interpretation in (13b) the 1sg. allomorph is *i-* in negative tenses. In this case the prevocalic negative allomorph *t-* is chosen. (Corresponding bimorphemic analyses are adopted by Kamba Muzenga 1981: 185, hence /s-i-/ for Luganda *si-*.) While this works in the present and general future tenses, where *t-i-* would be followed by a consonant, it does not work in the general past negative. As was seen in (14), we have to first allow the subject Vs to glide, as we also saw in Luganda in (7): Just as 2sg. /o-a-/ and (class 1) 3sg. /e-a-/ first become [wa] and [ya], an input /i-a/ would also have to become [ya], with the 1sg. and (class 1) 3sg. forms incorrectly becoming homophonous. Homophony would also result if the 1sg. allomorph were not /í-/, rather a segmentless high tonal morpheme /´/ which somehow requires the preceding *ti-* allomorph. The same problem arises if we assume the /ti-i-/ input in (13c). One could of course stipulate that the observed prevocalic *ty-* is somehow due to avoidance of homophony. However, there is another available solution which does not need to make this stipulation.

In the fourth analysis, in (13d), *ti-* is identified as the corresponding portmanteau morpheme to *si-* in Luganda (and Swahili). In other words, /ti-/ is not further segmented, rather it is a single morph representing both the negative and the first person singular SM. This explains why the form 'I didn't cultivate' is *ty-áà-lìm-á* in (14): /ti-/ spells out both "slots" at once and then undergoes the expected gliding + CL of the following TM *-a-*. This analysis seems the best and most direct way to account for the Lusoga facts, not requiring any stipulation beyond the one we were forced to make for Luganda. However, it was at first elusive: (13a–d) in fact represents the order in which I (and others I have shown the data to) first thought of each of the analyses. In (13a) it is tempting to generalize *ti-* as the negative marker throughout the paradigm (which *si-* could not be in Luganda), since it appears both in 1sg. and before consonantal SMs. In (13b) and (13c) the absence or deletion of the /i/ of the negative marker /t-/ or /ti-/ would automatically be triggered by 1sg. /i-/, exactly as it is by 2sg. /o-/ and (class 1) 3sg. /a-/. Both Kamba Muzenga (1981: 185–187, 206n) and Bastin (2006: 26–30) show that there is a 1sg. SM allomorph *i-* which shows up sporadically in various Bantu languages. However, as was shown, each of these proposals runs into complications which can be avoided if /ti-/ is analyzed as a 1sg. negative portmanteau morpheme.

4 Discussion and conclusion

In the preceding sections we have analyzed the 1sg. negative subject marking as a portmanteau morpheme *si-* in Luganda, *ti-* in Lusoga. While this interpretation was quite clear in Luganda, where *si-* differs from the *te-* found elsewhere in the (main clause) negative paradigm, three other (ultimately rejected) analyses seemed at first plausible in Lusoga. It was particularly the prevocalic realization *ty-* that pointed towards the ultimate solution. There are, however, additional data that were not addressed concerning the realization of the 1sg. SM with different negative markers in dependent clauses. As seen in the following present tense relative forms from Luganda, instead of initial *te-*, negation is marked by post-SM *-ta-* in relative clauses:

(15) Present tense relative clause marking in Luganda

	'...that I etc. cultivate'	'...that I etc. don't cultivate'
1sg	kyé ń-nímâ	kyé sí-límâ
2sg	ky' óó-límâ	ky' óó-tá-límâ
3sg.	ky' áá-límâ	ky' áá-tá-límâ
1pl.	kyé tú-límâ	kyé tú-tá-límâ
2pl.	kyé mú-límâ	kyé mú-tá-límâ
3pl.	kyé bá-límâ	kyé bá-tá-límâ

As seen, the post-SM -ta- occurs in all forms except the first person singular, where once again si- is observed. In other words, the portmanteau morpheme si- is not sensitive to the would-be difference in morpheme orders of the expected main and relative clause sequences *te-n- and *n-ta-. In other words, if the morphology is spelled out cyclically, both [NEG [1sg ...]] and [1sg [NEG ...]] are spelled out as si-.

As seen in (16), the negative marker is also post-SM -ta- in relative clauses in Lusoga.

(16) Present tense relative clause marking in Lusoga

	'...that I etc. cultivate'	'...that I etc. don't cultivate'
1sg	kyé ń-nímà	kyé ń-tá-límà
2sg	ky' óó-límà	ky' óó-tá-límà
3sg	ky' áá-ímà	ky' áá-tá-límà
1pl	kyé tú-límà	kyé tú-tá-límà
2pl	kyé mú-límà	kyé mú-tá-límà
3pl	kyé bá-límà	kyé bá-tá-límà

However, contrary to Luganda, the first singular negative is realized with the regular relative clause sequence n-ta- instead of portmanteau si-, which thus only occurs as a conflation of would-be main clause *ti-n-. While the different properties of si- can be modeled synchronically by adding a syntactic restriction on the Lusoga spell-out, this raises the issue of whether Lusoga 1sg. negative ti- was in fact a historical contraction of *ti-i-, with -i- being an allomorph of the first person SM. Correspondingly, could Luganda then have derived si- from *ti-i- where one or both vowels were degree 1 (often symbolized as Proto-Bantu *̣i), which historically spirantizes *t to [s]?

The problem is why the clausal distribution of the portmanteau differs in Luganda and Lusoga. The several questions are *where*, *why* and *how* did the 1sg. negative portmanteau first come into existence: in main clauses or in dependent clauses? Finding a solution to these questions is complicated by several factors.

First, although other Bantu languages have a negative marker *si-*, either general or restricted to first person singular, its properties vary considerably. In some it's limited to initial position, while in others it occurs in post-SM position. The latter is the case in Swahili, which uses *ha-* in main clauses, as seen in (1), but *-si-* in relative and subjunctive clauses, e.g. *mtu a-si-ye-som-a* 'a man who doesn't read' (Ashton 1944: 112), *tu-si-pig-e* 'that we may not beat' (Ashton 1944: 119). This raises the likelihood that there are multiple sources of negative *si-* in Bantu.

Although a number of Bantu languages show a portmanteau morpheme restricted to first person singular (Kamba Muzenga 1981: 204), the phonetic and distributional details vary. In Kirundi the negative marker is *nti-* in main clauses vs. *-ta-* in dependent clauses. However, it is only the former that is replaced by *si-* in the first person (English translations are my own):

(17) Negative marking in Kirundi (Meeussen 1959: 137, 140)
    a. main clause ("indicatif récent")
        i.   *nti-tw-aa-kubuura* 'nous ne balayions pas'
                                    (we weren't sweeping)
        ii. *si-n-aa-kubuura*   'je ne balayais pas'
                                      (I wasn't sweeping)
    b. dependent clause ("conjonctif récent"; /-ta-aa-/ → t-aa-)
        i.   *tú-t-aa-kubuura*   'sans que nous balayions'
                                      (without us sweeping)
        ii. *n-t-áa-kub uura*   'sans que je balaie'
                                      (without me sweeping)

It seems reasonable to parse Kirundi *sin-* into negative *si-* followed by the 1sg. SM *n-*. However, the opposite ordering obtains in Chibemba /n-si-/ → *nši-*, which consists of the first person singular SM *n-* followed by post-SM *-si-* (*n-shi-lee-tum-a* 'I am not sending') vs. the general initial negative marker *ta-* (*ta-tu-lee-pep-a* 'we are not praying') (Mwita 2016: 21). Evidence can thus be found for both an initial and post-SM negative marker *si*. Note finally that Swahili has a subjunctive and relative clause post-SM allomorph *-si-* which concatenates with the 1sg. SM *ni-*: *ni-si-som-e* 'shan't I read? mayn't I read?' (Ashton 1944: 120). By restricting the portmanteau *si-* to main clause negatives, it isn't necessary to cite the Repeated Morph Constraint (Menn and MacWhinney 1984) to rule out *si-si-som-e and avoidance of haplology to rule out *si-som-e.

One hypothesis for the *si-n-* of Kirundi (and closely related Kinyarwanda and Ha) is that *si-* may be a predicative marker (Kamba Muzenga 1981: 86–87). The Swahili polarity opposition of *ni/si* seen in (1) is found not only in the first person, but also in predicatives: *ni kitabu* 'it's a book', *si kitabu* 'it's not a book'. Initial *(n)ti-* and *si-* may therefore represent an innovation. Thus compare in Haya the predictative function of *ní* in *ní káto* 'it's Kato' vs. its aspectual function in *ni-ba-lím-a* 'they are cultivating' where *ni-* has been added as a progressive marker (cf. *ba-lím-a* 'they cultivate') (Hyman and Watters 1984: 260–261). Interestingly the 1sg. negative subject forms [si] and [ti] line up perfectly with the corresponding negative predicative markers in Luganda and Lusoga:

(18) Negative predicative markers
    a. Luganda: *sí kìtábó* 'it's not a book'
    b. Lusoga: *tí kìtábó* 'it's not a book'

If forms such as *si-*, *te-*, *ti-* and *nti-* could be shown to derive from predicative markers, this might account for why *t-o-* and *t-a-* are realized without compensatory lengthening. As Meeussen (1959: 33) explains concerning Kirundi: "L'élision se trouve normalement quand les deux voyelles en cause appartiennent à deux mots nettement distincts; mais on le trouve aussi à l'intérieur du mot avec ´*nti-* du négatif [. . .]." ['Elision normally occurs when the two vowels in question belong to two clearly distinct words; but one also finds it word-internally with the negative [marker] ´*nti-*.']

As opposed to Meeussen's "contraction", which occurs with CL within words, his cross-word "élision" refers to vowel deletion without CL. If *nti-* (and other such markers) were historically separated by a full word boundary, we would expect no CL, as is still the case in many Bantu languages. However, Luganda and Lusoga have CL even across words, as seen in the following Luganda phrases (Hyman and Katamba 1999: 352):

(19) Gliding + CL across words in Luganda
    a. *o-mu-limi # o-mû* → *ò-mù-lìmy' òò-mû* 'one farmer'
    b. *e-fúdu # e-mû* → *è-n-fúdw' èè-mû* 'one tortoise'

Thus, if the explanation for the shortness of the vowels of *t-o-* and *t-a-* has to do with there having been a word boundary between the negative marker and the SM, Luganda (and Lusoga) would have had to extend CL to phrasal contexts. (We would also have to explain why the marker is *te-* in Luganda vs. the predicative marker *sí-*.) This is why I proposed an allomorph solution beyond the portmanteaus: *t-* before a vowel, *te-* (Luganda) or *ti-* (Lusoga) before a consonant.

What the preceding discussion reveals is that there is considerable instability, variability, and diversity in negative marking in present-day Bantu languages. A particularly striking example comes from Lengola, spoken in Democratic Republic of Congo, which marks negatives with a postposed possessive pronoun corresponding to the subject. In addition, in the past tense singular (class 1) persons fuse with a preceding s- (Stappers 1971: 295):

(20) Past tense negative in Lengola
      singular   plural
1st   s-í-lìm-ámi   tú-lìm-ású   'I/we didn't cultivate'
2nd   s-ú-lìm-áyì   nú-lim-ánú   'you didn't cultivate'
3rd   s-á-lìm-ésé   bá-lim-ábó   '(s)he/they didn't cultivate'

Since Lengola doesn't spirantize before degree 1 *i, it is clear that the initial s- comes from Proto-Bantu *c rather than *t, although other cases may not be as clear (Kamba Muzenga 1981: 109). Finally, even if correspondences aren't exact, grammatical morphemes are often irregular. Thus, although the Standard Swahili negative marker ha- derives from *nka- (Nurse and Hinnebusch 1993: 365), it should instead be realized kha, as it is realized dialectally (Derek Nurse, pers. comm.) and in other languages, e.g. nkha- in Chizigula (Kamba Muzenga 1981: 141).

Which brings us to the question of reconstruction. There is general agreement that Proto-Bantu had multiple negative markers. Kamba Muzenga reconstructs initial *nka- in main clauses, and post-SM -ti- and -ta- in subjunctive and relative clauses, respectively. Güldemann's (1999) work has centered around explaining the correlation between the two positions and the clause types in which they are found. However, although I have only given a brief glimpse of this, the situation is more complicated than a simple binary positional contrast, not to mention the wide range of forms that are found (cf. Nurse 2008: 188–189). Even at the level of Luganda-Lusoga we are not sure if si and ti are cognate. If not, why did both languages develop a special form – and with different distributions? While I cannot resolve these diachronic questions, we can at least recognize that despite appearances and distributional differences, Lusoga 1sg. negative subject /ti-/ requires a strikingly similar synchronic portmanteau analysis to Luganda /si-/. This conclusion thus bears on where we began the discussion: that allomorphy is non-ideal – a violation of the preference that Vennemann termed "Humboldt's Universal". What's interesting in the Lusoga case is that either (13b) and (13c) must have been the historical situation – and similarly, pre-Luganda must have had si-i- as it is in Lengola in (20) or n-si- as it is in Chibemba. In order for the derivations to proceed regularly towards a portmanteau interpretation, it was necessary for speakers to eschew a natural phonological derivation with vowel or nasal deletion in favor of a grammatically conditioned one. This brings me to work I did in the early 1970s with my longtime and recently late friend, Russell Schuh, in which we published the following pronouncement: "Given the alternatives of analyzing a given synchronic alternation as conditioned by some abstract phonological unit or by a grammatical category, speakers will always choose the latter course" (Hyman and Schuh 1974: 94). In rereading this some decades later I was rather surprised to learn that we had made this proposal. However, as graduates of UCLA Russ and I had both been greatly influenced by Vennemann's natural generative phonology, especially Vennemann (1972b), which inspired Schuh (1972) and which I had to address in Hyman (1972: chapter 4), even though I wasn't quite ready to jump ship.[1] I thus suspect that we may have gotten the idea from Theo.

References

Ashton, E. O. 1944. *Swahili grammar*. London: Longmans.
Ashton, E. O., E. M. K. Mulira, E. G. M. Ndawula & A. N. Tucker. 1954. *A Luganda grammar*. London: Longmans Green & Co.
Bastin, Yvonne. 2006. Un PVi- à la première personne du singulier en bantou. *Africana Linguistica* 12. 25–36.
Clements, George. 1986. Compensatory lengthening and consonant gemination in Luganda. In Leo Wetzels & Engin Sezer (eds.), *Studies in compensatory lengthening*, 37–78. Dordrecht: Foris.
Güldemann, Tom. 1999. The genesis of verbal negation in Bantu and its dependency on functional features of clause types. In Jean-Marie Hombert & Larry M. Hyman (eds.), *Bantu historical linguistics: Theoretical and empirical perspectives*, 545–487. Stanford: C.S.L.I.
Hyman, Larry M. 1972. *A phonological study of Fe'fe'-Bamileke*. Los Angeles, CA: University of California, Los Angeles dissertation. *Studies in African Linguistics*, Supplement 4.
Hyman, Larry M. & Francis X. Katamba. 1990. Final vowel shortening in Luganda. *Studies in African Linguistics* 15. 233–273.
Hyman, Larry M. & Francis X. Katamba. 1999. The syllable in Luganda phonology and morphology. In Harry van der Hulst & Nancy Ritter (eds.), *The syllable: Views and facts*, 349–416. Berlin: de Gruyter.
Hyman, Larry M. & Russell G. Schuh. 1974. Universals of tone rules: Evidence from West Africa. *Linguistic Inquiry* 5. 81–115.
Hyman, Larry M. & John Robert Watters. 1984. Auxiliary focus. *Studies in African Linguistics* 15. 233–273.
Kamba Muzenga, J. G. 1981. *Les formes verbales négatives dans les langues bantoues*. Tervuren: Musée Royal de l'Afrique Centrale.

---

[1] Thus, I wrote back then: "I have greatly profited in phonology from long discussions with Prof. Vennemann, who may or may not agree with some of the solutions in this study, but who was always more than willing to give me a challenge and provoke new thoughts. While he may go on to greater things in the realm of syntax and semantics, I shall always remember Prof. Vennemann for the many long evenings in the G.L.C. [Graduate Linguistics Circle] Reading Room, where we fought tooth and nail over generative phonology." (Hyman 1972: *vii–viii*).

Katamba, Francis X. & Larry M. Hyman. 1991. Nasality and morpheme structure constraints in Luganda. *Afrikanistische Arbeitspapiere* 25. 175–211.

Meeussen, A. E. 1959. *Essai de grammaire rundi*. Tervuren: Musée Royal de l'Afrique Centrale.

Menn, Lise & Brian MacWhinney. 1984. The repeated morph constraint: Toward an explanation. *Language* 60. 519–541.

Mwita, Change. 2016. *A morphosyntactic verb inflection for tense and aspect in Bemba*. Nairobi: University of Nairobi dissertation.

Nurse, Derek. 2008. *Tense and aspect in Bantu*. Oxford: Oxford University Press.

Nurse, Derek & Thomas J. Hinnebusch. 1993. *Swahili and Sabaki: A linguistic history*. University of California Publications in Linguistics 121. Berkeley, Los Angeles & London: University of California Press.

Schuh, Russell G. 1972. Rule inversion in Chadic. *Studies in African Linguistics* 3. 379–397.

Stappers, Leo. 1971. Esquisse de la langue Lengola. *Africana Linguistica* 5. 256–307.

Stump, Gregory. 2017a. Rules and blocks. In Claire Bowern, Laurence Horn & Raffaella Zanuttini (eds.), *On looking into words (and beyond)*, 379–397. Berlin: Language Science Press.

Stump, Gregory. 2017b. Rule conflation in an inferential-realizational theory of morphotactics. *Acta Linguistica Academica* 64. 79–124.

Vennemann, Theo. 1972a. Phonetic analogy and conceptual analogy. In Theo Vennemann and Terence H. Wilbur (eds.), *Schuchhardt, the Neogrammarians, and the transformational theory of phonological change: Four essays by Hugo Schuchhardt, Theo Vennemann, Terence H. Wilbur*, 115–179. Frankfurt am Main: Athenäum.

Vennemann, Theo. 1972b. Rule inversion. *Lingua* 29. 209–242.

Vennemann, Theo. 1990. Language change as language improvement. In Vincenzo Orioles (ed.), *Modelli esplicativi della diacronica linguistica: Atti del Convegno della Società Italiana di Glottologia, Pavia, 15–17 settembre 1988*, 11–35. Pisa: Giardini Editori e Stampatori.

Irmengard Rauch
The laryngeal preference, Saussure, and his politics

Abstract: Foundational to Vennemann's Preference Laws is the concept of Universal Consonantal Strength propagated also by Saussure and others before and after him. A preference for resonants to be vowel-like, indeed, to engender vowels, lies at the heart of laryngeal theory as discovered by Sausssure. Both Vennemann and Saussure wrestle with prevailing status-quo phonological research, not only in arguing, agreeing and disagreeing, with their own reasoning (inner polemic), but with that of others, demonstrating the political nature of all language.

1 Introduction

Theo Vennemann inaugurated his comprehensive *Preference laws for syllable structure and the explanation of sound change* (1988) in a lecture presented in the German Department at the University of California, Berkeley, on April 22, 1985 (Vennemann 1988: 7). He writes that foundational to his treatment of syllable structure is the concept of Universal Consonantal Strength propagated in the 19th century by Sievers, Jespersen, Saussure, and others forward (Vennemann 1988: 9, 13). (The concept is often attributed to Jespersen as his "Sonority Hierarchy".) A preference for resonants to be vowel-like lies at the heart of laryngeal theory as discovered by Saussure. This paper recounts the known linguistic and semiotic legacy of Saussure, but from a viewpoint of Saussure the man, his ancestry, his temperament, his worries, and yes, his political in-fighting.

2 Saussure's family tree

Saussure himself begins his family tree in an undated, handwritten manuscript (Bibliothèque Genève MS fr. 3957/2, f. 34 v) with Jean-Baptiste de Saussure, who was born in 1575. However, John E. Joseph in his comprehensive 780-page biography (2012) chronicles another four generations before Jean Baptiste, starting

---

Irmengard Rauch, Department of German, Berkeley University of California, Berkeley/USA

https://doi.org/10.1515/9783110721461-009

with a Chouel de Saulxures-lès Nancy, place names serving as surnames in the 1940s. Joseph's biography is the principal source for the facts of Saussure's life. Chouel begat Mongin (born 1469), who begat Antoine (born 1514), who simplified the family name to Saussure. Antoine begat Jean (born 1546), the father of Jean-Baptiste, who begins Ferdinand's own genealogical account. This era is in the heart of the Reformation and it is precisely the factor which drove Antoine de Saussure to move the Saussure family out of France and to seek refuge in the sanctuary city of Geneva, the life-long home of Ferdinand except for three years in Berlin and Leipzig and ten years teaching in Paris. Antoine died at age 55; the only other Saussure dying young is Ferdinand.

Fast forward then another seven generations from Jean Baptiste to the father of Ferdinand, Henri Frederic Louis (born 1829, twelfth-generation Saussure). In the three centuries in between, the turmoil of the French Revolution and the Napoleonic Wars impacted lives, yet the intellectual pursuits of the Saussures are beginning to emerge. They were ever landowners, aristocracy, then elite bourgeoisie, as witnessed also in the emigrated South Carolina Dés-suh-sher, Henri, the great grandson of Jean Baptiste, and his descendants, whose plantation was destroyed by Sherman in the Civil War. One of these South Carolinian Dés-suh-shers includes an original trustee of the University of South Carolina (1801), which subsumes the present-day De Saussure College.

The tenth generation Horace Benedict, born 1740, great-grandfather of Ferdinand, shared with Ferdinand a short life, 54 and 56 years, respectively, compared with the other male Saussures living into their eighties. Horace Benedict was reputed to be the most famous Geneva scientist of the 18th century, having brought the Alps to the reading public through his four volume *Voyages into the Alps*, his fabled first person claim to set foot on the summit of Mont Blanc, his professorship at Geneva Academie and lectures on physics and metaphysics in Latin. Horace Benedict's daughter Albertine, great-aunt of Ferdinand, wrote three volumes on the acquisition of language, invoking foundational linguistic and semiotic concepts such as the *sign, sameness,* and *difference*. Ferdinand was familiar with this great-aunt's writing.

The library and unschooled amateur conversations on ethology and etymology with Ferdinand's maternal grandfather, Alexander-Joseph de Pourtalès (born 1810), stimulated Ferdinand's pursuit of language. Ferdinand would send his grandfather a copy of his breakthrough 1879 *Memoir on the original system of vowels in the Indo-European languages.*

While Ferdinand's mother, Louise-Elisabeth de Pourtalès (born 1837), was a classy lady, his father, Henri Frederic Louis de Saussure (born 1829), was a bit of a schemer. During an exploration in Mexico, Henri is known to have engaged in a scam in which he surreptitiously copied a 16th-century Mixtec codex for publication. He overreached in his scientific adventures and was never awarded an academic position but wrote and published out of his Geneva study. He supported his family through various and sundry investments, which at times required scheming.

Henri monitored the lives of his children closely. His diary entries recording his eldest son Ferdinand include e.g. an entry (cited by Joseph 2012: 117) of August 25, 1870 stating "What an unusually gifted boy is our Ferdinand. He learns with extreme ease, and he is not superficial as overly gifted children too often are". Another entry of May 5, 1876 (Joseph 2012: 117) reads, "As he grew, his faculties grew as well. He was always something of a man. From the age of twelve he read his newspaper regularly and took interest in general politics. His tastes were not those of youth. He sought the company of adults; he read everything he could get his hands on". Yet, the adolescent Ferdinand was not beyond drawing cartoons and passing notes in class.

3 Saussure's politics

"What Matters?" These two words are the opening sentence of Charles Krauthammer's 2013 Pulitzer Prize winning *Things that matter*, a mantra that infuses our current media discourse. Krauthammer (2013: 2) answers, "While science, medicine, art, poetry, architecture, chess, space, sports, number theory and all things hard and beautiful promise purity, elegance and sometimes even transcendence, they are fundamentally subordinate. In the end they must bow to the sovereignty of politics." This statement begs for a definition of politics, in itself a seeming mundane pursuit. However, Joseph in his 2006 *Language and politics*, in which Saussure's laryngeal plays no role, argues that "all language is political [. . .] from top to bottom [. . .] [since] disagreement is the mother of politics" (2006: ix, 17). Joseph (2006: 18) refers to the shopping list as "very political"; it is his "wife's list." Of the early infant babbling interpreted as commands, Joseph (2006: 18) writes, "It doesn't get more political than that." Similarly, we interpret computer commands or simply a copyright symbol with date which signal injunctions/imperatives.

All that is termed "political", from Old French *politique* into Late Middle English via Latin from Greek *politikos* meaning 'citizen' from *polis* 'city'. As *Google* informs, "political" refers to "the assumptions or principles relating to or inherent in a sphere, theory, or thing, especially when concerned with power and status in society." Indeed, that shopping list is political. Compare Julia Kristeva who in her *Intimate Politics* (2003) links politics with "revolt". Kristeva explains the etymology of revolt as having a distinctively political meaning from the French Revolution, but she considers its relevancy as changed in current times, that is, 2003. She writes, "I will start by situating the problematic of revolt within the context of our current concerns, both in terms of intimacy on which our notion of happiness depends and the social link that determines what we call politics" (Kristeva 2003: 3). That was 2003. Without entering into the "concerns" of 2021, what is to be gleaned from Kristeva's quotation is that universally the notions of intimacy and social life "determine" politics.

Where does Saussure fit in, in the midst of these definitions, and why is he foundational for the discussions of Joseph, Kristeva, and for most 20th-century linguists and semiotists? The answer resides to a great extent in Saussure's dichotomies of *langue* and *parole*, diachrony and synchrony, which engendered "disagreement" and "revolt" within Saussure himself to the end. Saussure's *langue* is held to be an abstract invariant system determined by social force, whereas his *parole* is the speech of an individual. In his book *Course in general linguistics* (1959: 8), we read: "Speech has both an individual and a social side and we cannot conceive of one without the other." Yet in his final lectures on general linguistics at Geneva, the then fifty-four-year-old Saussure still agonises over the collective mind determining *langue* and fixates on the fact that *parole* associates with the horizontal or static axis and that for the speaker diachrony, that is the vertical axis, extremely expressed, does not exist. He faults himself for "the looseness of this course" (Joseph 2012: 596). Even static linguistics cannot be pinned down in time; he admits change is always ongoing. As to formal politics, the thirty-seven-year-old Sausssurean declaration that he is "a convinced Dreyfusard" (Joseph 2012: 416) during the Dreyfus Affair of the 1890's reflects Saussure's anti-racist political convictions.

4 The celebrated case of academic politics: The laryngeal

We turn now to the celebrated case of academic politics, namely, the disagreement, revolt, and polemic of the young Saussure starting in his teens. A month short of the required age fifteen to enter Geneva University, in 1872 his father enrolled the disappointed Ferdinand in preparatory school into the classical and literary studies track, rather than the industrial, commercial track. In his diary of May 23, 1873 Ferdinand recounts the final exam a year later writing with condescension toward his examiners: "I don't give a damn about those oral exams" (Joseph 2012: 136), this in spite of graduating first in his class.

It was during that year at prep school in 1872–73 at age fifteen/sixteen that Ferdinand experienced the embryonic insight, an analogical abduction, to which he laid claim the rest of his life and which is the foundation of his Indo-European breakthrough to come. In reading Greek he encountered an alternate *tetákhatai* (3rd p. pl. perf. pass. 'to array') to **tetákhntai*, abducing that n of the latter equals a of the former. Saussure thus displayed the preference of the vowel-like quality, indeed, the vowel-producing quality of resonants, i.e. $n = a$, thus the sonant nasal, leading to the birth of the laryngeal.

From the prep school to the University of Geneva in 1873, and in 1874 at seventeen Ferdinand wrote his first linguistic essay on reducing the words of Greek, Latin and German to nine primitive roots composed of p, t, k and the vowel a. It foreshadows his algebraic and distinctive feature approach, concepts of *difference* and *system*, indeed of the laryngeal. Intent on language origin, Ferdinand derives the nine primitive roots from the basic consonants p, t, k, plus the vowel a. The first consonant to emerge is k, which came from aspiration h before vowel; it was laryngeal (which aligned with Semitic, believed to represent the oldest strain of human language). Taken as an essay on a universal language, Ferdinand's essay was not well received. After all, the powerful Linguistic Society of Paris, of which Ferdinand was to become a member two years after his essay, had banned ten years earlier already (1866) any present or future debates on the origin of language. In the first of many intellectual disputes with revered authority, Ferdinand questioned in 1876 some of the work of the sacred cow of French linguistics, Michel Bréal, while never abandoning his own seminal insights/concepts.

From the two years at the University of Geneva, Ferdinand was sent by his father to Leipzig, the then global centre for the science of linguistics, including the likes of Brugmann, Curtius, and Bopp. Here he learned of Brugmann's 1871 article on sonant nasals, detailing cases of Greek a derived from n, similar to Saussure's prep school monumental insight (above). Ferdinand exclaims in his recollections that "[I] suddenly and definitively realized that my ideas were not worse than those I saw taken seriously around me [in Leipzig]" (Joseph 2012: 187). Indeed, at age 18 ½ he reads Curtius, takes on Bopp, and claims "the sonant nasal which had been familiar to me a lot longer than it had to Brugmann" (Joseph 2012: 189).

Ever protective of his own ideas, Ferdinand recounts,

When in the autumn of 1877 I began to take a course of Mr. Brugman's, I paid a visit to Mr. Brugman to declare to him that I was starting to write something (Memoire on the System of Vowels) in which it might seem as though I was partially using his ideas, I was giving up being one of his auditors, and would he please take note [. . .]. (Joseph 2012: 199)

Active in the Linguistic Society of Paris as well at this time (1877) Ferdinand takes on Grassmann on the variable endings *io / eo* of the Sanskrit class 4 verbs, which Grassmann attributed to the length of the root syllable with exceptions (a thorn in the Neogrammarian Principle that sound laws know no exceptions). Ferdinand introduced meaning, assigning neutral meaning to -*io* verbs and active meaning to -*eo* verbs. Meaning in conjunction with sound is a step backward in the Neogrammarian mind which holds that the linguistic sign is arbitrary. The limiting of the arbitrariness of the sign was, of course, Ferdinand's goal in activating his semiological dictum that the linguistic sign is like a piece of paper with sound on the one side and meaning on the other. What was this nineteen year old brash, aloof kid from Geneva thinking, challenging the dominant Leipzig Neogrammarians?

Ferdinand recounts that he was perceived as an outsider, a French-speaking foreigner, who did not schmooze and did not attend the weekly pub meetings attended by Brugmann, Osthoff, Leskien, Braune, Sievers, and Verner. Ferdinand felt well-disposed toward Brugmann but was obsessed with ownership of his own ideas and the accusations of plagiarism and counter-plagiarism which were to infuse his second year at Leipzig in which he frantically wrote his *Memoir on the primitive system of vowels in Indo-European languages*. Ferdinand seized on Brugmann's concept of two PIE *a*'s: a_1 = an *e*-colored vowel and a_2 = an *o*-colored vowel, both yielding *a* in the Asian languages but *e* and *o* in the European. In his 1877 paper to the Linguistic Society of Paris, entitled "An attempt at distinguishing the different *a*'s of Indo-European", Ferdinand accounts for the *e* ~ *o* alternation but also for the long *ê*, *ô* as well as the zero grade, namely *i*, *u* and for the preference of the nasal to be vowel-like.

The 1877 paper was a foretaste to Ferdinand's 1879 *Memoire*, envisaged as sixty pages, but ending up as 300 pages, feverishly writing so that no one (not Brugmann, not Osthoff) would as chronicled by Ferdinand's father "get there first" (Joseph 2012: 221). In the middle (page 133) of his *Memoire*, Saussure repeats his 1874 claim, writing, "The phoneme a_1 [Brugmann a_1 = e] is the radical vowel of all roots. It can form the vocalic element of the root by itself or it can be followed by a second sonant which we have termed the 'sonant coefficient'", this last symbolized by Saussure as "A." The sonant coefficient was the cover term for the semivowels *i*, *u* and for the sonant consonants *m*, *n*, *ŋ*, *l*, *r*, hearkening back to the "sonant nasal" of the fifteen-year-old Ferdinand. His insight of an original proto-vowel *e* required that "Everything back to Bopp [. . .] had to be rewritten. Even Curtius's revelation [. . .] had to be reversed" (Joseph 2012: 230).

According to Saussure, Engl. *sing, sang, sung* occurs as the ablaut alternation *en* ~ *on* ~ *n* = the *e* ~ *o* ~ Ø grades. Greek evidence, ever the stereotypical ablaut examples, allows the *e* ~ *o* ~ Ø grades to be observed with *i* instead of *n*, that is, *ei* ~ *oi* ~ *i*, in, for example, Greek *eidó* 'I know'. To account for roots with basic long vowel in the root, parallel to *ei ~ oi ~ i* or *en ~ on ~ n*, we have *eA ~ oA ~ A* in, e.g., Greek *títhēmi* 'I put'. This, Ferdinand's brilliant abduction at age twenty-one is, according to Beekes (1995: 102): "the most important single discovery in the whole history of Indo-European linguistics" and *ceteris paribus* certainly one of the most important instances of stormy academic politics.

5 Conclusion

By his sonant coefficient, Ferdinand predicts the Hittite laryngeal, substantiated three decades later by the Hittite finds, deciphered in 1915, and connected to Ferdinand's sonant coefficient by Kuryłowicz in 1935. Needless to say, Ferdinand did not live to experience the confirmation of his abduction. In fact, the reception of his *Memoire* in Leipzig was miserable, endemic to academic politics. Joseph (2012: 245) writes:

> It is in some ways unfortunate that no one in Leipzig brought a legal case against Saussure, because this would have given him a public forum in which to defend himself. Instead, they subjected him to a whispering campaign, effectively condemning him of plagiarism without trial. It was a harsh irony, given that what had impelled him to work so feverishly was the fear of being denied credit for his own discoveries. On the whole he succeeded in his aim; the *Memoire* was widely recognized outside Leipzig as a work of immense originality.

To be sure, the *Memoire* did not yield a Ph.D. for Saussure. He moved on to Berlin, where he lived in 1878–79, and to the non-hot thesis topic of the Sanskrit genitive absolute, which he submitted in January 1880 at Leipzig for the Ph.D. at age twenty-two. In February 1880, two reviewers, Windisch and Curtius, separately approved Saussure's thesis *On the genitive absolute in Sanskrit*, assigning it the grade "*egregia*" 'outstanding'. Joseph (2012: 266) explains, "[T]he indications from these reports [of Windisch and Curtius] is that he [Saussure] would have received the doctorate for the *Memoire* had he submitted it. Indeed, perhaps the mention *egregia* was given as much for the *Memoire* as for the comparatively modest thesis on the Sanskrit genitive absolute."

Throughout his teens and early into adulthood, Ferdinand enjoyed an occasional love-life and the writing of poetry. At age thirty-four in March 1892 Saussure married Marie-Eugénie Faesch and in December they produced Jaques-Alexandre Bénédict – the fourteenth generation scion of de Saussures.

Vennemann (1988: 1) in opening his treatise states, "My conception of preference laws differs from most approaches to linguistic naturalness by characterizing linguistic structure not as good or bad (natural or unnatural, unmarked or marked), but as better or worse." The Consonantal Strength concept informs Vennemann's thinking just as it had Saussure's, who, likewise rejecting a consonant : vowel divide, considered early on the possibility of the consonantal nature of sonant coefficients. The intellectual "disagreement" of each of these two research giants with the *status quo* "matters." Each display their own genre of political language.

References

Beekes, Robert. 1995. *Comparative Indo-European linguistics: An introduction*. Amsterdam: John Benjamins.
Joseph, John. 2006. *Language and politics*. Edinburgh: Edinburgh University Press.
Joseph, John. 2012. *Saussure*. Oxford: Oxford University Press.
Kristeva, Julia. 2003. *Intimate revolt: The powers and limits of psychoanalysis*. Vol. 2. Ed. by Lawrence Kritzman. Transl. by Jeanine Herman. New York: Columbia University Press.
Krauthammer, Charles. 2013. *Things that matter*. New York: Crown Forum.
Saussure, Ferdinand. 1879. *Mémoire sur le système primitif des voyelles dans les langues indo-européennes*. Leipzig: Teubner.
Saussure, Ferdinand. 1959. *Course in general linguistics*. Ed. by Charles Bally and Albert Sechehaye. Transl. by Wade Baskin. New York: Philosophical Society.
Vennemann, Theo. 1988. *Preference laws for syllable structure and the explanation of sound change*. Berlin: de Gruyter.

Part III: **Comparative evaluation and the inherent "predictive" purpose of preferences**

Antoniy Dimitrov
Preference laws and a new interpretation of Modern Bulgarian "liquid metathesis"

Abstract: Preference theories in general and the Syllable Contact Law as discussed in Vennemann (1988) in particular may provide a more systematic view on the Law of rising sonority of Proto-Slavic and some "post-open-syllable" innovations, such as the paradigmatic alternation between ъr/rъ and ъl/lъ in Modern Bulgarian. The standard grammars of Bulgarian do not provide useful rules concerning the distribution of both variants. A new approach concerning a complex interdependence of phonological and morphological preferences, as well as a modern concept of the aspect system of Bulgarian, and triconsonantal stem vocalisation instead of metathesis may offer a more systematic understanding with possible benefits for learners and linguists alike due to improved analytical accuracy and predictive capability compared to former analyses.

1 Introduction

Liquid metathesis in Modern Bulgarian is a specific dynamic feature of this language. The English name of the phenomenon refers to the more general term *Slavic*[1] *liquid metathesis*, but in the Bulgarian grammarian tradition, it is called *подвижно ъ* 'ъ-mobile' or 'movable ъ'. In this case, both names focus on different properties, the participating liquids and vowel, respectively, while neither of them refers to the adjacent consonants. Indeed, both phenomena (Slavic metathesis and Bulgarian movable ъ) should describe the characteristic vocalisation patterns of TRT-sequences.[2] More precisely, Slavic liquid metathesis operates with

---

[1] The terms *Slavic* and *Slavonic* are sometimes used as synonyms. Here Slavic refers to the Proto-Slavic language, Common Slavonic and the early stages of the Slavonic languages, while Slavonic means the modern Slavonic languages.

[2] A TRT-sequence means a sequence of consonant-liquid-consonant. Its vocalisation includes the vowel or vowels inside this sequence or, in other words, the vowel(s) between the liquid and the consonantal parts of the sequence. The use of T instead of C for the consonant elements follows the tradition in Slavonic grammars. Indeed, these grammars usually use small Latin t for the consonants in the sequence. A second reason is the attempt to regard the sequence as a base

Antoniy Dimitrov, Department of German, Ludwig-Maximilians-Universität Munich, Munich/Germany

https://doi.org/10.1515/9783110721461-010

many vowels and provides vocalisations with one or two vowels (TVRT-, TRVT-, and TVRVT-sequences). Liquid metathesis in Modern Bulgarian, on the other hand, operates with only one single vowel with only two possible results: TRъT and TъRT. The results of Bulgarian metathesis depend on the sound environment of the TRT-sequence and other factors. More obviously, liquid metathesis in Modern Bulgarian has nothing in common with "die bekannte Liquidametathese -CVRC->-CRVC-" [the well-known metathesis of liquids] (Hill 2009: 235).[3] From a standard perspective, the Bulgarian vocalisation patterns may occur arbitrarily, and their correct use indeed represents difficulty from a learner's point of view. To grammarians and textbook authors, the deployment of a proper set of operational rules for the practical use issues a challenge. Therefore, an approach capable of explaining – or, according to Vennemann (1983: 8), describing more accurately – at least some of the cases viewed as arbitrary by standard rules should be beneficial.

The complexity of pattern distributions may indicate the impact of more than one set of rules governing its emergence.[4] The different sets of rules may be related hierarchically to each other. In this regard, Hugo Schuchardt points out that "all the thousands of etymological and morphological correspondences, the thousands of sound laws, [. . .] as long as they remain isolated, as long as they are not absorbed into higher relationships" (1972: 66) would not be very meaningful. Preference Theory, as introduced by Theo Vennemann (1986, 1988), offers a plausible solution postulating no good or bad options but only better and worse ones. Furthermore, Vennemann's approach also integrates a type of optimality where optimisation on one set of parameters can be suboptimal with regards to other parameters. Indeed, the optimisation on one parameter results in a deterioration of others. A morphological rule, for example, may generate suboptimal sound structures or a sound change may lead to ambiguity of grammatical forms (cf. Vennemann 1986: 32–34).

Indeed, the combination of phonological and morphological motivations in hierarchical order is an inextricable part of the Preference Theory itself. For

---

for vocalisation. The third reason is the role of affricates for the argumentation, which include a dental element.

3 Eugen Hill (2009) considers this particular TRT-sequence vocalisation prototypical for the *Tendenz zur Silbenöffnung im Slavischen* [Tendency towards open syllables in Slavic].

4 In German, for example, there are pairs like *Urlaub* 'holidays' and *erlauben* 'allow'. They are the result of the weakening of the unstressed vowels outside the root syllables of Middle High German to a schwa. Due to the different nominal and verbal accentuation patterns, the vowel became a schwa in the initial syllable of the verb but not in the noun. The rule of weakening is complex itself as it considers at least two parameters: the vowel being unstressed and outside the root.

example, the *Morpho-Syllabic Theorem for Contemporary Standard German* (Vennemann 1988: 41–42) shows a case where morphology has more influence than phonology (*Contact Law*) in some instances. In this context, the new approach to liquid metathesis in Modern Bulgarian drawing on a complex array of parameters is not just inspired by Vennemann's Preference Theory but indeed operates within the purposes of this theory. Beginning with some remarks on Slavic and Slavonic syllables and consonant cluster parameters and further proceeding with a description of the actual situation of vocalisation of TRT-sequences in Modern Bulgarian, this paper introduces a systematic analysis of this vocalisation and a discussion thereof. As there is still no other approach capable of systemically analysing or predicting vocalisation patterns of TRT-sequences in Modern Bulgarian, the new approach can provide benefits for grammarians and language learners due to its extended explanative capacity. Indeed, some phenomena seem to be *a priori* inexplicable by standard descriptions of Modern Bulgarian as they do not (and cannot) follow any single sound law. Therefore, only theories operating on a complexity level by default can more reasonably address the vocalisation of TRT-sequences.

2 Slavic (and Slavonic) syllables and consonant cluster complexity

The Proto-Slavic syllable has a typical structure of XV.XV.XV (where X=(0-3)C),[5] which is very close to the optimal hypothetic structure of CV.CV.CV. This stage of the syllable structure settled down over a two-phase process with its first phase leading to a shift in syllable breaks and a second phase not affecting them (Mareš 1999: 34). The open-syllable system was fully functional at least until the late 9th century, as the early Slavonic texts, written in either the Glagolitic or the Cyrillic alphabet, show. In all of the present-day spoken Slavic languages, structures other than XV are possible, including closed syllables with more than one consonant in the coda.

---

[5] The most common syllable is the CV one, while V, CCV, and CCCV are subject to various restrictions. For example, not every vowel may occur in a V-syllable, and for the CCC- cluster there is only one option: STR (a sequence of fricative-plosive-liquid in this order) when affricates are viewed as a composite of sounds and not sequences of two sounds. Even in the last case, the restriction would be STR or T^{S}R. And, of course, less prefered syllables like V or CCCV do not co-occur. Thus, structures like *V.V.V or *CCCV.CCCV.CCCV do not occur at all. For further information about the combinatory variants of Proto-Slavic, see Žuravlev (2007: 39–46 and 56–71).

2.1 Relevance of consonant clusters

In words like the Russian *борщ* 'borsch, borscht' (German: *Borschtsch*), for example, the coda consists of four consonants (-RSTS or -R^{S}T^S if an STS-sequence; the graph <щ> represents a complex structure with affricate elements). Indeed, this coda complexity is similar to that in German words like *Herbst* 'autumn' and less complex only compared to the relatively rare cases of even higher complexity in German like *Herbsts* 'autumn; Gen. Sg.', which is considered a very complex cluster in German. On the other hand, the general level of Modern Slavonic final-consonant-cluster complexity does not apply to Modern Bulgarian. Indeed, Modern Bulgarian has no final clusters of four or five consonants and even no triconsonantal clusters in native words. In certain cases, Modern Bulgarian has only one consonant in places where other Slavonic languages have two or three consonants, as in Bg. *солидарност* (solidarnost) 'solidarity' (the orthography preserves the final /-t/, but in the pronunciation, the word ends with a simple fricative: [-s]), Pol. *solidarność* 'idem' [-ɕtɕ] (or, respectively [-ʃtʲ]) and Russ. *солидарность* (solidarnost') 'idem' [-s't']'. Ruska Simeonova (1998: 220) points out, "Im Bulgarischen sind nur drei dreigliedrige Auslautverbindungen möglich: kst, ŋkt, ŋks, und zwar nur in Fremdwörtern. Mehrgliedrige Auslautstrukturen sind im Bulgarischen ausgeschlossen" [In the Bulgarian language only three triconsonantal final clusters are possible: kst, ŋkt, ŋks, and, to be sure, these occur in borrowed words only. More complex final structures are unacceptable]. Nonetheless, there are a few more triconsonantal final clusters in (more recent) borrowings from English or German, like [-rts/ -rt^s] or [-ntʃ/ -ntʲ].

The new feature means not just a reinvention or a return to the syllabic system of Indo-European but constitutes a system with parameters of its own. This system differs from the syllabic systems of other Indo-European languages (including Indo-European itself) in its very core as it deals differently with ambisyllabic consonants. On the other hand, heterosyllabicity (or, more commonly, *ambisyllabicity*) is considered a central feature of syllabic systems by Vennemann (1986: 12–13). Syllable preferences are indeed influential in cases where specific, non-tolerable consonantal clusters must be adopted. RTR-sequences (liquid-plosive-liquid) represented by the consonant sequence [-rtl(-)], which is common in Southern Germany and Austria, cannot exist inside a syllable in Modern Bulgarian, neither as head nor as a coda. Indeed, the Austrian place Name *Hartl* is adapted as *Хартъл* (Hartyl) in Bulgarian (Paraškevov 2015: 303) but as *Хартль* (Hartl')[6] in Modern Russian. However, in a non-final position, the sequence can

---

[6] Russian *Хартль* has only one vowel. The letter sequence <ль> is a digraph for the more palatal variant of the liquid.

be adopted without vowel epenthesis as in the proper name *Бертле* (Bertle) from German *Bärtle*. In this case, the syllabification of the word in Bulgarian (*Бер-тле* [Ber-tle]) is optimal in terms of Vennemann's Contact Law (Vennemann 1988: 40) with a syllable contact of /r$^$t/ while in German the word is morphologically segmented as *Bärt-le*, with the non-optimal syllable contact /t$^$l/. This segmentation is possible in Modern Bulgarian because the morphemic structure of the original word is not identifiable and especially because /tl-/ is a tolerable and even preferable (according to Vennemann's *Law of Initials* 1988: 32) head as in Bg. *тлъка* (tlyka)[7] 'gathering (in the evening)'. In German, on the contrary, /tl-/ is not a possible syllable head at all as demonstrated by Vennemann on German "*han/t/.lung* 'action'" (1988: 33). Indeed, different results in both languages arise from differences between the sets of parameters, on which the Preference Laws operate.

2.2 Tautosyllabity and affricates

Tautosyllabic and heterosyllabic properties, respectively, play a significant role in the analysis of syllable structures. Eugen Hill introduced a heterosyllabic analysis of Slavic syllable borders as evidence for the limitations of the scope of Preference Theory: "Da geschlossene Silben auf *s* in der Mitte des Wortes im Slavischen keine Modifikation erfahren (vgl. Lexeme wie aksl. *věsna* 'Frühling', *maslo* 'Öl', *město* 'Ort' etc.), ist der Schwund des *s* im Wortauslaut auf der Analyseebene der Silbe nicht zu motivieren, obwohl dieser Schwund zu einer drastischen Zunahme der Silben mit leichterem Auslaut führt" [As far as closed syllables ending in *s* do not undergo any changes in the middle of a word (cf. lexemes like O.Ch.Slav. *věsna* 'spring', *maslo* 'oil', *město* 'place' etc.), the loss of *s* in word-final position cannot be considered motivated on the level of syllable analysis, even though this loss leads to a drastic increase in the number of syllables with less complex auslaut] (2009: 236). This interpretation would work only if the Slavic consonant sequences were heterosyllabic in analogy to Germanic. Thus, a tautosyllabic solution would be preferable regarding the Preference Laws as it would lead to a CV-CCV-structure, and the CV-structure itself would be optimal in terms of the Law of Finals. In addition, this solution would be a more reasonable one because it would conform to

---

[7] In this word, the vocalisation pattern of the TRT-sequence is irregular. This irregularity may be the result of an attempt to avoid confusion with similar sequences in words like *тълковен* (tylkoven) 'explanatory' derived from a different Indo-European root. For the etymology of both roots, see also Pokorny (2005: 1062, 1088). Indeed, *tlyka* is an archaic word, not really used in Modern Bulgarian and often misspelt as "*tlaka*". The misspelling indicates that native speakers do not interpret the word as a case of a TRT-sequence with variable vocalisation any more.

the tendency for open syllables as well. More obviously, in places where a heterosyllabic solution was not possible at all, such as in VNC-sequences, the result was not a closed non-final syllable (CVN-CV) but rather an open one (CV^n-CV).[8] Additionally, consonant clusters not capable of tautosyllabicity could also be adapted to the open syllable preference in Proto-Slavic and in Common Slavic by the elimination or shifting of morpheme boundaries as described in Brackney (2007: 138–140). Čekman (1979: 211–213) describes for Proto-Slavic the mechanism of vowel syncope without creating closed syllables at all due to a regularity very similar to the Law of Initials. In the modern Slavonic languages closed syllables are common in all positions, and therefore heterosyllabic solutions may be the preferred option in certain cases. As for Bulgarian, both old and modern, at least some cases of biconsonantal sequences are explicitly marked as tautosyllabic due to the use of specific affricate letters. But there are certain cases where tautosyllabicity is indicated indirectly as in Bg. *гнездо* (gnezdo) 'nest', srb. *гнездо* (gnezdo) 'idem': in Serbian (according to the rule of "written as pronounced"), in a heterosyllabic allocation, due to the final devoicing, a voiceless fricative would occur instead of the voiced one. In English, on the other hand, a similar process takes place based on the Law of Finals. Consonant clusters like [ks] and [ps] are simplified to [z] and [s] in word-initial position and preserved where they can be ambisyllabic *or* tautosyllabic in coda position. The Greek word ἀνάπτυξις 'anaptyxis' has the hyphenation {an.ap.tyx.is} in English and {a.na.pti.ksis} in Bulgarian. If hyphenated in the same way as in Bulgarian, the English word would have a different pronunciation for the <x>: */ˌænəpˈtɪzɪs/. Both variants conform to the Preference Laws in their entirety but follow different pathways.

In the Glagolitic script, which is the oldest systematically developed alphabet in use both for Slavonic languages in general and for the Bulgarian language in particular, there are specific letters for several affricates, all of them containing a dental and a fricative. In Modern Bulgarian, only the three voiceless affricate letters are still in use.[9] In the Glagolitic script, a disbalance between voiced and voiceless affricates already existed, with no voiced counterpart of <щ>, which

---

[8] As predicted by the Law of Finals, -CV^n is a possible final syllable for Proto-Slavic and -CVC and -CVN are not.

[9] Interestingly, these three letters (щ, ч, ц) are directly or indirectly related to two Hebrew letters – *shin* (ש) and *tsade* (צ). The letters <ц> and <ч> represent tsade (the only affricate letter used in Modern Hebrew) with its two forms (word-final <ץ> and non-final <צ>) while <щ> is a ligature of <ш> (itself directly based on shin) and <т>. A coincidence emerges because the decision to keep these letters and to abandon the letters for the voiced affricates follows the attempt to adjust the orthography of Modern Bulgarian towards Russian. In Modern Serbian, the letters for the voiced affricates are still in use. The rendering of affricates or consonant clusters by a single letter is not a mandatory property of alphabetic writing. The Runic alphabet featured no affricate

itself was a ligature albeit a stable one, listed as a letter in the alphabet. All affricate letters except for <щ> refer to TS-sequences, while for the ST-sequences digraphs are used.[10] This allocation of letters and digraphs for the rendition of consonant sequences may refer to an interpretation as affricates and non-affricates, respectively.

As for Modern Bulgarian, affricates are defined by their tautosyllabic properties and contrast with both simple plosives and combinations of a plosive and a fricative capable of ambisyllabic allocation (Žečev 2015: 53). Indeed, there is an attempt to address the vocalisation of TRT-sequences by considering affricates equal to single consonants (Žečev 2015: 54–55). This attempt follows the standard rules that operate by counting the number of letters between R and the vowel of the following syllable with affricates spelt by a single letter (the voiceless ones). The examples listed by Georgi Žečev do not include the voiced affricates spelt by two letters. Indeed, this attempt cannot increase the analytic and predictive ability of the standard rules (cf. Section 4.2). However, it indicates an opposition of heterosyllabic and tautosyllabic allocations in Modern Bulgarian in contrast to Common Slavic or Old Bulgarian, which offered only the tautosyllabic option.

2.3 Syllable structures in Modern Bulgarian

The distribution of consonants in Modern Bulgarian rests upon the sonority of the intervocalic consonants or, in the terms used by Vennemann, upon their consonantal strength. Generally, a sequence with non-rising (i.e. constant or falling) sonority can become heterosyllabic, and a sequence with rising sonority becomes tautosyllabic and functions as the head of the following syllable. In Proto-Slavic, a sequence with rising sonority was not possible at all, and the sequences with non-rising sonority were possible only in the onset. Specific combinatory conditions additionally constrain the rule: For a contrastive overview of the possible initial and final clusters in Modern Bulgarian and Modern German, see Simeonova (1998: 218–221). According to this overview, there is a general preference for more complexity in the head position compared to the coda. An additional constraint is tautosyllabicity of affricates. In some cases, the tendency towards less complexity may be more influential than the rules themselves. The Bulgarian

---

letters or consonantal cluster letters at all, using, for example, the Phoenician/Punic Ṣade as a vowel letter (cf. Vennemann 2006: 410).

10 For all other frequent combinations, such as TV-, VT-, KS-, or SK-, digraphs are in use. On the other hand, Greek and Latin have single letters for some of these sequences, but the specific consonant clusters -ks- and -ps- are not tolerable in Common Slavic and Old Bulgarian.

adjective *гръцки* (grycki [grət^{s}ki]) 'Greek' is often misspelt "*гръдски*" (grydski).[11] The name of Greece itself is spelt (and pronounced) *Гърция* (Gyrciâ) – with an affricate. The misspelling of the adjective may result from a preference towards segmentation with a single consonant in the coda of the first syllable and a consonant cluster in the head of the second, because a cluster consisting of an affricate plus a consonant in the onset of the last syllable (*T^{S}CV) is not an optimal solution as well. A syllable border inside of an affricate is not an available option. Therefore, the best solution available in this case would be to "break" the affricate by decreasing the consonant strength[12] of its first component. A voiced plosive and a voiceless fricative *et vice versa* must, therefore, be separated by a vowel or by a syllable border. On the other hand, the final devoicing of Modern Bulgarian allows voiced consonants in the coda only on the graphic level. Thus, the spelling <-ds-> refers to a syllable border /t$^\$$s/ instead of the affricate /t^s/. For further examples, see Žečev (2015: 54).

The word *grycki* itself belongs to a specific formation class because its morphologically proper form should be **grycski* in analogy with *сръбски* (srybski) 'Serbian'. This form would indicate a syllable allocation as *{gryt^s.ski}. In terms of the Contact Law (Vennemann 1988: 40), this would be the less preferable variant as there would be no characteristic difference between the consonantal stress of both contact elements at all. Thus, the omission of one of the identical fricatives would be a preferable option. The standard orthography of Bulgarian optimises the syllable border by deleting the second fricative while retaining the affricate intact. This solution is beneficial in terms of morphological transparency and, thus, is a preferable one. However, even the standard orthography accepts the biconsonantal head solution in adjectives like *френски* (frenski) 'French' or *турски* (turski) 'Turkish'. Indeed, the derivation with the suffix *-ski* would produce the syllable contacts /nt^s.sk/ and /rt^s.sk/, respectively. A solution analogous to *grycki* would result in /nt^s.k/ and /rt^s.k/. This solution would produce a more complex coda and a simpler head, which is not a preferable option, especially in terms of Coda Law (Vennemann 1988: 20). Therefore, the deletion of the fricative element of the affricate would be the preferred option, resulting in /nt.sk/ and /rt.sk/, which is analogous to the process that accounts for the spelling *grycki*. Conventionally, in this case, the final post-consonantal deletion of dentals allows the avoidance of mis-

---

[11] Misspellings may be able to represent a more natural approach from the phonological point of view as they would be influenced by (historical) morphology to a lesser degree.

[12] "Decreasing the consonant strength" means the same as "increasing the sonority". A voiced plosive has more sonority and therefore less consonantal strength than its voiceless counterpart. As for an affricate, both elements have to be equal with regard to the voiced-voiceless-opposition.

spellings as the now bare dental disappears.[13] Thus there is no need to indicate a syllable border like /nt.sk/ or /rt.sk/ by *<ndsk> or *<rdsk> while /n.sk/ and /r.sk/ represent a preferable syllable contact situation. Indeed, this solution is optimal for the orthography because no "un-morphological" letter must follow, and it is optimal for native speakers as well. The difference between *grucki* and *frenski/ turski* is the consonant sequence TRT, which allows an additional option (alternative vocalisation CyRC- and CRyC-) unavailable to words with other consonant patterns. In Russian, this "problem" is solved by adding an epenthetic vowel (and thus an additional syllable), as in *турецкой* (tureckoj).

3 Liquid metathesis in Modern Bulgarian

The liquid metathesis of Modern Bulgarian is defined as "редуване [ър : ръ] и [ъл : лъ]" (an alternation of [yr : ry] and [yl : ly])[14] (Stoânov 1994: 16). In general, the position of the [y] in the sound groups[15] [tyrt] and [tylt][16] in poly-

---

13 This specific deletion is not a feature of the standard language and has no appropriate representation in the orthography. As for the spoken language, it is obligatory in some instances and facultative under other circumstances. However, this process does not include affricates with a dental element. In other Slavonic languages, the process excludes palatalised consonants. There might be a general tendency towards excluding the additionally featured (by palatalisation or affrication) consonants from the dental deletion, even though Modern Bulgarian itself does not allow any palatalised consonants in final position. The allocation of additionally featured and non-featured consonants has a significant impact on the phonological and morphological system, as discussed in Vennemann (1989).
14 Curved brackets are used for the translation in this specific case because of the use of squared brackets in the original text. The transliteration of Bulgarian follows the ISO 9: 1995 rule except for Bg. <ъ> which lacks a proper ISO sign (it is substituted by the sign <″>, not by a letter). Therefore, here the letter <y> replaces this <″>, mainly because the Russian <ы>, represented by the ISO letter <y>, does not exist in Bulgarian. Furthermore, in Russian, the Bulgarian <ъ> is transliterated by <ы>. The usual convention, in this case, would be to use the Cyrillic letter <ъ> in combination with Latin letters for the rest, such as tъrt, TъrT. In a text about Modern Bulgarian, the usage of a Latin letter for <ъ> allows better legibility. Bulgarian proper names are spelt according to ISO or according to the spelling used in the cited works themselves, as far as the texts provide this option.
15 These are in fact groups or "rows" of sounds because this is a pre-syllabic description. Indeed, the last consonant can switch to the following syllable. Basically, with regard to more traditional grammars of Bulgarian, *row* must be considered a synonym for 'sequence' and *group* for 'cluster'. Here the terms *row* and *group* are used for references on texts in Bulgarian and sequence/cluster in all other contexts.
16 The spelling tъrt/tъlt instead of TъRT is usual in Slavonic grammars. This notion does not refer to single phonemes but to groups of phonemes and is written in Latin letters in Cyrillic texts.

syllabic words depends on the number of consonants between the liquid and the following vowel (cf. Stoânov 1994: 16). In this standard[17] point of view, the rule for metathesis requests [tyrt] if a vowel follows and [tryt] if a consonant follows (Stoânov 1994: 16), which does not describe all the cases that exist in practice. Applying this rule would be possible only under postulation of multiple "exceptional cases", which can at some point get very numerous. Indeed, Townsend and Janda point out that there exist "keine völlig zufriedenstellenden Regeln, die die betreffenden Folgen in allen heutigen Wörtern erklären könnten" [no fully satisfactory rules which could explain the relevant sequences in all contemporary words] (2002: 225), especially as Modern Bulgarian differs from the reconstructed Late Common Slavic, where the simple rule seems to have been applicable.

3.1 Regular and irregular cases

The regular cases of liquid metathesis in Modern Bulgarian are limited to polysyllabic words as there is no rule for monosyllables. This feature is *prima facie* counterintuitive as the presence of the following syllable would offer more alternatives for syllable division by adjusting the syllable borders. Nevertheless, the rules are focused on the number of consonants between the liquid of a TRT-sequence and the vowel following the last T-element. Monosyllables with more than one consonant in place of the last T in the sequence are not very common. Examples are words like Bg. *пръст* (pryst) 'finger, soil',[18] but the consonant cluster <-st> is simply an orthographic convention with a silent letter. In native words, two consonants occur in this position mostly in the form of an affricate as in Bg. *гърч* [gərtʃ] 'convulsion' – for further examples, a description of the combinatory variants, and a comparison with German, see also Simeonova (1988: 193).[19]

---

17 This view represents the standard as it originates from a representative work, published by the Institute for Bulgarian Language of the Bulgarian Academy of Sciences.
18 This homonymy emerged due to the orthographic reforms of the late 1940s: *пръстъ* 'finger' from IE. *pr̥- 'forth' (Pokorny 2005: 813) and *пръстъ* 'soil' from IE. *pers- 'to spray' or *pr̥so-s- 'dust, ash' (Pokorny 2005: 823) were homophones only.
19 Simeonova (1988) is an earlier and shorter version of Simeonova (1998) without a separate syllable section. In this particular case, the representation in the earlier version seems to be more practical.

3.2 Standard Rule and non-standard verb forms

In Modern Bulgarian, the metathesis rule is not even called a metathesis but a *редуване* 'alternation' in scientific texts like Stoânov (1994: 15) or *подвижно ъ* 'movable y' in textbooks and reference works. Indeed, the rules include a hypothetical consonantal frame (CRXV) and two possible positions for the [y] (on both sites of the liquid) regulated by the number of consonants in the X-position. This vocalisation rule for a consonantal root initially resembles the rules of Semitic languages but has no significant grammatical implications and provides less eloquent results. The standard case would be to fill the first argument position (between the first consonant of the sequence and the liquid) when only one consonant follows (X=C), as in *гърне* (gyrne) 'pot', and when two or more consonants follow (X≥CC), as in *грънци* (grynci) 'pottery'. The second part of the rule is restricted by a "general irregularity" when the last consonant of the X-sequence is the -*v*- from an imperfective verbal suffix, as in Bg. *натъртвам* (natyrt**v**am) 'to stress'. Thus, a grammatical component has an impact on the vocalisation, while, due to numerous exceptions, the rule remains a tendency or a semi-regularity.

The "grammatical implement" would work mostly on circumfix or combined[20] forms like *na-tyrt-v-am*, where *na-* and -*v*- are the imperfectiveness elements. These are the more traditional forms, while more recent forms do not use prefixes, such as in *мълчиш* (mylčiš) 'to be silent, 2nd pers. sing. present, imperfective', *млъкваш* (mlykvaš) 'idem, iterative',[21] and *млъкнеш* (mlykneš) 'idem, perfective'.[22] Further examples for this phenomenon are indeed numerous with forms like *дърпаш* (dyrpaš) 'to draw, drag, 2nd pers. sing. present, imperfective', *дръпваш* (drypvaš) 'idem, iterative' and *дръпнеш* (drypneš) 'idem, perfective'. Here the vocalisation pattern for the TRT-frame depends on a grammatical feature (the verbal aspect), namely TyRT for

---

[20] Combined indicates, in this specific case, an imperfective verbal form built by adding a prefix and a suffix to the perfective root.

[21] These verbs are considered "secondary imperfective" in traditional grammars, but newer approaches tend to more innovative descriptions. For an overview of the traditional literature and a new methodical conceptualization, see Chakarova (2015a, 2015b).

[22] Traditionally, every aspect form of a verb is considered an independent word, a lemma of its own in the lexicon. From a learner's point of view, the solution is not a good one, especially referring to the more recent forms that seem to function as a single verb in Romance languages such as Spanish and not as a couple of different verbs. The actual formation patterns of Modern Bulgarian cannot be described precisely enough in terms of traditional perspectives, including a prototypical formation of imperfective verbs in Slavonic languages via circumfixes and with some lexical differences between the perfective and the imperfective verb.

imperfective and TRyT for iterative and perfective.[23] The correlation between stem vocalisation and verbal aspect does not represent any specific rule, but it shows a notable grade of regularity. Therefore these two phenomena may be interdependent and not only coexistent. Moreover, this relation seems more influential than the -v-rule of standard textbooks and even the X=C-rule. Nevertheless, the standard rules work properly on prefix verbs, especially when they are defective in terms of triple-aspect forms like, for example, *привършиш* (privyršiš) 'to finish sth., perf.' and *привършваш* (privyršvaš) 'idem, imperf.', without a uniquely iterative form.[24] Moreover, even the prefix derivations from triple-aspect verbs follow the standard rule, as in *издърпваш* (izdyrpvaš) 'to draw out' from *дръпваш*. Consequently, there must be another rule, according to which the standard or the grammatical vocalisation rule operates in a given case. The superior rule intervenes especially when the TRX sequence is not in the final position. If this is the case, the grammatical vocalisation rule, as defined above loses its influence and the standard rule *per definitionem* does not make predictions on the vocalisation of TRX without the following syllable.[25]

In the case of Bg. *държиш* (dyržiš) 'to hold, 2nd pers. sg. perf. indicative', *дръж!* (dryž!) 'idem, imperative', and all of its prefix derivations like *задържиш – задръж!* (zadyržiš – zadryž!) 'to hold back', both the standard and the vocalisation rule would explain the indicative, but neither of them would explain the imperative form. This modification due to a nongrammatical component (final position) may occur problematic in terms of formulating rules for a vocalisation controlled primarily by grammar. However, inside a verb paradigm of Modern Bulgarian, the 2nd pers. sing. of the athematic imperative is the only form at all, where a TRT-sequence occurs in final position. In the plural, the suffix without any thematic vowel produces a complex consonant cluster, as in *дръжте!* (dryzhte!) 'to hold, 2nd pers. plur. imperative'. Nonetheless, the plural is the less common form and therefore not the expected basis for a generalisation. Additionally, mood seems to be superior to aspect in this case as, unlike in the indicative, in the imperative all three aspects occur in the same type of sequences.[26]

---

[23] The traditional grammar divides Slavonic verbs into perfective and imperfective, whereby the imperfective class would include both imperfective and iterative verbal forms. With no distinction between these two verbal classes, it would be more challenging to address the vocalisation pattern adequately.

[24] This combination is, of course, defective only from a modern point of view. The bipolar pattern should be considered the prototypical one in terms of genuine Slavic morphology.

[25] Formally the standard rule does not make any predictions on monosyllables or polysyllables where there is no vowel after the TRT sequence.

[26] The different usage of the aspects is restricted to the present tense in declarative sentences. Imperatives, on the contrary, are restricted to exclamations. Therefore, the aspect restrictions cannot operate on imperative forms at all.

3.3 Vocalisation in verb paradigms

In other cases, the standard rule does not operate appropriately in Bg. *потвържд аваш* (potvyrždavaš)[27] 'to confirm, 2nd pers. sg. perf.', with an *-yr-* where the standard rule would predict *-ry-* as there are two consonants between the liquid and the following vowel. On a very formal level, this case might not be relevant because it does not consist of TRT or TRX but of XRX (CCRCC). In the case of a triple-aspect paradigm, on the other hand, XRX can become an analogue vocalisation pattern[28] as TRX: *хвъркаш, хвръкваш, хвръкнеш* (hvyrkaš, hvrykvaš, hvrykneš) 'to fly around, second pers. sg. – imperfective, iterative, perfective).

Table 1 shows the rules discussed above (except for the XRX case):

Table 1: Priorisation of rules operating on -TRX- verbal roots.

Highest-priority rules	Higher-priority rule	Middle-priority rule	Lower-priority rule	Result
A) TRT as a verbal root	I. Compound vocalisation rule (based on grammatical implements; verb conceptualisation with three aspects)	TRX-	Imperfective aspect	TyRX-
B) TRX (and not XRX)			Perfective or iterative aspect	TRyX-
C) T ≠ n-[29]		?-TRX-	Not a typical case as the modern rule applies typically to non-prefixed verbs. Within the group of prefixed triple-aspect verbs, there are examples for both the modern and the standard rule.	
		TRX -TRX	X=T (X>T not applicable to plain roots)	P(TRyT) – P(-TRyT) - few examples; always 2nd pers. sing. imperative[30]

---

27 Here *po-* is a prefix and *-tvyržd-* is the verbal root.
28 XRX represents the same vocalisation pattern (as CRC) in terms of the positions *-yr-* and *-ry-*, but with two consonants in front and behind it. The vowel is always next to the liquid.
29 As for the onset of the Modern Bulgarian, technically no liquid metathesis would be tolerable after n- in the initial position of a potential NRX- or CNRX-sequence and it always would be vocalised as NyRX or CNyRX.
30 There are only a few cases of plain root imperatives in Modern Bulgarian, and the imperatives composed of a prefix and plain verbal root may follow the form of the base verb. On the other hand, it is difficult to find counterexamples in this regard.

Table 1 (continued)

Highest-priority rules	Higher-priority rule	Middle-priority rule	Lower-priority rule	Result
	II. Traditional (standard) rule (no operative grammatical implements;[31] verb conceptualisation with two aspects)	TRX-	X=T	TyRT-
			X=T(C)C_{last}; C_{last}=v	TyRT(C)v- / ~~TyRT(C)v-~~ -numerous exceptions
			X=T(C)C_{last}; C_{last}≠V	-TRyT(C)C_{last}-
		-TRX-	X=T	-TyRT-
			X=T(C)C_{last}; C_{last}=v	-TyRT(C)v- / ~~TyRT(C)v-~~ -numerous exceptions, especially in prefixed triple-aspect verbs
			X=T(C)C_{last}; C_{last}≠V	-TRyT(C)C_{last}- / ~~TRyT(C)Clast-~~ - numerous exceptions[32]
		TRX -TRX	No rule at all as these cases do not match the standard rule *per definitionem*.	

The rules presented in the Table above are heterogeneous as they undergo many influences, from phonological up to grammatical. The predictive capability of these rules would be limited in general. On the other hand, in some cases, both rules seem to work correctly. The scope of the aspect vocalisation rule is considerably smaller because this rule operates only on a specific group of verbs. Within its scope, the aspect vocalisation rule seems to be superior to the standard rule. In other words, in cases with a choice between both rules, the aspect vocalisation seems to be the preferred option. This preference may be "better relative to one parameter or set of parameters [...] [and] worse relative to others" (Vennemann, 1988: 1). While weakening the general rule, the aspect vocalisation offers more regularity in a narrower set of cases.

---

[31] Formally the standard rule includes a grammatical implement as it defines -v- as a part of a verbal suffix. There are few cases where -v- is not a part of a verbal suffix, such as in Bg. църква (cyrkva) 'church', but these do not seem to underlie special rules. Additionally, in this case, the nonverbal cyrkva follows the standard rule, and its verbal counterpart цръква (crykva) 'to squirt/sprinkle, 3rd pers. sing.' does not as it follows the aspect vocalisation rule.

[32] There exist even minimal pairs of -TyRTv- and -TRyTv- verbs in this group: замръквам (zamrykvam) 'to be benighted/belated' and замъркваm (zamyrkvam) 'to start growling'.

3.4 Interconnection of vocalisation and grammar in verb paradigms

Both rules (standard and composite vocalisation, see Section 3.3) generate sound sequences that do not diverge from the general norms of Modern Bulgarian. However, only the aspect vocalisation might be functional, as the standard rule has no implications beyond pronunciation and orthography. The combination between a set of two parameters (the vocalisation) and another one including three (triple aspect) cannot provide a one-to-one correspondence. The allocation of the parameters can be considered arbitrary or functional. In this case, the arbitrary allocation would be a worse choice than the functional one because it would have the same complexity factor but a lower utility grade. The distribution of the TRyX and TyRX vocalisations among the three aspects may, *prima facie*, appear suboptimal because it refers to opposition between imperfective on the one hand and perfective/iterative on the other. This correlation differs from the traditional division of imperfective and perfective aspect, which considers iterative "a secondary imperfective", as mentioned above.

Nevertheless, only the actual contradictory allocation can be regarded as functional because perfective verb forms appear in contexts other than imperfective and iterative forms. In this manner, the different vocalisation pattern of imperfective and iterative verb forms contributes to their better distinction as an additional feature next to inflection. Perfective and iterative forms, on the other hand, do not appear in the same contexts, and an additional distinction between them would not bring any benefits. Moreover, the iterative aspect expresses the repetition of a perfective act, while being morpho-syntactically (in terms of context and inflection) more closely linked to imperfective forms. In this regard, the additional connection between iterative and perfective forms set by a similar vocalisation pattern of their roots can be considered a beneficial feature. In this way, the subsystem of triple-aspect liquid metathesis verbs becomes better balanced. A new systematic conceptualisation may be necessary in cases where the imperfective and the iterative forms belong to the same conjugation. Without the contrastive vocalisation, the only difference between them would be the suffix element -*v*- between the root and the inflection. The -*v*- is, of course, a sufficient differential element itself, but having an additional feature to support this functionality is preferable due to an expanded interpretation of the "Tendenz zur Maximierung der Kontraste im Interesse der besseren Verständlichkeit" [Tendency towards maximisation of contrasts on behalf of a better intelligibility] (Vennemann 1973: 38). Table 2 contains the forms of *дърпаш*, *дръпнеш*, and *дръпваш* discussed above.

Table 2: Vocalisation inside a triple-aspect verb paradigm.

Feature → Verb form ↓	Conjugational class	Aspect	Simple present declarative sentence	Vocalisation pattern
дърпаш	3rd: -aš	imperfective	YES	TyRT
дръпгаш	3rd: -aš	iterative	YES	TRyT
дръпнеш	1st: -eš	perfective	NO	TRyT

Within the verb system of Modern Bulgarian, liquid metathesis can consequently be determined by its position[33] inside the word, by its peripheral consonants,[34] by grammar, or by a combination of these factors. Grammatical influence is more substantial for the initial position of the TRT-sequence and weaker for the intermediate. The sound environment is more influential for intermediate positions than for final or initial. In the final position, which is less common, the few examples show a reliable link to a single grammatical feature. Hence, liquid metathesis is a dynamic and partially functional feature inside verb paradigms.

4 TRT-sequences in nominal paradigms

The inflection of Modern Bulgarian is not equally complex for nominal and verbal paradigms. As in modern Spanish, the Bulgarian verb system possesses synthetic features and a rich inflectional morphology, while the nominal system has become an almost entirely analytical one. Accordingly, the nominal system should show more definite tendencies towards invariability of stems, but the setting is ambiguous in reality. Some variable features like *umlaut* and movable accent (accent shift) seem to disappear from verb paradigms gradually but tend to be more stable in nominal paradigms.[35] Concerning the vocalisation of TRT-sequences,

---

[33] That is the position of the TRT-sequence, inside which the metathesis takes place, in the word. In this context, the position of the sequence is equal to the position of the syllable arising by the vocalisation of the sequence, or, in other words, the liquid metathesis syllable.

[34] These are all consonants between the liquid and the adjacent vowels, excluding the metathesis vowel itself.

[35] For example, the accent shift from the root to the inflectional ending as a characteristic of the past simple tense is considered archaic by recent textbooks of Modern Bulgarian. In this way, the accent pattern difference between the present and the past simple tense disappears. Therefore, the umlaut also disappears in this case as it is an accent-sensitive feature in Bulgarian. In the nominal paradigm, on the contrary, accent shift and umlaut are very common and can occur in correlation with number, case, gender, or definiteness. The preference for accent shift and um-

the situation within the nominal system is more complicated. Indeed, numerous nouns consist of (or end in) a TRT-sequence. These cases are considered *a priori* irregular by the standard set of rules as they conceptually operate on a single word and derive the vocalisation from the sound structure of the word itself.[36] As seen in the verbal system, influences beyond the sound patterns of any specific word can affect the vocalisation as well. In some contexts, these "external" influences can be more preferred than considerations of sound structure, such as in the case of triple-aspect verb forms. Consequently, an approach considering more parameters has more potential to explain and predict the vocalisation patterns in some cases.

Within the range of grammatically tolerable forms (determined by the rules), preferences can have an impact on the selection of an option to be realised. Multiple preferences can also operate simultaneously and affect each other, providing a result not explicable by a single preference alone. Possible preferences having an effect on the choice of a vocalisation pattern for a TRT-sequence in Modern Bulgarian include euphony, a tendency towards columnarity (avoiding stress shifts for different inflections of a word), grammar, and lexical analogy. The results from the first three are interrelated, and lexical analogy has an additional influence of its own.

Euphony is the core feature of the standard rule. These euphony rules are themselves derived from the syllable-structure preferences of Modern Bulgarian. They indeed operate, even though not explicitly, based on the juncture of syllables. However, the juncture itself is a function of the preferences for the structure of the resulting syllables. Nevertheless, the standard rules represent a quantitative approach that does conform with the syllable preferences in several cases. More precisely, the cases where the standard rule operates appropriately refer to a bundle of preferences. This bundle includes general preferences for covered and for mono-consonantally closed root syllables. Some preferences related to the consonant combinations in the head and the coda may be incorporated. In essence, the observations on polysyllables cannot be repeated on monosyllables because there are no syllable junctures. The syllable-structure preferences themselves are, as a matter of course, identical but the base they operate on may be different due to the changes in the quality and quantity of consonants and consonant combinations to be considered. Moreover, there are different sets of

---

laut in the nominal paradigm is indeed very dominant. Even verb forms like the past indefinite tense or the narrative mode show these features as they are formally built equal to nominal verb forms (participles) used in the place of a finite verb.

[36] This is primarily the case because, within the standard concept, the presence of a vowel following the TRT-sequence is crucial.

"external" factors operating on monosyllables and polysyllables. Hence, the disparity among the paradigms may be one of the reasons why standard rules exclude monosyllables from their scope.

4.1 Paradigmatic implements

A paradigmatic approach to the analysis of the vocalisation of TRT-sequences in nouns in Modern Bulgarian has to operate with two types of paradigms. The first type consists of only polysyllabic forms. In the second type, there are monosyllabic and polysyllabic forms. There is no nominal paradigm consisting of only monosyllables.[37] As for the strictly polysyllabic paradigms, the standard rules are supposed to operate appropriately on them, except for the deverbal nouns, which often represent the verbal vocalisation pattern of their base verb. Among the second set of paradigms, some subtypes need to be distinguished and analysed separately. Indeed, there are paradigms with and without identical vocalisation of the monosyllabic and polysyllabic forms. Within the same vocalisation subtype, there are two possible subvarieties as well.

As the vocalisation of the TRT-sequences in Modern Bulgarian seems to still be a productive process, it needs a classification. From a strictly formal point of view, the different vocalisation patterns resemble a transfix phenomenon. Another possible explanation may include two *ablaut*-positions inside a TRT-pattern. Undoubtedly these concepts are uncommon for a modern Indo-European language. On the other hand, especially from a synchronic point of view, there is no clear phonological justification for the stem variability. In terms of a preference theoretical analysis "for the overt morphological marking of conversion, i.e. category switching, having affixation alone is preferred to having mutation, either alone or in addition to affixation" (Vennemann 1983: 12). A form that is less preferred in terms of one parameter is thus supposed to be optimal concerning others. In this context, each of the multiple vocalisation types can be viewed as optimal to a specific preference parameter without the need to find a simple principle or law describing all of them. Similar to Aristotle's theory of the four causes, Preference Theory operates on multiple parameters with one of

---

[37] Modern Bulgarian provides the structure for this feature, because some of the inflectional endings, such as the definite plural ending, are polysyllabic themselves. Thus, even nouns with no vowel in their root, like Bg. *дните* (dnite) 'the days', are polysyllabic in this form due to the ending *-ite*.

them being dominant in a specific case. Accordingly, each particular vocalisation achieves a specific phonological, contemporary or historical, preference.

4.1.1 Paradigms with vocalisation shift

A representative case for a paradigm with nonidentical vocalisation of the monosyllabic and polysyllabic forms would be that of Bg. *гръб* (gryb) 'back, spine' – *гърбът* (gy**r**byt) 'idem, definite' and *гърбове* (gy**r**bove) 'idem, plural'. Here the polysyllabic forms follow the standard rule. In this case, all syllables are preferred ones: closed by one consonant in the root syllable, all covered and all including a non-falling sonority pattern. Expectations are to have the same results in derived forms, which are not part of the declension paradigm itself but still closely related to the base word. For derived substantives such as *гръбче* (grybče) 'back, spine – diminutive', *гърбище* (gyrbiŝe) 'idem – amplificative',[38] *гърбина* 'idem – pejorative',[39] or *гръбнак* (grybnak) 'backbone',[40] this seems to be the case. All derivations belong to the polysyllabic-only class as the derivative suffixes themselves always contain at least one vowel.

However, among the derived adjectives, such as *гръбен* (gryben) 'spinal, masc. sing. – indefinite' and *гръбния* (grybniâ) 'idem – definite, objective case', there is a non-preferable form with an open root syllable, which is also irregular according to the standard rules. Indeed, adjectival paradigms of Modern Bulgarian have more forms than substantives. In the case of the adjectives derived using the suffix *-en*, there is only one form with CRCV-structure (masculine, singular, indefinite) while all other forms have a CRCV-structure. As a result, the tendency to invariability increases in these paradigms and outperforms the syllable preferences. This columnar effect seems to be shared among this adjective class and should be considered a systematic irregularity or a predictable exception. Besides, the presence of the specific suffix itself may explain the "irregular" form. Adjectives derived by other suffixes, such as *гърбав* (gyrbav) 'humpbacked', do not show any irregular forms, akin to the phenomenon explained in the next section. Last but not least, in this case, *-en* is also the suffix for a verbal participle, *гърбен, гърбения* (gyrben, gyrbeniâ), which follows the verbal vocalisation and has no forms with a CRCCV-structure at all.

---

38 Amplificative derivations are, just like diminutives, a systemic feature of Modern Bulgarian.
39 Pejorative forms are not a system feature. In this case, the word is a feminine derivation.
40 The word *гръбнак* is a derivation. The resemblance to English compounds like *backbone* or *redneck* is only apparent.

4.1.2 Paradigms with columnar vocalisation

The most complicated situation involves a group of substantives that have identical vocalisation of their monosyllabic and polysyllabic forms. A part of these paradigms generalises the commonly preferred vocalisation in the monosyllabic form, while some other paradigms generalise the polysyllabic form. At least for the first case, there is no explanation in terms of the general columnar tendency because it operates in cases where a single form is adjusted to the vast majority of forms and not on the reverse process. Some of these irregular cases may be the result of a specific set of syllable-structure sub-preferences or of lexical analogy. In the paradigm of Bg. *плъх* (plyh) 'rat', the polysyllabic forms like the plural *плъхове* (plyhove) are suboptimal and irregular in terms of standard rules.

The root *plyh-* is limited to this word, and there are no further derivatives from it. On the other hand, *плъх* belongs to the columnar stressed heterosyllabic heterobasic[41] subgroup of the declension of masculine substantives with monosyllabic base form.[42] Other words in this group include *кръг* (kryg) 'circle' and *прът* (pryt) 'rod' with the plural forms *кръгове* (krygove) and *прътове* (prytove). These words have the same irregularity in their plural forms and seem, *prima facie*, to contradict the rules. However, this is a fallacy produced by the orthography reforms in the late 1940s. As the ancient orthography (*кržгъ* and *prżтъ*) showed, these words could not participate in the liquid metathesis because the nasalised vowel cannot precede a liquid.[43] Thus, the paradigms of *kryg* and *pryt* are regular and represent the general preference for the avoidance of tautosyllabic n+liquid-sequences.[44] In this case, the lexical analogy seemingly

---

41 Heterobasic means that the base of the substantive is different in the singular (athematic) and the plural (thematic) forms. Indeed, in this case, the singular base represents the plain Indo-European root only and the plural base the root with a thematic vowel. Inflectional endings (for case, number, and definiteness) succeed the base. From a synchronic point of view, the base is the plain root and the thematic vowel serves as a part of the plural inflection. The use of the diachronic terminology, however, allows a more straightforward classification.
42 The base form is the undefined subjective case of the singular.
43 The historical pronunciation of /ə/ would be [oⁿ] like Polish /ą/. The standard pronunciation of Modern Bulgarian is [ə], but in dialects it varies from [u] to [əⁿ]. In this context, the denasalisation of the old nasalised vowels can be considered a still-incomplete process. Concerning this, the aftermath of the former nasalisation can still be influential. As for the other Slavonic languages, the pronunciation of the Proto-Slavic nasalised vowels also shows many variations.
44 This sequence can be avoided only by having a vowel or a syllable border between n- and the adjacent liquid. In a *TVNRT-sequence, the second solution is not available because RT- is not a tolerable syllable head in Modern Bulgarian.

conveys the results of a syllable-structure preference.⁴⁵ This conclusion has reliable explanatory power but little predictive capability in a synchronic approach. However, this word is feminine in some dialects, just as its etymological cognates in other Slavonic languages are, such as Slovc. *plha* 'idem'. In this context, Bg. *плъх, плъхта* (plyh, plyhta) 'rat; indefinite, definite' (older orthography: *плъхъ, плъхъта*) may function as a case of a (not yet fully completed) gender shift that still has not obtained the proper vocalisation according to its new grammatical features.⁴⁶ The analogy to *kryg* and *pryt* may be the reason for the irregular plural *plyhove* as the singular has the old TRyTь-pattern.

Inside the same declension subtype, there is a second and even larger group of cases where the polysyllabic vocalisation pattern gets over-generalised. Their monosyllabic base forms have sub-preferred features like complex codas. Indeed, speakers of Modern Bulgarian vocalise some of these forms consistently with the natural syllable preferences and not according to the orthography. Thus, learners, even native speakers, have to learn how to vocalise correctly in written texts. Modern Bulgarian is, similarly to Modern German, based on some specific dialects but artificially enriched with forms and features from others. A preferences approach cannot adequately describe the features of an artificial system itself. Different preferences may be operational in the same position, and therefore the results may stay unpredictable without additional information. As for the vocalisation pattern of TRT-sequences, the dialects of Modern Bulgarian have slightly different syllable-structure preferences caused by the differences in their phoneme inventories. These differences originate primarily from unequal stages in the process of elimination of the Slavonic palatalised consonants as well as from the unequal stage of vowel reduction in unstressed syllables. Most obviously, a T'R-sequence would be the less preferred option in a system with palatal consonants, as this sequence is hardly pronounceable. In reality, the noun *дълг* (dylg) 'debt, obligation' and the adjective *длъжен* (dlyžen) 'obliged' are both irregular forms in terms of standard rules and syllable preferences of

---

45 More precisely, the analogy affects the morphological features of the target word as well, such as its attribution to a specific declination type.
46 Standard attempts do not take these forms into account. Saskia Pronk-Tiethoff reconstructs a Proto-Slavic Form *pьlhъ* '(edible) dormouse' as the basis for a borrowing into Germanic, represented by German *Bilche* 'idem' (2013: 70). Other attempts interpret the German word as a borrowing from Slavic (cf. Duridanov 1999: 374–375). Nevertheless, the German word is also feminine while the reconstructed Proto-Slavic form has the masculine ending -ъ. Therefore, a feminine variant should be considered at least possible if not probable. The *Bulgarian etymological dictionary* (Duridanov 1999: 375) lists a TYRT-vocalisation as *пълф* [pylf] (with [f] representing [h] following sound laws and not influencing the syllable structure) for some western dialects as well.

the standard variety of Modern Bulgarian. The pronunciation of these forms is [dlyg, dlyžen] in some western dialects and [dylg, dylžen, *or even*: d'ylg, d'ylžen] in some eastern ones.

4.2 Complex vocalisation rules in nominal forms

The standard vocalisation patterns of Modern Bulgarian were indeed not set in order to produce a maximum of sub-preferable syllables. They, in most cases, follow the conception of 19th-century historical orthography. From this point of view, a grammatical rule would be superior to the actual syllable preferences while representing the natural preferences from an earlier period. A TRT-sequence becomes its vocalisation according to the rules as TyRT for masculine substantives with columnar accentuation, adjectives with monosyllabic base form, and polysyllabic adjectives, except for those derived by the suffix *-en*. Feminine substantives with a monosyllabic base form and masculine adjectives with a polysyllabic base derived by *-en* would be vocalised as TRyT. Thus, a stable connection between vocalisation and orthography of the mute vowel characters emerged, in particular TRyTь and TyRTъ.[47] In this context, every paradigm containing one of the variants would follow the relevant rule. As for the examples above, the spelling *дългъ* represents TyRTъ with the final <-ъ>, and *длъженъ*[48] (dlyženъ) represents TRyTь following other forms in its paradigm like the feminine form *длъжъна* (dlyžьna). More precisely, the distinctive feature was the presence or absence of TRyTь-sequences in a given paradigm because the paradigms without it would behave like the TyRTъ-containing paradigms, as in *дългов* (dylgov) 'related to debts'. Accordingly, the general distinction would have the form TRyTь versus TyRT(ъ) or directly (+ь) versus (-ь). The chances are that at an earlier stage, anterior to the loss of the short vowels in some positions, this was a productive intersyllabic rule. This concept provides results with very few exceptions. Nevertheless, the writing of <-ь-> in some positions disappeared in the late 19th century.

---

47 The use of the Latin letter y for the transliteration of Modern Bulgarian ъ provides the opportunity to use the Cyrillic signs <ъ> and <ь> for the transliteration of the mute sounds.
48 There were also attempts to write *длъжънъ* instead of *длъженъ* in this position following the historical orthography.

Table 3: Analytical accuracy and predictive capability of vocalisation rules.

	Validity		Compound rule parameter				
	Standard rule (n. a. = monosyllabic)	Compound vocalisation rule	Columnar vocalisation	Gender/ Number	Columnar accent	derived by -en- or resulting from sound shift (o^n>ə)	word class
гръб	n. a.	+	–	M. Sg.	–	–	Subst.
гърбове	+	+	–	M. Pl.	–	–	Subst.
дълг	n. a.	+	+	M. Sg.	+	–	Subst.
дългове	+	+	+	M. Pl.	+	–	Subst.
длъжен	–	+	+	M. Sg.	+	+	Adj.
длъжна	+	+	+	F. Sg.	+	+	Adj.
дългов	+	+	+	M. Sg.	+	–	Adj.
длъж	n. a.	+	+	F. Sg.	–	.	Subst.
длъжта	+	+	+	F. Sg. (def.)	–	–	Subst.
кръг	n.a.	+	+	M. Sg.	+/–[49]	(!)[50]	Subst.
кръгове	–	+	+	M. Pl.	+/–	(!)	Subst.
кръгов	–	+	+	M. Sg.	+	(!)	Adj.
окръжен	–	+	+	M. Sg.	+	++[51]	Adj.
окръжни	+	+	+	M. Pl.	+	++	Adj.
плъх	n.a.	–/+	+	M. Sg.	+	–	Subst.
плъхове	+	–/+[52]	+	M. Pl.	+	–	Subst.

From a synchronic point of view, the grammatical rules discussed above are still operational but not supported by the orthography in a proper way. Their predictive force for learners without knowledge of historical grammar or, at least,

---

[49] The whole paradigm of *kryg* has a columnar accent, except for the definite forms of subjective [or: nominative] and objective case. This irregularity should be considered a specific feature of this word (due to its use in mathematical contexts and therefore a need for better distinction between definite singular and distributive [numeric] plural) without any impact on the vocalisation pattern itself.
[50] Synchronically there is no explicit marker for the historical sound shift.
[51] Here both parameters (derived and resulting) are valid but only the derivation is marked.
[52] A diachronic gender shift can explain the singular vocalization. The plural form, however, has a new, masculine inflection. Therefore, this case may represent an analogy to another subgroup, where the regular plural forms arise due to the similarity among the singular forms. This explanation is plausible for the irregular forms but cannot be regarded as a special rule. Thus, the complex rule operates on this particular case under some specific restrictions.

orthography would be restricted. Especially the orthographical reforms of the late 1940s conceal the phonetic structures on which the preferences responsible for the emergence of actual patterns operated. Hence, the grammatical rules inside the nominal system of Modern Bulgarian represent the syllable-structure preferences of earlier stages of language development. These rules provide different results than actual syllable-structure preferences would. Therefore, an approach considering only the actual preferences would not be able to explain all vocalisation patterns. Inside the verbal system, on the other hand, grammar-driven rules are productive in terms of setting a vocalisation pattern due to the more complex verbal morphology of Modern Bulgarian. Inside the nominal system, the grammar rules reliably apply to TRT-sequences, and inside the verbal system, they operate on both TRT- and TRX- and probably even on XRX-sequences. In the cases where a grammar rule does not set the vocalisation, the syllable preferences of Modern Bulgarian take effect.

5 Conclusion

Certain phonological phenomena in Proto-Slavic and modern Slavonic languages, especially in Modern Bulgarian, can be addressed by the Preference Laws as described by Vennemann. The interdependence of syllable structure, phoneme inventory, and morphological factors rests on processes underlying specific preferences. An approach based on Preference Theory operates with more adequate concepts of the Proto-Slavic syllable, as it does not assume "irregular cases" like the hypothesis about the existence of word-medial closed syllables in Proto-Slavic proposed by more traditional attempts.

The Preference Laws operate on a higher complexity level and can, therefore, apply in a more suitable way to complex phenomena that cannot be described by a single rule. Within the Preference Laws concept, different specific sets and hierarchies are feasible. Thus, individual languages (and even dialects) may develop seemingly different phonological phenomena due to using their specific sets of preferences with or without a modified hierarchy, having divergent phoneme inventories, or both. Nevertheless, as for the cases discussed above, there is no evidence for processes to which the Preference Laws would not apply at all.

The liquid metathesis of Modern Bulgarian, also called alternation, is considered a partly (or mostly) irregular process by standard attempts. Any irregular phenomenon is a problem for learners and students. The interpretation of this process as triconsonantal frame vocalisation rather than as a metathesis allows a more systematic approach. Thus, there would be no movement of the vowel around the liquid but an ambiguous, empty frame disambiguated by a particular vocalisation pattern in specific sound environments or due to specific morphological features. This method offers a possibility of systematic description with a higher grade of analytical accuracy and predicational capability, which benefits learners and grammarians.

The systematic analysis of the vocalisation patterns for TRT-sequences in Modern Bulgarian includes the consideration of phonological, morphological, historical, and analogical factors, each of them preferred under specific circumstances. The phonological preferences, such as preferable syllables or tolerable consonant clusters, apply for all cases, but the morphological impact differs depending on the word class. Thus, the complex influence analysis splits into a verbal and a nominal part. As for verbs, the combination of a modern theoretical approach considering verb-aspect forms built by any combination of suffixes and conjugation shift being a part of one single verb paradigm (and not independent verbs/lemmata) allows a description of the correlation between the aspect (and mode) of a verb form and the vocalisation of its TRT-root. This correlation seems to be functional, productive, and, even though not without restrictions, capable of properly describing certain cases where the standard rules deliver false results.

Inside the nominal paradigms, the standard rules apply to polysyllables and exclude monosyllable forms *per definitionem*. Moreover, even inside the polysyllabic forms of certain paradigms, the standard rules tend to fail. An analysis of the forms considering the word class, declension type, accentuation pattern, morphological features, *and* a historical reference shows a strong correlation between these factors and the vocalisation of the TRT-root. Nevertheless, some of these factors are morphological or phonological preferences referring to earlier stages of Bulgarian. The analytical capability of this approach may be significantly higher than that of the standard rules. Therefore, the nominal word classes seem to feature a stronger tendency towards a systematic use of TRT-vocalisation patterns than the verbal class.

The new analysis of the vocalisation of TRT-clusters in Modern Bulgarian is a combinatory attempt as it addresses a phonological problem using additional morphological and diachronic proposals. This method is an integrative part of Preference Theory as introduced by Vennemann. The new approach demonstrates the utility of application of the Preference Laws for the description of complex phenomena. As the attempt itself still exists on an introductory theoretical level, further elaboration and incorporation into didactic concepts may prove beneficial if it is implemented in practice.

References

Brackney, Noel. 2007. *The origins of Slavonic: Language contact and language change*. Munich: Lincom Europa.
Čekman, Valerij. 1979. *Issledovanija po istoričeskoj fonetike praslavjanskogo jazyka* [Research on the historical phonetics of Proto-Slavic]. Minsk: Nauka i Technika.
Chakarova, Krassimira. 2015a. On some specific problems of teaching verb aspect (with regard to teaching Bulgarian as a foreign language). *Scientific works of University of Food Technologies* LXII. 877–881. http://uft-plovdiv.bg/site_files/file/scienwork/scienworks_2015/docs/09_Лингвистика%20и%20обучение/Лингвистика%20и%20обучение/01_Chakarova_UHT_2015.pdf (accessed 10 December 2017).
Chakarova, Krassimira. 2015b. More on the issue of teaching the verb aspect category in Bulgarian and its acquisition by foreigners. *Scientific works of University of Food Technologies* LXII. 882–887. http://uft-plovdiv.bg/site_files/file/scienwork/scienworks_2015/docs/09_Лингвистика%20и%20обучение/Лингвистика%20и%20обучение/02_Chakarova_UHT_2015.pdf (accessed 10 December 2017).
Duridanov, Ivan (ed.). 1999. *Bălgarski etimologičen rečnik*. Vol. 5: *padèž – pùska* [Bulgarian etymological dictionary]. Sofia: Drinov.
Hill, Eugen. 2009. Die Präferenztheorie in der historischen Phonologie aus junggrammatischer Perspektive. *Zeitschrift für Sprachwissenschaft* 28. 231–263.
Mareš, František (ed.). 1999. *Diachronische Phonologie des Ur- und Frühslavischen*. Frankfurt am Main: Lang.
Paraškevov, Boris. 2015. *Bălgarska transkripcija na nemski imena: Bulgarische Transkription deutscher Namen*. Sofia: Iztok-Zapad.
Pokorny, Julius. 2005. *Indogermanisches etymologisches Wörterbuch*, 5th ed. Tübingen: Francke.
Pronk-Tiethoff, Saskia. 2013. *Germanic loanwords in Proto-Slavic*. Amsterdam: Rodopi.
Schuchardt, Hugo. 1972. On the sound laws: Against the Neogrammarians. In Theo Vennemann & Terence Wilbur (eds.), *Schuchardt, the Neogrammarians, and the transformational theory of phonological change: Four essays*, 39–72. Frankfurt am Main: Athenäum.
Simeonova, Ruska. 1988. *Grundzüge einer kontrastiven Phonetik Deutsch/Bulgarisch*. Sofia: Nauka i Izkustvo.
Simeonova, Ruska. 1998. *Grundzüge einer kontrastiven Phonetik und Phonologie: Deutsch/Bulgarisch*. Sofia: Svjat. Nauka.
Stoânov, Stoân (ed.). 1994. *Slavjanski ezici: Gramatični očerci* [Slavonic languages: Essays on grammar]. Sofia: Izdatelstvo na Bălgarskata Akademia na Naukite.
Townsend, Charles & Laura Janda. 2003. *Gemeinslavisch und Slavisch im Vergleich: Einführung in die Entwicklung von Phonologie und Flexion; vom Frühurslavischen über das Spätgemeinslavische bis in die slavischen Einzelsprachen; mit besonderer Berücksichtigung des Russischen, Polnischen, Tschechischen, Serbischen/Kroatischen, Bulgarischen*. Munich: Sagner.
Vennemann, Theo. 1973. Linguistik und Phonetik. In Renate Bartsch & Theo Vennemann (eds.), *Linguistik und Nachbarwissenschaften*, 21–44. Kronberg: Scriptor.
Vennemann, Theo. 1983. Causality in language change: Theories of linguistic preferences as a basis for linguistic explanations. *Folia Linguistica Historica* 17. 5–26.
Vennemann, Theo. 1986. *Neuere Entwicklungen in der Phonologie*. Berlin: de Gruyter.

Vennemann, Theo. 1988. *Preference laws for syllable structure and the explanation of sound change: With special reference to German, Germanic, Italian, and Latin*. Berlin: de Gruyter.

Vennemann, Theo. 1989. Phonological and morphological consequences of the 'Glottalic Theory'. In Theo Vennemann (ed.), *The new sound of Indo-European: Essays in phonological reconstruction*, 107–116. Berlin: de Gruyter.

Vennemann, Theo. 2006. Germanische Runen und Phönizisches Alphabet. In *Sprachwissenschaft* 31. 367–429.

Žečev, Georgi. 2015. *Aspekti na palatalizaciite: Romanski i slavjanski fonologični procesi* [Aspects of the palatalisations: Romance and Slavonic phonological processes]. Sofia: Universitetsko izdatelstvo "Sv. Kliment Ochridski".

Žuravlev, Vladimir 2007. *Teorija gruppofonem: Razvitie gruppovogo singarmonizma v praslavjanskom jazyke* [Theory of cluster-phonemes: The development of cluster harmony in Proto-Slavic]. Moskva: LKI.

Raymond Hickey
Syllable structure and sonority in Modern Irish

Abstract: The use of a sonority hierarchy to reach principled explanations of many syllabic phenomena received a considerable impetus from Vennemann (1982) and later, in more general form, in Vennemann (1988). In this contribution, two specific phenomena from the sound structure of Irish, namely epenthesis and metathesis, are examined with a view to gaining insights into the conditions which trigger them in the phonology of the modern language. The analysis shows that an account in terms of the relative sonority of the segments involved in both processes yields the most parsimonious and accurate explanation for their occurrence. Epenthesis is most favoured in clusters of high sonority and least in those with low sonority where it is in fact blocked. Apart from relative sonority, other factors also play a role, such as place of articulation and relative stress of the syllables involved.

1 Introduction

During the 1970s and into the 1980s phonologists began to realise that the linear phonology found in such seminal works as Chomsky and Halle's *The sound pattern of English* (1968) failed to capture many generalisations about the phonologies of languages and that other considerations were required. This led to a revalorisation of the concept of the syllable and of the sonority values shown by segments occupying key positions of this structure. Various authors were active in promoting non-linear views of sound structure for the world's languages, not least of whom was Theo Vennemann, whose work in this sphere (see Vennemann 1982) on German syllable structure culminated in the publication of Vennemann (1988).

For the present study the preferred structures of syllables in Modern Irish and the sonority[1] values of the segments in these structures are to be scrutinised. By

---

[1] For a comprehensive list of relevant studies, see the online *Bibliography of resources on sonority* by Steve Parker, Graduate Institute of Applied Linguistics and SIL International (last updated on January 29, 2018).

Raymond Hickey, General Linguistics and Varieties of English, Department of Anglophone Studies, University of Duisburg and Essen, Germany

'preferred' is meant here the statistical tendency across the language for words to show phonotactics which is determined by the increase in sonority from edge to centre (Hickey 2014: 177–234). At least two major volumes have been dedicated to the role of the syllable in phonology (see van der Hulst and Ritter 1999 and Cairns and Raimy 2011) while in both editions of the *Handbook of phonology* (Goldsmith 1995, Goldsmith, Riggle, and Yu 2014) there are central chapters on the syllable, see Blevins (1995) and Goldsmith (2014) as well as monograph studies such as Duanmu (2009: 36–71).

A discussion of the syllable involves clarifying two central questions to begin with (cf. Goldsmith 2014: 168–171).

(1) (i) What constituents are assumed for syllables?
 (ii) Can the internal composition of these constituents be optimally characterised by the relative sonority of their segments?[2]

Characterisations of the syllable (Fudge 1969: 273, 1987, Hooper 1976: 199, Fallows 1981, Selkirk 1984, Maddieson 1985, Picard 1987, Vennemann 1988, van der Hulst and Ritter 1999: 22–29) generally assume two major constituents with a further subdivision of the second, i.e. (1) an onset and (2) a rhyme with the latter divided into (2a) nucleus and (2b) coda. Both the onset and the coda can be internally complex with a maximum of three segments in an initial and of two segments in a coda in Modern Irish, reflecting divisions which are deemed by many phonologists to apply to all languages.

(2)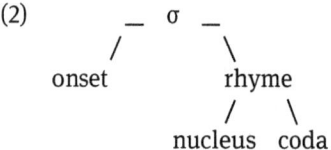

There are many aspects of Irish phonology and morphonology which support this division. Consider the domains of the two chief morphonological processes in Modern Irish (1) initial mutation and (2) polarity reversal (palatalisation or velarisation depending on the value for [palatal] of the input). Here there is

---

2 Vennemann (1988: 11–56) sets out a series of laws which he then employs to account for several items of language change. In the present contribution, the first three of these laws, the Head Law, the Coda Law, and the Nucleus Law, are used to assist in the synchronic analysis of epenthesis and metathesis.

an absolute division of syllables into onset on the one hand and rhyme on the other, for instance, such that polarity reversal never affects the onset and initial mutation never the coda of a syllable.

Table 1: Domains of morphonological processes in Modern Irish by syllable position.

initial mutation		vowel gradation	polarity reversal
		rhyme	
onset		nucleus	coda

The question of the composition of syllable constituents primarily concerns onsets and codas. These constituents are consonantal while the nucleus is usually vocalic but can also show a syllabic nasal as in the second syllable of English *button* [bʌtn̩] or Munster Irish *maidin* [madʲn̩] 'morning'.

Sonority-based analyses of onsets and codas (Zec 1995) assume that, preferentially, a syllable consists of a maximum onset and a minimum coda with an increase in sonority within an onset and a decrease in a coda should these positions be segmentally complex in a given syllable (Dogil 1988, 1992, Dogil and Luschützky 1990, Daland et al. 2011: 198). The preference for maximum onsets probably derives from the perceptual recognition of the beginnings of phonological words which it promotes (Flemming 2004, 2005) while the decrease in the coda is also taken to refer to prosodic domains above the syllable, i.e. to phrases and clauses, cf. Flack (2009: 270).

'Maximum'/'increase' and 'minimum'/ 'decrease' refer in this context to the value of segments on a scale of sonority (vowel-like quality, the opposite of consonantality). Such scales have been an established instrument in analyses in recent decades, see Hooper (1976) and Vennemann (1982) as representative examples for the re-establishment of sonority scales in phonology. These scales go back at least to Jespersen: his scale (Jespersen 1913: 191) is only slightly different from that in Hooper (1976: 196, 206), and in his use of the term *Schallfülle* 'sonority' Jespersen (1913: 190) is close to late twentieth-century understandings of sonority (Nathan 1989: 60–62, Rice 1992: 65). A maximally differentiated sonority scale could be arranged as follows, with a few contestable positions, e.g. those of voiced stops and voiceless fricatives.

Table 2: Classification of sounds by sonority.

vowels	0	greatest sonority
semi-vowels	1	
/r/	2	
/l/	3	
nasals	4	
voiced fricatives	5	
voiceless fricatives	6	
voiced stops	7	
voiceless stops	8	greatest consonantality

In phonological literature of the 2000s there has been much criticism of sonority scales. This criticism is largely centred around the lack of predictability which sonority shows (see Blevins 2006: 159–164 and Harris 2006 as typical examples of such criticism). There is some justification in rejecting sonority should any predictive power be attributed to it or should explanations of phonological change be regarded as always deriving from considerations of sonority. However, as a heuristic tool by means of which one can account for tendencies across languages and local distributions of segments within syllables for individual languages, the notion of sonority is useful (see the chapter on Danish by Basbøll, this volume). In Modern Irish epenthesis and syncope as well as phonotactic distributions can be accounted for satisfactorily by appealing to the sonority values of segments (Fudge 1976). Nonetheless, bilingual speakers in Ireland with comparable competence in Irish and English will produce Irish *banbh* 'piglet' as [banəv] or *tarbh* 'bull' as [tarəv] and have *swerve* [swɚːv] when speaking English and not necessarily [swɛrəv]. So the sonority-motivated epenthesis of Irish does not necessarily carry over into Irish English, i.e. it lacks predictive power for Irish English, though historically, due to the much stronger position of Irish, there was transfer into Irish English, cf. pronunciations like *term* [tɛrəm] and *girl* [gɛrəl] (in maximally sonorous codas consisting of sonorants) which are well attested both diachronically and in many rural varieties today.

A first division of syllable constituents would assume an onset, nucleus, and coda (see above). In Irish, metathesis offers support for an extra slot, the medial, consisting of one or two consonants, yielding the following structure (see section 3 below).

(3)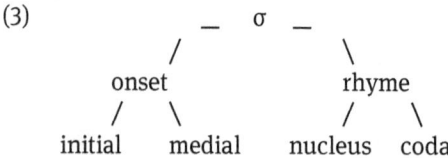

Irish can have mono-, bi-, or trisegmental onset clusters, and with the latter two the segments which constitute them must have sonority values which, if not adjacent to each other, are at least ordered consecutively on the following sonority scale going from right to left in an onset (and from left to right in a coda).

Table 3: Sonority scale for onset clusters in Irish.

vowels	0
semi-vowels	1
/r/	2
/l/	3
nasals	4
voiced fricatives	5
voiceless fricatives	6
voiced stops	7
voiceless stops	8

This is true for all onset clusters with the one exception of those which have initial /s/ which can be followed by stops (*sp- st- sk-*). Here the primacy of the alveolar point of articulation among segments allows a consonantally weaker segment (/s/) to stand before stronger segments (stops) in syllable onsets.

2 Epenthesis in Modern Irish

Epenthesis is the addition of phonetic substance to a word, either vocalic or consonantal. It may be either obligatory – as in the case of vowel epenthesis in Irish (Ní Chiosáin 1997) – or it may be merely probable, i.e. it need not of necessity occur when the conditions for epenthesis are met. This is generally the case with consonantal epenthesis in Irish as in *arís* [əˈrʲiːʃtʲ] 'again' (Western Irish).

The following account of vowel epenthesis appeals to the notion of coda sonority. This should not be understood as something which is absolute across all languages but which has local significance in Irish and which furthermore has varying degrees of significance in the different dialects of the language (how the sonority-based restrictions on codas in Irish arose historically cannot be determined now and so will not be addressed here).

Vowel epenthesis is known from pronunciations of Irish English, e.g. *film* [fɪləm] (Hickey 2007: 307–308), and from languages like Dutch, e.g. *melk* [mɛlək] 'milk' (Hickey 1985). Essentially, it is similar in Irish, but here it is necessary to distinguish epenthesis from a related but distinct phenomenon, syncope. The latter is the loss of a vowel between two consonants when a vowel follows the second, e.g. *cosain*[3] [kʌsənʲ] 'defend', *cosnaím* [kʌsnʲiːmʲ] 'I defend'. Epenthesis on the other hand is a general restriction which is due to phonotactic rules which apply globally for the language. Certain statements can be made for epenthesis as a general phenomenon in Irish.

Table 4: Conditions for vowel epenthesis in Irish.

---
1) An epenthetic vowel never carries lexical information.[4]
2) An epenthetic vowel never indicates a grammatical category.
3) The values for [palatal] with both the preceding and the following consonant always agree.
4) An epenthetic vowel is never stressed.

The likely purpose of an epenthetic vowel is to break up a phonotactically inadmissible cluster by re-syllabifying its members (see Smith, this volume). The clusters which are broken up by an epenthetic vowel show a characteristic segmental structure as seen in the following examples.

(4) a. *borb* [bʌrəb] 'fierce, violent'
    b. *corb* [kʌrəb] 'to corrupt'
    c. *lorg* [lʲʌrəg] 'search'
    d. *bolg* [bʌlʲəg] 'belly'

Epenthesis involves two-segment clusters in the coda of a stressed syllable. If the segments of the coda cluster are homorganic then no epenthesis takes place. In essence, this means that the second element must be labial or velar as in the above examples. The first element must furthermore be a sonorant, and due to the distribution of sonorants in syllable codas in Irish, these are always coronal. This means that a coronal sonorant followed by a voiced non-coronal obstruent (velar or labial) triggers epenthesis: *seilbh* [ʃɛlʲɪvʲ] 'possession', *banbh* [banʲəv] 'piglet'.

The conditions for epenthesis can be deduced from the attested forms which show it. For instance, the failure of epenthesis with clusters showing (i) a sonorant and (iia) a voiceless or (iib) a homorganic obstruent (sometimes both)

---

[3] <ai> in this word represents a schwa preceded by a non-palatal and followed by a palatal consonant.
[4] An epenthetic vowel is (if one agrees with the terminology) a post-lexical rule which always applies, irrespective of the grammatical or lexical status of a word.

is confirmed by forms such as the following, (iia): *gort* [gʌrt] 'field', *feilt* [fʲɛlʲtʲ] 'felt', *corp* [kʌrp] 'body', *folc* [fʌlˠk] 'downpour', *olc* [ʌlˠk] 'evil', *port* [pʌrt] 'port, harbour; tune', and (iib): *bord* [baurd] 'table'.

It is obvious from monosyllables without epenthesis that a coda cluster must have a sonorant as first element for this to occur: *toisc* [tʌsʲkʲ] 'journey, purpose', *tost* [tʌst] 'silence'. However, the required nature of the second element is not as obvious. Words such as the following show epenthesis regularly: *ainm* [anʲɪmʲ] 'name', *arm* [arəm] 'army', *feilm* [fʲɛlʲɪmʲ] 'farm'. These instances would seem to indicate that epenthesis is triggered where the second element is at least as sonorous as a voiced obstruent. This would include sonorants as second element, a postulation which is vindicated by the forms just quoted.

Epenthesis does not occur before voiceless stops. As epenthesis is the development of a short unstressed vowel, then this can arise preferentially in an environment which is voiced and where the cluster-final consonant is lenis. With stops, voicelessness sets in immediately at the end of the sonorant or slightly before this, thus reducing the likelihood of epenthesis, cf. *olc* [ʌlˠk], *[ʌlˠək] 'evil'. However, epenthesis is attested before voiceless fricatives, e.g. *seilf* [ʃɛlʲɪfʲ] 'shelf'. The phonetic nature of voiceless stops also explains their position at the lowest point on a sonority scale thus demonstrating the interrelationship of phonotactics and syllable structure.

There are two further conditions on epenthesis apart from the relative sonority of the segments of the coda in which it occurs: (1) the cluster must consist of heterorganic segments, and (2) there must be no morpheme boundary between the elements of a cluster. This holds for Cois Fharraige Irish (although Southern Irish allows slight leakages, Breatnach 1947: 127), so that forms like *greannmhar* /gʲrʲɑːnˠ#vər/ 'funny' or *cionmhar* /kʲʌnˠ#vər/ 'proportional' do not show epenthesis.[5]

If one now orders the consonants of Irish on a hierarchy according to their relative sonority, then one can recognise that there is a cut-off point for epenthesis between voiced and voiceless plosives so that the latter cannot trigger epenthesis in a syllable coda with a preceding sonorant.

---

5 Southern Irish does have limited epenthesis across morpheme boundaries, e.g. *an-mhaith* /an#va/ > [anəva] 'very good'.

Table 5: Preferential environments for epenthesis in Irish.

a)	sonorants and sonorants
b)	sonorants and voiced fricatives
c)	sonorants and voiceless fricatives
d)	sonorants and voiced stops
e)	[sonorants and voiceless stops]

2.1 Motivation for epenthesis

Epenthesis is governed by the phonotactics of syllable codas in Irish. All the clusters which show epenthesis contain a sonorant and a further sonorous element. These are instances of heavy clusters in Irish. If the preceding stressed vowel is short, then the weight of the coda cluster is resolved by inserting an epenthetic vowel which resyllabifies the word. The final element of the input coda cluster is shifted to the second syllable created by epenthetic vowel insertion forming a single-element coda in this new syllable.

(5) Coda resyllabification on epenthesis
  bolg /bʌlg/ > [.bʌl.əg.] 'belly'

There could be a case for the sonorant after a short stem vowel being ambisyllabic in the new epenthetic structure and thus support the general expectation that VCV structures syllabify as V.CV. Whether or not this is the case is not of relevance for the current discussion. The main point is that the second element of the coda in the lexical form is no longer in the stem syllable after epenthesis but forms a separate, second syllable.

Evidence for the status of epenthetic vowels as syllable nuclei is found in Irish where these vowels, before non-palatal /v/, can vocalise to /u:/ which is most definitely a separate syllable.

(6) Vocalisation of epenthetic syllable coda
  garbh /garv/ > [.gar.əv.] > [.gar.u:.]   'rough'

Given that vowel epenthesis serves the function of resyllabification, its lack of lexical or grammatical significance is to be expected. The resyllabification interpretation gains credence if one examines those instances in which epenthesis does not occur. Consider the following instances where the elements of the central clusters belong to different syllables.

(7) a. *céimnigh* /kʲeːmʲ.nʲə/   'to step'
     b. *téarma* /tʲeːr.mə/   'term'
     c. *corrdhuine* /kaur.ɣinʲə/   'occasional person'
     d. *fiordhrochlá* /fʲiːr.ɣrʌx.lˠɑː/ 'very bad day'
     e. *cúlchaint* /kuːlˠ.xanʲtʲ/ 'bad talk'
     f. *fuarchúis* /fuːr.xuːsʲ/   'apathy'

But there is a further condition required to explain the attestations just given. Epenthesis is blocked in polysyllabic forms if the vowel before the potential epenthetic cluster is long. In the following forms this vowel is short, triggering epenthesis.

(8) *dorcha*   /dʌr.xə/   > [dʌrəxə]   'dark'
     Donncha /dʌnˠ.xə/   > [dʌnˠəxə]   'Denis'
     Murchú   /mʌrxuː/   > [mʌrəxuː]   'Murphy'
     simléar /sʲɪmʲ.lʲeːr/ > [ʃɪmʲɪlʲeːr] 'chimney'

The stipulation that epenthesis does not occur after long vowels is upheld by compounds. There are a large number of these with the qualifying element *mór-* 'big'. None of them show epenthesis though in the first word epenthesis may be found in the head of the compound: *mórbholgach* [moːrvʌlˠəgəx] 'big-bellied', *mórchuid* [moːrxɪdʲ] 'large amount', *mórga* [moːrgə] 'exalted, majestic', but: *morgadh* [mʌrəgə] 'corruption, putrefaction'. In addition, if the lexical form of a word is monosyllabic and the nucleus vowel is long, then epenthesis is indeed present in the phonetic realisation, e.g. *táirg* [tɑːrʲɪgʲ] 'manufacture' with epenthesis just like *tairg* [tarʲɪgʲ] 'offer'.

Unstressed central vowels between segments,[6] which would form heavy clusters in Irish, are found across the board in the lexicon of the language. The status of these vowels would on closer inspection seem to show differences despite superficial similarities. Consider the following forms which show [-lˠəv]: *folamh* [fʌlˠəv] 'empty', *ollamh* [ʌlˠəv] 'professor'. In these cases the schwa is part of the lexical structure of a word and the flanking consonants can differ in terms of their value for [palatal] in certain inflectional cases. This means that these words are different from epenthesis-triggering forms like *bolg* [bʌlˠəg] 'belly', *banbh* [banˠəv] 'piglet' in one essential respect: when the final consonant is palatalised, e.g. in the genitive case, then the sonorant before this is not palatalised, e.g. *Leabhar nua an ollaimh.* [. . . ʌlˠɪvʲ] 'The professor's new book', *Dath an bhuidéil*

---

[6] Phonetically, this can be schwa [ə] between non-palatal consonants or [ɪ] between palatal ones.

fholaimh [... ʌlˠɪvʲ] 'The colour of the empty bottle'. An absolute rule of Irish phonology is that all clusters – except /-xtʲ/, /-rdʲ/, and /-rtʲ/ – agree in the value for [palatal]. Seeing as how the [lˠ] and the [vʲ] of the second syllable of the forms just quoted differ in this respect, palatalisation must have operated on an input[7] which already contained a vowel between [lˠ] and [vʲ], otherwise the outcome would have been /ʌlʲvʲ/ yielding *[ʌlʲɪvʲ] by epenthesis, which is not the case. The second vowel in the form *folamh* is thus lexical. It may be deleted via syncope when a palatalising suffix is added to the base form, e.g. in the comparative *níos foilmhe* 'emptier'. Syncope, however, brings the lateral and the voiced fricative together, palatalising the former and then satisfying the input condition for epenthesis on phonetic realisation.

(9) a. *folamh* /fʌlˠəv/ 'empty'
    + palatalising suffix *e* for the comparative
    b. *foilmhe* /fɛlʲvʲə/ > [fɛlʲɪvʲə] 'emptier'

2.2 Epenthesis and syncope

In Modern Irish, syncope always occurs where the input for resyllabification is satisfied by suffixation. In instances like the following, the /-dl-/ must be split between two syllables as such a sequence cannot occur in a monosyllable in Irish. It violates the sonority cline for codas, which demands that sonorants come before obstruents word-finally in monosyllables.

(10) a. *codail* /kʌdɪlʲ/ 'sleep'
     b. *codlaím* /kʌd.lˠiːmʲ/ 'I sleep'

After syncope has applied to /kʌdɪlʲ/, the liquid is non-palatal (/kʌdlˠiːmʲ/, not */kʌdʲlʲiːmʲ/). The reason why the /vʲ/ in the word *foilmhe* 'emptier' remains palatal is that the palatalisation is a morphophonological process (here: formation of the comparative) which cannot be reversed by a low-level rule like assimilation. In the case of the verb for 'sleep' one can see, looking at a whole series of verbs, that the stem is /kʌd/ and the /-ɪlʲ/ is an ending, one of a group of sonorant endings, which characterises the imperative and the past (with lenition): *codail* /kʌd/ + /ɪlʲ/ 'sleep', *oscail* /ʌsk/ + /ɪlʲ/ 'open', *iomair* /ʌm/ + /ɪrʲ/ 'row', *cosain* /kʌs/ + /ɪnʲ/ 'defend', *cigil* /kʲɪgʲ/ + /ɪlʲ/ 'tickle', *imir* /ɪmʲ/ + /ɪrʲ/ 'play', *taitin* /tatʲ/ + /ɪnʲ/ 'please'.

---

7 By input here I mean the phonological form which is subject to phonetic realisation.

Any low-level rule such as assimilation cannot alter the phonological composition of a lexical stem. Thus the sonorant stem endings do not alter the value for [palatal] with the stem-final segment when syncope deletes the vowel of the ending. This principle applies vacuously to the last three verbs just listed as their stems end in palatal consonants anyway.

3 Metathesis in Modern Irish

Metathesis is well attested throughout the history of many languages, not least in English. Its manifestations and effects have been investigated quite often (Bailey 1970, Hogg 1977, Ultan 1978, Hock 1985, Hume 1998, 2001, Buckley 2011), and it has been postulated as a stage in underlying structures to account for surface forms. The manifestations of metathesis are often presented as taxonomies, for example in the various traditional grammars of Old English, such as Campbell (1959: 184–186) and Luick (1940: 917–920). It is widely documented for the varieties of Irish, and all the dialect studies which were published during the twentieth century (Hickey 2011: 88–90) treat metathesis in dedicated sections.

Metathesis has no obvious cause and some linguists admit to the difficulties in determining its possible motivation (Hogg 1977: 174, Alexander 1985) while others ascribe it to a *lapsus linguae* (see the summary of views on metathesis in Thompson and Thompson 1969: 213). Another opinion, outlined in Ultan (1978: 373, 383–394), is that metathesis has the function of preserving phonological segments from deletion. The view that metathesis is due to a *lapsus linguae* links up with research done on slips of the tongue (Fromkin 1973) which have been shown not to be irregular, although in any given instance they would not be predictable. Slips of the tongue, it would seem, occur on the basis of syllable organisation (Crompton 1981: 689–690). The same would appear to be true of metathesis which has the syllable as its domain. Syllable structure does not account for all cases of metathesis, but it can provide a framework for describing attested instances of metathesis in Irish with considerable consistency and regularity.

In order to deal with metathesis, a sufficient number of instances of it are required. With modern standard languages, as a result of regularised orthography and universal education, metathesis is not in evidence. If it occurs then it is confined in its nature and extent, cf. the simple *r*-vowel metathesis in Irish English *modern* [mʊdrən], which is the only type found in supraregional Irish English. However, place-names are a fruitful source of metathesis in Ireland, e.g. *Ballytruckle* from Irish *Baile an Turcail* with [...tʌrk...] appearing as [...trʌk...], in turn from Scandinavian 'Torkell's town' (Sommerfelt 1952: 228).

Dialect material is useful for the study of metathesis (Hickey 2011: 150–153) as it shows forms within a single language which vary geographically and which are independent of orthographical or standardising influences. One of the few detailed treatments of metathesis is that of Grammont (1971 [1933]: 339–357), which takes as its material dialect realisations, mainly of standard French word forms and of words from other Romance languages.

3.1 Delimiting metathesis

Attestations of metathesis point to it being a phonological phenomenon which affects the ordering of segments in words. It is essentially non-phonetic as can be seen from the most common case of metathesis, that of *r* and a vowel – e.g. Irish English V+/r/ > /r/+V, *pattern* /pætərn/ > [pætrən]. The metathesised form has an alveolar fricative (Cruttenden 2008: 181–185) for the sequence /tr/ while the non-metathesised form has a rhotacised central vowel [ɚ]: phonetically this is not a sequence of a vowel followed by an /r/ articulation.

The recognition of metathesis may sometimes present difficulties, particularly as it may co-occur with further processes or, indeed, one of these can be misinterpreted as metathesis. For instance, with the Irish word *spioraid* 'spirit', the first vowel may be deleted with the /r/ forming a cluster with the initial /sp-/: /sʲpʲɪrədʲ/ > [sʲpʲrʲɪdʲ]. This is not a case of *r*-vowel metathesis (note that the /r/ palatalises when it joins the palatal onset and that the second vowel /ə/ when stressed becomes /ɪ/ between palatal consonants). There are many similar instances in Irish, e.g. *furasta* 'simple' with /fʌrəstə/ > [frʌstə] or *turas* 'journey' /tʌrəs/ > [trʌs] (Southern Irish).

3.2 Metathesis and other processes

Metathesis consists of a linear reordering of segments. It may occur between various syllable positions and be found twice within a single word. Although it is true that metathesis never involves the deletion of a phonological segment, phonetic substance may be deleted as a consequence of metathesis having applied. Irish has a system of epenthesis (see previous section) which introduces an epenthetic vowel /ə/ in a cluster of /r/ and voiced stop (among many other types of clusters). Thus one has /krɪɣʲarg/ 'blood-red' (*croidhearg*) (in former West Cork Irish, see Ó Cuív 1944: 128), where the phonetic realisation shows an epenthetic vowel which splits up and thus resyllabifies the final cluster: /krɪ.ɣʲarg/ > [krɪ.jarək] (the phonotactic restriction states that a sequence of sonorant and heterorganic voiced stop cannot share the same syllable coda). However, with *r*-vowel metathesis the surface form is disyllabic as the underlying form after metathesis no longer meets the structural description for epenthesis: /krɪɣʲarg/ > /krɪɣʲrak/, /krɪɣʲ.rag/ > [krɪj.rak] (the phonetic forms vary across dialects of Irish and occasionally within dialect areas).

Metathesis may also block another process which fortifies voiced stops to voiceless ones in homorganic post-sonorant word-final position. If the sonorant is removed from its immediately pre-stop position through metathesis, this fortition (McCone 1981) can be reversed: /malˠərʲtʲ/ > /malˠrədʲ/ 'opposite' (*malairt*) (de Bhaldraithe 1945: 116).

3.3 The domain of metathesis

Metathesis appears to be only phonological. There would seem to be no cases where it has been co-opted for grammatical purposes, though there may be one language in which vowel-vowel metathesis seems to indicate grammatical categories. This is Kasem (also Kasim, Kasena), a language of the Niger-Congo phylum spoken by about 250,000 mostly in northern Ghana and Burkina Faso, see the discussion in Anderson (1974: 152–160) and in Phelps (1975), who refutes the analysis as metathesis. One case where it co-occurs with, but is not determined by, a grammatical category is found in Lithuanian where an alveolar or palatal fricative and a velar stop are reversed in sequence before a further obstruent: *mezg-a* 'knitted' (third person past) *meks-ti* 'to knit' (Kenstowicz 1971: 22).

A number of generalisations about metathesis can be made, all of which have consequences for its manifestation.

(11) a. Metathesis never obscures the grammatical structure of a word
 b. Metathesis does not occur in inflections
 c. Metathesis is only found in lexical stems

These three conditions are closely interrelated. The first is an observation made from cross-linguistic examinations, but there is no way of claiming that it is a universal. The second and the third are mirror images of each other. All three generalisations on metathesis derive from its grammatically afunctional nature.

3.4 Possible motivation for metathesis

Although metathesis has no grammatical function (Janda 1984), scholars often take the view that it has at least an incidental function on a phonological level. Thus when referring to metathesis of /r/ and a sibilant in Armenian, Winter (1962: 260–261) notes that "metathesis occurs when the regular developments would lead to a deviation from the established pattern". When discussing historical French *r*-vowel metathesis, Ultan (1978: 389) postulates that it was motivated by a tendency to develop open syllables in French (but Ultan also notes exceptions to this), e.g. *troubler* 'to disturb' < *torbler,* but: *pour* 'for' < *pro.*

In Classical Greek, intervocalic /h/ (from Indo-European */s/) was retained prevocalically but lost elsewhere. The preterite augment /e/ when added to a stem beginning with /h/ then metathesised to place /h/ in a prevocalic position even after prefixation: *heipomen* 'we followed' < **ehepoman* (Ultan 1978: 385). Given the lack of intervocalic /h/ in Greek, the metathesis restored /h/ after prefixation of /e/ to its preferred position before an initial vowel. Thus metathesis in this instance led to a structure more in keeping with the preferred structure, i.e. phonotactics of Greek.

In terms of syllable structure a voiceless fricative is preferred in initial position (in accordance with the greater degree of consonantality of syllable onsets) than in intervocalic medial position. An implication of this is that languages should show a tendency to lose intervocalic /h/; this is the case, for example, in Old English where /h/ was lost medially but retained initially, pre-Old English *sexan* > Old English *seon* /seːon/ 'to see', *xus* > *hus* /huːs/ 'house'. In the Irish of Cois Fharraige, /h/ has also been lost medially but retained initially (de Bhaldraithe 1945: 120), e.g. /boːhər/ > /boːər/ 'road' (*bóthar*), /hatə/ > /hatə/ 'hat' (*hata*). In Spanish /h/ which derives from the lenition of /s/ (Malmberg 1962: 64–65) is lost entirely in many dialects (Southern Spain and large parts of Spanish-speaking America): *pasta* [pahta] > [pata] 'pastry', *casas* [kasah] > [kasa] 'houses'.

3.5 Metathesis and syllable structure

Principles of syllable structure state that onsets are preferentially maximally consonantal (Vennemann 1982: 283, Vennemann 1988: 57, Blevins 1995: 210–212, Goldsmith 2014: 180–182): they start with a strong segment, i.e. one which displays little sonority. The increase in sonority towards the nucleus implies a steady decrease in consonantal strength within the onset towards the nucleus. Thus fricatives are not to be expected before stops in syllable onsets, subject to the qualification that this does not hold for the fricative at the most natural point of articulation, the alveolar ridge. This means that one would not expect initial clusters such as /xt/, /hp/, /fk/ but that a cluster such as /sk/ or /sp/ is natural due to the place of articulation qualification. In this view /sp/ conforms to preferred syllable structure but /hp/ does not. In the following a few examples from other languages are discussed to show the general principles of syllable structure and preferences underlying the analysis of Irish in this contribution.

In Old Armenian, Indo-European intervocalic */s/ was lost. The loss of /s/ in a language often implies a sequence /s/ > /h/ > Ø. Indo-European */sp/, however, appears as /p'/ in Old Armenian: *p'oit'* 'haste' (cf. Greek *spondḗ*) The ejective /p'/ can be regarded as having arisen from the absorption of /h/ (Ultan 1978: 385). But this could only have followed the stop if there was metathesis of a sequence /hp/ to /ph/, the preceding /h/ deriving from the lenition of /s/. The metathesis can be viewed as having been triggered by the relative unnaturalness of the syllable onset /hp/ in comparison to the onset /sp/ from which it arose.

Other instances of metathesis can be accounted for in terms of syllable structure, e.g. Persian *surx* 'red', *garf* 'deep', cf. Zend *suxra*, *jafra*. Ultan (1978: 388) maintains that apocope of the final vowels of the Persian forms led to metathesis of the earlier fricative and liquid cluster. But the question here is why should this be the case? If the forms *surx*, *garf* and *suxra*, *jafra* have the following syllabification: /.surx./ vs. /.su.xra/, /.garf./ vs. /.ga.fra/ then there is an obvious explanation in terms of syllable structure. A syllable coda, if it contains two or more segments, will preferably show an increase in consonantal strength away from the nucleus. The forms /.suxr./ and /.gafr./ would show a decrease in consonantal strength with the /r/. The attested metathesis, however, led to a syllable structure in which there is a gradual decrease in sonority from nucleus to right-most element in the coda, i.e. /-urx/ and /-arf/.

4 Conclusion

Examining the phonotactics of Modern Irish shows that the syllable slots in which segments can occur is determined largely by their sonority values, on a scale which is largely language-independent. Furthermore, the common subphonological processes of epenthesis and metathesis can be shown to crucially depend on the sonority values of the segments affected by these processes with elements of high sonority preferentially triggering them. The examination of epenthesis and metathesis shows clearly that a consideration of syllable structure and sonority leads to linguistically significant generalisations in Modern Irish which would not be attainable otherwise.

References

Alexander, James. 1985. R-metathesis in English: A diachronic account. *Journal of English Linguistics* 18. 33–40.
Anderson, Stephen. 1974. *The organization of phonology*. New York: Academic Press.
de Bhaldraithe, Tomás. 1945. *The Irish of Chois Fhairrge, Co. Galway*. Dublin: Institute for Advanced Studies.
Bailey, Charles. 1970. Towards specifying constraints on phonological metathesis. *Linguistic Inquiry* 3. 347–349.
Blevins, Juliette. 1995. The syllable in phonological theory. In John Goldsmith (ed.), *The handbook of phonological theory*, 206–244. Oxford: Blackwell.
Blevins, Juliette. 2006. *Evolutionary phonology: The emergence of sound patterns*. Cambridge: Cambridge University Press.
Breatnach, Risteard. 1947. *The Irish of Ring, Co. Waterford*. Dublin: Dublin Institute for Advanced Studies.
Buckley, Eugene. 2011. Metathesis. In Marc van Oostendorp, Colin Ewen, Elizabeth Hume & Keren Rice (eds.), *The Blackwell companion to phonology*, 1380–1407. Malden, MA: Wiley Blackwell.
Cairns, Charles & Eric Raimy (eds.). 2011. *Handbook of the syllable*. Leiden: Brill.
Campbell, Alasdair. 1959. *Old English grammar*. Oxford: Clarendon Press.
Chomsky, Noam & Morris Halle. 1968. *The sound pattern of English*. New York: Harcourt Brace Jovanovich.
Crompton, Andrew. 1981. Syllables and segments in speech production. *Linguistics* 19. 663–716.
Cruttenden, Alan. 2008. *Gimson's pronunciation of English*. 7th ed. London: Arnold.
Daland, Robert, Bruce Hayes, James White, Marc Garellek, Andrea Davis & Ingrid Norrmann. 2011. Explaining sonority projection effects. *Phonology* 28. 197–234.
Dogil, Grzegorz. 1988. Phonological configurations, natural classes, sonority and syllabicity. In Harry van der Hulst and Norval Smith (eds.), *Features, segmental structure and harmony processes (part I)*, 79–193. Dordrecht: Foris Publications.
Dogil, Grzegorz. 1992. Underspecification, natural classes, and the sonority hierarchy. In Jacek Fisiak and Stanisław Puppel (eds.), *Phonological investigations*, 329–412. Amsterdam: John Benjamins.
Dogil, Grzegorz & Hans Christian Luschützky. 1990. Notes on sonority and segmental strength. *Rivista di Linguistica* [Linguistics Review] 2. 3–56.
Duanmu, San. 2009. *Syllable structure: The limits of variation*. Oxford: Oxford University Press.
Fallows, Deborah. 1981. Experimental evidence for English syllabification and syllable structure. *Journal of Linguistics* 17. 309–317.
Flack, Kathryn. 2009. Constraints on onsets and codas of words and phrases. *Phonology* 26. 269–302.
Flemming, Edward. 2004. Contrast and perceptual distinctiveness. In Bruce Hayes, Robert Kirchner & Donca Steriade (eds.), *Phonetically-based phonology*, 232–276. Cambridge: Cambridge University Press.
Flemming, Edward. 2005. Speech perception and phonological contrast. In David Pisoni & Robert Remez (eds.), *The handbook of speech perception*, 156–181. Oxford: Blackwell.
Fromkin, Victoria (ed.). 1973. *Speech errors as linguistic evidence*. The Hague: Mouton.
Fudge, Erik. 1969. Syllables. *Journal of Linguistics* 5. 253–286.

Fudge, Erik. 1976. Phonotactics and the syllable. In Alphonse Juilland (ed.), *Studies offered to Joseph Greenberg. Vol. 2: Phonology*, 381–398. Saratoga, CA: Anma Libri.
Fudge, Erik. 1987. Branching structure within the syllable. *Journal of Linguistics* 23. 359–377.
Goldsmith, John. 2014. The syllable. In John Goldsmith, Jason Riggle & Alan Yu (eds.), *The handbook of phonological theory*, 164–196. 2nd ed. Malden, MA: Wiley-Blackwell.
Goldsmith, John (ed.). 1995. *The handbook of phonological theory*. Oxford: Blackwell.
Goldsmith, John, Jason Riggle & Alan Yu (eds.). 2014. *The handbook of phonological theory*, 2nd ed. Malden, MA: Wiley-Blackwell.
Grammont, Maurice. 1971 [1933]. *Traité de Phonétique*. Paris: Librairie Delagrave.
Harris, John. 2006. The phonology of being understood: Further arguments against sonority. *Lingua* 116. 1483–1494.
Hickey, Raymond. 1985. The interrelationship of epenthesis and syncope: Evidence from Dutch and Irish. *Lingua* 65. 229–249.
Hickey, Raymond. 2007. *Irish English: History and present-day forms*. Cambridge: Cambridge University Press.
Hickey, Raymond. 2011. *The dialects of Irish: Study in a changing landscape*. Berlin: de Gruyter.
Hickey, Raymond. 2014. *The sound structure of Modern Irish*. Berlin: de Gruyter.
Hock, Hans Henrich. 1985. Regular metathesis. *Linguistics* 23. 529–546.
Hogg, Richard. 1977. Old English *r*-metathesis and generative phonology. *Journal of Linguistics* 13. 165–175.
Hooper, Joan. 1976. *An introduction to natural generative phonology*. New York: Academic Press.
van der Hulst, Harry & Nancy Ritter. 1999. Theories of the syllable. In Harry van der Hulst & Nancy Ritter (eds.), *The syllable: Views and facts*, 13–52. Berlin: de Gruyter.
van der Hulst, Harry & Nancy Ritter (eds.). 1999. *The syllable: Views and facts*. Berlin: de Gruyter.
Hume, Elizabeth. 1998. Metathesis in phonological theory: The case of Leti. *Lingua* 104. 147–186.
Hume, Elizabeth. 2001. Metathesis: formal and functional considerations. In Elizabeth Hume, Normal Smith & Jeroen van de Weijer (eds.), *Surface syllable structure and segment sequencing*, 1–25. Leiden: Holland Institute of Generative Linguistics.
Janda, Richard. 1984. Why morphological metathesis rules are rare: On the possibility of historical explanation in linguistics. *Proceedings of the Annual Meeting of the Berkeley Linguistics Society* 10, 87–103.
Jespersen, Otto. 1913. *Lehrbuch der Phonetik*. Leipzig: Teubner.
Kenstowicz, Michael. 1971. *Lithuanian phonology*. University of Illinois at Urbana-Champaign dissertation.
Luick, Karl. 1940. *Historische Grammatik der englischen Sprache*. 2 vols. Stuttgart: Tauchnitz.
Maddieson, Ian. 1985. Phonetic cues to syllabification. In Victoria Fromkin (ed.), *Phonetic linguistics: Essays in honor of Peter Ladefoged*, 203–221. Orlando, FL: Academic Press.
Malmberg, Bertil. 1962. *Spansk fonetik*. Lund: Liber Läromedel.
McCone, Kim. 1981. Final /t/ to /d/ after unstressed vowels, and an Old Irish sound law. *Ériu* 32. 29–44.
Nathan, Geoffrey. 1989. Preliminaries to a theory of phonological substance: The substance of sonority. In Roberta Corrigan, Fred Eckman & Michael Noonan (eds.), *Linguistic categorization*, 55–67. Amsterdam: John Benjamins.

Ní Chiosáin, Maire. 1997. Patterns of epenthesis in Irish. In Anders Ahlqvist & Vera Čapková (eds.), *Dán do Oide: Essays in Memory of Conn R. Ó Cléirigh 1927–1995*, 367–377. Dublin: Linguistics Institute of Ireland.

Ó Cuív, Brian. 1944. *The Irish of West Muskerry, Co. Cork*. Dublin: Dublin Institute for Advanced Studies.

Parker, Steve. 2018. *Bibliography of resources on sonority*. Dallas, TX: Graduate Institute of Applied Linguistics and SIL International.

Phelps, Elaine. 1975. Abstractness and rule ordering in Kasem: A refutation of Halle's Maximizing Principle. *Linguistic Analysis* 5. 29–68.

Picard, Marc. 1987. Conditions and constraints on syllable division. *Linguistics* 25. 361–382.

Rice, Keren. 1992. On deriving sonority: A structural account of sonority relationships. *Phonology* 9. 61–99.

Selkirk, Elisabeth. 1984. On the major class features and syllable theory. In Mark Aronoff & Richard Oehrle (eds.), *Language sound structure: Studies in phonology presented to Morris Halle by his teacher and students*, 107–136. Cambridge, MA: MIT Press.

Sommerfelt, Alf. 1952. Norse-Gaelic contacts. *Norsk Tidskrift for Sprogvidenskap* 16. 226–236.

Thompson, Laurence & M. Terry Thompson. 1969. Metathesis as a grammatical device. *International Journal of American Linguistics* 35. 213–219.

Ultan, Russell. 1978. A typological view of metathesis. In Joseph Greenberg (ed.), *Universals of Human Language. Vol. 2: Phonology*, 367–402. Stanford: Stanford University Press.

Vennemann, Theo. 1982. Zur Silbenstruktur der deutschen Standardsprache [On the syllable structure of standard German]. In Theo Vennemann (ed.), *Silben, Segmente, Akzente: Referate zur Wort-, Satz- und Versphonologie anläßlich der vierten Jahrestagung der Deutschen Gesellschaft für Sprachwissenschaft, Köln, 2. - 4. März, 1982*, 261–305. Tübingen: Max Niemeyer.

Vennemann, Theo. 1988. *Preference laws for syllable structure*. Berlin: de Gruyter.

Winter, Werner. 1962. Problems of Armenian phonology III. *Language* 38. 254–262.

Zec, Draga. 1995. Sonority constraints on syllable structure. *Phonology* 12. 85–129.

Donka Minkova
Preference theory and the uneven progress of degemination in Middle English

Abstract: Old English, like its West Germanic relatives, is reconstructed as having contrastive consonantal length: *bane,* n. 'destroyer, bane' - *bannen,* v. 'to ban'. Geminates never occurred in word-initial position, and their loss in word- and syllable-final position is consistently reconstructed as a late Old English change. Also by late Old English, pre-geminate long vowels were shortened, so that by early Middle English (12th c.), geminates could appear only between two short vowels, though paradigmatic analogy may reintroduce orthographic doubling elsewhere.

Building on the premise that the presence or absence of geminates in the system is related to preferences on syllable structure (Vennemann 1988), this study identifies and discusses the conflicting parameters involved in degemination. It provides some background on consonantal length in Old English and Present-Day English and elaborates on the evidential value of Middle English double consonant spellings. Four theoretical issues emerge as central to the history of degemination: the phonological testability of the consonantal length contrast, the low functional load of minimal pairs, the relationship between consonantal strength and degemination, and the interaction between the bias for syllabic well-formedness and the existence of length contrasts in various word positions and word-types. Brief comments on language contact and degemination are followed by a discussion of the results, highlighting the unevenness of the singleton-geminate alternation across the nominal and verbal paradigms. The relative stability of disyllabic forms in the verbal paradigm is a previously unrecognized intermediate phase in the course of degemination in English and opens up a new perspective on the interaction between syllable structure and morphological complexity in the account of the change.

Acknowledgements: For Theo, a life-time professional role model and a family friend, whose foundational *Preference Theory* formulates the link between parametric universality and local gradualness of language change, a major conceptual forerunner of constraint-based theories of phonology.

Donka Minkova, Department of English, University of California, Los Angeles (UCLA), Los Angeles/USA

https://doi.org/10.1515/9783110721461-012

1 The singleton-geminate dichotomy in phonology

Gemination is the term used for consonantal quantity: prosodically, vowels are short or long, and consonants are singletons or geminates. Parallel to the way that long and short vowels interact with syllable structure and syllable weight, consonantal quantity also affects syllable structure and weight. A geminate consonant differs from a short consonant in that the former is underlyingly moraic while the latter is non-moraic.

The dichotomy of singleton vs. geminate consonants is an issue at the core of any phonological theory.[1] Phonetically, segmental length is greatly variable; the IPA has a special modifier diacritic for vocalic "half-length". No such notation is available for the singleton-geminate phonetic continuum. The length, or acoustic closure duration of geminates, in the languages that have them contrastively, ranges from one and a half time to three times the duration of the singleton stops in careful speech (Ladefoged and Maddieson 1996: 91–93). The length of geminates varies from language to language: singletons can range from 3:1, as in Cypriot Greek or Japanese, to a low of 1.85:1 in Italian, or 1.68:1 in Russian.[2]

In diachrony, the basic criterion for the categorisation of length is phonological behavior. Building on the premise that geminates improve the inter-syllabic contact by providing equal strength on both sides of the boundary and should therefore be structurally preferred (Vennemann 1988: 43–50), the goal of this study is to identify and discuss previously unidentified factors involved in the loss of gemination in Middle English (ME). After providing some background on consonantal length in Old English (OE) and Present-Day English (PDE), the endpoints of the process, Section 3 turns to one gnarly empirical concern: the evidential value of ME double consonant spellings. Section 4 examines some of the theoretical issues in the account of ME degemination: the phonological testability of the length contrast (4.1), the importance of minimal pairs (4.2), the relationship between consonantal strength and degemination (4.3), and the interaction between the bias for syllabic well-formedness and the existence of length con-

---

[1] Kubozono (2017) is an important collection of studies on the interaction between phonetic and phonological factors in the synchronic treatment of geminates. For accounts in terms of weight vs. length see Ringen and Vago (2011). Ryan (2019: 64–81) offers a comprehensive treatment of geminates in terms of weight.

[2] See Muller (2001), Idemaru and Guion (2008: 184), Davis (2011), and Dmitrieva (2017, 2018) on Russian.

trasts in various word positions and word-types (4.4). Section 5 comments briefly on ME degemination and language contact, and Section 6 offers thoughts relating the process to Vennemann's (1988) Contact Law, Weight Law, the Head Law, and the Coda Law and concludes with suggestions for further research.

2 Gemination before and after Middle English

2.1 Sources of long consonants in OE

The sources of long consonants in OE are listed in (1):

(1) Sources of long consonants in OE:
a. Assimilation (Inherited):
Proto-Germanic (PrG): PrG *huln-i-z* > OE *hyll* 'hill'; **farza* > OE *fearr* 'ox, bull'
West Germanic Gemination (WGG): -V̆C₁jV- > -V̆C₁C₁V- : Goth. *sal-jan* > OE *sellan* 'to give'; Goth. *sibja* > OE *sibb* 'relationship'; **apl* > *æppel* 'apple'[3]
Paradigmatic attestations of gemination: *fremme* 'perform' 1ˢᵗ pers. sg. pres. ind., pres. sg. subj. - *freme* imper. sg.[4]; *cyn(n)* 'race', nom.sg. - *cynnes* gen. sg.
b. Variables attested within OE:
Across stems and inflectional morphemes: Weak verbs ending in dental stops: *lædan* 'to lead' > 3ʳᵈ sg. *læd+þ* > *lædt* > *læt(t)* 'leads'; *cȳþan* > *cydde* 'said'; *fēdan* > *fēdde* 'fed'; *hȳdan* > *hydde* 'hid'; *āgen+e* > *āgene* ~ *āgenne* 'own, adj. pl.'; *ōþer+a* > *ōþera* ~ *ōþerra* 'of others'; comparatives: *dēop+re* > *dēopre* ~ *dēoppre* 'deeper'; *hāt+ost* > *hātost* ~ *hāttost* 'hottest'; *sēl+ra* > *selra* ~ *sella* 'better'
Across stems and derivational morphemes: *atelic* ~ *atollic* 'horrible'; *eorlic* ~ *eorllic* 'noble', *hlāforddom* ~ *hlāfordom* 'lord-dom'; *geornnes* ~ *geornis* 'eagerness'
c. Compounding: *goddohtor* 'goddaughter'; *gafolland* 'gavel-land, leased land'

---

3 WGG is triggered regularly by /j/, infrequently by /r, l/, and rarely before /w, m/. For full details see Fulk (2018: 126–129). While /j/ triggers gemination across the lexicon, the share of verb forms with geminates is very large, e.g. 73% of the items listed as having geminates in OE in Lucas (1991: 38) are verbs. The causative suffix /-j/ may also trigger gemination: settan 'to set' < *sat-jan; cwellan 'to kill' < cwelan 'die'.
4 The imperative sg. goes back to WG *fremi (Hogg and Fulk 2011: 260–263).

d. "Expressive" gemination:
Otto < *Odoberht*; *Offa* < *Ōsfrið*; *Eadda* < *Eadhelm*; *Wuffa* ~ *Wulf-*; *Eappa* ~ *Earp*; *galan* 'to sing' – *gyllan* 'to yell'; "pet"-names: *frogga* 'frog'; *stagga* 'stag'; *sugga* 'sparrow'; *crabba* 'crab'; *budda* 'beetle' (Minkoff 1967: 81, Hogg 1982, Hogg 1992: 32–33, 42–43, Lass 1994: 250, Colman 2014: 139–147, Fulk 2018: 115[5]). (Inherited and synchronic)

The mixture of inherited and synchronically productive geminations underlies the reconstruction of the OE consonant system as in Table 1:

Table 1: The early OE consonant system.

			Labial	Lab-Den	Dental	Alveolar	Palatal	Velar
Obstruent	STOPS		p(:) b(:)			t(:) d(:)		k(:) g(:)
	AFFRICATES							
	FRICATIVES			f(:)	θ(:)	s(:)	(ʃ)?	x(:)
Sonorant	NASALS		m(:)			n(:)		
	Approximants	Lateral				l(:)		
		Central	w			r(:)	j	

Parenthesized length marks (:) point to one of the most significant systemic differences between early OE and PDE. The later affricates [t͡ʃ] and [d͡ʒ] are left out because they function as clusters in OE, see Minkova (2019).[6] The post-alveolar fricative [ʃ] is probably still allophonic; in any case, there are no instances of contrasting [ʃ] and [ʃʃ] in OE.

WGG, the most prominent diachronic source of OE geminates, required a short vowel preceding the geminate, so the V̆C₁C₁- string is overwhelmingly more common in the lexicon even prior to the late OE pre-geminate vowel shortening (2b). Very importantly, the largest lexical set subject to WGG are weak

---

[5] Forms showing expressive consonantal gemination can be treated as affective or emphatic forms of address and endearment. Colman draws attention to the assimilated type, e. g. *Æffa* and *Beonna*, < *Ælf, Beorn-*, respectively (Colman 2014: 144), and notes the 'blended' type, e. g. *Beoffa* < *Beorhtfrið*; *Ċěolla* < *Ċěollāf*.

[6] Although the clusters /tʃ/ and /dʒ/ may derive from historical geminates, the absence of functionally singleton affricates /t͡ʃ/ and /d͡ʒ/ makes positing and testing OE affricate gemination moot.

verbs.[7] As for the overall presence of forms with geminates, we don't have detailed statistics, but Mailhammer (2010) estimates that 15% of the words in his limited OE corpus have syllables of the shape $\breve{V}C_1C_1$.

Phonologically, long consonants share a lot with clusters. (2) lists similarities and differences between geminates (C_1C_1) and clusters (C_1C_2) in OE.[8]

(2) Similarities and differences between geminates (C_1C_1) and clusters (C_1C_2)
a. Similarities:
$\acute{V}$CCV- strings syllabified $\acute{V}$C.CV-; $\acute{V}$C. is heavy (H)

    mo**n.n**a   cy**n.n**es   'of mankind'   *Jul* 470a
    æ**f.t**er   weo**r.þ**an   'after (to) befall'   *Jul* 197a

$\acute{V}VC_1C_1$ and $\acute{V}VC_1C_2$ both allowed in early OE[9]
    bītt < **bīdþ, bīdeþ* 'awaits', 3rd pers. sg.; *blīss* < *blīþs* 'bliss'
    ēast 'east'; *ǣlc* 'each, ilk'; *ǣht* 'possession'; *nāht* 'naught'; *ōxn* 'arm-pit'; *rūst* 'rust'

b. Differences:
Stem-internal epenthesis OK in -C_1C_2 ~ -C_1VC_2: *hærfest ~ hærefest* 'autumn'; *culfre ~ culufre* 'dove'; *wylf ~ wylif* 'wulf', but NOT: C_1C_1 ~ C_1VC1; *hyll* 'hill', but *hylel

Lengthening OK before homorganic clusters (+son + obstr) -VC_1C_2 > VV C_1C_2 (*feld > fēld, blind > blīnd*), but NOT - VC_1C_1 > VVC_1C_1 (*fell* 'skin, hide' > *fēll; *cinn* 'chin' > *chīn)

Regular pre-geminate shortening: VVC_1C_1 > VC_1: Late OE *blīss > bliss*; *mētte > met*[10], but cluster specific restricted VVC_1C_2 > VC_1C_2, comp. OE *lǣst* 'least', *ēast* 'east', but *rūst* 'rust'

---

7 The most frequent weak verbs with geminates in the stem are class 1 *-jan* verbs, but we cannot exclude class 2 *-ian* verbs because of the blurring of boundaries/transfers as in the causative *ferian < faran* or just variable *fremman ~ fremian* 'perform', *hwītan ~ hwītian* 'whitewash', *andettan ~ andettian* 'confess'.
8 The traditional notation in the literature is CC, used for both a sequence and a geminate (Hogg 1992: 44). In line with the theoretical position of geminates contributing a single mora to weight, a common notation is also G (Morén 2013, Ryan 2019).
9 Wright and Wright (1925: §150).
10 The shortening of the vowel in the set of weak verbs cannot be dated with precision, comp. For þis meting þat I wiþ *met* {\}I dide he saide þe forto *fette*. Edinburgh, Royal College of Physicians, MS of *Cursor Mundi*, hand C, fols. 37r-50v Date: C14a; Awai he ran and sar he *gret* {\} And wit a wo(m)man son he *met*, Edinburgh, Royal College of Physicians, MS of *Cursor Mundi*, hand B, fols. 16r-36v: Extracts from the *Northern Homily Collection*, C14a.

The effect of intervocalic CC's on weight is the same: the stressed syllable in V́C.CV-strings counts as heavy in the verse (Minkova 2015). Indeed, Britton (2012: 232) explicitly states that "geminates, though undoubtedly long in duration, were essentially clusters [. . .] they are to be regarded as heterosyllabic sequences of identical consonants." Lutz (1986) also finds that they behave similarly in word division in OE. Also, OE allowed both V́VC$_1$C$_1$ and VVC$_1$C$_2$, though such "overlong" syllables were distributionally marginal.

VC$_1$C$_1$ and VVC$_1$C$_2$ may also behave asymmetrically, depending on the consonantal properties. Epenthesis is disallowed only in geminates.[11] The so-called "homorganic" clusters such as *-nd, -mb, -ld* can trigger lengthening, while *truly* homorganic clusters, i.e. geminates, not only disallow lengthening but block it. Moreover, the pre-geminate shortening of long vowels in (2b) is "regular", while shortening before clusters is variable and morphologically circumscribed.

2.2 Distribution of long consonants in OE

Geminates in English, or in any older Germanic language have never occurred stem-initially, and they were unstable at best in word-final position, e.g. <*bridd ~ brid*> 'chick, bird'; <*brocc ~ broc*> 'badger, brock'; <*dell ~ del*> 'dell'.

(3) Distribution of geminates in OE at stem edges:
a. Stem-initial: *#C$_1$C$_1$
b. Stem-final orthographic variability: <*bridd ~ brid*> 'chick, bird', <*brocc ~ broc*> 'badger', <*dell ~ del*> 'dell'; *grim* (x42) ~ *grimm* (x3) (The DOE lists the <-mm> spelling as the "main" entry)

The lack of stem-initial geminates (3a) would inhibit syllable-initial geminates, see Vennemann's *Law of Initials* (1988: 32–33). Stem-internal sequences of the type *VrttV-, *VlppV- are not found in OE. The absence of domain-initial geminates is taken as a given in Germanic,[12] though diachronic descriptions of English

---

[11] See Schein and Steriade (1986) on the impossibility of splitting up geminates and discrete treatment of participating consonants. Hogg (1992: 236) separates the epenthetic processes in OE in two sets: (a) genuine epenthesis in liquid + labial or velar, as in *wylf ~ wylif* (DM's examples *deorf ~ ðeorif*, 'bold'; *hærfest ~ hærefest* 'autumn'), and (b), obstruent + sonorant sequences where a syllabic sonorant alternates with schwa: *bēacen ~ bēacn̩ ~ bēanc* 'sign'; *beb̩r ~ beber ~ bebir ~ bebor* 'beaver'. On the second type see further Hogg (1992: §6.38–41).

[12] A notable exception recorded in Germanic is initial gemination of stops in Thurgovian Swiss German, where geminates and singletons are perceptually neutralized (Kraehenmann 2001).

do not comment on this fact. Phonetically, closure duration, the acoustic correlate of gemination, is least perceptible in onset position (Ladefoged and Maddieson 1996: 91–95).[13]

Consonantal weakening in codas at word boundaries (3b) is also phonetically motivated. While right-edge vocalic length is increased cumulatively from lower to higher prosodic domains, there is no parallel consonantal strengthening at the right edge in English. Geminates in word-final position cannot be reconstructed with confidence for *any* period of English, and word-final geminates are most likely orthographic by the time we get to "classical" OE, c. 1000 AD.

(4) Word-final and preconsonantal degemination in OE:
"In stressed positions [. . .] *all geminates were shortened finally* [. . .] geminate spellings were most probably due to orthographic influence from inflected forms" (Hogg 1992: 288–289).
"At word-end, or before any consonant, *geminate consonants are reduced phonologically to nongeminates*" (Fulk 2014: 42). [italics DM]

My counts shown in Table 2 confirm Hogg's and Fulk's positions: the spelling of OE word-final geminates in *The Linguistics Atlas of Early Middle English* (LAEME), which includes a number of texts that have very archaic features, and cuts off at c. 1315, indicates complete loss of word-final geminates by the end of the 13th century, but the process was under way much earlier.[14]

---

13 The absence of geminate-singleton contrast domain-initially invites a parallel between studies of boundary marking in OE and in PDE. The general principle of initial strengthening, which correlates with lengthening and increased articulatory magnitude, would favor gemination. However, "different aspects of prosodic structure (domain boundary vs. prominence) are differentially encoded" (Cho and Keating 2009: 482); apparently, any singleton in any period of English is sufficient to encode a simplex-word boundary.

14 The token counts in Tables 2 and 3 are from the *Dictionary of Old English Web Corpus* (*DOEC*) (http://tapor.library.utoronto.ca/doecorpus/) *Word Wheel* and from *LAEME* (http://www.lel.ed.ac.uk/ihd/laeme2/laeme2.html). The counts exclude <-VC$_1$C$_1$V># and <-VCV># forms. *Ormulum* forms such as <mann>, <sibb>, <mihhte>, <reccned> are not counted because of the unique problems posed by the text's spelling for the interpretation of degemination, see the overview in Murray (2000), who takes the position that that text shows degemination. In treating the *Ormulum* data separately from the rest of the corpus, I follow Britton (2012: 238–239), who finds Kurath's (1956) and all subsequent claims that the text shows degemination 'ill-founded'. Britton counts eleven "actual or potential 'minimal pairs'" in that text.

Table 2: Word-final orthographic degemination in OE and early ME.

	OE data from *DOEC*		OE-ME data from *LAEME*	
	<-VC$_1$C$_1$>#	<-VC>#	<-VC$_1$C$_1$>#	<-VC>#
bed(d) 'bed'	48	104	5	31
cin(n) 'chin'	3	5	0	4
man(n) 'man'	1200	7413	2	>1000
rib(b) 'rib'	10	19	0	3
sib(b) 'relative'	126	137	0	5
web(b) 'web'	6	11	0	3

Table 3: Syllable-final orthographic degemination in OE and early ME.

	OEDC		LAEME	
	<-VC$_1$C$_1$C$_2$V>#	<-VC$_1$C$_2$V>#	<-VC$_1$C$_1$C$_2$V>#	<-VC$_1$C$_2$V>#
al(l)re	435	2397	1	173
ful(l)ne	12	172	0	1

For paradigmatic syllable-final degemination the orthographic evidence is also convincing, as the LAEME spellings for gen. pl. of 'all': *allre/ealre* and the acc. sg. of 'full': *fullne/fulne* attest.

Phonetically, word-final stops in PDE are often unreleased, thus *dog* [-g̚], *robe* [-b̚], *lack* [-k̚] (Cruttenden 2014: 169–170). The lack of an audible release stage is particularly noticeable in homorganic clusters: think of *lump, kiln, stamp*, the history of word-final *-mb, -ng*. Geminates are by definition homorganic; lack of release provides a plausible phonetic grounding for the early dating of degemination at a right prosodic boundary. Phonemically, degemination is an "instantiation of lenition on the basis of constriction duration" (Zuraw 2009: 14).

The only position in which the reconstruction of contrastive consonantal length *can* be posited in late OE is intervocalic: all consonants, except the central approximants /w/ and /j/, appeared as contrastive geminates in intervocalic position.

(5) Contrastive singletons and geminates in OE:
    bite 'bit, morsel, cut' *bitte* 'bucket'
    cyre 'choice' *cyrre* 'occasion, chore'
    hopian 'to hope' *hoppian* 'to hop'
    manu 'mane, acc. sg.' *mannan* 'person, acc. sg.'

sæpe 'sap, dat. sg.'   sæppe 'spruce, fir'
sete 'set!'   sette 'set' 1ˢᵗ pers. sg. pres. ind.
tela 'well, thoroughly'   tellan 'to (re)count'

In sum: by early ME, etymological word-final geminates in base forms and syllable-final geminates were non-contrastive, and so were $VVC_1.C_2$- : $VVC_1C_1.C_2$- forms. However, in $\check{V}C_1.C_1VC\#$ and $\check{V}C_1.C_1ə\#$ forms alternating with $\check{V}C_1\#$, the contrast persisted.

2.3 Gemination in PDE

In PDE consonantal length is non-contrastive, though phonetic consonantal length may be significantly increased if two identical consonants occur at word and morpheme boundaries; the result is commonly referred to as "false" geminates, also "fake" geminates (Oh and Redford 2012, Kotzor et al. 2016), or "morphological geminates" (Ben Hedia and Plag 2017, Ben Hedia 2019).[15] The variables that can influence the realization of length are many: type of boundary, type of affix, type of consonant, stress, rate of speech, orthography. One of the possible factors, not tested in the studies consulted above, is lexical frequency. By way of a preliminary check, (6) shows some examples of long consonants as recorded in the OED; the numbers in parentheses in 6 (b) indicate the frequency band for the headword:[16]

(6) "False" geminates in PDE:
a. Across word boundaries: *bank causes* [-kk-]; *mass symptoms* [-ss-]; *lame move* [-mm-]; *snappea* [-p- or -pp-]
b. Across morpheme boundaries: *dissatisfied* (4) [-ss-] vs. *disseminate* (5) [-s-]; *innovation* (6) [-n-] vs. *unknown* [-nn-] (6) vs. *inness* (2) [-n(n)-]; *really* [-l-] (7); *illy* [-ll-](3); *dully* [-ll-](4); *fully* [-l-] (6), *wholly* Brit. [-ll-], U.S. [-l(l)-] (6); *palely* [-(l)l-] (3); *smally* [-l-] (2); *novelly* (2) [-(l)l-]; *vilely* (3) Brit. /-ll-/, U.S. /-l(l)-/.

---

15 On phonological degemination without phonetic shortening for e.g. *apple, copper, bitter, otter, middle* in PDE, see Goblirsch (2010), who does not, however, cite supporting phonetic data for this claim.
16 The OED uses 8 frequency bands; the highest frequency for words with long consonants is 7, which means "words which occur between 100 and 1000 times per million words in typical modern English usage". At the other end of the range are band 3 (0.01 and 0.1 times per million words) and band 2 (< 0.01 times per million words).

Lengthening across word boundaries is quite systematic while word-internal historical degemination is greatly variable. The edges of the frequency continuum: *really* at Band 7[17] with no gemination vs. *illy* at band 3 or *dully* at Band 4 with gemination, appear to correlate with frequency, but then *wholly* and *fully* are within the same frequency band (6), yet only *wholly* seems to vary. The current research question for PDE is why does degemination affect the outputs differently. The question is still unsettled, but it links to the basic research goal in this study: in early ME a contextually restricted phonotactic contrast between intervocalic singletons and geminates was in the process of disappearing, so when and why did the older system evolve into the system we know today? What are some possible ME variables involved in the process?

3 Orthographic doubling vs. phonological quantity

The issue of orthographic vs. phonological doubling of consonants in ME is directly linked to the recovery of the fate of consonantal length. Here is how the *Corpus of Narrative Etymologies* (CoNE) addresses this issue:

(7) CoNE on OE gemination ((OEG)):
 In [...] lOE and ME (e.g. Nth *eatta* EAT, *LAEME* GODD GOOD) *the apparent geminate may be a diacritic for shortness of the preceding vowel (see ((OGASV)))*.[18] *Indeed, ... it is not clear to what extent this may hold over the whole set of such spellings* (italics DM).

This takes us directly to the so-called Northumbrian gemination, which bears on the shakiness of the orthographic argumentation in the reconstruction of a systemic contrast across the board:

---

[17] Other band 7 singleton [-l-]'s are found in *usually, especially, generally, actually*.
[18] ((OGASV)) stands for "Orthographic gemination after short vowel". Nth stands for Northumbrian Old English.

(8) The Northumbrian geminates:
"[I]m Nordhumbrischen, namentlich in Li [...] finden sich in weitem Umfange die harten Verschlusslaute *p, t, c,* und *m,* seltener *d* und *s,* wenn sie intervokalisch nach Kürze stehen, verdoppelt geschrieben. [...] Die Deutung dieser Erscheinung ist aber schwierig, weil die Folgeentwicklung nur unsichere Hinweise gibt." [In Northumbrian, namely in Li [*Lindisfarne Gospels*], Old English, *p, t, c,* and *m,* and more rarely *d* and *s,* are doubled in writing intervocalically after a short vowel. The significance of this phenomenon is difficult to interpret.] (Luick 1964: §670).
"[. . .] consonant length may have been nonphonemic in Northumbrian [. . .] as early as the tenth century" as in the gloss of the *Lindisfarne Gospels* (Kuhn 1970: 49).

The combination of a weight-based quantitative change and an attendant orthographic practice of doubling etymological singletons makes spelling an unreliable basis for reconstructing degemination.[19] The interpretation I am following is articulated explicitly in Fulk (1996: 498):

(9) The significance of orthographic geminates in OE-ME:[20]
"[Rather], internally, *double consonants in Old English seem to indicate syllable boundaries* (italics DM), a function that is probably phonetically indistinguishable from that of indicating actual consonant length" (Fulk 1996: 498).

For the transitional period between OE and ME, and indeed all the way into late ME, orthographic doubling of consonants is a way of marking syllable structure which is directly related to the length of the preceding vowel, hence the long tradition of associating the phonological account of degemination with

---

[19] Compare Minkova (2015: 156 and references there): "[. . .] in Present-Day English: 66% of disyllabic English words with one medial consonant that contain a stressed lax vowel in the first syllable are written with a geminate (e.g., *rabbit, grammar*)."
[20] Vennemann's theory of syllable cuts (see Vennemann [2000] and the references there) has been applied to the interpretation of orthographic doubling of consonants after short vowels in the *Ormulum* as a manifestation of the typological transition from quantity to syllable cut in Middle English (Murray 1995, 2000; Mailhammer 2007). These interpretations rely on the assumption that in Orm's language degemination was completed, a claim shown to be "ill-founded" by Britton (2012) – see note 14. Page (2006) argued against the application of the syllable cut theory to the English historical data, while he found the theory applicable to the history of Dutch.

ME compensatory lengthening (MECL).[21] Section 4 looks into MECL and other phonological correlates of degemination.

4 The Early Middle English geminates: How much do we know?

> "[. . .] not everything that can be counted counts, and not everything that counts can be counted."[22]

What we teach is familiar: The singleton-geminate contrast was *gradually* lost in ME.[23] Since both -C_1C_1- and -C_1C_2- strings triggered shortening of the preceding stressed long vowel in late OE as in (2b), geminates show up only in -$\acute{V}C_1C_1\breve{V}(C)$- environments as in (5).

4.1 Phonological tests for consonantal quantity contrast: MECL

The similarities between intervocalic clusters and geminates were noted in (2a); in OE they have the same effect on weight: all -$\acute{V}CCV$- strings are syllabified $\acute{V}C.CV$-, and the stressed syllables are treated as heavy in the meter.[24] The moraic value of geminates is the same as any -CC- sequence (see 2.1); we know this because both types cause shortening historically.

Some asymmetries between clusters and geminates were cited in (2b): unlike clusters, geminates are cohesive, and the effect on the weight of the preceding syllable for clusters is consonant-specific. By the 12th century geminates are phonotactically restricted to intervocalic position and they can appear only between two short vowels. Since singletons also appear in these positions, the only compelling argument for contrastive consonantal length comes from a small set of

---

[21] See Minkova and Lefkowitz (2020) for the acronym MECL in preference to the more familiar MEOSL.
[22] Cameron (1967: 13). This quote is often misattributed to Einstein.
[23] "This shortening or degemination began in the north ca 1200, and extended southwards over the next two centuries, probably completing in London around 1400" (Lass 1992: 59) is a typical characterization of the change.
[24] This applies also to the cohesive clusters /sp-, st-, sk/ which alliterate as single units but are treated as heterosyllabic word-medially, as in *fæs.te hæf.de* 'firmly had' *Beo* 554b.

minimal pairs in which non-high vowels remain short if followed by an etymological geminate but could lengthen if there was no geminate.

(10) Singleton-geminate consonants and MECL:

	OE	EME		LME		
a.	bana	<ban(e)>	/ba.n(ə)/	/baːn/	'slayer, doom, bane'	(MECL)
b.	bannan	<bann(en)>	/ban.n(ə)/	/ban/	'to summon, ban'	(no MECL)

Since lengthening did not apply before geminates, it is a key diagnostic for the survival of contrastive geminates beyond late OE; this is not new or controversial. But the account in (10) presents a difficult ordering conundrum:

(11) The ordering conundrum: MECL precedes /-ə/ apocope[25]
a.   Lengthening precedes /-ə/ apocope:
     /ba.n(ə)/   /baːn/   'slayer, doom, bane'
     /ban.n(ən)/   /ban/   'to summon, ban'
     Problems:
     97.5% of (C)V.CəT items unlengthened: *claret, habit, palate, planet, radish, relic, rocket*...
     77% of (C)V.CəR items unlengthened: *camel, father, gravel, Latin, seven*...
b.   /-ə/ apocope precedes MECL:
     /ba.n(ə)/   */ban/   */ban/   'slayer, doom, bane'
     /ban.n(ən)/ */bann/   /ban/   'to summon, ban'
     Problems: Late ME */ban/ 'doom'; ME */bann/ 'to summon, ban'

In (11a), ordering MECL as an independent first change, we find a contradiction in that open-syllable lengthening in English is attested practically only in items with second-syllable apocope. Put differently, if lengthening precedes or is unrelated to apocope, the account faces the problem of an unexpected 97.5% of (C)V.CəT obstruent-final forms and 77% of sonorant-final forms remaining short in spite of meeting the conditions of initial stress on a short non-high vowel in an open sylla-

---

[25] Here and below 'T' stands for an obstruent and 'R' stands for a sonorant. The degeminating effect of apocope is ultimately similar to the effect of syncope in inflected forms: $\acute{V}C_1 \cdot C_1 \partial C(C) > \acute{V}C_1 \cdot C_1 C(C)$ destroys the only environment in which geminates are (marginally) viable, but see 4.4 below.

ble and a single intervocalic consonant. These conditions alone are not sufficient to characterize the non-lengthening in forms such as *claret, habit, camel, mother*.

(11b), ordering schwa loss first, does not work either: the apocopated schwa entails loss of consonantal length distinction at the right edge, so we have to date MECL *after* schwa loss, but of course *after* schwa loss the inputs will both be identical, e.g. /ban/; the different results remain unexplained. We could posit a difference between singletons and geminates based on the degree of lenition at the right edge, i.e., if one of the factors behind OE *bana* > /bɛm/ 'bane', but OE *bannan* > /ban/ 'ban' is not the presence or absence of a true "long" consonant, but a matter of a different degree of consonant lenition. However, this requires a synchronically untestable contrast between */ban/ and */bann/ (see the references in (4)), and makes the lengthening in the former unmotivated. Thus, the survival of geminates still relates to both open-syllable lengthening and apocope.

Positing the third option, concurrent ongoing variability of schwa apocope, compensatory lengthening, and degemination, which is an often-unarticulated assumption in the voluminous literature on the subject, does avoid the problems in (11b),[26] but some factors add to the complexity and granularity of the interplay between these variables; they will be discussed in the next sections.

4.2 Minimal pairs as a factor for the loss of consonantal quantity contrast

The lack of distinctive geminates at word edges raises the question of the phonemic status for the surviving geminates in intervocalic position in ME. Britton (2012: 232) rightly treats such contrasts as phonotactically restricted "geminate clusters", leaving the notion of a "classical phonemic" contrast out of the picture. Either way, the loss of stem-internal -$VC_1C_1V(C)$- is a phonological change in need of an explanation. A somewhat quixotic suggestion over fifty years ago (Peters, 1967; 1968: 86, fn. 2) is that the idea of a phonemic contrast between OE singletons and geminates should be abandoned.[27] This was prompted by his rather conservative count of "a low total of only sixteen apparent minimal pairs" in the 35,000 headwords in the *Clark Hall-Meritt Dictionary*. Britton (2012), the most

---

26 Minkova and Lefkowitz (2020) address the variable results of lengthening in disyllabic (C)V.CVC and show that conventional OT constraints can correctly predict variation in the (C)V.TəR stems and categorical lengthening or non-lengthening in other input disyllabic stems.

27 "[...] phonic short and long consonants are in complementary distribution. [...] Thus, medial double consonantals in morph final position represent phonic short consonants. This conclusion negates the case for phonemic long consonants in Old English" (Peters 1967: 3).

recent discussion of ME degemination in these terms, recognized the unsatisfactory state of affairs regarding its causation and shifted the explanatory focus onto the functional load of the contrast. Examining an idealized, *Ormulum*-like East Midland variety of Early ME of the late 12th century, he put together an impressively detailed hands-on list of items that might have constituted minimal pairs, i.e. the bedrock of what we see as distinctive entities. Excluding "false" geminates in derivatives and compounds and unstressed *þis(s)es*, *þis(s)um* 'this', he found only 11 actual or potential "minimal pairs" in the *Ormulum*. All items included in his new database are disyllabic trochees of the shape $(C)\acute{V}C_1(C_1)V(C)$. The list of what he cautiously calls "quasi minimal pairs" (Britton 2012: 238) is extensive, but it includes "oblique forms with final *–e* [. . .] preserved in formulaic phrases" (Britton 2012: 239, fn. 15) such as *bedd(e)* 'bed', *mann(e)* 'man', *socc(e)* 'sock', as well as pairs with high vowels such as *wine* 'friend' : *winne (n)* 'to win'; these also include "oblique forms" as in OE *smiþ(e)* 'smith' : *smiþþ(e)* 'smithy'.[28] French loans and rare or manifestly regionally restricted items are excluded.

Although his database is significantly broader than Peters', Britton still finds the contrastive role of geminates "vastly weakened" (2012: 243), since only forms with input geminates can have a short (non-high) vowel. The central claim, which bears on the labeling and the analysis of the early ME long consonants, is that the *functional load* of geminates even before the lengthening of the non-high vowels and at a very early stage of schwa apocope was minimal.

Britton's sally into documenting the potential functional load of geminates before the 13th century reveals a new angle in the reconstruction of degemination: the lingering contrastiveness is not fully functional and the distribution is mostly complementary. His tentative suggestion is "to regard degemination as a general process of diffusion, involving the selection of the weakened/simplified variants" (2012: 243). The selection would occur at very little communicative cost. Bermúdez-Otero (2012: 193) elaborates on this suggestion, adding that the low functional load means that "a potential systemic obstacle in the path of phonetically driven reduction was nearly absent". This is a convincing point: the absence of evidence for systemic contrasts would enable and expedite phonetically driven reduction. This aspect of the ME degemination record brings up further empirical and theoretical questions: were some geminate consonants more prone to reduction, and was degemination proceeding at the same rate across the lexicon?

---

[28] The inclusion of the high vowels is uninformative with respect to MECL; there is one single relevant surviving pair: lengthened *week*, vs. unlengthened *wicked*. A lowered/lengthened form of *week* is not recorded in *LAEME*, there is no rhyme evidence, practically all *LAEME* forms are monosyllabic, while all instances of *wicked* are minimally disyllabic (no attestations in rhyme).

Britton's study provides the largest empirical foundation for the reconstruction of degemination; I approached that valuable database with these questions in mind.

4.3 Degemination and consonantal strength

Typologically, the maintenance of length contrast can be hypothesized to relate to the type of intervocalic consonants: perceptually, different consonants have different durations which could affect the confusability of C: CC and therefore the stability of the geminate. In principle, inherent phonetic properties can result in uneven rates of gemination and degemination. One line of inquiry is the potential influence of consonantal strength (Vennemann 1988: 8–9), the phonetic inverse of sonority, with /p, t, k/ at the top of the scale. Consonantal strength arguably accounts for the fact that WGG before liquids is restricted to voiceless stops (Vennemann 1988: 43–45). On the other hand, the *loss* of consonantal length from Latin to Hispano-Romance is reconstructed as affecting the obstruents first, then the sonorants, leading to a proposal of a direct link of the process to sonority (Holt 1999).[29] The native vocabulary of Japanese allows only voiceless stops as geminates, while voiced stops are not geminated (Morén 2013: 80), which runs against the idea that it is only and always the manner feature of sonority that is implicated in degemination. With respect to the obstruent-sonorant variable, Morén (2013: 17–18) references languages which have distinctively moraic obstruent geminates but no sonorant geminates, languages in which the more sonorous liquids, but not nasal sonorants, geminate, and languages which have the Japanese-type pattern as a preference for voiceless obstruents, though not categorically. The conclusion is that "distinctive consonant weight is fairly free" with respect to sonority (Morén 2013: 18). If sonority is taken out of the picture, however, a correlation between the laryngeal feature of voicing and gemination for obstruents is a very widely attested cross-linguistic pattern – see Hayes, Kirchner, and Steriade (2004: 6–18), who formulate an implicational law whereby "the presence of a voiced obstruent geminate in a given language implies, in any context, that of the corresponding voiceless geminate."

This parameter has not been looked at for the English diachronic data, so I checked its applicability to the records in Britton (2012). One prediction for ME degemination would be that simplification of <bb, dd, gg> would be more advanced than that of <pp, tt, kk>. For the voiced velar and labial geminate-

---

[29] Also, geminate voiced stops (and [ff]) in Holt's data are rare as inputs to degemination. Language-specific patterns are expected; in Russian Dmitrieva (2017: 52) found the voiced stops' resistance to degemination an "idiosyncrasy".

singleton contrast, the prediction is borne out by default. The contrast between /gg/ and /g/ was non-existent in early ME since the velar in <-VgV-> strings was vocalized: OE *boga* > Late OE *boue* ~ *bowe* 'bow'; OE *sǣge* Late OE *sei(e)*, 'say, imp.' (Minkova 2014: 82–84). By inheritance, there were no singleton tautomorphemic intervocalic [-b-]'s in OE either, thus PrG *VbV > OE [v], as in PrG. **uberi* > OE *ofer* 'over'. That leaves [-VddV-] vs. [-VdV-] in a total of six pairs in Britton (2012: 241), all of which are problematic in some way.[30] The lack of lexical basis for acquiring the contrast places the diachronic English data within the range of predictions on obstruent voicing and gemination.[31]

As for the voiceless geminate stops <pp, tt, kk>, the lexical input picture appears to be more stable: *nape* 'nape' : *nappe(n)* 'nap'; *hipe* 'hip' : *hippe(n)* 'jump'; *mete* 'meat' : *mette* 'meet', past sg.; *hace* 'hake, hook' : *hakke(n)* 'to hack. Even with the generous inclusion of inflected nouns and adjectives and forms with alternate late OE spellings, as well as items with high vowels, the numbers of minimal pairs are still low: /p/:/pp/ (x7); /t/:/tt/ (x8); /k/:/kk/ (x12). One observation, discussed in 4.4, is that in the majority of the pairs the contrast crosses word classes, an a priori syntactic and semantic contextual limitation on the value of minimal pairs as phonological contrast diagnostics.

The fricatives are irrelevant for the history of degemination in English. As seen in Table 1, [voice] is not distinctive for the fricatives; there are no voiced intervocalic fricative geminates in OE. Hogg (1982) makes a strong case for the lack of [ff] already in OE, and Britton's search confirms that. For the dental fricative, the contrast can only be posited for *smiþ(e)*, n. obl. 'smith' : *smiþþ(e)* 'smithy' and *laðe(n)* 'to invite', *laðe* 'barn, ON *hlaða* : *laþþe* 'lath', n., OE *lætt*; the posited contrasting form **læþþe* is of obscure origin (OED). For /s/ [z] : /ss/, both pairs include post-1300 items.

The cumulative evidence for the geminate-singleton contrast for /r, l, n/[32] is more extensive than for the obstruents, though once again the contrast does cross word-class boundaries: *mere* 'horse' : *merre(n)* 'hinder'; *bane* 'destroyer' : *banne(n)*

---

[30] This includes inflected forms such as *rade* 'quick' (also <ræd, red>), *bedde* 'bed', where the <-dd->'s value cannot be sustained, also *ladde* 'lad', only attested after c. 1300 and "of obscure origin" (OED). All six contrasts include verbal forms with paradigmatic vowel length alternations: *bide(n)*, the past part. of *bīdan* 'to await' : vs. *bidde(n)* 'to pray' inf., also OE *rīdan* 'to ride', *cȳðan* 'to make known', where the quantity of the vowel would be a salient signal of the grammatical difference by itself.

[31] Kirchner's (2000; 2004: 326–327, 342) effort-based ranking of geminates shows the voiceless stops as always the least effortful; whether the OE lexicon reproduces this phonetic bias accidentally or not is an open question.

[32] Britton (2012: 242) lists two possible <m : mm> pairs, but their evidential value is questionable: the posited *brime(n)* 'bear fruit' and *brimme(n)* 'be in heat' are variants of the same verb

'ban'. These appear side by side with a few "genuine" minimal pairs such as *spare(n)* 'to spare' : *sparre(n)* 'to close'. All noun-based pairs include "oblique forms", e.g. *bale* 'evil' : *bal* n. 'ball', obl. *ball(e)* > unattested OE **beall* (OED); *mane* n. 'mane' : *manne*, n. obl. 'man'.

In sum, the pre-1200 evidence shows gemination already not only phonotactically restricted to intervocalic position but also practically limited to two subsets of the consonant system: voiceless stops and three sonorants (/r, l, n/). Consonantal strength, either seen in relation to the sonority scale, or in terms of voicing, failed to shed light on the path of degemination. There is no obvious common denominator for place of articulation of the handful of consonants which may have provided the learning basis for contrastive gemination by the beginning of the 13th century.[33]

4.4 Degemination across the lexicon

If apocope and MECL unfolded in parallel, as is reasonable to assume (Section 4.1), with both processes more advanced in the north than in the south, there should be forms with post-apocope degemination (-VCØ), forms without apocope preserving geminates (-VC$_1$C$_1$ə), and degeminated forms but no apocope (-VCə), the latter possibly triggering MECL. The variability of forms with and without apocope is typologically predictable; this is what one expects to find in "real" language data. Taking a very broad view of the period between late OE and late ME, Table 4 illustrates these options:

Table 4: Variability of late OE -VC$_1$C$_1$ə forms in ME.

-VC$_1$C$_1$V	Degemination	Apocope	MECL	OE *croppa* 'crop'
-VC$_1$C$_1$ə	–	–	–	ME *croppe*
-VCØ	√	√	–	ME *crop*
-VCə	√	–	√	ME ***crope, croupe*** (?)

Examining closely the various attestation of forms with reconstructed input geminates, we find more information on their variability in the ME lexicon, where OE -VC$_1$C$_1$V inputs result in -VC$_1$C$_1$ə ~ VC ~ VCə and possibly even VVC(ə):

(MED); similarly *hame* 'skin' : *hamme* 'ham' is problematic because the OE base form for 'ham' is *hamm ~ hom ~ ham* (DOE).

[33] For Modern Italian Payne (2005: 167) found that coronal sonorants and voiced stops are more prone to potential perceptual overlap, but such a correlation is clearly missing from our English data.

(12) Lengthened -VC₁C₁ə noun forms in ME (MED headwords):
DOE *cott ~ cotte*;   MED *cŏt*(e n.(1) ~ *cod ~ coth ~ **cout*** 'hovel, hut'
DOE *croppa ~ crop*;   MED *crop ~ croppe ~ **crope** ~ **croupe*** 'sprout'
DOE *gnætt ~ gnæt*;   MED *gnat ~ gnatte ~ **gnait** ~ **gneat*** 'gnat'
DOE *dokke ~ dokka*;   MED *doc, dok, **doke*** 'dock, weedy herb'
DOE *hearra ~ herra*;   MED *herre ~ her ~ here ~ **heere** ~ **hair** ~ **heir** ~ **heyr*** 'lord'
OE *pott*;   MED *pot ~ potte ~ **poot(e)** ~ **pote** ~ **poat** ~ **poatte** ~ **pootte*** 'pot'
OE *toll*;   MED *tolle ~ **toale** ~ **thol(e** ~ (early) **theol** ~ **tōl***
OE *web ~ webb*;   MED *web ~ web(b)e ~ **weob*** 'web'
OE *wella* (rare);   MED *wel ~ **weelle** ~ **wele** ~ **weyle*** 'wall'[34]

All items in (12) are cited in their OE nom. sg. form. Entries like OE *pott* 'pot', *toll* 'toll' are included because orthographic geminates, possibly from inflected forms, appear in the base forms (headwords) in the OED and the MED. It should be emphasized that for nouns, as well as for adverbs and adjectives, <-e> is by far the most frequently used inflection. Six out of the seven possible grammatical functions for nouns in early ME could be signaled by <-ə> (Minkova 1991: 126), including gen. sg. for feminine nouns and u-stems, fem. and neuter nom. acc. plurals, all gen. plurals, including the weak nouns. The only inflection without a possible /-ə/# allomorph is the OE dat. pl. <-um>, which was in the process of merging with /(ə)n/ by late OE - early ME. Put differently, we can expect the geminates in nouns, adverbs, and adjectives to be simplified frequently due to apocope.

Was the rate of degemination the same across the lexicon? Apocope in ME does not affect various word classes at the same rate.[35] Syncope triggers degemination too (Section 2.2), and -əC(C)# suffixes are more common in the verb paradigms where syncope may or may not apply. Table 5 shows the options for -VC₁.C₁əC(C) inputs:

Table 5: Variability of late OE -VC₁C₁əC(C) forms in ME.

-VC₁C₁VC	Degemination	Syncope	MECL	OE *hnappeþ* 'nap, 3 sg.'
-VC₁C₁əC	–	–	–	ME *nappeth*
-VC₁C	√	√	–	ME *napt*
-VC₁əC	√	–	?	ME *napeth? (not att.)

---

34 Regional (Northumberland) ***weel ~ weil*** (OED entry on 'wall').
35 The unevenness of apocope is discussed in Minkova (1991: Chapter 5) where nouns are found to be the most "precocious" group with respect to final schwa loss (1991: 150).

Syncope in $VC_1C_1əC(C)$ early ME forms results in $VC_1C_1əC(C)$ ~ $VC_1C(C)$ ~ $VC_1əC(C)$ destroying the only environment in which geminates are (marginally) viable, so *$VC_1C_1C(C)$ is not included. The form in the last row, *$napeth$ is not attested in *LAEME*, *MED*, the *MED Corpus*, or the *OED*. In this example, all forms preserving an orthographic -VC# inflected form have <-pp->, making it more likely that the geminate was still viable in this environment. -$VC_1əC(C)$ is also the environment where lengthening operates variably *only* for -$VC_1əR$, i.e. if the unstressed syllable coda is a sonorant, making MECL a very low-odds option.[36]

In an attempt to compare the potential effect of apocope vs. syncope, I checked the attested ME variable forms in Britton (2012) for class membership in the minimal pairs. The unexpected yet suggestive finding was that verbs with OE geminates generally do not show lengthened forms in ME:

(13) Unattested lengthening in OE -$VC_1C_1ə$ in verb forms (headwords in the MED):
OE *hnappian* > */naːp/ 'to nap'; OE *wellen* */wɛːl/ 'to boil, to well'
Similarly: ME *bannan* 'summon'; *cwellen* 'kill'; *droppen* 'drop', *fellen* 'fell'; *ferren* 'depart'; *hakkian* 'hack'; *hoppen* 'hop'; *kennen* 'make known'; *merren* 'hinder'; *nappen* 'nap'; *rekken* 'have interest in'; *sakken* 'put in a sack'; *soppian* 'sop'; *setten* 'set'; *spellen* 'speak'; *stellen* 'establish'; *sparren* 'close'; *sperren* 'close'; *waggen* 'wag'; *wannen* 'grow dark'

The verbs listed in (13) are exhaustive; the only exception in Britton's (2012) set is OE *dwellan* 'to tarry', recorded also as *dwelen*, *dweillen* (not in *LAEME*). This observed discrepancy in the potential lengthening is also seen in minimal pairs in surviving items where both the verb and the noun are taken in their headword form, i.e. uninflected, with the infinitives possibly n-less:

(14) -$VC_1C_1ə(n)$ verbs vs. -Və nouns in ME minimal pairs

OE	ME	Gloss
bannan ~ bonnan	*banne(n) ~ bonne(n) ~ banni*	'to summon'
bana ~ bona	*bāne*	'bane'
merran	*merr(en)*	'to mar'
mere ~ mǣre (Angl.)	*mĕare*	'mare'
(tō)haccian	*hakk(en)*	'to hack'
haca	*hāke* (MED 1252)	'hake-fish'

---

[36] The suffix <en> /(ə)n is a prominent grammatical marker for all classes, including weak nouns, dative plurals, infinitives, and past plurals, but these forms will not be discussed further here because of - (ə)n's early loss and/or substitution by existing allomorphs, see Minkova and Lefkowitz (2019).

spittan	spitte(n) ~ spytt(i)(n)	'to spit'
spitu	spite ~ spete ~ **speet**(e) ~ speit(e) ~ speat(e)	'spit, a sharp rod'
wællan ~ wellan	well(en)	'to well'[37]
wela	wele ~ weel(e)~ weyl(e) ~ weale	'weal, wealth'

Again, (14) shows a textbook solid pattern: MECL shifted the function of contrastiveness in e.g. OE *bana* 'bane' vs. *bannan* 'to summon' onto the stressed vowel. Additionally, there is asymmetry in the retention of geminates in ME: in pre-lengthening minimal pairs and even minimal pairs with high vowels as in *spit*, the shaded geminate providing the evidence for length contrast appears predominantly in verb forms.[38] Unlike nouns, where /-əs/# is limited to strong masc. and neuter nouns in gen. sg. and masc. nom. acc. plural, /-əC/# for verb forms is more wide-spread: 2nd and 3rd pers. sg. and all plurals in pres. tense, all past tense forms of weak verbs, all non-finite forms. Recall from Section 4.1 that 97.5% of (C)V.CəT obstruent-final forms and 77% of sonorant-final forms resist lengthening in spite of meeting the conditions of initial stress on a short non-high vowel in an open syllable and a single intervocalic consonant. If verb forms meet that description more often than noun forms, we can hypothesize that the maintenance of disyllabicity within the paradigm is one of the factors determining the course of degemination.

The forms cited in (12–14) cover most of the relevant data in Britton (2012), with added examples. They are nevertheless samples, and a fully comprehensive survey of the inputs to degemination is still missing. The grain of newness here is that allophonic long consonants are not distributed equally across the lexicon in ME: since their realization depends positionally on adjacency to vowels on both sides and prosodically on the maintenance of a disyllabic word template, the more advanced state of schwa apocope in nouns entails that the history of degemination in ME should be detailed further: degemination in nouns vs. degemination in verbs, with the former a more advanced process than the latter.

This proposal gets analytical credibility in light of the PDE distributional facts and the comparison of learnability and acquisition of nouns vs. verbs. Sereno and Jongman (1997) attest to the "the skewed distribution of noun and verb base form

---

[37] Compare: OE *well ~ wella*, n. 'well', MED: *wel(le, wēl(la, weile*, (early, chiefly SWM) *wæl(le, wealle*.
[38] Sporadic lengthening in some verb forms may be analogical, e.g. ME *grippen* v. also *grēpe* may have been influenced by the OE noun *gripe, gripa*, attested 38 times vs. a single attestation of the verb *grippan* in the DOE.

frequencies in English" (1997: 428). They find that "[. . .] the relative frequency of *un*inflected compared with inflected forms is greater for nouns than for verbs" (1997: 425). While in PDE the plural noun -*(e)s* might hold learning advantages over the 3rd person sg. pres. tense -*(e)s* in verbs (Hsieh, Leonard, and Swanson 1999), the pre-syncope ME distributional facts about the verb inflections, including 2nd person sg. /-əs(t)/, weak past tense /-əd/, and pres. participles /-ənd/ would make the disyllabic stimuli much stronger in the acquisition and transmission of geminates in verbal forms.

On the hypothesis that geminate reduction is a phonetically driven process that led to the loss of a phonological distinction between $-VC_1V-$ and $-VC_1C_1V-$, the ordering of processes in ME will look like this:

(15) Morphologically-based ordering of degemination in ME:
        Nouns   Verbs
EME: $-VC_1C_1$ə $-VC_1C_1$ə(C)
LME $-VC$Ø $-VC_1C_1$ə(C) ~ - VC_1CØ

Britton (2012: 236) argued that "both the separate areal processes and the stage by stage loss of geminates are unnecessary postulates". I have also ignored areal differences in the ME records, in agreement with Britton, but I believe that even within the limited set of minimal pairs/minimal functional load of the contrast, the loss occurred in stages, affecting forms subject to apocope first, mostly nouns and adjectives, and then forms with syncope, mostly verbs. The long-term difference between these stages is obscured by paradigmatic analogy, but a truly detailed reconstruction of degemination should include a reference to morphological classes.

5 Degemination and language contact

Degemination in this study has been addressed as a system-internal change, yet some comments on contact-based influences are in order. Old Norse (ON), a major source of "other Germanic" lexical and grammatical influences in the transition period, had only velar gemination, i.e. /gg/, /kk/, in addition to many "long" consonants due to assimilation (Robinson 1992: 88). The voiced velar geminate /-gg-/ was rare in OE and contact with ON would have reinforced its presence (Hogg 1982; Lucas 1991). After apocope and degemination it became the source of /-g/#, which continues to be a very-low-frequency word-final phoneme in English.

Contact with ON is also behind the relative robustness of the early ME length contrast for the voiceless velar /-kk-/ : /-k-/.

In a bi- and tri-lingual scribal culture, Latin and Anglo-Norman must have been important models in manuscript preparation and copying. The merger of Late Latin geminates with the corresponding singletons is dated to c. 9th–11th century (Pope 1934: 147). The earlier voiceless geminate stops, e.g. *cuppa* 'cup', *gutta* 'drop', and *bucca* 'mouth', were shortened in Romance and remained voiceless: *copa*, *gota*, *boca*, *tera*; nevertheless, traditional spelling was often maintained (Pope 1934: 147, 281). Geminates were disallowed in Anglo-Norman, but more to the point, "the doubling of consonants came to be employed as a device for showing the open quality of the ę-sound" (Pope 1934: 287). The doubling of consonants as a diacritic in the Anglo-Norman practice may have strengthened the OE and ME tendency to use double consonants after short vowels (Section 3), which survives as a major orthographic pattern in English (fn. 19).

6 Discussion of results and envoy

In terms of syllable structure, the OE inherited and synchronically generated geminates satisfy Vennemann's Weight Law (1988: 30–32): the stressed syllable is bimoraic in accord with the universal preference for stress-to-weight correspondence. The Contact Law (Vennemann 1988: 40–50) is satisfied only weakly: ideally, across a syllable boundary the onset should be of higher consonantal strength than the coda, but by being of equal strength geminates do not violate the Contact Law and can be seen as a compromise in inputs with really low onset strength, as in WGG. Geminates are also in agreement with the first part of the Head Law, the preference for a syllable head with a single consonant, which would be in line with the early degemination in -$VC_1C_1C_2V$ forms (2.2. and Table 3). Degemination in English thus emerges as a diachronic process in which a preferential syllable structure is destabilized and ultimately abandoned stem-internally in favor of domain-final phonetically motivated changes, a language- and period-specific option which Vennemann also envisages (1988: 1–2, 43–49).[39] However,

---

[39] Compare the ME loss of geminates to the High German Consonant Shift in Old High German (Robinson 1992: 239–244, Fulk 2018: 133–137), which modified and generated geminates so that the intra-syllabic contact was either maintained or improved. Commenting on the possibility of the preference laws to express conflicting tendencies, and the impossibility of optimizing the system on all parameters at once, Vennemann (1988: 65) is in effect anticipating one of the main developments in the last decade of the 20th century based on the interaction of differently ranked and weighted phonological constraints.

one aspect of a more detailed scrutiny of degemination in English can be linked directly to the effect of the Contact Law.

The loss of final unstressed vowels in early ME -$\breve{V}C_1C_1$ə# eliminated the $\acute{V}$-V# environment where geminates were perceived as "long", leading to positional neutralization of -$\breve{V}C_1C_1$# and -$\breve{V}C$#. As argued in Britton (2012), the paucity of minimal pairs attested only with ten consonants, i.e. low functional load, had already "vastly weakened" the contrastiveness of geminates by c. 1200. The functional peripherality of the consonantal length contrast facilitated phonetically driven lenition.

The survey of geminate histories in the context of consonantal properties (Section 4.3) did not reveal any systematic or typologically coherent patterns. Since geminates are equal in consonantal strength, the Head Law and the Coda Law (Vennemann 1988: 13–27) would be in conflict in disyllabic -$\breve{V}C_1.C_1V$- structures, so no preference with respect to geminate longevity can be formulated. After apocope, the Head Law is no longer applicable, and the Coda Law applies vacuously. The coda is also the position of the highest degree of confusability, which is attested by sonorants (Wright 2004). The data available so far do not provide the empirical evidence for evaluating the relative weight of these factors in ME degemination.

The link between degemination and the Weight Law should also be noted. While apocope and word-final degemination keep the outcome in compliance with the Weight Law, one possible outcome of syncope violates that law: -$\breve{V}C_1.C_1VC_2$ ~ -$\breve{V}.C_1VC_2$ (see 4.4 and the last row in Table 5). If post-degemination -$\breve{V}.C_1VC$ forms survive, their longevity can be related to the preference for a filled onset, i.e. the Head Law, but the first syllable violates the Weight Law. The majority of the outcomes are -$\breve{V}.C_1C_2$ in conformity with the Weight Law, thus *banned*, *marred*, *hacked*; the exception being forms where syncope is blocked by the constraint on word-final *C_1C_1#, as in *kisses*, *misses*, where phonotactics overrides the Weight Law.

Finally, there is the previously unaddressed question of the interplay between morphological class and degemination. The lopsided lexical input for consonantal length in nouns and in verbs renders verb forms apparently more resistant to degemination (Section 4.4.). This provides a possible new insight into how the preference for geminates in terms of syllable contact (Vennemann 1988) was manifested in the course of the change. If we take into consideration the disproportionate rate of schwa-final forms in nouns and adjectives vs. paradigmatic stability of disyllabic forms in verbs, we can connect the morphologically conditioned persistence of -$\breve{V}C_1C_1$əC to the preference for a better syllabic structure in the disyllabic form. In an account along these lines, the Contact Law continues to be satisfied, while degemination violates it, though this advantage in terms of syllable structure was epiphenomenal and not sufficient to safeguard the geminates after the independent process of syncope.

The proposed step-wise loss of geminates is tentative and requires further corroboration. An important component in the reconstruction is inter-paradigmatic analogy, referred to in all studies of degemination but not documented in any systematic way. Similarly, stems used both as nouns and as verbs would have grammatically ambiguous forms and potentially lengthened variants noun forms such as *crope*, *croup* 'crop' would be rendered even more peripheral by the unlengthened disyllabic verb forms; e.g. all four cases and tokens of the verb 'to crop' in LAEME are disyllabic. The relationship between degemination, lenition, and ambisyllabicity is another direction of inquiry that warrants attention. The frequency of apocope vs. syncope in elision environments needs to be considered in detail. We also lack quantifiable information on individual frequencies and lexical and semantic specificity which could affect the rate of degemination. Variables such as speech styles and speech rate are beyond recovery.

By way of an *envoi*: "[. . .] it is difficult to decide when a change happened, or whether an apparent trend is a fact or an illusion" (Bermúdez-Otero 2012: 192). Still, we can search for and maybe identify new patterns, giving us a fuller idea of the preferences active before, during, and after the operation of a diachronic change and more generally allowing us to test theories of lexical access and diachronic stability in language.

References

Ben Hedia, Sonia. 2019. *Gemination and degemination in English affixation: Investigating the interplay between morphology, phonology and phonetics*. Berlin: Language Science Press.

Ben Hedia, Sonia & Ingo Plag. 2017. Gemination and degemination in English prefixation: Phonetic evidence for morphological organization. *Journal of Phonetics* 62. 34–49.

Bermúdez-Otero, Ricardo. 2012. Introduction to Part IV: When a knowledge of history is a dangerous thing. In David Denison, Ricardo Bermúdez-Otero, Christopher McCully & Emma Moore, with the assistance of Ayumi Miura (eds.), *Analysing Older English*, 187–194. Cambridge: Cambridge University Press.

Britton, Derek. 2012. Degemination in English, with special reference to the Middle English period. In David Denison, Ricardo Bermúdez-Otero, Christopher McCully & Emma Moore, with the assistance of Ayumi Miura (eds.), *Analysing Older English*, 232–244. Cambridge: Cambridge University Press.

Cameron, William Bruce. 1967. *Informal sociology: A casual introduction to sociological thinking*. New York: Random House.

Cho, Taehong & Patricia Keating. 2009. Effects of initial position versus prominence in English. *Journal of Phonetics* 37. 466–485.

Colman, Fran. 2014. *The Grammar of names in Anglo-Saxon England: The linguistics and culture of the Old English onomasticon*. Oxford: Oxford University Press.
CoNE: *A corpus of narrative etymologies from Proto-Old English to Early Middle English and accompanying corpus of changes*. Compiled by Roger Lass, Margaret Laing, Rhona Alcorn and Keith Williamson. http://www.lel.ed.ac.uk/ihd/CoNE/CoNE.html. Version 1.1, 2013–. Edinburgh: The University of Edinburgh.
Cruttenden, Alan. 2014. *Gimson's pronunciation of English*. 8th ed. London: Routledge.
Davis, Stuart. 2011. Geminates. In Marc van Oostendorp, Colin Ewen, Elizabeth Hume & Keren Rice (eds.), *The Blackwell companion to phonology*, 873–897. Malden, MA: Blackwell.
Dmitrieva, Olga. 2017. Production of geminate consonants in Russian: Implications for typology. In Haruo Kubuzono (ed.), *The phonetics and phonology of geminate consonants*, 34–66. Oxford: Oxford University Press.
Dmitrieva, Olga. 2018. The role of perception in the typology of geminate consonants: Effects of manner of articulation, segmental environment, position, and stress. *Language and Speech* 61. 43–70.
DOEC: *Dictionary of Old English corpus*. http://tapor.library.utoronto.ca/doecorpus/.
Fulk, Robert. 1996. Consonant doubling and open syllable lengthening in the Ormulum. *Anglia: Zeitschrift für englische Philologie* 114. 481–513.
Fulk, Robert. 2014. *An introductory grammar of Old English*. Tempe: Arizona Center for Medieval & Renaissance Studies.
Fulk, Robert. 2018. *A comparative grammar of the early Germanic languages*. Amsterdam: John Benjamins.
Goblirsch, Kurt. 2010. A historical typology of the English obstruent system. *Anglia* 127. 176–207.
Hankamer, Jorge & Aditi Lahiri. 1988. The timing of geminate consonants. *Journal of Phonetics* 16. 327–338.
Hayes, Bruce, Robert Kirchner & Donca Steriade. 2004. *Phonetically based phonology*. Cambridge: Cambridge University Press.
Hogg, Richard. 1982. Two geminate consonants in Old English? In John Anderson (ed.), *Language form and linguistic variation: Papers dedicated to Angus McIntosh*, 187–202. Amsterdam: John Benjamins.
Hogg, Richard. 1992. *A grammar of Old English*. Vol. 1. Oxford: Blackwell.
Hogg, Richard & Robert Fulk. 2011. *A grammar of Old English*. Vol. II: Morphology. Malden, MA: Wiley-Blackwell.
Holt, Eric. 1999. The moraic status of consonants from Latin to Hispano-Romance: The case of obstruents. In *Advances in Hispanic linguistics: Papers from the Second Hispanic Linguistics Symposium*, 166–181. Somerville, MA: Cascadilla Press.
Hsieh, Li, Laurence Leonard & Lori Swanson. 1999. Some differences between English plural noun inflections and third singular verb inflections in the input: The contributions of frequency, sentence position, and duration. *Journal of Child Language* 26. 531–543.
Idemaru, Kaori & Susan Guion. 2008. Acoustic covariants of length contrast in Japanese stops. *Journal of the International Phonetic Association* 38. 167–186.
Kirchner, Robert. 2000. Geminate inalterability and lenition. *Language* 76. 509–545.
Kirchner, Robert. 2004. Consonant lenition. In Bruce Hayes, Robert Kirchner & Donca Steriade (eds.), *Phonetically based phonology*, 313–345. Cambridge: Cambridge University Press.

Kotzor, Sandra, Benjamin Molineaux, Elanor Banks & Aditi Lahiri. 2016. "Fake" gemination in suffixed words and compounds in English and German. *The Journal of the Acoustical Society of America* 140. 356–367.

Kraehenmann, Astrid. 2001. Swiss German stops: Geminates all over the word. *Phonology* 18. 109–145.

Kubozono, Haruo (ed.). 2017. *The phonetics and phonology of geminate consonants*. Oxford: Oxford University Press.

Kuhn, Sherman. 1970. On the consonantal phonemes of Old English. In James Rosier (ed.), *Philological essays: Studies in Old and Middle English language and literature in honour of Herbert Dean Meritt*, 16–49. Mouton: The Hague.

Kurath, Hans. 1956. The loss of long consonants and the rise of voiced fricatives in Middle English. *Language* 32. 435–445.

Ladefoged, Peter & Ian Maddieson. 1996. *The sounds of the world's languages*. Oxford: Blackwell.

LAEME: *A linguistic atlas of Early Middle English*, 1150–1325. Compiled by Margaret Laing. http://www.lel.ed.ac.uk/ihd/laeme2/laeme2.html. Version 3.2, 2013. Edinburgh: The University of Edinburgh.

Lass, Roger. 1992. Phonology and morphology. In Norman Blake (ed.), *The Cambridge History of the English Language*, 23–155. Vol. 2. Cambridge: Cambridge University Press.

Lass, Roger. 1994. *Old English: A historical linguistic companion*. Cambridge: Cambridge University Press.

Lucas, Peter. 1991. Some aspects of the historical development of English consonant phonemes. *Transactions of the Philological Society* 89. 37–64.

Luick, Karl. 1914–1940. *Historische Grammatik der englischen Sprache*. Leipzig: Tauchnitz. 1964 reprint. Oxford: Basil Blackwell.

Lutz, Angelika. 1986. The syllabic basis of word division in Old English manuscripts. *English Studies* 67. 193–210.

Mailhammer, Robert. 2007. On syllable cut in the Orrmulum. In Christopher Cain & Geoffrey Russom (eds.), *Studies in the history of the English language III. Managing chaos: Strategies for identifying change in English*, 37–61. Berlin: de Gruyter.

Mailhammer, Robert. 2010. Thoughts on the genesis and the development of syllable cut in English. *Anglia: Zeitschrift für englische Philologie* 127. 261–282.

MED: Online edition in *Middle English Compendium*. Frances McSparran et al. (eds.), Ann Arbor: University of Michigan Library, 2000–2018. http://quod.lib.umich.edu/m/middle-english-dictionary/.

Minkoff, Marco. 1967. *English historical grammar*. Sofia: Naouka I Izkoustvo.

Minkova, Donka. 1991. *The history of final vowels in English*. Berlin: de Gruyter.

Minkova, Donka. 2014. *A historical phonology of English*. Edinburgh: Edinburgh University Press.

Minkova, Donka. 2015. Metrical resolution, spelling, and the reconstruction of Old English syllabification. In Michael Adams, Laurel Brinton & Robert Fulk (eds.), *Studies in the history of the English language VI: Evidence and method in histories of English*, 137–160. Berlin: de Gruyter.

Minkova, Donka. 2019. Examining the evidence for phonemic affricates: Middle English /tʃ/, /dʒ/ or [t-ʃ], [d-ʒ]? In Rhona Alcorn, Joanna Kopaczyk, Bettelou Los & Benjamin Molineaux (eds.), *Historical dialectology in the Digital Age*, 156–184. Edinburgh: Edinburgh University Press.

Minkova, Donka & Michael Lefkowitz. 2019. The history of /-n/ loss in English: Phonotactic change with lexical and grammatical specificity. *Folia Linguistica* 40. 203–230.

Minkova, Donka & Michael Lefkowitz. 2020. Middle English open syllable lengthening (MEOSL) or Middle English compensatory lengthening (MECL)? *English Language and Linguistics* 24. 1–26.

Morén, Bruce. 2013. *Distinctiveness, coercion and sonority: A unified theory of weight.* New York: Routledge.

Muller, Jennifer. 2001. The phonology and phonetics of word-initial geminates. Columbus, OH: Ohio State University dissertation.

Murray, Robert. 1995. Orm's phonological-orthographic interface and quantity in Early Middle English. In *Quantitatsproblematik und Metrik: Greifswalder Symposion zur germanischen Grammatik.* [Special issue]. *Amsterdamer Beitrage zur älteren Germanistik* 42. 125–147.

Murray, Robert. 2000. Syllable cut prosody in Early Middle English. *Language* 76. 617–654.

Oh, Grace & Melissa Redford. 2012. The production and phonetic representation of fake geminates in English. *Journal of Phonetics* 40. 82–91.

Page, Richard. 2006. The diachrony and synchrony of vowel quantity in English and Dutch. *Diachronica* 23. 61–104.

Payne, Elinor. 2005. Phonetic variation in Italian consonant gemination. *Journal of the International Phonetic Association* 35. 153–181.

Peters, Robert. 1967. Phonic and phonemic long consonants in Old English. *Studies in Linguistics* 19. 1–4.

Peters, Robert. 1968. *A linguistic history of English.* Boston: Houghton Mifflin.

Pope, Mildred Katharine. 1934. *From Latin to Modern French with especial consideration of Anglo-Norman: Phonology and morphology.* Manchester: Manchester University Press.

Ringen, Catherine & Robert Vago. 2011. Geminates: Heavy or long? In Charles Cairns & Azra Ali (eds.), *Handbook of the syllable*, 155–169. Leiden: Brill.

Robinson, Orrin. 1992. *Old English and its closest relatives: A survey of the earliest Germanic languages.* London: Routledge.

Ryan, Kevin. 2019. *Prosodic weight: Categories and continua.* Oxford: Oxford University Press.

Schein, Barry & Donca Steriade. 1986. On geminates. *Linguistic Inquiry* 17. 691–744.

Sereno, Joan & Allard Jongman. 1997. Processing of English inflectional morphology. *Memory & Cognition* 25. 425–437.

Wright, Joseph & Elizabeth Mary Wright. 1925. *Old English grammar.* 3rd ed. Oxford: Oxford University Press.

Wright, Richard. 2004. A review of perceptual cues and cue robustness. In Bruce Hayes, Robert Kirchner & Donca Steriade (eds.), *Phonetically based phonology*, 34–57. Cambridge: Cambridge University Press.

Vennemann, Theo. 1988. *Preference laws for syllable structure and the explanation of sound change.* Berlin: de Gruyter.

Vennemann, Theo. 2000. From quantity to syllable cuts: On so-called lengthening in the Germanic languages. *Italian Journal of Linguistics* 12. 251–282.

Zuraw, Kie. 2009. Treatments of weakness in phonological theory. In Donka Minkova (ed.), *Phonological weakness in English*, 9–28. Basingstoke: Palgrave Macmillan.

Patrizia Noel Aziz Hanna
The principle of scopal serialisation: Wackernagel position and mirrored Wackernagel position

Abstract: According to Vennemann's principle of natural serialisation (1983), ideally, all constituent operators are placed on the same side of their operands/heads, that is, [Operator [Operand]] in OV languages and [[Operand] Operator] in VO languages. In this paper, unidirectional serialisation is extended to scopal ordering of elements in Wackernagel position and in the sentence-final "mirrored" Wackernagel position. The "principle of scopal serialisation", which claims that everything else being equal, having scopal serialisation in the Wackernagel positions is preferred to not having scopal serialisation, is introduced as a part of syntactic preference theory. Different directions of serialisation are discussed with respect to their contribution to syntactic iconicity.

1 Preference theory in syntax: Placement and directionality

Preference theory implies that syntactic structures stand in evaluable relations to each other. Comparative value concepts can either be "better" or "equal in value to"; there is either (strict) preference or indifference (Halldén 1957; cf. Hansson and Grüne-Yanoff 2018 for an overview). In language contact situations, left-headed syntax can turn into right-headed syntax and vice versa (cf. Vennemann 2003), which shows that the order of meaningful elements is open to change for speakers – within limits. One of the factors constraining syntactic order is directionality. Directionality is part of the cognitive foundations of languages and a major variable in the production of connected speech (cf. e.g. Levelt 1989 for the real time restriction on speech planning as well as look-ahead and Lee, Brown-Schmidt, and

---

Acknowledgements: For my teacher Theo Vennemann on the occasion of his 80th birthday. I would like to thank Laura Catharine Smith (Provo/UT) and Yeonsuk Yun (Bamberg) as well as the anonymous referees for valuable comments.

Patrizia Noel Aziz Hanna, Department of German Linguistics, Otto-Friedrich-Universität Bamberg, Bamberg/Germany

https://doi.org/10.1515/9783110721461-013

Watson 2013 for a discussion of ways of looking ahead in language production). Consistent word order is unidirectional. As has often been noted, unidirectionality is not the rule in the languages of the world; it is understood in this article as a preference. The analysis presented in this paper concentrates on two aspects: 1) anchor points and 2) direction of serialisation. More precisely, serialisations and anchor points are investigated for the Wackernagel position[1] and the "mirrored" Wackernagel position (Figure 1). An "anchor point" indicates the starting point of the structure under investigation, while "direction of serialisation" refers to its unidirectional orientation.

Wackernagel position	"Rest of sentence"	Mirrored Wackernagel position

Figure 1: Simplified sentence pattern with respect to Wackernagel position.

The directions of serialisation will be observed with respect to the two Wackernagel positions and the "rest of sentence". The term "rest of sentence" is used here in a pretheoretical sense as the part of the sentence that is "embraced" by the Wackernagel position and the mirrored Wackernagel position.

In the rest of sentence, the order of meaningful elements, as a preference, follows from unidirectional serialisation. Indeed, it was by interpreting insights from Greenberg (1963) and Lehmann (1972) that Vennemann extracted the principle of natural serialisation. According to this principle, all constituent operators are ideally placed on the same side of their operands/heads, that is, [Operator [Operand]] in OV languages and [[Operand] Operator] in VO languages[2] (Bartsch and Vennemann 1972: 136, Vennemann 1974: 347), cf. Figure 2:

---

[1] Although Wackernagel elements (e.g. co-ordinating sentence conjunctions, question particles, adverbial connectors, and object pronouns) do not belong to the same word class, they shared their placement in second position in the oldest Indo-European languages (Wackernagel 1892). In a large number of today's Indo-European languages, a subset of their etymological or functional continuations occurs in first position (cf. Noel Aziz Hanna 2015). In both scenarios – first and second position – Wackernagel position refers to sentence beginnings, whereas the "mirrored" Wackernagel position refers to the endings of sentences.

[2] The operator is a specifier of the operand. [Operator [Operand]] is preferred in OV languages, which are therefore called "right-headed". [[Operand] Operator] is preferred in VO languages, which are therefore called "left-headed". The preferred relative order of adposition and noun phrase serves as an example. According to the principle of natural serialisation, the preferred relative order is hypothesised to be adposition before noun phrase in VO languages; VO languages are post-specifying. In OV languages, the preferred relative order of adposition and noun phrase is hypothesised to be noun phrase before adposition; OV languages are pre-specifying.

{Operator {Operand}} ⇒ { [Operator [Operand]] in OV languages
                         [[Operand] Operator] in VO languages

Figure 2: Principle of natural serialisation.

More generally, Vennemann's principle of natural serialisation formulates preferred directionality in syntax:

> Everything else being equal, having unidirectional serialization is preferred to not having unidirectional serialization.
> (Vennemann 1983: 12).

The principle of natural serialisation has been debated repeatedly (e.g. Hawkins 1984, Ehala 1999, Roberts 2007: § 2.5). For the relative position of object, verb, and adposition, the plausibility of a serialisation principle governing the relative order of syntactic constituents has been confirmed on a broad typological basis (Dryer 2013b). For an illustration of this theory of basic word order, cf. (1). The example shows natural serialisation in the German subordinate clause, with numbers indicating the order of specificational application. Serialisation in the unmarked Modern German sentence is organised according to the serialisation of the subordinate clause, which has OV syntax. In the example, the constituent with the next higher number is the operator of the respective (following) operand (Vennemann 1984: 630).

(1) Natural serialisation in the German subordinate clause

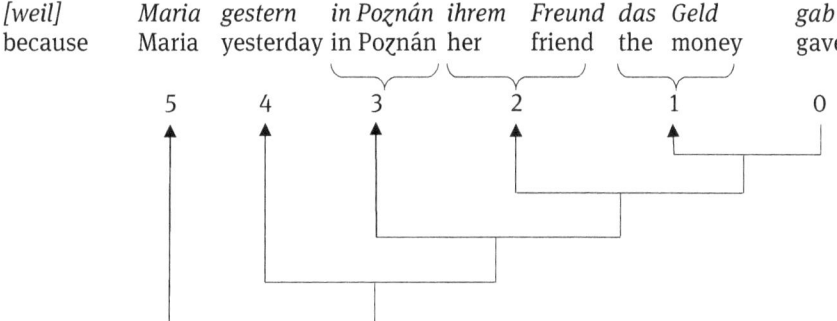

'because Maria gave the money to her friend in Poznán yesterday'

The principle of natural serialisation encompasses two components determining basic word order. The first one, obviously, is serialisation. The second one is position, since the principle implicitly relates to the "anchor", the orientation point from which serialisation starts.

To give an example, the syntax of Proto-Indo-European is usually reconstructed as right-headed (e.g. Lehmann 1974, Baldi 1979). Thus, the highest heads are expected to be placed at the end of the sentence. There are, however, systematic exceptions, since some heads can introduce sentences in old Indo-European languages. For instance, old Indo-European question particles behave strangely with respect to their placement in the sentence. Traditionally, the special placement of the question particle in prepositional old Indo-European languages has been classified as a manifestation of Wackernagel's Law, cf. (2) for the example of Latin -*ne*.

(2) Cicero, In Catilinam 1, 1,14
*non-**ne*** *etiam* *alio* *incredibili* *scelere* *hoc* *scelus*
not-Q even another- incredible- crime- this- crime-
 AblSgN AblSgN AblSgN AkkSgN AkkSgN
cumulavisti?
pile-2SgPerfIndAct
'Didn't you even top this crime with another incredible crime?'

It may be that the conspicuous early placement of clitics like the question particle in OV languages was the reason why Wackernagel position was even discovered by Delbrück (1878) and Wackernagel (1892) – sentence-initial placement of syntactic heads in VO languages would have been rather unspectacular.[3] Instead of the expected sentence-final anchor, Greenberg's Universal 9 applies, with Proto-Indo-European predominantly having prepositions.

> *Universal 9.* With well more than chance frequency, when question particles or affixes are specified in position by reference to the sentence as a whole, if initial, such elements are found in prepositional languages, and, if final, in postpositional.
> (Greenberg 1963)

Greenberg's Universal 9 is well documented. In left-headed Classical Arabic, for instance, the question particle introduces the sentence (3); in right-headed Japanese, the question particle is placed at the end of the sentence (4).

(3) Arab. *hal* *al-* *waladu* *sagheer?*
 Q the boy small?
 'Is the boy small?'
 (https://en.wikibooks.org/wiki/Arabic/YesNoQuestions; 08.08.19)

---

[3] Sentence-initial placement of syntactic heads, which are specified by the rest of sentence, is expected according to the principle of natural serialisation, since VO languages are post-specifying.

(4) Jap. *Zuhyoo no shita ni   ano kaigyoo maaku   deteimasu deshoo   ka*
Table NO below NI that paragraph mark appear-ASP-CONJ-fml INT
'Is there the carriage mark displayed?' (Teruya 2006: 173)

In accordance with Universal 9, old Indo-European question particles occur sentence-initially; the placement of the question particle is harmonic with adpositional placement (here: prepositions). Adpositional placement, however, has been confirmed on a cross-linguistic basis (see above) to be harmonic with the placement of object and verb, which means that natural serialisation and Universal 9 cannot be reconciled for old Indo-European languages. In addition, Greenberg's data-driven Universal 9 is surprising, since the position of the verb has to be excluded in order to fit the data. How can this be motivated?

I will propose extending unidirectional serialisation to the scopal ordering of elements in both Wackernagel position and in the sentence-final mirrored Wackernagel position. This means two possible anchor points: the beginning and the end of a sentence. Figure 3 gives the different directions of serialisation resulting from unidirectionality for natural and scopal serialisation, which will be discussed in the subsequent sections.

Wackernagel position	"Rest of sentence"	Mirrored Wackernagel position
Scopal serialisation ⟶	Natural serialisation OV ⟵ VO ⟶	Scopal serialisation ⟵

Figure 3: Natural and scopal serialisation.

After an account of the Wackernagel position and the mirrored Wackernagel position in the framework of preference theory is provided, the principle of scopal serialisation will be introduced. Opposing serialisation directions will be discussed with respect to their contribution to syntactic iconicity. Observations with respect to the functions of elements in Wackernagel positions are closely related to studies on sentence-final discourse particles (cf. e.g. the surveys in Hancil, Post, and Haselow 2015 and Beeching and Detges 2014a) as well as to 19th century studies in Indo-European syntax.

2 Wackernagel position and the principle of scopal serialisation

Wackernagel's Law leads to a close observation of sentence beginnings and endings as anchor points from which the serialisation of elements starts.

2.1 Anchor point

Wackernagel's Law (as outlined in Jakob Wackernagel's original version) refers to elements[4] such as co-ordinating sentence conjunctions, question particles, adverbial connectors, and object pronouns, which in the oldest Indo-European languages occur sentence-initially or more precisely as the second word (5). Functionally, the German co-ordinating sentence conjunction *oder* can be related to Latin *-ve* 'or' in Wackernagel position, German *nämlich* to Latin *enim* 'namely' in Wackernagel position, and German *aber* 'but' to Latin *autem*. In a number of modern Indo-European languages, etymologically or functionally equivalent elements occur in first instead of second position; some occur in both positions (5').

(5) Positions of Wackernagel elements
his　　　***autem***　*de*　　*rebus*　　　　*sol*
this-ABL.PL　but　　about　thing-ABL.PL.F　sun-NOM.SG.M
me　　　　*ille*　　　　　*admonuit*
me-AKK.SG　THAT-NOM.SG.M　admonish-3SG.PRF.IND.ACT.
'that sun, however, admonished me about these things'
Cicero, De oratore 3, 209 (cf. Wackernagel 1892: 408)

(5') ***Aber*** *sie*　 (***aber***)　*erinnerte*　*mich*　*an*　*die*　*erste*
but　 she　　(but)　　reminded　me　　on　　the　　first
Zweitligasaison　　　　　　*nach*　*dem*　*Zwangsabstieg*
season in the second division　after　the　　forced relegation
'**but** it reminded me of the first season in the second division after the forced relegation'
(https://zebrastreifenblog.wordpress.com/tag/fc-st-pauli/; 08.04.19)

---

4 Only some of the elements are indeed clitics according to phonological standards. For others, clitichood was (and is still) stipulated because of their second placement. Taking phonology seriously, it is clear that clitichood does not result in second placement but is a local effect.

The placement of Wackernagel elements "as soon as possible" in the sentence means the beginning of the sentence as an anchor point for serialisation. Second position placement is derivable for Wackernagel elements as an interaction between information structure, phonology, and syntax and is from a typological perspective best generalised as the placement of Wackernagel elements "as soon as possible" – thus including first and even later sentence-initial position placement besides second position of functionally equivalent elements (for an overview of theoretical positions and for the interplay of factors motivating this difference in position, cf. Noel Aziz Hanna 2015). According to the principle of natural serialisation, heads such as co-ordinating sentence conjunctions and interrogative particles are expected to be placed at the end instead of the beginning of sentences in OV languages. Why, then, can Wackernagel elements be placed at all in sentence-initial position rather than their expected sentence-final position in Indo-European languages?

The answer is in the function of elements. The whole set of sentence-initial Wackernagel elements contributes to coherence and cohesion as well as to recipient-directed discourse organisation. For the recipient's sentence comprehension, it is only reasonable that a sentence is indicated as, for instance, interrogative, conjoined, or pronominally tied to the pretext as early in the sentence as possible. A co-ordinating sentence conjunction at the ending of the second sentence, sentence-final interrogative particles, or thematic object pronouns at the endings of sentences do not offer the same benefits for the above-mentioned functions when compared to their initial placement. Nevertheless, there are occurrences of these elements in sentence-final position; furthermore, they do not represent exceptions (cf. section 3).

2.2 Direction of serialisation

Apart from the anchor point, the serialisation of Wackernagel elements has been a focus of attention from the beginning, i.e. starting with Delbrück's and Wackernagel's descriptions of the phenomenon. Negation particles precede object pronouns (Wackernagel 1892: 336), and particles precede enclitics (Delbrück 1900: § 22). Since those early studies, a scopal order of Wackernagel elements has been established for Hittite (Luraghi 1990, 1997). A corpus analysis[5] (Noel Aziz Hanna

---

5 SQL database with texts from Old High German to Early New High German (119 texts of different length and genre, > 190,000 sentences, > 1,900,000 words). I would like to thank Christian Riepl (IT Group LMU Munich) for creating the structure of the database.

2015) revealed the same organisational principle for German: a fixed serialisation of elements throughout German language history. Unlike the old Indo-European Wackernagel chain, however, the German chain is "virtual", since it is interrupted, for instance, by other function words (6), by the prefield, and by the finite verb in V2 position (7 with Figure 4):

(6) Old High German <u>Endi</u> so   ir   <u>auur</u> dhuo <u>ni</u>   uuas huuerfandi
                      and   so   he   but   then   not   was   turn back
'And so he did not turn back then' (*Isidor* XXIX, 11–13)

(7) Standard German <u>Und</u> nun <u>also</u> hat <u>ihm</u> der Geist Gottes
                     and   now   so   has   him   the   spirit God–GEN
                     heimgeleutet.
                     lead.home
'And now the spirit of God led him home.' (https://predigten.evangelisch.de/predigt/ predigt-zu-apostelgeschichte- 9431021-35-von-heinrich-braunschweiger, 18.03.19)

co-ordinating sentence conjunction	(interrupted chain)	adverbial connectors	(interrupted chain)	object pronoun
	↑		↑	
	prefield		V2	
und	nun	also	hat	ihm

Figure 4: Interrupted Wackernagel chain.

Since chains like Old High German *endi* 'and', *auur* 'but', and *ni* 'not' and Standard German *und* 'and', *also* 'so', and *ihm* 'him' are interrupted, the Wackernagel chain is no longer as obvious as it was in the old Indo-European languages. The old Indo-European languages had chains of adjacent Wackernagel elements, which because of their contiguity and (for some elements) because of their clitichood formed conceptual groups in the sense of Langacker (1997: 1). Nevertheless, the corpus analysis showed that the order of elements in the Wackernagel chain is without exception for the German data. The chain has been stable throughout the centuries with respect to the serialisation principle and at the same time dynamic with respect to the lexical elements filling this position. Figure 5 illustrates the results of the serialisation query, supplemented by Gothic data.

| co-ordinating sentence conjunctions | sentence mood markers | adverbial connectors | object pronouns |

Figure 5: Preferred serialisation in the Wackernagel chain[6].

Co-ordinating sentence conjunctions precede sentence mood markers. The latter are followed by adverbial connectors, then the sentence negation, and then object pronouns. As a matter of course, this selection of Germanic Wackernagel elements does not represent the complete chain of universally possible Wackernagel elements. Their order, however, is derivable – Wackernagel elements follow strict scopal serialisation. The scope of the more peripheral element is larger than the less peripheral one. Co-ordinating sentence conjunctions relate to two clauses and thus have the widest scope. Sentence mood markers like the Gothic interrogative particle -*u* or Latin -*ne* mark the state of sentence by determining sentence mood. Thus they are the second-highest heads in the above-mentioned hierarchy. Adverbial connectors follow this group. With respect to scope, object pronouns are the lowest in the hierarchy of German Wackernagel elements.

Complementing the serialisation data by Wackernagel, Delbrück, and Luraghi with the German data, I suggest the principle of scopal serialisation as a syntactic preference:

> Principle of scopal serialisation:
> Everything else being equal, having scopal serialisation in the Wackernagel positions is preferred to not having scopal serialisation.

Deviations from this principle require an explanation. To give an example of such a deviation, Dunkel (1992: 165–166) notes that while the chain of sentence-initial particles in the Anatolian languages was still transparent, the particles were continued in Late Indo-European as "frozen" pronominal stems or adverbs, while a new generation of particle chains evolved in the individual languages.

The obvious question is what unidirectionality means with respect to scope in the Wackernagel positions. Does unidirectionality pertain to the complete sentence or are chains of Wackernagel elements unidirectional but show asymmetric serialisation at beginnings and endings of sentences? What are the cognitive advantages of either solution from the perspective of preference theory?

---

6 Topicalised object pronouns were excluded from observation, since they do not occur in Wackernagel position.

3 The mirrored Wackernagel position

Apart from sentence-initial position, co-ordinating sentence conjunctions, interrogative particles, and adverbial connectors do occur in sentence-final position as part of core grammar. Sentence-final particles are typical of the languages of East Asia, like Japanese, Korean, and Cantonese; recently, they have also been investigated as sentence-final (discourse) particles of European languages (e.g. Beeching and Detges 2014a, Hancil, Post, and Haselow 2015[7]). In this section, Wackernagel's Law will be connected to research on East Asian final particles and on Indo-European final particles. The sentence-final location of Wackernagel elements will be referred to as the "mirrored" Wackernagel position. Both the principle of scopal serialisation in the mirrored Wackernagel position and the function of elements in this position will be addressed.

3.1 Anchor point

The mirrored Wackernagel position is generalised as the placement of Wackernagel elements "as late as possible", including final, penultimate, etc., placement, with the ending of the sentence as an anchor point. Placement in the mirrored Wackernagel position does not support the default function of Wackernagel position elements, i.e. cohesion, coherence, and recipient-directed discourse organisation. Preference theory predicts better options to be preferred over worse ones, which means that there has to be a good reason for the systematic occurrence of conventionalised or emergent sentence-final placement.

At this point, it is necessary to state commonalities and differences with respect to the categorical status of Wackernagel elements vs. discourse particles. Wackernagel elements, like co-ordinating conjunctions, adverbial connectors, and object pronouns, form a historically derived class that serves established functions. Unlike prototypical discourse particles like extra-sentential *well* or *I mean*, which are items "defined in relation to units of talk, rather than a more finely defined unit such as sentence, proposition, speech act, or tone unit" (Schiffrin 1987: 31), Wackernagel elements are typically integrated into the sentence and not necessarily optional. Discourse particles include optional sentence-final interjections like Dutch *hoor* 'hear' and *zeg* 'say' (van der Wouden and Foolen 2015), sentence-final adverbs like Norwegian *da* 'then' (Fretheim 2015), and sentence-final disjuncts like

---

[7] Beeching and Detges (2014b) investigate the functions of utterance-final vs. utterance-initial placement of discourse particles. Hancil, Post, and Haselow (2015) aim at demonstrating that sentence-final particles form a category of their own.

naturally and *probably* (Gómez-Moreno 2015), which are clearly not Wackernagel elements. Nevertheless, there is an overlapping of categories, since connectors like Korean *nuntey* 'but' (Sohn 2015) and sentence mood markers like the Japanese conditional particle *-ba* (Shinzato 2015) form part of the discussion of discourse particles and represent typical functions of Wackernagel elements. Therefore, the topics of sentence-final discourse particles and elements in the mirrored Wackernagel position converge; Wackernagel position and the mirrored Wackernagel position are related to, but not identical to, the position of discourse particles discussed in the context of the left and right sentence peripheries.

In the Indo-European languages, co-ordinating sentence conjunctions belong to the second of the conjoined sentences.[8] Sentence-final co-ordinating sentence conjunctions at the end of the second conjunct are counterintuitive, essentially because they cannot fulfil their default linking function at the end of a sentence or even at the end of an utterance. Despite this seeming functional disadvantage, they do occur in final position. Mulder and Thompson (2008) observed systematic placement of *but* in Australian English and, with this observation, started the interest in the sentence-final placement of Indo-European particles (8).

(8) Got a few mates who play jazz. Not my kind of music, **but**. And them musos drink like wharfies, a man can't hardly keep up with them. I'll come round about lunchtime tomorrow, all right? Today, I mean,' said Bert, noting that the church clock said half past twelve. (Greenwood, *Murder in Montparnasse*; Mulder and Thompson 2008: 180)

In comparing initial and final Australian English *but*, Mulder and Thompson note that sentence-final *but* has developed into a particle for Australian speakers. The particle is often followed by a substantial pause and considered by the speaker to end a turn (Mulder and Thompson 2008: 188) with "no implication of semantically contrastive material left "hanging" by the final *but*" (2008: 191). The same has been observed for regional usage of the German sentence-co-ordinating conjunction *aber* 'but', which can also end an intonation unit and a turn and has been recorded occurring in sentence-final position, for example in the region of Brandenburg (9). Haselow (2015: 91) comments that final *aber* "restricts the validity of X which it accompanies, as it implies the presence of a proposition Y that works against X." Sentence-final *aber* can be prosodically integrated into the sentence. Another German sentence-co-ordinating conjunction, *oder* 'or', has been described in sentence-final position for Swiss German (10). Sentence-final

---

[8] According to Ross (1986: 100), this applies to all clitic conjunctions.

oder is in this function clearly not used as a tag question; typical tag questions are tentative in nature and non-integrated. For Dutch, van der Wouden and Foolen list a sentence-final adverbial connector, "link[ing] the utterance to an earlier one" (2015: 231). The correspondent to Dutch sentence-final *namelijk* (11) is also attested in German with sentence-final *nämlich*:

(9) *Also wenn du mal gegenditscht ist nicht so 'schlimm aber.* (0.34) (Haselow 2015: 90)
'It is not a problem if you accidentally bump against the foam rubber mat from time to time *aber*.'

(10) *Dann gehen Sie zuerst geradeaus oder, dann links in die Bahnhofstraße, und dann auf der rechten Seite sind Sie da oder.* (Heine, Kaltenböck, and Kuteva 2015: 127)
'Then you go first straight on, then turn left into the Bahnhofstraße, and then on the right side you are there *oder*.'

(11) *et smaakt alsof het losse thee is namelijk.* (van der Wouden and Foolen 2015: 233)
'because it tastes like tea leaves *namelijk*.'

Wackernagel elements, just like typical sentence-final particles (Hancil, Post, and Haselow 2015: 16), are prosodically integrated into the clause and not focused. In addition, neither the occurrence of Wackernagel elements nor the occurrence of final particles depends on basic word order. Wackernagel elements are integrated into "basic syntax" (or at least interact with it as in the case of vocatives, cf. Noel Aziz Hanna 2019); in contrast to typical sentence-final particles (Hancil, Post, and Haselow 2015: 16), they participate in the organisation of sentence structure. This will be demonstrated by the example of German *und und und* "and and and" in the mirrored Wackernagel position.

Sentence-final *und und und* is a multipart co-ordinating sentence conjunction. As a sentence conjunction, *und* has wide scope. Since the function of co-ordinating sentence conjunctions is linkage, the limitation of triple *und* to final position is, at first, confusing. This is reflected by the fact that native speakers argue against its use[9] and also by the wish to clarify the normative aspect of

---

[9] 'Please resist the temptation of ending a listing with the words *und und und*! It is grammatically incorrect, stylistically hackneyed und has no meaning (http://www.texten.at/und-und-und-drei-worter-null-bedeutung/; 04.12.17; transl. PN).

whether commas should be inserted between *und und und* or not.[10] The intonation and prosody of *und und und* with even a "built-in" pause explicitly signals the end of sentence. The pause is built-in, because the third *und* is rhythmically prominent, which regularly means that a pause (the drop, metrically speaking) follows before the next sentence or utterance starts. For an example of an encoded pause in a written text see (12) in which the punctuation, besides indicating emotionality, signals the pause. *Und und und* is both prosodically and syntactically integrated into the preceding sentence.

(12) *Wie im Himmel ist sowas :) ein Wunder der Natur und ein Geschenk Gottes! Geniesst es und und und...! :) Vielleicht les ich ja doch nochmal von dir! :)*
http://www.sommersprossenzeit.at/2016/02/17/papa-mama-dein-grosser-bruder-und-du/ (04.12.17)
'It's like in heaven :) A miracle of nature and a gift of God! Enjoy it *"und und und"*! Maybe I will hear from you again! :) '

(13) is an example of spoken language, also displaying an annotated pause after *und und und* (*Datenbank für gesprochenes Deutsch* DGD):

(13)   Sentence-final *und und und*, DGD, BW--_E_00042_SE_01_T_01
    0158 ROLF und eh * na ja da ham wir dann eben och * vieles noch eh versucht zu improvisieren um ihnen da erstmal aus der patsche zu helfen.
    0159 UM hmhm, hmhm;
    0160 ROLF zum beispiel schulbücher die bei uns eben nich mehr so: unbedingt jebraucht wurden dann rüber das se dann erstmal mit arbeiten konnten **und und und** (2.0)
    0161 UM und wie warn da so die kontakte zwischen den kollegen? ehm kam man da ganz gut mitnander aus oder?
'And uh well, then we have tried to improvise in order to help them. – hmhm, hmhm – Schoolbooks, for example, which are not needed here so much any more, then to them, so they could start working with them *und und und*. – And how were contacts between colleagues? Uh did one get on well?'

The triple co-ordinating sentence conjunction *und und und* is an element of the mirrored Wackernagel position. While Latin *-que* is a Wackernagel clitic and just

---

[10] A platform answered with reference to a reference book on orthography that commas should be placed. (https://www.korrekturen.de/forum.pl/md/read/id/42418/sbj/und-und-und/; 04.12.17)

like its functional equivalent German *und* occurs in the beginning of the sentence, *und und und* ends a sentence and regularly an utterance as in (13). Obviously, it does not carry the same function as sentence-initial *und*. It refers to a (long) list, and the producer takes the recipient to be able to complement its implications. In this way, *und und und* refers to shared knowledge. Thus, apart from a conjunction, *und und und* is also an emotive marker, calling on the addressee's solidarity.

A second example is the German adverbial connector *nämlich* 'namely'. Its functional correspondent Lat. *enim* has been classified by Wackernagel (1892: 416) as a Wackernagel element occurring in second position. Just like Lat. *enim*, *nämlich* can be placed in second position (14):

(14) *Der Direktor war froh, dass der Flughafen bestehen bleiben konnte. Er nämlich wusste den Charme des Althergebrachten zu schätzen.* (http://www.elk.ee/?page_id=13102; 07.12.17)
'The director was glad that the airport was kept on. He appreciated the charm of the traditional.'

Nämlich in Wackernagel position ties up to the preceding context and, at the same time, focuses the sentence-initial element (in this case: *er* 'he'). Obviously, the function of *nämlich* in the mirrored Wackernagel position is significantly different from the sentence-initial one, as (15) illustrates:

(15) Sentence-final *nämlich*, DGD, FOLK_E_00229_SE_01_T_01_DF_01
```
0012   AS   dass natürlich des bekannteste genommen wird
0013        (0.37)
0014   AS   e kleines fläschje mit zehn em el [is des]
0015   EM                                     [klein is okay j]a genau
0016        (1.24)
0017   AS   so (.) des macht schön die nase frei gell ma kann wieder atmen
0018        (1.1)
0019   AS   un[d kann auch d]ann gut einschlafe nä[mlich]
0020   EM     [das will ich hoffen]
0021   EM                                         [he] h[e he]
```
'That the most well-known is bought. (0.37) That's a a little flask with ten ml is this. – Small is ok, yes, ok. – (1.24) – So. This clears the nose, right, one can breathe again (1.1) and can easily fall asleep *nämlich*. – I do hope so. Hehehe.'

Apart from the obvious differences, both Wackernagel and mirrored Wackernagel position share a recipient-directed function. Wackernagel position is recipient-directed because cohesion, coherence, and discourse-organising strategies are employed in order to assist recipients with the correct interpretation of a sentence by explicitly setting it in context. In contrast to sentence-initial elements in Wackernagel position, however, elements in the mirrored Wackernagel position are involved in turn-taking in its wider sense. The mirrored Wackernagel position is recipient-directed, handing over the turn by means of e.g. a question particle, by lexically closing the turn, or by modalising discourse-structuring (stance) (cf. Beeching and Detges 2014b for a discussion of sentence-initial vs. sentence-final position of discourse markers).

It is not trivial to cross-linguistically assume functional identity for sentence-initial and sentence-final particles. This becomes clear, for instance, in Japanese question particles.[11] The functional motivation of the late placement of these particles is their part in communicative interaction:[12]

> The Negotiator is realized at the end of the clause where the speaker is just about to hand over to the addressee [...]; both Predicator and Negotiator thus create the "finale" of the clause as an interactive move. (Teruya 2006: 48–49)

The interactional function of sentence-final particles seems to collide with the functional motivation of early particle placement in Wackernagel position. Negotiators are typically placed sentence-finally (Teruya 2006: 169), which in the case of question particles means that at least the lexical indication of sentence mood is delayed. According to Dryer (2013a), most question particles occur sentence-finally, which is in need of a motivation.[13] In the context of this paper,

---

11 "[T]he negotiator is realized by various interpersonal particles, such as *ka* か, *ne* ね, *yo* よ, etc., with each adding different interpersonal negotiatory value to the clause. The negotiator is generally located at the end of the clause, immediately after the Predicator. [...] *ka* か is the prototypical question particle, in the sense that it is comparatively less restricted in the type of mood it can turn into a question." (Teruya 2006: 169)

12 A number of publications focus on the grammaticalisation of sentence-final particles, which take their origin in sentence-initial ones (cf. e.g. Hancil, Post, and Haselow 2015 for references). The question arises whether this is a generalisation based on Indo-European evidence. Onodera (2004: 157) argues that the Japanese interjections/markers of involvement "*ne* and *na* first emerged in sentence-final and sentence-internal positions, then later began to occur in initial positions as interjections and discourse markers" (cf. also Iida 2018: 72). Another open question addressed by Yap, Yang, and Wong (2014) is whether there is a difference in grammaticalisation paths between languages with sentence-final particles and VO vs. OV basic word order.

13 Out of 884 languages, 181 have sentence-initial question particles (including second position placement), while 314 have sentence-final question particles. This combines with VO/OV word order (456 hits for both features in the WALS database, with 406 OV languages and 403 VO languages) in the following way: sentence-initial question particle and VO: 102; sentence-initial

this constellation leads to the question of why elements in the mirrored Wackernagel position are frequent, i.e. why they are not dispreferred.

One answer is phonological signalling. For Japanese, Teruya notes that interrogative mood may be signalled by intonation. This is also the case for the tone language Cantonese, which has a number of sentence-final question particles; it has been argued that statement and question intonation was mainly identified by the final syllable. Ma, Ciocca, and Whitehill (2011: 1014) criticise that the non-final part of a sentence was rarely discussed in the perception of questions and hypothesise that "listeners would be equally accurate in identifying the intonation of the complete sentences and of the isolated final syllables, and that they would perform more poorly for the carriers [sentences without the final syllable; PN]". Their results supported their hypothesis.[14] In addition, they propose that Cantonese listeners can make use of intonation cues in carriers to correctly identifying intonation questions, despite the fact that these cues are not as important as those of final syllables (2011: 1021).[15] Phonological signalling has also been described for Mandarin questions. In a study on the pragmatics and intonation patterns of the sentence-final Mandarin question particle *ma*, Lee (2000) investigated neutral *ma*-particle questions and compared them to declarative sentences. The data typically demonstrate that "the overall pitch of *ma*-particle questions is higher than that of declaratives sentences" (2000: 54); some utterances provide evidence for "a globally rising trend" (2000: 56, 113).

What follows with respect to sentence-final question particles is that the question of comprehension, i.e. the point in time when a listener understands a sentence to have interrogative mood, requires more than syntactical observations. The signalling of questions by means of sentence-final particles does not seem to rely exclusively on these particles but rests upon subsystem interactions, since intonation foreshadows interrogative sentence mood. Therefore, the anchor point is likely to have an influence on signalisation strategies.

---

question particle and OV: 60; sentence-final question particle and VO: 154; sentence-final question particle and OV: 140 (https://wals.info/combinations/92A_83A#2/22.4/152.8; 16.04.2019).

14 The results are in line with findings by Peters and Pfitzinger (2008) for German. Peters and Pfitzinger (2008: 68), in addition, note "strong individual differences in the ability to linguistically classify stimuli with a voicing duration of 40ms or less". 25% of the subjects even classified statements vs. questions correctly in the 20ms duration series.

15 Ma, Ciocca, and Whitehill (2011: 1013) also comment on the fact that, in contrast to Mandarin, all tones in the final position of intended questions have a rising F0 contour in Cantonese. "By contrast, the increase in overall F0 level may be a stronger cue in Mandarin than in Cantonese because questions appear to be mainly marked by global changes in Mandarin".

3.2 Direction of serialisation

As will be demonstrated, the serialisation of elements in a "chain", too, is instructive besides their anchor points. Do the elements in the mirrored Wackernagel position follow natural serialisation or scopal serialisation? The serialisation effect will be illustrated with data from Korean, Cantonese, and German.

With the widest possible scope, the German mirrored Wackernagel position has the adverbial connector *nämlich* before the co-ordinating conjunction *und und und* (16). "Sentence-co-ordinating conjunctions" follow "adverbial connectors" in the mirrored Wackernagel position.

(16) *Man kann wieder atmen und dann gut einschlafen <u>nämlich</u> <u>und und und</u>.*
 (elicited)
 'One can breathe again and then fall asleep better again *nämlich und und und*'

The same principle, an element with larger scope following an element with lower scope, has been reported for Korean:[16] the sentence-final clause connective *kuntey* 'but' is prosodically integrated into the sentence and follows question particles (Sohn and Kim 2014: 234; cf. also Sohn 2015 for the utterance-final connective *nuntey* 'but'):

(17) *moksoli- ka   mwe-   nya   kuntey*
 voice-   NM   what-   Q   but
 'What's with your voice kuntey?'

Does the order in the mirrored Wackernagel position follow the principle of natural serialisation or the principle of scopal serialisation? In OV languages like Korean and German, the principles of natural serialisation and scopal serialisation have the same effect on word order in the mirrored Wackernagel position: co-ordinating sentence conjunctions are predicted to follow adverbial connectors/question particles. Thus the question of which of the principles actually applies cannot be decided for these languages.

In VO languages, however, the serialisation directions formulated by the principle of scopal serialisation and the principle of natural serialisation do not coincide in the mirrored Wackernagel position. Just as scopal serialisation in Wackernagel position becomes distinct in OV languages, the serialisation princi-

---

[16] I would like to thank Yeonsuk Yun (Bamberg) for her valuable advice in interpreting the Korean data.

ple is expected to become distinct for VO languages in the mirrored Wackernagel position. Cantonese has been chosen for illustration, since it has a co-occurrence of both VO syntax and core grammar sentence-final particles.

(18) shows the Cantonese chain of sentence-final particles (as suggested by Busch 2011: 64[17]), in which two or more particles can be combined (Chan 2008: 5). Most elements taking part in the sentence-final (virtual) chain of elements described for the languages of East Asia do not have an equivalent in the old Indo-European Wackernagel position, with question particles as an obvious exception.[18]

(18) ge3 < aa3 < zaa3 < gwaa3 < maa3 [Q]
                  ze1   me1 [Q]
                  laa3   aa4 [Q]
                  lo1   ha2/ho2 [Q]
                                   waa2 [Q]
                                   ne1/le1 [Q?]
                                   wo3/bo3
                                   wo5
                                   aa1maa3
                                   aa1
                                   aak8
                                   zek7

The rigid order is "conspicuous" with respect to the direction of serialisation. Cantonese question particles occur last in the chain. It has been demonstrated that speaker-oriented final particles precede addressee-oriented ones in Cantonese, since the question particle *me1* precedes the question particle *ho2* (Lam 2014: 64, Lan 2017: 20). Lam (2014: 76) notes, "[S]cope facts and clause-typing restrictions conclude that *ho2* is syntactically higher than *me1*". *ge3*, a particle marking assertion, which is not restricted to declaratives (Busch 2011: 46–48), starts the chain.

---

17 The sentence mood markers proposed differ slightly from those suggested by Kwok (1984: 41–42; see 21–22 for co-occurrence restrictions), which, however, does not change the proposal made here.

18 *Ge3*: epistemic particle, *aa3*: contextualisation particle, *zaa3*: restrictive particle, *ze1*: restrictive particle, *laa3*: inchoative particle *lo1*: epistemic particle, *gwaa3*: epistemic particle, *wo3*: indexical particle, *bo3*: indexical particle, *wo5* evidentiality particle, *aa1maa3*: epistemic particle, *aa1*: contextualisation particle, *aak8*: contextualisation particle, *zek7*: restrictive particle; *maa3*, *me1*, *aa4*, *ha2/ho2*, *waa2*, and possibly *ne1/le1* (coll.) (debated): question particles (see Busch 2011 for a discussion and classification).

ge3 and the question particle *aa4* are combined in *gaa4* (Busch 2011: 49–50), the combinations reflecting scopal serialisation. *ge3*, *aa3*, and *laa3* have narrow scope (Busch 2011: 59), while question particles, naturally, have wide scope over the complete sentence, "changing a statement into a question" (Kwok 1984: 17). Clearly, question particles have wider scope than epistemic particles.

A question that emerges immediately is whether it is useful to compare the functions of the above-mentioned East Asian languages with those of Indo-European final particles. Obviousness, mirativity, and assertion, which are typically encoded in sentence-final East Asian particles, have also been listed for not-yet-codified Indo-European sentence-final particles (obviousness: Cantonese *lo1*, *aa1maa3*, cf. Wakefield 2010: 96; cf. Haselow 2015: 17–18 for German *ja*; mirativity: Cantonese *me1*, cf. Busch 2011: 22; cf. Del Gobbo, Munaro, and Poletto 2015: 374 for Venetian *ciò*; assertion: Cantonese *ge3*, cf. Yip and Matthews 2003: 159; cf. Lenker 2010: 210 for English *though*). It has to be taken into account, however, that there are restrictions of occurrence; the Japanese final particle *shi* 'and, and so' (type IV in McGloin and Konishi 2010) which unlike other uses of *shi* adds emotional tone or affect, combines neither with the question particle nor with any other particles, possibly because the final particle *shi* is used to express the speaker's immediate sentiment at the discourse site (although often negative), and the speaker's intention is not to seek agreement from or rapport with the listener (Naomi McGloin, p.c.).[19] Iida (2018: 67) argues that there should be more research on the properties of sentence-final particles of Asia before they are treated as a universal category. Irrespective of whether they form a universal category, it is obvious from the perspective of natural serialisation that the order of sentence-final particles is non-arbitrary, with heads like question particles in the extreme right position of VO languages and in the extreme left position of OV languages. In summary, the examples given show the highest heads, i.e. the elements with the widest scope, at the extreme end of the chain. The next section deals with the function of serialisation directions.

---

19 I would like to thank Naomi McGloin for her valuable comments on the serialisation of *shi*. The particle *shi* in a usage classified as a different construction type (Stage III) by McGloin and Konishi (2010: 573–574) precedes the sentence particles *ne* and *sa*, with *ne* giving rapport and *sa* indicating mild assertion. "*Shi* is a co-ordinate conjunction and thus more propositional/objective than subjective. While *shi* has developed a sentence-final usage, it still works as a conjunction also. In Japanese, more subjective expressions, such as mood and stance markers, come toward the end of the sentence" (Naomi McGloin, p.c.).

4 Iconicity

Wackernagel elements form a defined and typologically established set of elements, which can be compared cross-linguistically, despite the obvious difficulties. For Indo-European languages, the systematics in the syntactic placement of sentence-final Wackernagel elements suggests itself. When looking at the German data, the mirrored Wackernagel position is not fully conventionalised. The phenomenon is below the attention threshold even for widely diffused sentence-final elements, although lay questions referring to language usage (see the use and spelling of *und und und*) show an emerging awareness or even unease with this position.

The illustrated systematics in both lexical material and placement provide evidence that the use of elements in the mirrored Wackernagel position is more than just a repair in an incremental production process (for other examples of placement consolidation in the German post-field, like adjectives, intensifiers, and deictics, cf. Imo 2011). The mirrored Wackernagel position in German is a performance phenomenon in the sense that performance constitutes the system (cf. Stetter 2015[20]). Sentence-final occurrences like German *nämlich* and *und und und* are not part of core grammar; instead, the mirrored Wackernagel position is available as a position that can be used individually and creatively. As a consequence, the transition from entrenchment to conventionalisation can currently be observed.

The syntactic principles in the background, which govern the order of elements, are syntactic preferences interacting with each other. Scopal serialisation in both Wackernagel position and mirrored Wackernagel position is independent of a language's basic word order type. Categorising this principle as preference implies that the order of elements at beginnings and endings of sentences is non-arbitrarily unidirectional. A chain starts with the element with the widest scope or the highest head and ends with the element with the smallest scope or lowest element, with the beginning and end of the sentence as anchor points.

The interrelation of the principles of natural and scopal serialisation contributes to syntactic iconicity (cf. the repetition of Figure 3 for ease of reading). There are four possible combinations in a simplified scenario with either only Wackernagel position or the mirrored Wackernagel position: 1) Scopal serialisation (Wackernagel position) plus natural VO serialisation, 2) Scopal serialisation (mirrored Wackernagel position) plus natural OV serialisation, 3) Scopal serialisation

---

[20] Each single act of performance leaves the system in the state in which it actually is. Together, they change the system (Stetter 2015: 6).

Wackernagel position	"Rest of sentence"	Mirrored Wackernagel position
Scopal serialisation ─────────▶	Natural serialisation OV ◀─────── VO ───────▶	Scopal serialisation ◀─────────

Figure 3: Natural and scopal serialisation.

(Wackernagel position) plus natural OV serialisation, 4) Scopal serialisation (mirrored Wackernagel position) plus natural VO serialisation. In the constellations 1) and 2), unidirectionality economically ranges over the complete clause; there is only one direction of serialisation, either consistently from left to right, or consistently from right to left. In contrast, the opposite serialisation directions in the constellations 3) and 4) result with respect to syntactic iconicity in a demarcation of functionally determined fields (Figure 6).

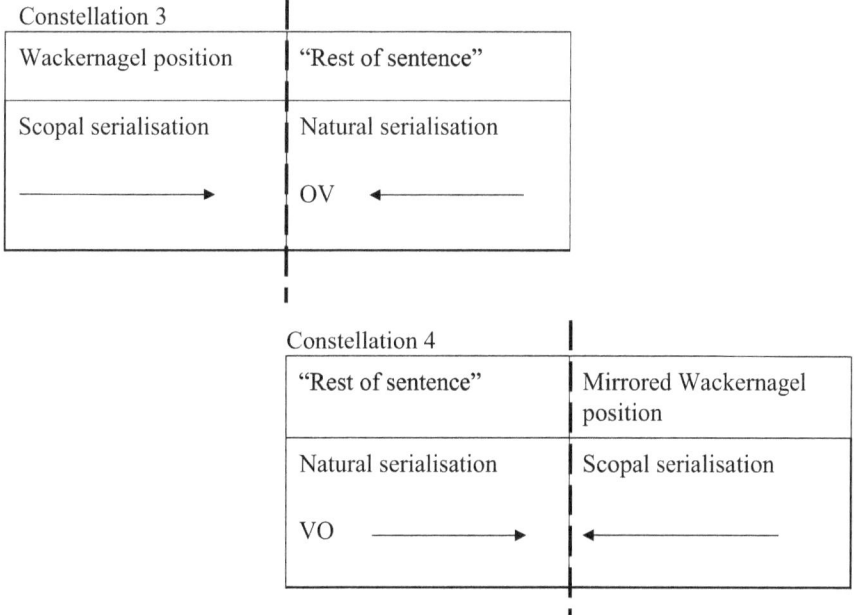

Figure 6: Opposite directions of natural and scopal serialisation: Demarcation of fields.

Iconicity in syntax is, according to Peirce (1906: 513), mandatory with respect to comprehension: "The arrangement of the words in the sentence [...] must serve as Icons, in order that the sentence may be understood. The chief need for the

Icons is in order to show the Form of the synthesis of the elements of thought". Jakobson (1965: 29) added with reference to Peirce's insight the different dimensions of connectedness, i.e. "the initial and the final limit of the sequence, the immediate neighbourhood and distance, the centrality and peripherality, the symmetrical and asymmetrical relations as linguistic properties". Examples of iconicity are on a large scale "natural" and thus usually escape attention; strict serialisation is the expression of an iconic strategy, with contents apt for natural serialisation conforming to special types of discourse strategies (Leiss 1992: 6, 9).

What becomes obvious with respect to opposite directions of natural and scopal serialisation is the demarcation of syntactic positions that correlate with disparate functions. The demarcation signals the different functions of elements associated with these positions. The degree to which this kind of iconicity shows depends on, first of all, whether the language is OV or VO and, second, whether the language has conventionalised more strongly the Wackernagel position or the mirrored Wackernagel position.

5 Summary

Serialisation strategies form evaluable relations. The paper dealt with two principles of unidirectional serialisation: the principle of natural serialisation and the principle of scopal serialisation, according to which everything else being equal, having scopal serialisation in the Wackernagel positions is preferred to not having scopal serialisation. The focus was laid on 1) anchor points and 2) the direction of serialisation in Wackernagel position and the here introduced "mirrored" Wackernagel position. Both syntactic positions show a preference for unidirectional serialisation within their domains. The resulting structures are conceived in the context of preference theory as observed choices that surface both in typologically unmarked structures and language change. With respect to the direction of serialisation, scopal serialisation may diverge from natural serialisation. In OV languages, scopal serialisation in Wackernagel position and natural serialisation have opposite directions, while in VO languages scopal serialisation in the mirrored Wackernagel position and natural serialisation have opposite directions. Opposite directions highlight syntactic iconicity, separating syntactic "fields" with different functions from each other. Thus what is displayed in natural languages is an encoding of functions of sentence positions.

References

Baldi, Philip. 1979. Typology and the Indo-European prepositions. *Indogermanische Forschungen* 84. 49–61.
Bartsch, Renate & Theo Vennemann. 1972. *Semantic structures: A study in the relation between semantics and syntax*. Frankfurt am Main: Athenäum.
Beeching, Kate & Ulrich Detges. 2014a. *Discourse functions at the left and right periphery: Crosslinguistic investigations of language use and language change*. Leiden: Brill.
Beeching, Kate & Ulrich Detges. 2014b. Introduction. In Kate Beeching & Ulrich Detges (eds.), *Discourse functions at the left and right periphery: Crosslinguistic investigations of language use and language change*, 1–23. Leiden: Brill.
Busch, Jerra Lui. 2011. *Syntaktische Einbettung kantonesischer Satzpartikel*. Vienna: University of Vienna diploma thesis.
Chan, Szeman. 2008. *The acquisition of Cantonese sentence-final particles by native Mandarin speakers*. Hong Kong: The Chinese University of Hong Kong MA thesis.
Del Gobbo, Francesca, Nicola Munaro & Cecilia Poletto. 2015. On sentential particles: A crosslinguistic study. In Sylvie Hancil, Alexander Haselow & Margje Post (eds.), *Final particles*, 359–386. Berlin: de Gruyter.
Delbrück, Berthold. 1878. *Syntaktische Forschungen III: Die altindische Wortfolge*. Halle: Buchhandlung des Waisenhauses.
Delbrück, Berthold. 1900. *Vergleichende Syntax der indogermanischen Sprachen. 3. Theil*. Straßburg: Trübner.
Dryer, Matthew 2013a. Position of polar question particles. In Matthew Dryer & Martin Haspelmath (eds.), *The world atlas of language structures online*. Leipzig: Max Planck Institute for Evolutionary Anthropology. http://wals.info/chapter/92 (accessed 16 April 2019).
Dryer, Matthew 2013b. Relationship between the order of object and verb and the order of adposition and noun phrase. In Matthew Dryer & Martin Haspelmath (eds.), *The world atlas of language structures online*. Leipzig: Max Planck Institute for Evolutionary Anthropology. http://wals.info/chapter/95 (accessed 6 May 2014).
Dunkel, George. 1992. Die Grammatik der Partikeln. In Robert Beekes, Alexander Lubotsky & Jos Weitenberg (ed.), *Rekonstruktion und relative Chronologie*, 153–177. Innsbruck: Institut für Sprachwissenschaft der Universität Innsbruck.
Ehala, Martin. 1999. Stable states and impossible changes: The limits of teleological explanation in diachronic linguistics. *Trames* 3. 203–214.
Fretheim, Thorstein. 2015. A relevance-theoretic perspective on the Norwegian utterance-final particles *da* and *altså* compared to their English counterpart *then*. In Sylvie Hancil, Alexander Haselow & Margje Post (eds.), *Final particles*, 249–283. Berlin: de Gruyter.
Gómez-Moreno, Pedro Ureña. 2015. Sentence-final adverbials: Recurrent types and usage. In Sylvie Hancil, Alexander Haselow & Margje Post (eds.), *Final particles*, 39–54. Berlin: de Gruyter.
Greenberg, Joseph. 1963. Some universals of grammar with particular reference to the order of meaningful elements. Report of a Conference held at Dobbs Ferry, New York, April 13–15, 1961. In Joseph Greenberg (ed.), *Universals of language*, 73–113. Cambridge: MIT Press.
Halldén, Sören. 1957. *On the logic of "better"*. Lund: Library of Theoria.

Hancil, Sylvie, Margje Post & Alexander Haselow. 2015. Introduction: Final particles from a typological perspective. In Sylvie Hancil, Alexander Haselow & Margje Post (eds.), *Final particles*, 1–35. Berlin: de Gruyter.

Hansson, Sven Ove & Till Grüne-Yanoff. 2018. Preferences. In Edward Zalta (ed.), *The Stanford encyclopedia of philosophy*. https://plato.stanford.edu/archives/sum2018/ entries/ preferences/ (accessed 25 November 2019).

Haselow, Alexander. 2015. Final particles in spoken German. In Sylvie Hancil, Alexander Haselow & Margje Post (eds.), *Final particles*, 77–107. Berlin: de Gruyter.

Hawkins, John. 1984. Modifier-head or function-argument relations in phrase structure? The evidence of some word order universals. *Lingua* 63. 107–138.

Heine, Bernd, Gunther Kaltenböck, and Tania Kuteva (2015), Some observations on the evolution of final particles. In Sylvie Hancil, Alexander Haselow & Margje Post (eds.), *Final particles*, 111–140. Berlin: de Gruyter.

Iida, Maki. 2018. Sentence-final particles in Cantonese and Japanese from a cross-linguistic perspective. *Media and Communication Studies* 71. 65–93.

Imo, Wolfgang. 2011. Ad hoc-Produktion oder Konstruktion? Verfestigungstendenzen bei Inkrement-Strukturen im gesprochenen Deutsch. In Alexander Lasch & Alexander Ziem (eds.), *Konstruktionsgrammatik III*, 241–256. Tübingen: Stauffenburg.

Jakobson, Romans. 1965. Quest for the essence of language. *Diogenes* 13. 21–37.

Kwok, Helen. 1984. *Sentence particles in Cantonese*. Hong Kong: Centre of Asian Studies, University of Hong Kong.

Lam, Zoe Wai-Man. 2014. A complex ForceP for speaker- and addressee-oriented discourse particles in Cantonese. *Studies in Chinese Linguistics* 35. 61–80.

Lan, Yingjie. 2017. Probing higher layers: What Singaporean English particles might show us. *JATLaC Journal* 12. 15–26.

Langacker, Ronald. 1997. Constituency, dependency, and conceptual grouping. *Cognitive Linguistics* 8. 1–32.

Lee, Eun-Kyung, Sarah Brown-Schmidt & Duane. Watson. 2013. Ways of looking ahead: Hierarchical planning in language production. *Cognition* 129. 544–562.

Lee, Ok Joo. 2000. *The pragmatics and intonation of ma-particle questions in Mandarin*. Ohio: Ohio State University MA thesis.

Lehmann, Winfred. 1972. Proto-Germanic syntax. In Frans van Coetsem & Herbert Kufner (eds.), *Toward a grammar of Proto-Germanic*, 239–268. Tübingen: Niemeyer.

Lehmann, Winfred. 1974. *Proto-Indo-European Syntax*. Austin: University of Texas Press. https://liberalarts.utexas.edu/lrc/resources/books/pies/index.php (accessed 10 April 2019).

Leiss, Elisabeth. 1992. *Die Verbalkategorien des Deutschen*. Berlin: de Gruyter.

Lenker, Ursula. 2010. *Argument and rhetoric: Adverbial connectors in the history of English*. Berlin: de Gruyter.

Levelt, William. 1989. *Speaking: From intention to articulation*. Cambridge: MIT Press.

Luraghi, Silvia. 1990. *Old Hittite sentence structure*. London: Routledge.

Luraghi, Silvia. 1997. *Hittite*. Munich: Lincom.

Ma, Joan, Ciocca Valter & Whitehill. 2011. The perception of intonation questions and statements in Cantonese. *Journal of the Acoustical Society of America* 129. 1012–1023.

McGloin, Naomi & Yumiko Konishi. 2010. From connective particle to sentence-final particle: A usage-based analysis of *shi* 'and' in Japanese. *Language Sciences* 32. 563–578.

Mulder, Jean & Sandra Thompson. 2008. The grammaticization of *but* as a final particle in English conversation. In Ritva Laury (ed.), *Crosslinguistic studies of clause combining: The multifunctionality of conjunctions*, 179–204. Amsterdam: John Benjamins.

Noel Aziz Hanna, Patrizia. 2015. *Wackernagels Gesetz im Deutschen: Zur Interaktion von Syntax, Phonologie und Informationsstruktur*. Berlin: de Gruyter.

Noel Aziz Hanna, Patrizia. 2019. Vocative in Standard German – a 'syntagmatic category'. *Sprachwissenschaft* 44. 257–278.

Onodera, Noriko. 2004. *Japanese discourse markers: Synchronic and diachronic discourse analysis*. Philadelphia: John Benjamins.

Peirce, Charles. 1906. Prolegomena to an apology for pragmaticism. *The Monist* 16. 492–546.

Peters, Benno & Hartmut Pfitzinger. 2008. Duration and F0 interval of utterance-final intonation contours in the perception of German sentence modality. In *Proceedings of the Interspeech, Brisbane, Australia, 22–26 September 2008*, 65–68. Adelaide, South Australia: Causal Productions.

Roberts, Ian. 2007. *Diachronic syntax*. Oxford: Oxford University Press.

Ross, John Robert. 1986. *Infinite syntax*. Norwood: Ablex Publishing Corporation.

Schiffrin, Deborah. 1987. *Discourse markers*. Cambridge: Cambridge University Press.

Shinzato, Rumiko. 2015. Two types of conditionals and two different grammaticalization paths. In Sylvie Hancil, Alexander Haselow & Margje Post (eds.), *Final particles*, 157–180. Berlin: de Gruyter.

Sohn, Sung-Ock. 2015. The emergence of utterance-final particles in Korean. In Sylvie Hancil, Alexander Haselow & Margje Post (eds.), *Final particles*, 181–195. Berlin: de Gruyter.

Sohn, Sung-Ock & Stephanie Hyeri Kim. 2014. The interplay of discourse and prosody at the left and right periphery in Korean: An analysis of kuntey 'but'. In Kate Beeching & Ulrich Detges (eds.), *Discourse functions at the left and right periphery: Crosslinguistic investigations of language use and language change*, 221–249. Brill: Leiden.

Stetter, Christian. 2015. System und Performanz. In Christa Dürscheid & Jan Georg Schneider (eds.), *Handbuch Satz, Äußerung, Schema*, 3–16. Berlin: de Gruyter.

Teruya, Kazuhiro. 2006. *A systemic functional grammar of Japanese*. Vol. 1. London: Continuum.

Vennemann, Theo. 1974. Topics, subjects, and word order: From SXV to SVX via TVX. In John Anderson & Charles Jones (eds.), *Historical linguistics: Proceedings of the First International Congress of Historical Linguistics, Edinburgh, September 1973*, 339–376. Vol. 2. Amsterdam: North-Holland.

Vennemann, Theo. 1983. Causality in language change: Theories of linguistic preferences as a basis for linguistic explanations. *Folia linguistica historica* 6. 5–26.

Vennemann, Theo. 1984. Verb-second, verb late and the brace construction: Comments on some papers. In Jacek Fisiak (ed.), *Historical syntax*, 627–636. Berlin: de Gruyter.

Vennemann, Theo. 2003. Syntax und Sprachkontakt: Mit besonderer Berücksichtigung der indogermanischen Sprachen des Nordwestens. In Alfred Bammesberger & Theo Vennemann (eds.), *Languages in prehistoric Europe*, 333–364. Heidelberg: Carl Winter.

Wackernagel, Jacob. 1892. Über ein Gesetz der indogermanischen Wortstellung. *Indogermanische Forschungen* 1. 333–436.

Wakefield, John. 2010. *The English equivalents of Cantonese sentence-final particles: A contrastive analysis*. Hong Kong: The Hong Kong Polytechnic University dissertation.

van der Wouden, Ton & Ad Foolen. 2015. Dutch particles in the right periphery. In Sylvie Hancil, Alexander Haselow & Margje Post (eds.), *Final particles*, 221–247. Berlin: de Gruyter.

Yap, Foong Ha, Ying Yang & Tak-Sum Wong. 2014. On the development of sentence final particles (and utterance tags) in Chinese. In Kate Beeching & Ulrich Detges (eds.), *Discourse functions at the left and right periphery: Crosslinguistic investigations of language use and language change*, 179–220. Brill: Leiden.

Yip, Virginia & Stephen Matthews. 2003. *Intermediate Cantonese: A grammar and workbook*. London: Routledge.

Tabula Gratulatoria

Henning Andersen	University of California at Los Angeles
Maria Giovanna Arcamone	Università di Pisa/University of Pisa
John Ole Askedal	Universitetet i Oslo/University of Oslo
Peter Auer	Albert-Ludwigs-Universität Freiburg
Philip H. Baldi	Pennsylvania State University
Renate Bartsch	Universiteit van Amsterdam
Hans Basbøll	Syddansk Universitet/University of Southern Denmark
Rolf Bergmann	Otto-Friedrich-Universität Bamberg
Pier Marco Bertinetto	Scuola Normale Superiore di Pisa
Dagmar Bittner	Leibniz-Zentrum Allgemeine Sprachwissenschaft
Georg Bossong	Universität Zürich
Kurt Braunmüller	Universität Hamburg
Donatella Bremer	Università di Pisa/University of Pisa
Walter Breu	Universität Konstanz
Joan Bybee	The University of New Mexico
Gerald F. Carr	California State University, Sacramento
Michela Cennamo	Università degli Studi di Napoli Federico II/University of Naples Federico II
Carolin Cholotta	Otto-Friedrich-Universität Bamberg
Bernard Comrie	University of California, Santa Barbara
Stuart Davis	Indiana University
Martin Dewey-Findell	University of Nottingham
Tonya Kim Dewey-Findell	University of Nottingham
Antoniy Dimitrov	Ludwigs-Maximilian-Universität München
Wolfgang U. Dressler	Universität Wien
Andreas Dufter	Ludwig-Maximilians-Universität München
Katarzyna Dziubalska-Kołaczyk	Uniwersytet im. Adama Mickiewicza w Poznaniu/Adam Mickiewicz University
Lutz Edzard	Friedrich-Alexander-Universität Erlangen-Nürnberg
Konrad Ehlich	Freie Universität Berlin
Ludwig Eichinger	Universität Mannheim
Peter Eisenberg	Universität Potsdam
Stig Eliasson	Johannes Gutenberg-Universität Mainz
Stefan Engelberg	Institut für Deutsche Sprache, Mannheim
Dankmar Enke	Ludwig-Maximilians-Universität München
Peter Erdmann	Technische Universität Berlin
Elisabetta Fava	Universita' degli Studi di Ferrara/University of Ferrara
Anna Helene Feulner	Humboldt-Universität zu Berlin
Markku Filppula	Itä-Suomen yliopisto/University of Eastern Finland
Livio Gaeta	Università degli Studi di Torino/University of Turin
Claudia Gerstner-Link	Ludwig-Maximilians-Universität München
Dafydd Gibbon	Universität Bielefeld
Paolo di Giovine	Sapienza – Università di Roma/Sapienza University of Rome

Elvira Glaser	Universität Zürich
Hans Götsche	Aalborg Universitet/Aalborg University
Hartmut Haberland	Roskilde Universitet/Roskilde University
Stephanie Hackert	Ludwig-Maximilians-Universität München
Angela Hahn	Ludwig-Maximilians-Universität München
SJ Hannahs	Newcastle University
Jonathan Harrington	Ludwig-Maximilians-Universität München
Dietrich Hartmann	Ruhr-Universität Bochum
Martin Haspelmath	Max-Planck-Institut für Menschheitsgeschichte
Volker Heeschen	Ludwig-Maximilians-Universität München
Wilhelm Heitzmann	Ludwig-Maximilians-Universität München
Klaus von Heusinger	Universität zu Köln
Raymond Hickey	Universität Duisburg-Essen
Armin Höfer	Universität Augsburg
Phil Hoole	Ludwig-Maximilians-Universität München
Grover Hudson	Michigan State University
Bernhard Hurch	Universität Graz
Larry M. Hyman	University of California, Berkeley
Joachim Jacobs	Bergische Universität Wuppertal
Neil Jacobs	Ohio State University
Ernst Håkon Jahr	Universitetet i Agder/University of Agder
Richard Janney	Ludwig-Maximilians-Universität München
Michael Job	Georg-August-Universität Göttingen
Karel Jongeling	Gouda
Edward Keenan	University of California at Los Angeles
Andreas Kemmerling	Universität Heidelberg
Robert Martin Kerr	Universität des Saarlandes
Juhani Klemola	Tampereen Yliopisto/Tampere University
Ekkehard König	Freie Universität Berlin
Thomas Krefeld	Ludwig-Maximilians-Universität München
Manfred Krifka	Leibniz-Zentrum Allgemeine Sprachwissenschaft
Manfred Kropp	Johannes Gutenberg-Universität Mainz
Jurij Kusmenko	Humboldt-Universität zu Berlin
Aditi Lahiri	University of Oxford
Stephen Laker	Kyushu University
Roger Lass	University of Cape Town
Minhaeng Lee	Yeonse Daehakgyo/Yonsei University, Seoul
Christian Lehmann	Universität Erfurt
Reinhard G. Lehmann	Johannes Gutenberg-Universität Mainz
Jürgen Lenerz	Universität zu Köln
Hans-Heinrich Lieb	Freie Universität Berlin
Katrin Lindner	Ludwig-Maximilians-Universität München
Michele Loporcaro	Universität Zürich
Angelika Lutz	Friedrich-Alexander-Universität Erlangen-Nürnberg
Utz Maas	Universität Osnabrück
Monica Macaulay	University of Wisconsin-Madison
Robert Mailhammer	University of Western Sydney

Ferdinand von Mengden	Freie Universitaet Berlin
Guido Mensching	Georg-August-Universität Göttingen
Aurelia Merlan	Ludwig-Maximilians-Universität München
Donka Minkova	University of California at Los Angeles
Peter-Arnold Mumm	Ludwigs-Maximilian-Universität München
Pamela Munro	University of California at Los Angeles
Robert Murray	University of Calgary
Benedicte Nielsen Whitehead	Københavns Universitet
Patrizia Noel Aziz Hanna	Otto-Friedrich-Universität Bamberg
Thomas Olander	Københavns Universitet/University of Copenhagen
Birgit Anette Olsen	Københavns Universitet/University of Copenhagen
Susan Olsen	Humboldt-Universität zu Berlin
Magnús Pétursson	Universität Hamburg
Marc Pierce	University of Texas
Erich Poppe	Philipps-Universität Marburg
Renate Raffelsiefen	Institut für Deutsche Sprache, Mannheim, und Freie Universität Berlin
Anna Ramat	Università degli studi di Pavia/University of Pavia
Paolo Ramat	Università degli studi di Pavia/University of Pavia
Irmengard Rauch	University of California, Berkeley
Angelika Redder	Universität Hamburg
Uwe Reichel	Magyar Tudományos Akadémia/Hungarian Academy of Sciences
David Restle	Ludwig-Maximilians-Universität München
Claudia Maria Riehl	Ludwig-Maximilians-Universität München
Nikolaus Ritt	Universität Wien
Katrin Röder-vom Scheidt	München
Elke Ronneberger-Sibold	Katholische Universität Eichstätt-Ingolstadt
Anthony Rowley	Bayerisches Wörterbuch, Bayerische Akademie der Wissenschaften
Joseph Salmons	University of Wisconsin-Madison
Christopher David Sapp	Indiana University
Hans Sauer	Ludwig-Maximilians-Universität München
Oliver Schallert	Ludwig-Maximilians-Universität München
Hannes Scheutz	Paris-Lodron-Universität Salzburg
Kurt Schier	Ludwig-Maximilians-Universität München
Katharina Schuhmann	The Pennsylvania State University
Christoph Schwarze	Universität Konstanz
Ulrich Schweier	Ludwig-Maximilians-Universität München
Guido Seiler	Universität Zürich
Thomas Shannon	University of California, Berkeley
Birgit Sievert	De Gruyter Mouton
Elena Smirnova	Université de Neuchâtel/University of Neuchâtel
Laura Catharine Smith	Brigham Young University
Gabriele Sommer	Universität Bayreuth
Barbara Sonnenhauser	Universität Zürich
Elisabeth Stark	Universität Zürich

Dieter Stein	Heinrich Heine Universität Düsseldorf
Wolf-Dieter Stempel	Ludwig-Maximilians-Universität München
Anita Steube	Universität Leipzig
Stefanie Stricker	Otto-Friedrich-Universität Bamberg
Stephan Sudhoff	Universiteit Utrecht/Utrecht University
Sarah Thomason	University of Michigan
Hans G. Tillmann	Ludwig-Maximilians-Universität München
Carolina Trautmann	Ludwig-Maximilians-Universität München
Robert Vetterle	München
Letizia Vezzosi	Università degli Studi di Firenze/University of Florence
Ulrich Wandruszka	Alpen-Adria-Universität Klagenfurt
Gaby Waxenberger	Ludwig-Maximilians-Universität München
Thilo Weber	Institut für Deutsche Sprache, Mannheim
Iva Welscher	Markt Schwaben
Richard Wiese	Philipps-Universität Marburg
Geirr Wiggen	Universitetet i Oslo/University of Oslo
Dietmar Zaefferer	Ludwig-Maximilians-Universität München

Index

Abduction 5, 11, 213, 215
Ablaut 17, 20, 22, 24, 38, 39, 40, 43–44, 214, 236
Aerodynamic constraints 171–194
Affixation 17–18, 20, 117, 123, 236
Algic 24, 26, 29, 30
Algonquian 17–48
Allomorphy 51, 195–207
Amurdak 49–69
Anaptyxis. See epenthesis
Apocope 118–122, 127, 129–130, 261, 277–279, 282–286, 288–289
Arabic 17, 33–34, 43, 110, 296
Articulatory coordination 171–194

Bulgarian 219–245

Cantonese 308, 310–311
Chibemba 204, 206
Chizigula 206
Coda Law 111, 226, 248, 267, 288
Compensatory lengthening. See lengthening
Consonant clusters 43, 50, 55–56, 61–62, 87, 131, 171–194, 222–225
Consonantal strength. See sonority hierarchy
Consonants
– consonant clusters. See consonant clusters
– geminates. See geminates
– liquids. See liquids
– syllabic consonants. See syllabic consonants
Constraints 4, 20, 71–108, 127, 173, 204
– See aerodynamic constraints
Contact Law 49–69, 111, 221, 223, 226, 287–288
Cree 24, 26–30, 39

Danish 143–170
Degemination 64, 265–292
Diachronic maxim 9, 66, 112, 117, 130, 137
Dutch 85, 130–133, 251, 275, 302, 304

Edges 25, 34–37, 39, 43–44, 74, 93, 97, 124–126, 132, 176–177, 186, 248, 271, 278. See sentence also periphery
English
– Irish English 250–251, 257–258
– Middle English 265–292
– Modern English 9, 74, 153, 155–156, 174, 179, 181, 185, 189, 222, 224, 249–251, 257, 273–274, 303
– Old English 122, 260, 265, 275
Epenthesis 19–20, 183–184, 192, 199, 223, 247, 250–259, 261, 269–270
Extra-prosodicity 151, 154–161, 166–168

Feature [±peripheral] 84, 86–91, 94–95, 99, 105–106
Final particles 302–314
Foot structure 37, 40, 44, 71, 73–75, 85, 88, 90–93, 102–103, 105, 109–139
French 86, 153, 155–157, 171, 180–184, 258, 260
Frisian
– Modern Frisian dialects 129
– Old Frisian 109, 127–130, 136
– Wangeroog dialect 129
– Wursten dialect 129
Functional load 265, 279, 286, 288

Geminates 105–106, 129, 152, 198, 265–292
Georgian 173, 178–179
German
– Middle High German 133–134, 220
– Modern German 9, 61, 71–108, 144–145, 154–155, 171–172, 174–184, 189–190, 213, 220, 222–223, 239, 270, 295, 298–301, 303–307
– Old High German 109–111, 117–127, 133–134, 136
– See plural formation
– See shortening
– See Wackernagel positions
Greek
– Ancient Greek 155, 213–215, 260

Haya 205
Head Law 9, 37, 88, 111, 248, 267, 287–288
Humboldt's universal 195, 206

Iamb 37, 43
Iconicity 293, 297, 312–314
Ilgar/Garig 54–55
Initial change 17–48
Irish
– Modern Irish 247–264
– See also Irish English
Iwaidja 50, 52–57, 59, 62, 64–65, 67
Iwaidjan 51–52, 54–57, 59, 63–65, 67

jan-verbs 109, 111, 117, 122–127, 136–137
Japanese 144, 266, 280, 296–297, 302–303, 307–308, 311

Karuk 30
Kasem 259
Kinyarwanda 204
Kirundi 204–205
Korean 302–303, 309

Languages. See under specific language
– Algic
– Algonquian
– Amurdak
– Arabic
– Bulgarian
– Cantonese
– Chibemba
– Chizigula
– Cree
– Danish
– Dutch
– English
– Irish English
– Middle English
– Modern English
– Old English
– French
– Frisian
– Modern Frisian dialects
– Old Frisian
– Wangeroog Frisian
– Wursten Frisian
– Georgian
– German
– Middle High German
– Modern German
– Old High German
– Ancient Greek
– Haya
– Modern Irish
– Ilgar/Garig
– Iwaidja
– Iwaidjan
– Japanese
– Kasem
– Karuk
– Kinyarwanda
– Kirundi
– Korean
– Latin
– Lengola
– Luganda
– Lusoga
– Mandarin
– Mawng
– Menominee
– Meskwaki
– Nishnaabemwin
– Ojibwe
– Saanich
– Sanskrit
– Old Saxon
– Shawnee
– Slavic
– Slavonic
– Slovak
– Swahili
– Yurok

Laryngeal 143, 173, 179, 183, 209, 211–215
Laryngealisation 25, 153, 163, 165–166
Latin 154–155, 211, 213, 225, 277, 280, 287, 296, 298, 301, 305
Law of Finals 223–224
Law of Initials 223–224, 270
Lengola 205–206
Lengthening 37, 41, 73–74, 81, 90–92, 145, 269–271, 274, 277–279, 284–285
– Compensatory lengthening 197, 199, 202, 205, 276–278

Index — **325**

– Open syllable lengthening 145, 277–278
Liquid metathesis 219–243
Liquids 50, 58, 61–62, 66, 88, 133, 145–146, 149, 185–188, 219–243, 256, 261, 270, 280
Luganda 195–208
Lusoga 195–208

Mandarin 308
Markedness 2, 5–7, 9, 71, 73–77, 82–84, 86–87, 89, 92, 96, 103, 106, 151, 153–155
Mawng 52–55, 57, 59, 64–65
Menominee 18–19, 21–22, 24, 26, 28–29, 35, 37, 39, 41–43
Meskwaki 24, 27–30, 39, 42–43
Metathesis 25, 32–33, 38, 180–181, 219–243, 247–248, 250, 257–261
– See also liquid metathesis
Minimal foot 112, 116, 119–121, 125–126
Mora 91, 112–122, 125, 130–131, 136, 143–170, 266, 269, 276, 280, 287
Morphological class 122, 132, 136, 286, 288
Morphophonemic alternations 49–67

Nasalisation 171–172, 188–191, 238
Natural generative phonology 8, 207
Natural serialisation. See serialisation
Naturalness 2–4, 7–8, 112, 125, 146, 149, 178, 191, 206–207, 215, 226, 239, 240, 260–261, 293–297, 299, 309, 311–314
Negation 202–203, 299, 301
Negative (paradigms) 195–208
Nishnaabemwin 21–22, 28
Nonconcatenative morphology 17–18, 20, 26, 34, 38, 44–45
Non-Stød Model 144, 153–168
Nucleus Law 248

Ojibwe 21, 23–24, 28–29, 42–43
Old Saxon 109–111, 114–123, 127, 130, 136
Open syllable lengthening. See lengthening
Optimality Theory 4, 71–106, 181, 278
Orthographic doubling 265, 274–275

Palatalisation 227, 248, 256
Phonemic representation 71–106, 227
Phonotactics 49–67, 111, 113, 117, 125–127, 146, 248, 250, 252–254, 259–261, 274, 288

Plural formation 109, 117–118, 122, 130–136
Politics 209–216
Portmanteau 195–208
Preference Laws 60–67, 109–111, 113, 137, 143, 168, 209, 215, 219, 223–224, 242–243, 287
– See Coda Law
– See Contact Law
– See Head Law
– See Law of Finals
– See Law of Initials
– See Nucleus Law
– See Prokosch's Law
– See Strength Assimilation Law
– Theory 1–2, 5–10
– See Weight Law
Preference Theory
– Comparative evaluation 1–2, 5–6
– Gradience and scales 2–3, 9–10
– Observed choices 2, 4–5, 314
– "Predictive" and explanatory purpose 6–7
– Preference ranking 2–4, 85
– Prioritisation 2, 5
– Syntax 293–297
Principle of natural serialisation. See serialisation
Principle of scopal serialisation. See serialisation
Prokosch's Law. See Weight Law
Prosodic hierarchy 109, 113, 127, 136
Prosodic morphology 20, 32, 110
Prosodic templates 3, 17–45, 110, 116–117, 137

Question particles 294, 296–298, 307–311. See final particles

Reconstruction 23–26, 29–31, 39–40, 44–45, 52, 63–64, 67, 206, 268, 272, 274, 279–280, 286, 289
Reduplication 17–45, 62, 117

Saanich 38, 43
Sanskrit 214–215
Saussure de 209–216
Scopal serialisation. See serialisation
Sentence-final particles. See final particles

Serialisation
- Direction of 294, 299–301, 309–314
- Principle of natural serialisation 293–297, 299, 309, 311, 313–314
- Principle of scopal serialisation 293, 297–302, 309, 311–314

Shawnee 20, 39, 43–44
Shortening 71–106, 115, 120–121, 125, 130, 136, 159–160, 163, 268–270, 273, 276
Sievers' Law 40, 41
Slavic 219–245
Slavonic 219–245
Slovak 171, 185–188
Strength hierarchy. See sonority hierarchy
Sonority. See sonority hierarchy
Sonority hierarchy 3, 8–9, 60–62, 65, 81, 87–88, 145–146, 148–153, 163–167, 209, 216, 226, 260–261, 265, 280–282, 287–288
Stød 143–170
Strength Assimilation Law 49, 63–67
Subject marking 202
Suppletion 155, 195
Swahili 195–199, 202, 204, 206
Syllabic consonants 171–172, 185–188
Syllable
- Syllable structure 8, 25, 37, 55, 63, 65–67, 79–81, 87, 91–92, 109, 113, 151, 163, 166, 168, 209, 221, 223, 225–227, 235, 238–239, 242, 247–261, 265–266, 275, 287
- Syllable weight 37, 74, 85, 91, 110, 114–116, 118, 123, 129, 130–131, 144–145, 151–154, 168, 254, 266–267, 269–270, 275–276, 280, 287–288

Synchronic maxim 62, 111–112
Syncope 28, 122–123, 126–127, 224, 250–251, 256–257, 277, 283–284, 286, 288–289
Syntactic headedness 293–294, 296
Syntactic iconicity. See iconicity
Syntactic principles. See serialisation

Taps 61–62
Templates. See prosodic templates
Trochee 74, 76, 80, 82–83, 85–86, 92, 94, 96, 98, 102, 105, 109, 111, 113, 138, 177, 279

Universals 1, 4, 8, 11, 74, 209, 259, 287, 296–297, 311
- See Humboldt's universal

Velarisation 248
Vocalisation 89, 103, 122, 158, 162, 219–221, 223, 225, 227, 229–243, 254
Vowel balance 109, 122, 127–130, 136–137
Vowel length 28, 85–87, 91, 128, 143–145, 151–152, 157–161, 166, 185, 281

Wackernagel positions 293–318
- Traditional 298–301
- Mirrored 302–311
Weight Law 96, 115, 118, 143–145, 267, 287–288
Word prosody 88

Yurok 24, 29–30, 44

www.ingramcontent.com/pod-product-compliance
Lightning Source LLC
Chambersburg PA
CBHW071735150426
43191CB00010B/1580